MICROSOFT Excel 2000

Comprehensive Course

Mastering and Using

H. Albert Napier
Philip J. Judd

VISIT US ON THE INTERNET
www.swep.com

South-Western Educational Publishing
an International Thomson Publishing company I(T)P®
www.thomson.com

Cincinnati • Albany, NY • Belmont, CA • Bonn • Boston • Detroit • Johannesburg • London • Madrid
Melbourne • Mexico City • New York • Paris • Singapore • Tokyo • Toronto • Washington

Copyright © 2000
By SOUTH-WESTERN EDUCATIONAL PUBLISHING
Cincinnati, Ohio

ALL RIGHTS RESERVED

The text of this publication, or any part thereof, may not be reproduced or transmitted in any form or by any means, electronic or mechanical, including photocopying, scanning, recording, storage in an information retrieval system, or otherwise, without the prior written permission of the publisher.

> **WARNING:** Reproducing the pages of this book by any means, without the prior written permission of the publisher, may be a violation of applicable copyright laws. Illegal copying robs authors and publishers of their proper revenues and makes educational materials more expensive for everyone. South-Western Educational Publishing is interested in knowing about violations of copyright law. If you know of materials being illegally copied and distributed, please contact us.

You can request permission to use material from this text through the following phone and fax numbers: Phone: 1-800-730-2214, Fax: 1-800-730-2215, or visit our web site at http://www.thomsonrights.com.

ISBN: 0-538-42613-6

1 2 3 4 5 6 7 XX 03 02 01 00

Managing Editor: Carol Volz
Project Manager/Editor: Cheryl L. Beck
Marketing Manager: Larry Qualls
Consulting Editor: Robin Romer, Pale Moon Productions
Production Services: GEX Publishing Services
Graphic Designer: Brenda Grannan, Grannan Graphics
Fee Writer: Benjamin Rand

I(T)P®
International Thomson Publishing

South-Western Educational Publishing is a division of International Thomson Publishing, Inc. The ITP logo is a registered trademark herein used under license by South-Western Educational Publishing.

The names of all commercially available software and other products mentioned herein are used for identification purposes only and may be trademarks or registered trademarks of their respective owners.

South-Western Educational Publishing disclaims any affiliation, association, connection with, sponsorship, or endorsement by such owners.

Mastering and Using

Microsoft® Excel 2000 Comprehensive Course for Windows®

Journey into the Future . . .

Our NEW Napier & Judd series™, *Mastering and Using Microsoft Excel 2000 Comprehensive Course* is the most comprehensive, instructional tool designed for the user who wants to master and use the application software. This expertly written product provides all the instruction necessary to be certified as a Microsoft Office User Specialist (MOUS) Core and Expert user.

Mastering and Using Microsoft Excel 2000 Comprehensive
- Student Text (perfect bound, soft cover) — 0-538-42613-6
- Student Text/data CD-ROM Package — 0-538-42615-2
- Activities Workbook (perfect bound, soft cover) — 0-538-42624-1
- Electronic Instructor Package (Manual and CD-ROM) — 0-538-42614-4
- Testing Package — 0-538-42673-X

A new feature is the Electronic Instructor, a CD-ROM which includes lesson plans, SCAN correlations, scheduling charts, presentations slides, and much more! Books complementary to this book include the following:

Mastering and Using Microsoft Excel 2000 Beginning Course
- Student Text (perfect bound, soft cover) — 0-538-42808-2
- Student Text/data CD-ROM Package — 0-538-42805-8
- Activities Workbook (perfect bound, soft cover) — 0-538-42624-1
- Electronic Instructor Package (Manual and CD-ROM) — 0-538-42614-4
- Testing Package — 0-538-42673-X

Mastering and Using Microsoft Excel 2000 Intermediate Course
- Student Text (perfect bound, soft cover) — 0-538-42809-0
- Student Text/data CD-ROM Package — 0-538-42806-6
- Activities Workbook (perfect bound, soft cover) — 0-538-42624-1
- Electronic Instructor Package (Manual and CD-ROM) — 0-538-42614-4
- Testing Package — 0-538-42673-X

Mastering and Using Microsoft Excel 2000 Advanced Course
- Student Text (perfect bound, soft cover) — 0-538-42810-4
- Student Text/data CD-ROM Package — 0-538-42807-4
- Activities Workbook (perfect bound, soft cover) — 0-538-42624-1
- Electronic Instructor Package (Manual and CD-ROM) — 0-538-42614-4
- Testing Package — 0-538-42673-X

For more information about these South-Western products and others:
Join us On the Internet at www.swep.com

What's New in Excel 2000

Office

- Different Office 2000 suites
- Personalized menus and toolbars
- Multi-language support
- Web-based analysis tools
- Improved Office Assistant
- Online collaboration with NetMeeting and Web discussions from inside Office applications
- E-mail from inside Office applications
- Collect and Paste and Office Clipboard toolbar
- New Open and Save As dialog box features
- Saving directly to Web server
- New Clip Gallery format and new clips

Excel

- See-through selection shading
- Euro currency symbol added to number formats
- Four-digit date formats
- List AutoFill automatically extends formatting of lists to new items
- PivotChart reports created from PivotTable reports
- Display units can be modified on charts
- Open and save HTML documents natively
- Create interactive PivotTables for the Web
- Create PivotTable reports directly on the worksheet
- Indented PivotTable report format
- PivotTable AutoFormat
- Row and column fields list arrow to hide or display items
- Create PivotTable reports using information stored in OLAP data cubes
- Create OLAP data cubes based on queries from other databases
- Digital signing of macros to ensure virus-free status
- Insert pictures directly from a scanner

Napier & Judd

In their over 48 years of combined experience, Al Napier and Phil Judd have developed a tested, realistic approach to mastering and using application software. As both academics and corporate trainers, Al and Phil have the unique ability to help students by teaching them the skills necessary to compete in today's complex business world.

H. Albert Napier, Ph.D. is the Director of the Center on the Management of Information Technology and Professor in the Jones Graduate School of Administration at Rice University. In addition, Al is a principal of Napier & Judd, Inc., a consulting company and corporate trainer in Houston, Texas, that has trained more than 90,000 people in computer applications.

Philip J. Judd is a former instructor in the Management Department and the Director of the Research and Instructional Computing Service at the University of Houston. Phil now dedicates himself to corporate training and consulting as a principal of Napier & Judd, Inc.

Philip J. Judd

H. Albert Napier, Ph.D.

Preface

At South-Western Educational Publishing, we believe that technology will change the way people teach and learn. Today there are millions of people using personal computers in their everyday lives—both as tools at work and for recreational activities. As a result, the personal computer has revolutionized the ways in which people interact with each other. The Napier and Judd series combines the following distinguishing features to allow people to do amazing things with their personal computers.

Distinguishing Features

All the textbooks in the *Mastering and Using* series share several key pedagogical features:

Case Project Approach. In their more than twenty years of business and corporate training and teaching experience, Napier and Judd have found that learners are more enthusiastic about learning a software application if they can see its real-world relevance. The textbook provides bountiful business-based profiles, exercises, and projects. It also emphasizes the skills most in demand by employers.

Comprehensive and Easy to Use. There is thorough coverage of new features. The narrative is clear and concise. Each unit or chapter thoroughly explains the concepts that underlie the skills and procedures. We explain not just the *how*, but the *why*.

Step-by-Step Instructions and Screen Illustrations. All examples in this text include step-by-step instructions that explain how to complete the specific task. Full-color screen illustrations are used extensively to provide the learner with a realistic picture of the software application feature.

Extensive Tips and Tricks. The author has placed informational boxes in the margin of the text. These boxes of information provide the learner with the following helpful tips:

- Quick Tip. Extra information provides shortcuts on how to perform common business-related functions.
- Caution Tip. This additional information explains how a mistake occurs and provides tips on how to avoid making similar mistakes in the future.
- Menu Tip. Additional explanation on how to use menu commands to perform application tasks.
- Mouse Tip. Further instructions on how to use the mouse to perform application tasks.
- Internet Tip. This information incorporates the power of the Internet to help learners use the Internet as they progress through the text.
- Design Tip. Hints for better presentation designs (found in only the PowerPoint book).

End-of-Chapter Materials. Each book in the *Mastering and Using* series places a heavy emphasis on providing learners with the opportunity to practice and reinforce the skills they are learning through extensive exercises. Each chapter has a summary, commands review, concepts review, skills review, and case projects so that the learner can master the material by doing. For more information on each of the end-of-chapter elements see page viii of the How to Use this Book section in this preface.

Appendixes. *Mastering and Using* series contains three appendixes to further help the learner prepare to be successful in the classroom or in the workplace. Appendix A teaches the learner to work with Windows 98. Appendix B teaches the learner how to use Windows Explorer; Appendix C illustrates how to format letters; how to insert a mailing notation; how to format envelopes (referencing the U.S. Postal Service documents); how to format interoffice memorandums; and how to key a formal outline. It also lists popular style guides and describes proofreader's marks.

Microsoft Office User Specialist (MOUS) Certification. The logo on the cover of this book indicates that these materials are officially certified by Microsoft Corporation. This certification is part of the MOUS program, which validates your skills as a knowledgeable user of Microsoft applications. Upon completing the lessons in the book, you will be prepared to take a test that could qualify you as either a core or expert user. To be certified, you will need to take an exam from a third-party testing company called an Authorization Certification Testing Center. Call **1-800-933-4493** to find the location of the testing center nearest you. Tests are conducted at different dates throughout the calendar year. To learn more about the entire line of training materials suitable for Microsoft Office certification, contact your South-Western Representative or call **1-800-824-5179**. Also visit our Web site at *www.swep.com*. To learn more about the MOUS program, you can visit Microsoft's Web site at *www.microsoft.com/train_cert/cert/*.

SCANS. In 1992, the U.S. Department of Labor and Education formed the Secretary's Commission on Achieving Necessary Skills, or SCANS, to study the kinds of competencies and skills that workers must have to succeed in today's marketplace. The results of the study were published in a document entitled *What Work Requires of Schools: A SCANS Report for America 2000*. The in-chapter and end-of-chapter exercises in this book are designed to meet the criteria outlined in the SCANS report and thus help prepare learners to be successful in today's workplace.

Instructional Support

All books in the *Mastering and Using* series are supplemented with the following items:

Instructor's Resource Package. This printed instructor's manual contains lesson plans with teaching materials and preparation suggestions, along with tips for implementing instruction and assessment ideas; a suggested syllabus for scheduling semester, block, and quarter classes; and SCANS workplace know how. The printed manual is packaged with an Electronic Instructor CD-ROM. The Electronic Instructor CD-ROM contains all the materials found in the printed manual as well as:

- ▶ Student lesson plans
- ▶ Data files
- ▶ Solutions files
- ▶ Test questions
- ▶ Transparencies
- ▶ PowerPoint presentations
- ▶ Portfolio assessment/worksheets
- ▶ Learning styles strategies
- ▶ Career worksheets
- ▶ Tech prep strategies

Testing Tools Package. Testing Tools is a powerful testing and assessment package that enables instructors to create and print tests from test banks designed specifically for South-Western Educational Publishing titles. In addition, instructors with access to a networked computer lab (LAN) or the Internet can administer, grade, and track tests online. Learners can also take online practice tests.

Course. Course is a template-based platform to deliver a Web-based syllabus. It allows instructors to create their own completely customized online syllabus, including lesson descriptions, dates, assignments, grades, and lesson links to other resources on the Web. To access this Web tool, an instructor must be a South-Western customer and contact sales support at 1-800-824-5179 for an access code. After the instructor has set up the online syllabus, students can access the Course.

Learner Support

Activity Workbooks. The workbook includes additional end-of-chapter exercises over and above those provided in the main text.

Data CD-ROM. To use this book, the learner must have the data CD-ROM (also referred to as the Data Disk). Data Files needed to complete exercises in the text are contained on this CD-ROM. These files can be copied to a hard drive or posted to a network drive.

How to Use This Book

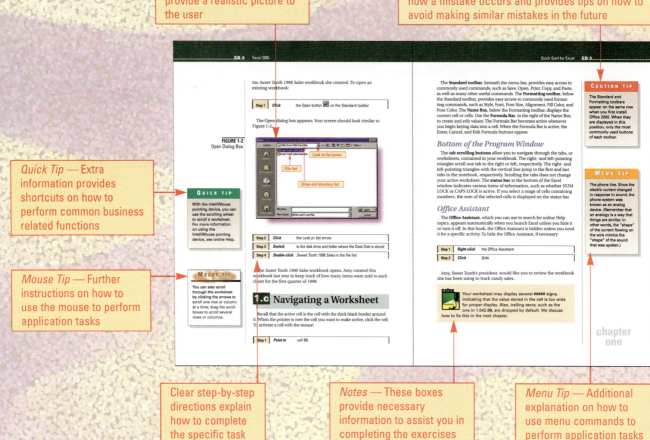

Learning Objectives — A quick reference of the major topics learned in the chapter

Chapter Overview — A concise summary of what will be learned in the chapter

Case profile — Realistic scenarios that show the real world application of the material being covered

Full color screen illustrations provide a realistic picture to the user

Caution Tip — This additional information explains how a mistake occurs and provides tips on how to avoid making similar mistakes in the future

Quick Tip — Extra information provides shortcuts on how to perform common business related functions

Mouse Tip — Further instructions on how to use the mouse to perform application tasks

Clear step-by-step directions explain how to complete the specific task

Notes — These boxes provide necessary information to assist you in completing the exercises

Menu Tip — Additional explanation on how to use menu commands to perform application tasks

End-of-Chapter Material

Summary — Reviews key topics discussed in the chapter

Commands Review — Provides a quick reference and reinforcement tool on multiple methods for performing actions discussed in the chapter

Concepts Review — Multiple choice and true or false questions help assess how well the reader has learned the chapter material

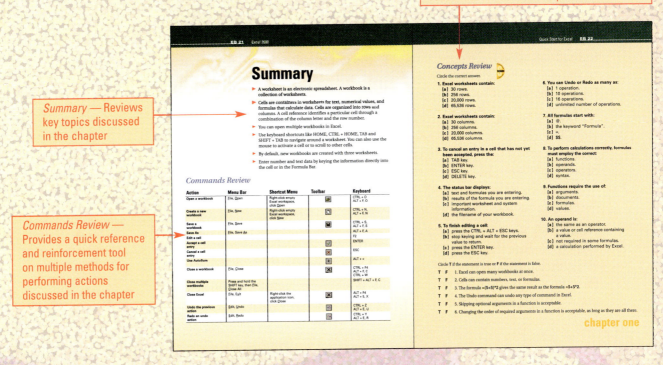

Skills Review — Hands-on exercises provide the ability to practice the skills just learned in the chapter

SCANS icon — Indicates that the exercise or project meets a SCANS competencies and prepares the learner to be successful in today's workplace

Case Projects — Asks the reader to synthesize the material they learned in the chapter and complete an office assignment

Internet Case Projects — Allow the reader to practice using the World Wide Web

MOUS Certification icon — indicates that the exercise or project meets Microsoft's certification objectives that prepare the learner for the MOUS exam

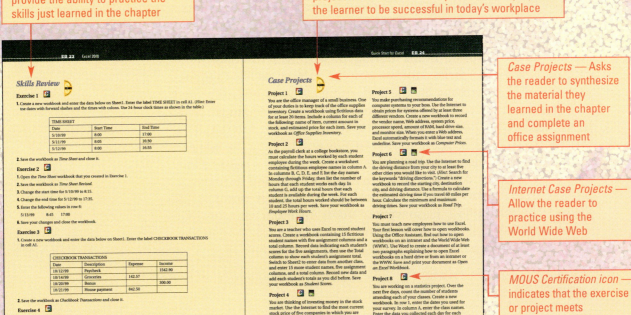

Acknowledgments

We would like to thank and express our appreciation to the many fine individuals who have contributed to the completion of this book. We have been fortunate to have a reviewer whose constructive comments have been so helpful: Kathy Koppy.

No book is possible without the motivation and support of an editorial staff. Therefore, we wish to acknowledge with great appreciation the project team at South-Western Educational Publishing: Cheryl Beck, project manager; Mike Broussard, art and designer coordinator; Angela McDonald, production coordinator; Kathy Hampton, manufacturing coordinator, and Carol Volz, managing editor.

We are very appreciative of the personnel at Napier & Judd, Inc., who helped prepare this book. We acknowledge, with great appreciation, the assistance provided by Ollie Rivers and Nancy Onarheim in preparing the Office unit and Appendixes for this book. We gratefully acknowledge the work of Benjamin Rand in writing the Excel unit for this series.

H. Albert Napier
Philip J. Judd

Thoreau wrote, "Most men live lives of quiet desperation." He obviously didn't have an editor and deadlines when he was writing, because there was nothing "quiet" about the desperation. First and foremost, my biggest debt of gratitude is owed to my wife, Erika, and my two wonderful boys, Casey and Jordan. Having Daddy home was elevated to the status of "Event" during the writing of this book, but they were never less thrilled for the rarity of it. Next, I'd like to thank everyone at ITP for giving me the opportunity to work on this project. To Kitty, my editor, can we meet on Jeopardy next, or would we have to stay up late/get up early studying for that? I also need to thank Mike and Karl for getting me started writing and helping me make the connections that are so important in this business. Thanks a lot (you know how to take that). I have to thank my dad and business partner for letting me go on "sabbatical" for a couple of months while I worked on this project. I also want to thank my mom who continues to believe in her children and what they can accomplish. And finally, to my friends who haven't seen me at all, I got next game.

Benjamin Rand

Contents

Napier & Judd — v

Preface — vi

OFFICE UNIT — OF 1

1 Getting Started with Microsoft Office 2000 — OF 2
   a. What Is Microsoft Office 2000? — OF 3
   b. Hardware and Software Requirements — OF 4
   c. Identifying Common Office Elements — OF 4
   d. Starting Office Applications — OF 7
   e. Getting Help in Office Applications — OF 11
   f. Closing Office Applications — OF 16

2 Working with Menus and Toolbars — OF 20
   a. Working with Personalized Menus and Toolbars — OF 21
   b. Viewing, Hiding, Docking, and Floating Toolbars — OF 25
   c. Customizing the Menu Bar and Toolbars — OF 27
   d. Viewing and Customizing the Office Shortcut Bar — OF 28

3 Working With Others Using Online Collaboration Tools — OF 35
   a. Scheduling an Online Meeting — OF 36
   b. Participating in Web Discussions — OF 42

4 Introduction to the Internet and the World Wide Web — OF 50
   a. What Is the Internet? — OF 51
   b. Connecting to the Internet — OF 52
   c. Challenges to Using the Internet — OF 55
   d. Using Internet Explorer — OF 56
   e. Using Directories and Search Engines — OF 59

EXCEL UNIT — EB 1

1 Quick Start for Excel — EB 2
   a. Exploring the Excel Components — EB 3
   b. Locating and Opening an Existing Workbook — EB 5
   c. Navigating a Worksheet — EB 6
   d. Entering Text, Dates, and Numbers — EB 7
   e. Selecting Cells — EB 9
   f. Editing Cell Content — EB 11
   g. Clearing Contents and Formatting of Cells — EB 13
   h. Using Undo and Redo — EB 13
   i. Entering Formulas and Functions — EB 14
   j. Saving Workbooks — EB 18
   k. Closing Workbooks and Exiting Excel — EB 20

2 Formatting Worksheets — EB 28
   a. Merging Cells to Create a Worksheet Title — EB 29
   b. Working with a Series to Add Labels — EB 30
   c. Modifying the Size of Columns and Rows — EB 32
   d. Changing Fonts and Font Styles — EB 33
   e. Modifying the Alignment of Cell Contents — EB 35
   f. Rotating Text and Changing Indents — EB 36
   g. Applying Number Formats — EB 37
   h. Applying Cell Borders and Shading — EB 40

3 Organizing Worksheets Effectively — EB 52
   a. Performing Single and Multi-level Sorts — EB 53
   b. Copying and Moving Data Using Drag and Drop — EB 54
   c. Renaming a Worksheet — EB 56
   d. Inserting, Moving, Copying, and Deleting Worksheets — EB 56
   e. Copy and Move Data Using Cut, Copy, and Paste — EB 58
   f. Inserting and Deleting Cells, Rows, and Columns — EB 61
   g. Using Absolute, Relative, and Mixed References in Formulas — EB 62
   h. Creating and Using Named Ranges — EB 65
   i. Freezing and Unfreezing Rows and Columns — EB 67
   j. Using Grouping and Outlines — EB 68
   k. Check Spelling in a Worksheet — EB 71

4 Previewing and Printing Worksheets — **EB 80**
- a. Previewing and Modifying Page Setup Options — EB 81
- b. Inserting and Removing Page Breaks — EB 88
- c. Printing an Entire Workbook — EB 90

5 Creating Charts — **EB 98**
- a. Using Chart Wizard to Create a Chart — EB 99
- b. Formatting and Modifying a Chart — EB 102
- c. Previewing and Printing Charts — EB 105
- d. Working with Embedded Charts — EB 106

EX Integrating Excel with Office Applications and the Internet — **EX 1**
- a. Integrating Excel with Word and PowerPoint — EX 2
- b. Integrating Excel with Access — EX 9
- c. Importing Data from Other Applications — EX 15
- d. Sending a Workbook via E-mail — EX 16
- e. Integrating Excel with the Internet — EX 20

6 Drawing in Excel — **EI 1**
- a. Using Clip Art and AutoShapes — EI 2
- b. Adding and Modifying Text and Line Objects — EI 9
- c. Adding Shadow and 3-D Effects to Objects — EI 12
- d. Modifying Stack Order and Grouping Objects — EI 15
- e. Creating WordArt — EI 17

7 Using Worksheet Functions — **EI 26**
- a. Using Worksheet Functions — EI 27
- b. Using Paste Function and the Formula Palette — EI 27
- c. Creating Natural Language Formulas — EI 32
- d. Using Date and Time Functions — EI 33
- e. Using Financial Functions — EI 38
- f. Using Logical Functions — EI 44
- g. Using Statistical Functions — EI 50
- h. Using Engineering Functions — EI 53
- i. Using Lookup and Reference Functions — EI 55
- j. Using Text Functions — EI 59

8 Formatting Worksheets with Styles and Custom Formats — EI 70
- **a.** Creating Custom Number Formats — EI 71
- **b.** Using Conditional Formatting — EI 79
- **c.** Applying AutoFormats — EI 84
- **d.** Defining, Applying, and Removing Styles — EI 86

9 Summarizing Data with Data Maps, PivotTables, and PivotCharts — EI 100
- **a.** Using Data Map — EI 101
- **b.** Using Data Analysis — EI 109
- **c.** Creating PivotTable Reports — EI 113
- **d.** Modifying a PivotTable Report — EI 119
- **e.** Formatting a PivotTable Report — EI 123
- **f.** Creating PivotChart Reports — EI 126

10 Linking Multiple Worksheets and Workbooks — EI 136
- **a.** Grouping Worksheets to Share Data, Formatting, and Formulas — EI 137
- **b.** Linking Worksheets and Using 3-D References — EI 140
- **c.** Printing Multiple Worksheets — EI 143
- **d.** Working with Multiple Workbooks — EI 144
- **e.** Linking Workbooks — EI 147
- **f.** Inserting Hyperlinks — EI 150

11 Customizing Excel Templates, Toolbars, and Menus — EI 162
- **a.** Using and Editing Templates to Create a New Workbook — EI 163
- **b.** Creating Custom Templates — EI 171
- **c.** Viewing, Hiding, and Docking Toolbars — EI 175
- **d.** Customizing Toolbars — EI 178
- **e.** Creating a Custom Menu — EI 182

12 Sharing Workbooks with Others — EA 1
- **a.** Protecting Worksheets and Workbooks and Using Passwords — EA 2
- **b.** Sharing a Workbook — EA 4
- **c.** Tracking Changes — EA 5
- **d.** Changing Workbook Properties — EA 8
- **e.** Merging Workbooks — EA 9
- **f.** Creating, Editing, and Removing Comments — EA 11

13 Using Lists in Excel	**EA 20**
a. Identifying Components of a List	EA 21
b. Using Data Validation	EA 22
c. Using the Data Form	EA 32
d. Applying Data Filters	EA 34

14 Auditing a Worksheet	**EA 50**
a. Using Range Finder to Check and Review Data	EA 51
b. Identifying Relationships Between Precedent and Dependent Cells	EA 53
c. Tracing Errors	EA 58
d. Identifying Invalid Data	EA 59

15 Automating Excel with Macros	**EA 66**
a. Recording a Macro	EA 67
b. Running a Macro	EA 69
c. Editing a Macro	EA 70
d. Using Workbooks Containing Macros	EA 74
e. Adding Visual Basic Functions to a Macro	EA 76

16 Using What-If Analysis	**EA 89**
a. Creating Data Tables	EA 90
b. Using Goal Seek and Solver	EA 94
c. Creating Scenarios	EA 101

APPENDIX — AP 1

A Working with Windows 98	**AP 1**
a. Reviewing the Windows 98 Desktop	AP 2
b. Accessing Your Computer System Resources	AP 3
c. Using Menu Commands and Toolbar Buttons	AP 5
d. Using the Start Menu	AP 6
e. Reviewing Dialog Box Options	AP 7
f. Using Windows 98 Shortcuts	AP 8
g. Understanding the Recycle Bin	AP 10
h. Shutting Down Windows 98	AP 10

B. Managing Your Folders and Files Using Windows Explorer — AP 11
- a. Opening Windows Explorer — AP 12
- b. Reviewing Windows Explorer Options — AP 13
- c. Creating a New Folder — AP 14
- d. Moving and Copying Folders and Files — AP 15
- e. Renaming Folders and Files — AP 15
- f. Creating Desktop Shortcuts — AP 16
- g. Deleting Folders and Files — AP 16

C. Formatting Tips for Business Documents — AP 17
- a. Formatting Letters — AP 18
- b. Inserting Mailing Notations — AP 22
- c. Formatting Envelopes — AP 24
- d. Formatting Interoffice Memorandums — AP 26
- e. Formatting Formal Outlines — AP 28
- f. Using Proofreader's Marks — AP 30
- g. Using Style Guides — AP 31

Microsoft Office 2000

Office 2000

Getting Started with Microsoft Office 2000

Chapter Overview

Microsoft Office 2000 provides the ability to enter, record, analyze, display, and present any type of business information. In this chapter you learn about the capabilities of Microsoft Office 2000, including its computer hardware and software requirements and elements common to all its applications. You also learn how to open and close those applications and get help.

Learning Objectives

- Describe Microsoft Office 2000
- Determine hardware and software requirements
- Identify common Office elements
- Start Office applications
- Get help in Office applications
- Close Office applications

For more information on how to prepare for the MOUS certification exam, check out the MOUS certification grids located on the data CD-ROM under the MOUS correlation folder for each book.

chapter one

1.a What Is Microsoft Office 2000?

Microsoft Office 2000 is a software suite (or package) that contains a combination of software applications you use to create text documents, analyze numbers, create presentations, manage large files of data, create Web pages, and create professional-looking marketing materials. Table 1-1 lists four editions of the Office 2000 suite and the software applications included in each.

Applications	Premium	Professional	Standard	Small Business
Word	X	X	X	X
Excel	X	X	X	X
PowerPoint	X	X	X	
Access	X	X		
Outlook	X	X	X	X
Publisher	X	X		X
FrontPage	X			

TABLE 1-1
Office 2000 Editions

> **CAUTION TIP**
>
> This book assumes that you have little or no knowledge of Microsoft Office 2000, but that you have worked with personal computers and are familiar with Microsoft Windows 98 or Windows 95 operating systems.

The **Word 2000** software application provides you with word processing capabilities. **Word processing** is the preparation and production of text documents such as letters, memorandums, and reports. **Excel 2000** is software you use to analyze numbers with worksheets (sometimes called spreadsheets) and charts, as well as perform other tasks such as sorting data. A **worksheet** is a grid of columns and rows in which you enter labels and data. A **chart** is a visual or graphic representation of worksheet data. With Excel, you can create financial budgets, reports, and a variety of other forms.

PowerPoint 2000 software is used to create **presentations,** a collection of slides. A **slide** is the presentation output (actual 35mm slides, transparencies, computer screens, or printed pages) that contains text, charts, graphics, audio, and video. You can use PowerPoint slides to create a slide show on a computer attached to a projector, to broadcast a presentation over the Internet or company intranet, and to create handout materials for a presentation.

Access 2000 provides database management capabilities, enabling you to store and retrieve a large amount of data. A **database** is a collection of related information. A phone book or an address book are common examples of databases you use every day. Other databases include a price list, school registration information, or an inventory. You can query (or search) an Access database to answer specific questions about the stored data. For example, you can determine which customers in a particular state had sales in excess of a particular value during the month of June.

> **QUICK TIP**
>
> Microsoft Office 2000 is often called Office and the individual applications are called Word, Excel, PowerPoint, Access, Outlook, Publisher, and so on.

chapter one

Outlook 2000 is a **personal information manager** that enables you to send and receive e-mail, as well as maintain a calendar, contacts list, journal, electronic notes, and an electronic "to do" list. **Publisher 2000** is desktop publishing software used to create publications, such as professional-looking marketing materials, newsletters, or brochures. Publisher wizards provide step-by-step instructions for creating a publication from an existing design; you also can design your own publication. The **FrontPage 2000** application is used to create and manage Web sites. **PhotoDraw 2000** is business graphics software that allows users to add custom graphics to marketing materials and Web pages.

A major advantage of using an Office suite is the ability to share data between applications. For example, you can include a portion of an Excel worksheet or chart in a Word document, use an outline created in a Word document as the starting point for a PowerPoint presentation, import an Excel worksheet into Access, merge names and addresses from an Outlook Address Book with a Word letter, or import a picture from PhotoDraw into a newsletter created in Publisher.

> **MENU TIP**
>
> Publisher tutorials are a series of hyperlinked windows providing a brief introduction to a specific topic. Each window contains a series of hyperlink buttons at the bottom of the window you use to advance to the next tutorial page or return to the main tutorial menu. To review the online tutorials, open Publisher, click the Help menu, and then click Publisher Tutorials.

1.b Hardware and Software Requirements

You must install Office 2000 applications in Windows 95, Windows 98, or Windows NT Workstation 4.0 with Service Pack 3.0 installed. The applications will not run in the Windows 3.x or the Windows NT Workstation 3.5 environments.

Microsoft recommends that you install Office on a computer that has a Pentium processor, at least 32 MB of RAM, a CD-ROM drive, Super VGA, 256-color video, Microsoft Mouse, Microsoft IntelliMouse, or another pointing device, and at least a 28,800-baud modem. To access certain features you should have a multimedia computer, e-mail software, and a Web browser. For detailed information on installing Office, see the documentation that comes with the software.

> **QUICK TIP**
>
> If you store your files and documents on diskette, make sure you have the proper type of diskette for your computer. A disk storage box is a good way to store and protect diskettes you are not using.

1.c Identifying Common Office Elements

Office applications share many common elements, making it easier for you to work efficiently in any application. A **window** is a rectangular area on your screen in which you view a software application, such as Excel. All the Office application windows have a similar look and arrangement of shortcuts, menus, and toolbars. In addition, they share many features, such as a common dictionary to use for spell checking your work and identical menu commands, toolbar buttons, shortcut menus, and keyboard shortcuts that enable you to perform tasks such as copying data from one location to another. Figure 1-1 shows the common elements in the Office application windows.

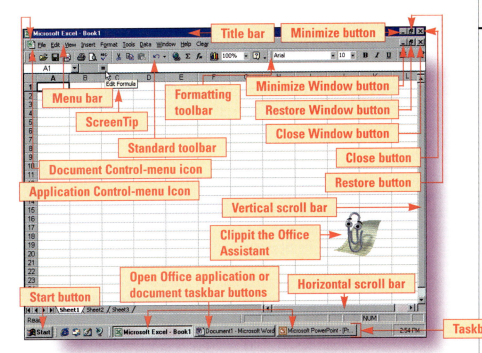

FIGURE 1-1
Common Elements in Office Application Windows

Title Bar

The application **title bar** at the top of the window includes the application Control-menu icon, the application name, the filename of the active document, and the Minimize, Restore (or Maximize), and Close buttons.

The **application Control-menu** icon, located in the left corner of the title bar, displays the Control menu. The Control menu commands manage the application window, and typically include commands such as: Restore, Move, Size, Minimize, Maximize, and Close. Commands that are currently available appear in a darker color. You can view the Control menu by clicking the Control-menu icon or by holding down the ALT key and then pressing the SPACEBAR key.

The **Minimize** button, near the right corner of the title bar reduces the application window to a taskbar button. The **Maximize** button, to the right of the Minimize button, enlarges the application window to fill the entire screen viewing area above the taskbar. If the window is already maximized, the Restore button appears in its place. The **Restore** button reduces the application window size. The **Close** button, located in the right corner of the title bar, closes the application and removes it from the computer's memory.

CAUTION TIP

In order to save hard disk space, Office installs many features and components as you need them. Shortcuts, toolbar buttons, and menu commands for these features appear in the application window or dialog boxes, indicating that the feature is available.

chapter one

> **QUICK TIP**
>
> Office 2000 file formats (except Access) are compatible with the previous version of Office (Office 97), which means Office 97 users can open Office 2000 files without a converter, although some Office 2000 formatting features will be lost. For a list of Office 2000 formatting features not supported by Office 97, see online Help in each application.

Menu Bar

The **menu bar** is a special toolbar located below the title bar and contains the menus for the application. A **menu** is list of commands. The menus common to Office applications are File, Edit, View, Insert, Format, Tools, Window, and Help. Each application may have additional menus.

The **document Control-menu** icon, located below the application Control-menu icon, contains the Restore, Move, Size, Minimize, Maximize, and Close menu commands for the document window. You can view the document Control menu by clicking the Control-menu icon or by holding down the ALT key and pressing the HYPHEN (-) key.

The **Minimize Window** button reduces the document window to a title-bar icon inside the document area. It appears on the menu bar below the Minimize button in Excel and PowerPoint. (Word documents open in their own application window and use the title bar Minimize button.)

The **Maximize Window** button enlarges the document window to cover the entire application display area and share the application title bar. It appears on the title-bar icon of a minimized Excel workbook or PowerPoint presentation. (Word documents open in their own application window and use the title bar Maximize button.) If the window is already maximized, the Restore Window button appears in its place.

The **Restore Window** button changes the document window to a smaller sized window inside the application window. It appears to the right of the Minimize Window button in Excel and PowerPoint. (Word documents open in their own application window and use the title bar Restore button.)

The **Close Window** button closes the document and removes it from the computer's memory. It appears to the right of the Restore Window or Maximize Window button. (In Word, the Close Window button appears only when one document is open. Otherwise, Word uses the title bar Close button.)

> **MOUSE TIP**
>
> If you are left-handed, you can switch the operation of the left and right mouse buttons in the Mouse Properties dialog box. Double-click the My Computer icon on the desktop, double-click the Control Panel folder, and then double-click the Mouse icon to display the dialog box.

Default Toolbars

The **Standard** and **Formatting toolbars,** located on one row below the menu bar, contain a set of icons called buttons. The toolbar buttons represent commonly used commands and are mouse shortcuts used to perform tasks quickly. In addition to the Standard and Formatting toolbars, each application has several other toolbars available. You can customize toolbars by adding or removing buttons and commands.

When the mouse pointer rests on a toolbar button, a **ScreenTip** appears identifying the name of the button. ScreenTips, part of online Help, describe a toolbar button, dialog box option, or menu command.

Scroll Bars

The **vertical scroll bar,** on the right side of the document area, is used to view various parts of the document by moving, or scrolling, the document up or down. It includes scroll arrows and a scroll box. The **horizontal scroll bar**, near the bottom of the document area, is used to view various parts of the document by scrolling the document left or right. It includes scroll arrows and a scroll box.

Office Assistant

The **Office Assistant** is an animated graphic you can click to view online Help. The Office Assistant may also anticipate your needs and provide advice in a balloon-style dialog box when you begin certain tasks, such as writing a letter in Word.

Taskbar

The **taskbar,** located across the bottom of the Windows desktop, includes the Start button and buttons for each open Office document. The **Start button,** located in the left corner of the taskbar, displays the Start menu or list of tasks you can perform and applications you can use.

You can switch between documents, close documents and applications, and view other items, such as the system time and printer status, with buttons or icons on the taskbar. If you are using Windows 98, other toolbars—such as the Quick Launch toolbar—may also appear on the taskbar.

> **QUICK TIP**
>
> You can use the keyboard to access Office application features. This book lists all keys in uppercase letters, such as the TAB key. This book lists keystrokes as: Press the ENTER key. When you are to press one key and, while holding down that key, to press another key, this book lists the keystrokes as: Press the SHIFT + F7 keys.

1.d Starting Office Applications

You access the Office applications through the Windows desktop. When you turn on your computer, the Windows operating system software is automatically loaded into memory. Once the process is complete, your screen should look similar to Figure 1-2.

notes The desktop illustrations in this book assume you are using Windows 98 with default settings. Your desktop may not look identical to the illustrations in this book. For more information on using Windows 98 see Appendix A or information provided by your instructor.

chapter one

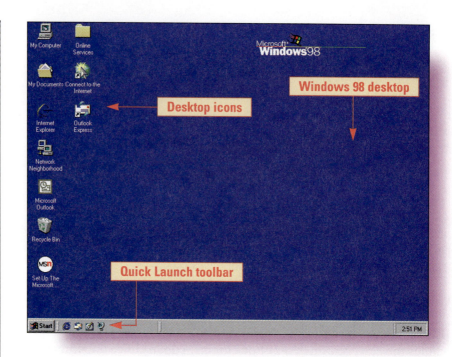

FIGURE 1-2
Default Windows 98 Desktop

MOUSE TIP

This book uses distinct instructions for mouse operations. **Point** means to place the mouse pointer on the specified command or item. **Click** means to press the left mouse button and then release it. **Right-click** means to press the right mouse button and then release it. **Double-click** means to press the left mouse button twice very rapidly. **Drag** means to press and hold down the left mouse button and then move the mouse on the mouse pad. **Right-drag** means to press and hold down the right mouse button and then move the mouse on the mouse pad. **Scroll** means to use the application scroll bar features or the IntelliMouse scrolling wheel.

You begin by opening the Excel application. To use Start button to open Excel:

Step 1	Click	the Start button [Start] on the taskbar
Step 2	Point to	Programs
Step 3	Click	Microsoft Excel on the Programs menu

The Excel software is placed into the memory of your computer and the Excel window opens. Your screen should look similar to Figure 1-1.

You can open and work in more than one Office application at a time. When Office is installed, the Open Office Document command and the New Office Document command appear on the Start menu. You can use these commands to select the type of document on which you want to work rather than first selecting an Office application. To create a new Word document without first opening the application:

Step 1	Click	the Start button [Start] on the taskbar
Step 2	Click	New Office Document
Step 3	Click	the General tab, if necessary

The dialog box that opens should look similar to Figure 1-3.

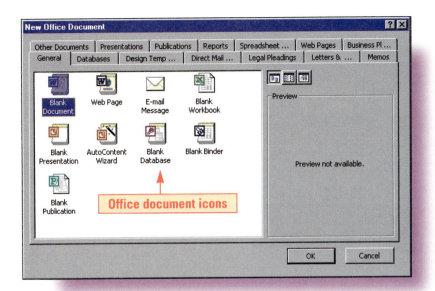

FIGURE 1-3
General Tab in the New Office Document Dialog Box

QUICK TIP

A **dialog box** is a window that contains options for performing specific tasks. The New Office Document dialog box contains **icons** (or pictures) for creating a blank Word document, Web page (in Word), e-mail message (using Outlook or Outlook Express), Excel workbook, PowerPoint presentation, Access database, or Publisher publication. The available icons depends on the Office applications you have installed.

To create a blank Word document:

| Step 1 | Click | the Blank Document icon to select it, if necessary |
| Step 2 | Click | OK |

The Word software loads into your computer's memory, the Word application opens with a blank document, and a taskbar button appears for the document. Your screen should look similar to Figure 1-4.

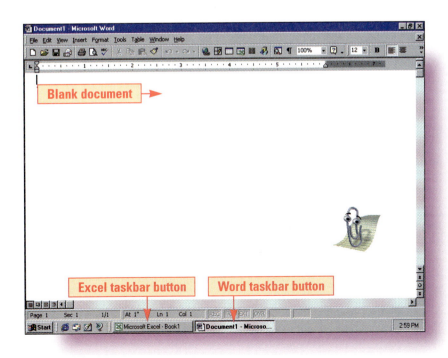

FIGURE 1-4
Word Application Window

Mouse tip

Double-clicking an icon is the same as clicking it once to select it and then clicking the OK button.

Next you open a blank presentation. To open the PowerPoint application and a blank presentation:

Step 1	Open	the New Office Document dialog box using the Start menu
Step 2	Double-click	the Blank Presentation icon
Step 3	Click	OK in the New Slide dialog box to create a blank title slide, as shown in Figure 1-5

FIGURE 1-5
Blank PowerPoint Presentation

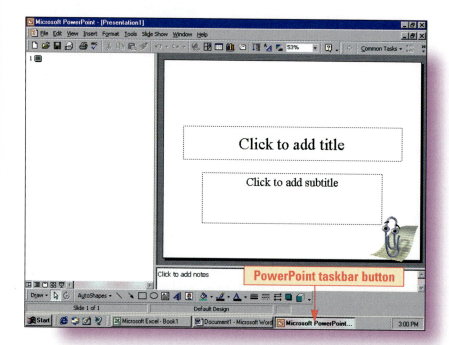

Quick tip

You can have multiple Excel workbooks, PowerPoint presentations, and Word documents open at one time. Each open workbook, presentation, and document has its own taskbar button. Your computer's resources determine the number of documents, workbooks, and presentations you can have open at once. You can open only one Access database at a time.

You can also open an Office application by opening an existing Office document from the Start menu. To open an existing Access database:

Step 1	View	the Start button 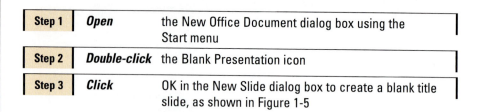 on the taskbar
Step 2	Click	Open Office Document
Step 3	Click	the Look in: list arrow in the Open Office Document dialog box
Step 4	Switch	to the disk drive and folder where the Data Files are stored
Step 5	Double-click	*International Sales* to open the Access application and database, as shown in Figure 1-6

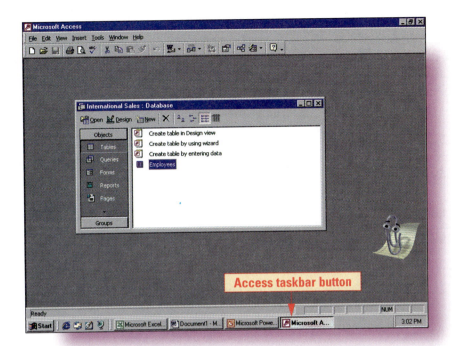

FIGURE 1-6
International Sales Database in Access Window

You can switch between open Office documents by clicking the appropriate taskbar button. To switch to the Excel workbook and then the Word document:

Step 1	Click	the Excel button on the taskbar
Step 2	Observe	that the Excel window and workbook are visible
Step 3	Click	the Word Document1 button on the taskbar
Step 4	Observe	that the Word window and document are visible

1.e Getting Help in Office Applications

There are several ways to get help in any Office application. You can display the Office Assistant, get context-sensitive help, or launch your Web browser and get Web-based help from Microsoft.

Using the Office Assistant

The **Office Assistant** is an interactive, animated graphic that appears in the Word, Excel, PowerPoint, and Publisher application windows. When you activate the Office Assistant, a balloon-style dialog box

> **QUICK TIP**
>
> If multiple windows are open, the **active window** has a dark blue title bar. Inactive windows have a light gray title bar.

chapter one

> **MENU TIP**
>
> You can display the Office Assistant from the Help menu. You can also press the F1 key.

opens containing options for searching online Help by topic. The Office Assistant may also automatically offer suggestions when you begin certain tasks. As you begin to key a personal letter to Aunt Isabel, the Office Assistant automatically asks if you want help writing the letter. To begin the letter:

Step 1	Verify	the Word document is the active window
Step 2	Click	the Microsoft Word Help button on the Standard toolbar, if the Office Assistant is not visible
Step 3	Key	Dear Aunt Isabel: (including the colon)
Step 4	Press	the ENTER key

The Office Assistant and balloon appear. Your screen should look similar to Figure 1-7.

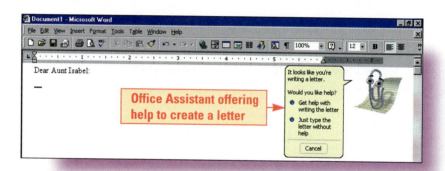

FIGURE 1-7
Office Assistant Balloon

The Office Assistant balloon contains three options you can click with the mouse. If you click the "Get help with writing the letter" option, the Letter Wizard dialog box opens. A **wizard** is a series of dialog boxes you can use to complete a task step-by-step. If you click the "Just type the letter without help" option or the Cancel option, the balloon closes.

Step 5	Click	Cancel to close the balloon

If you prefer to use the Microsoft Help window to access online Help, you can choose to show or hide the Office Assistant or you can turn off the Office Assistant completely. To hide the Office Assistant:

Step 1	Right-click	the Office Assistant
Step 2	Click	Hide

> **CAUTION TIP**
>
> After you cancel the balloon, the letter-writing help options will not appear again until you create a new, blank document.

You can activate the Office Assistant at any time to search online help for specific topics or to customize the Office Assistant. Custom options affect all Office applications. To review the Office Assistant customization options:

Step 1	Click	the Microsoft Word Help button on the Standard toolbar
Step 2	Click	the Office Assistant to view the balloon, if necessary
Step 3	Click	Options in the Office Assistant balloon
Step 4	Click	the Options tab, if necessary

The dialog box that opens should look similar to Figure 1-8.

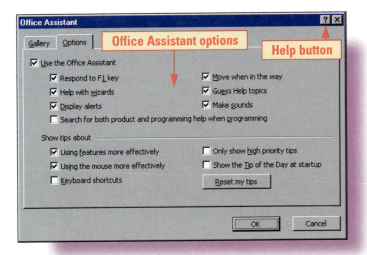

> **MENU TIP**
>
> You can hide the Office Assistant by clicking the Hide the Office Assistant command on the Help menu. You can redisplay the Office Assistant by clicking the Show the Office Assistant on the Help menu.

FIGURE 1-8
Options Tab in the Office Assistant Dialog Box

To learn about dialog box options, you can use the dialog box Help button or you can right-click an option. To view the ScreenTip help:

Step 1	Drag	the Office Assistant out of the way, if necessary
Step 2	Right-click	the Keyboard shortcuts option
Step 3	Click	What's This? to view a ScreenTip help message for this option
Step 4	Press	the ESC key to close the ScreenTip help message

> **MOUSE TIP**
>
> You can drag the Office Assistant to a new location with the mouse pointer.

The default Office Assistant image is Clippit. But you can select from a gallery of animated images. To view the Office Assistant image options:

Step 1	Click	the Gallery tab

chapter one

| Step 2 | **Click** | the Next> and <Back buttons to view different image options |
| Step 3 | **Click** | Cancel to close the dialog box without changing any options |

You can use the Office Assistant to search an application's online Help. Suppose you want to learn how to turn off the Office Assistant. To search online Help:

Step 1	**Click**	the Office Assistant to activate the balloon
Step 2	**Key**	turn off the Office Assistant in the text box
Step 3	**Press**	the ENTER key to view a list of help options in the balloon dialog box
Step 4	**Click**	the Hide, show, or turn off the Office Assistant option

The Microsoft Word Help window opens and contains information about how to manage the Office Assistant. Your screen should look similar to Figure 1-9.

FIGURE 1-9
Microsoft Word Help Window

You can scroll the Help window to view all the information. You can click the Show button to view the Contents, Answer Wizard, and Index tabs that access other help topics. If you have Internet access, you can view a Microsoft Help Web page from inside the Help window. To view the additional tabs:

| Step 1 | Click | the Show button in the Help window, if necessary, to display the Contents, Answer Wizard, and Index tabs |
| Step 2 | Click | the Close button ☒ in the upper-right corner of the window |

Using the Help Menu

The Help menu provides commands you can use to view the Office Assistant or Help window, show or hide the Office Assistant, connect to the Microsoft Web site, get context-sensitive help for a menu command or toolbar button, detect and repair font and template files, and view licensing information for the Office application. To review the Help menu commands:

Step 1	Click	Help
Step 2	Observe	the menu commands
Step 3	Click	in the document area outside the menu to close the Help menu

> **QUICK TIP**
>
> You can press the ESC key to close a menu.

Using What's This?

You can get context-sensitive help for a menu command or toolbar button using the What's This? command on the Help menu. This command changes the mouse pointer to a help pointer, a white mouse pointer with a large black question mark. When you click a toolbar button or menu command with the help pointer, a brief ScreenTip help message appears describing the command or toolbar button. To a ScreenTip help message for a toolbar button:

Step 1	Press	the SHIFT + F1 keys
Step 2	Observe	that the help mouse pointer with the attached question mark
Step 3	Click	the Save button 💾 on the Standard toolbar
Step 4	Observe	the ScreenTip help message describing the Save button
Step 5	Press	the ESC key to close the ScreenTip help message

chapter one

1.f Closing Office Applications

There are many ways to close the Access, Excel and PowerPoint applications (or the Word application with a single document open) and return to the Windows desktop. You can: (1) double-click the application Control-menu icon; (2) click the application Close button; (3) right-click the application taskbar button and then click the Close command on the shortcut menu; (4) press the ALT + F4 keys; or (5) click the Exit command on the File menu to close Office applications (no matter how many Word documents are open). To close the Excel application from the taskbar:

| Step 1 | *Right-click* | the Excel button on the taskbar |
| Step 2 | *Click* | Close |

You can close multiple applications at one time from the taskbar by selecting the application buttons using the CTRL key and then using the shortcut menu. To close the PowerPoint and Access applications:

Step 1	*Press & Hold*	the CTRL key
Step 2	*Click*	the PowerPoint button and then the Access button on the taskbar
Step 3	*Release*	the CTRL key and observe that both buttons are selected (pressed in)
Step 4	*Right-click*	the PowerPoint or Access button
Step 5	*Click*	Close

Both applications close, leaving only the Word document open. To close the Word document using the menu:

Step 1	*Verify*	that the Word application window is maximized
Step 2	*Click*	File
Step 3	*Click*	Exit
Step 4	*Click*	No in the Office Assistant balloon or confirmation dialog box to close Word without saving the document

Summary

- The Word application provides word processing capabilities for the preparation of text documents such as letters, memorandums, and reports.
- The Excel application provides the ability to analyze numbers in worksheets and for creating financial budgets, reports, charts, and forms.
- The PowerPoint application is used to create presentation slides and audience handouts.
- You can use Access databases to organize and retrieve collections of data.
- Publisher provides tools for creating marketing materials, such as newsletters, brochures, flyers, and Web pages.
- The Outlook application helps you send and receive e-mail, maintain a calendar, "to do" lists, organize the names and addresses of contacts, and perform other information management tasks.
- One major advantage of Office suite applications is the ability to integrate the applications by sharing information between them.
- Another advantage of using Office suite applications is that they share a number of common elements, such as window elements, shortcuts, toolbars, menu commands, and other features.
- You can start Office suite applications from the Programs submenu on the Start menu and from the Open Office Document or New Office Document commands on the Start menu.
- You can close Office applications by double-clicking the application Control Menu icon, clicking the application Close button on the title bar, right-clicking the application button on the taskbar, pressing the ALT + F4 keys, or clicking the Exit command on the File menu.
- You can get help in an Office application by clicking commands on the Help menu, pressing the F1 or SHIFT + F1 keys, or clicking the Microsoft Help button on the Standard toolbar.

chapter one

Concepts Review

Circle the correct answer.

1. ScreenTips do not provide:
 [a] the name of a button on a toolbar.
 [b] help for options in a dialog box.
 [c] context-sensitive help for menu commands or toolbar buttons.
 [d] access to the Office Assistant.

2. To manage a Web site, you can use:
 [a] Outlook.
 [b] FrontPage.
 [c] PhotoDraw.
 [d] Publisher.

3. The title bar contains the:
 [a] document Control-menu icon.
 [b] Close Window button.
 [c] Standard toolbar.
 [d] application and document name.

4. The Excel application is best used to:
 [a] prepare financial reports.
 [b] maintain a list of tasks to accomplish.
 [c] create newsletters, brochures, and flyers.
 [d] create custom graphics.

Circle **T** if the statement is true or **F** if the statement is false.
T F   1. You use Publisher to create newsletters and brochures.
T F   2. Excel is used to create presentation slides.
T F   3. The default Office Assistant graphic is Clippit.
T F   4. Access is used to create and format text.

Skills Review

Exercise 1
1. Identify each common element of Office application windows numbered in Figure 1-10.

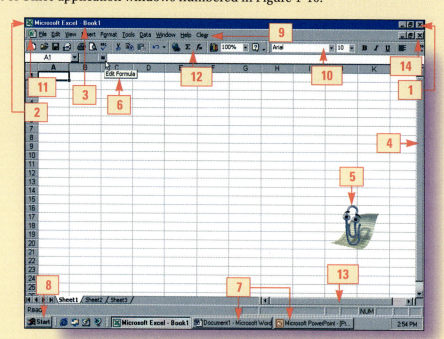

FIGURE 1-10
Excel Application Window

Exercise 2
1. Open the Word application using the <u>P</u>rograms command on the Start menu.
2. Close the Word application using the taskbar.

Exercise 3

1. Open the Excel application and then the PowerPoint application using the Programs command on the Start menu.
2. Open the Access application and the *International Sales* database using the Open Office Document command on the Start menu.
3. Switch to the PowerPoint application using the taskbar button and close it using the Close button on the title bar.
4. Close the PowerPoint and Access applications at the same time using the taskbar.

Exercise 4

1. Create a new, blank Word document using the New Office Document command on the Start menu.
2. Create a new, blank Excel workbook using the New Office Document command on the Start menu.
3. Switch to the Word document using the taskbar and close it using the title bar Close button.
4. Close the Excel workbook using the taskbar button.

Exercise 5

1. Open the Word application using the Start menu.
2. Show the Office Assistant, if necessary, with a command on the Help menu.
3. Hide the Office Assistant with a shortcut menu.
4. Show the Office Assistant with the Microsoft Word Help button on the Standard toolbar.
5. Search online Help using the search phrase "type text." Open the Type text help page.
6. Click the underlined text typing text to view a help page of subtopics. Scroll and review the help page.
7. Close the Help window. Hide the Office Assistant with a shortcut menu.

Case Projects

Project 1

You are the secretary to the marketing manager of High Risk Insurance, an insurance brokerage firm. The marketing manager wants to know how to open and close the Excel application. Write at least two paragraphs describing different ways to open and close Excel. With your instructor's permission, use your written description to show a classmate several ways to open and close Excel.

Project 2

You work in the administrative offices of Alma Public Relations, and the information management department just installed Office 2000 Professional on your computer. Your supervisor asks you to write down and describe some of the Office Assistant options. Open the Options tab in the Office Assistant dialog box. Review each option using the dialog box Help button or the What's This? command. Write at least three paragraphs describing five Office Assistant options.

Project 3

As the new office manager at Hot Wheels Messenger Service, you are learning to use the Word 2000 application and want to learn more about some of the buttons on the Word toolbars. Open Word and use the What's This? command on the Help menu to review the ScreenTip help for five toolbar buttons. Write a brief paragraph for each button describing how it is used.

Project 4

As the acquisitions director for Osiris Books, an international antique book and map dealer, you use Publisher to create the company's catalogs and brochures. A co-worker, who is helping you with a new brochure, opened Publisher and did not know why the Catalog window appeared. She has asked you for an explanation. Open the Publisher application and review the Catalog window. Close the Catalog window leaving the Publisher window open. Use the Office Assistant to find out more about the Catalog by searching online Help using the keyword "catalog." Write your co-worker a short note explaining how the Catalog is used.

Office 2000

Working with Menus and Toolbars

Chapter Overview

Office 2000 tries to make your work life easier by learning how you work. The personalized menus and toolbars in each application remember which commands and buttons you use, and add and remove them as needed. In this chapter, you learn how to work with the personalized menus and toolbars, how to customize the menu bar and toolbars, and how to view and customize the Office Shortcut Bar.

Learning Objectives

- Work with personalized menus and toolbars
- View, hide, dock, and float toolbars
- Customize the menu bar and toolbars
- View and customize the Office Shortcut Bar

chapter two

2.a Working with Personalized Menus and Toolbars

A **menu** is a list of commands you use to perform tasks in the Office applications. Some commands also have an associated image, or icon, shown to the left of a command. A **toolbar** contains a set of icons (the same icons you see on the menus) called **buttons** that you click with the mouse pointer to quickly execute a menu command.

When you first open Excel, Word, or PowerPoint, the menus on the menu bar initially show only a basic set of commands and the Standard and Formatting toolbars contain only a basic set of buttons. These short versions of the menus and toolbars are called **personalized menus and toolbars**. As you work, the commands and buttons you use most frequently are stored in the personalized settings. The first time you select a menu command or toolbar button that is not part of the basic set, it is added to your personalized settings and appears on the menu or toolbar. If you do not use a command for a while, it is removed from your personalized settings and no longer appears on the menu or toolbar. To view the personalized menus and toolbars in PowerPoint:

Step 1	Click	the Start button ⊞ Start on the taskbar
Step 2	Click	the New Office Document command on the Start menu
Step 3	Click	the General tab in the New Office Document dialog box
Step 4	Double-click	the Blank Presentation icon
Step 5	Click	OK in the New Slide dialog box to create a blank title slide for the presentation
Step 6	Click	Tools on the menu bar
Step 7	Observe	the short personalized menu containing only the basic commands, as shown in Figure 2-1

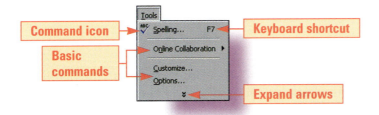

FIGURE 2-1
Personalized Tools Menu

CAUTION TIP

The activities in this chapter assume the personalized menus and toolbars are reset to their default settings. In this chapter, you select menu commands and toolbar buttons by clicking them with the mouse pointer. You learn how to use menu commands and toolbar buttons to perform tasks in the application chapters.

QUICK TIP

FrontPage and Access also provide the personalized menus and toolbars options. When you first open FrontPage, you see the Standard and Formatting toolbars. When you first open Access, you see only the Standard toolbar. Publisher does not provide the personalized menus and toolbars options.

chapter two

If the command you want to use does not appear on the short personalized menu, you can expand the menu by pausing for a few seconds until the menu expands, clicking the expand arrows at the bottom of the menu, or double-clicking the menu name.

| Step 8 | *Pause* | until the menu automatically expands, as shown in Figure 2-2 |

FIGURE 2-2
Expanded Tools Menu

> **QUICK TIP**
>
> You can also use keyboard shortcuts to perform tasks in Office applications. Many of these keyboard shortcuts are shown on the menus to the right of the menu command.

You move a menu command from the expanded menu to the personalized menu, simply by selecting it. To add the AutoCorrect command to the short personalized Tools menu:

Step 1	*Click*	AutoCorrect
Step 2	*Click*	Cancel in the AutoCorrect dialog box to cancel the dialog box
Step 3	*Click*	Tools on the menu bar
Step 4	*Observe*	the updated personalized Tools menu contains the AutoCorrect command, as shown in Figure 2-3

FIGURE 2-3
Updated Personalized Tools Menu

When you first open Word, Excel, or PowerPoint, the Standard and Formatting toolbars appear on one row below the title bar and some default buttons are hidden. You can resize a toolbar to view a hidden button by dragging its **move handle**, the gray vertical bar at the left edge of the toolbar, with the **move pointer,** a four-headed black arrow. To resize the Formatting toolbar:

Step 1	Move	the mouse pointer to the move handle on the Formatting toolbar
Step 2	Observe	that the mouse pointer becomes a move pointer
Step 3	Drag	the Formatting toolbar to the left until nine Formatting toolbar buttons are visible
Step 4	Observe	that you see fewer buttons on the Standard toolbar

The buttons that don't fit on the displayed area of a toolbar are collected in a More Buttons list. To view the remaining the Standard toolbar default buttons:

Step 1	Click	the More Buttons list arrow on the Standard toolbar
Step 2	Observe	the default buttons that are not visible on the toolbar, as shown in Figure 2-4

CAUTION TIP

When updating the personalized Standard or Formatting toolbar with a new button, a button that you have not used recently might move to the More Buttons list to make room for the new button.

FIGURE 2-4
More Buttons List

Step 3	Press	the ESC key to close the More Buttons list

If you want to display one of the default buttons on a personalized toolbar, you can select it from the More Buttons list. To add the Format Painter button to the personalized Standard toolbar:

Step 1	Click	the More Buttons list arrow on the Standard toolbar
Step 2	Click	the Format Painter button
Step 3	Observe	that the Format Painter button is turned on and added to the personalized Standard toolbar, as shown in Figure 2-5

FIGURE 2-5
Updated Personalized Standard Toolbar

| Step 4 | Click | the Format Painter button on the Standard toolbar to turn it off |

If you want to view all the menu commands instead of a short personalized menu and all the default toolbar buttons on the Standard and Formatting toolbars, you can change options in the Customize dialog box. To show all the toolbar buttons and menu commands:

Step 1	Click	Tools
Step 2	Click	Customize
Step 3	Click	the Options tab, if necessary

The dialog box that opens should be similar to Figure 2-6.

FIGURE 2-6
Options Tab in the Customize Dialog Box

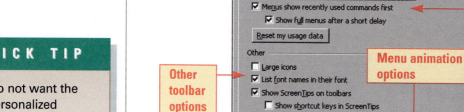

QUICK TIP

If you do not want the short personalized menus to expand automatically when you pause, remove the check mark from the Show full menus after a short delay check box. Then, to show the full menu, double-click the menu or click the expand arrows at the bottom of the menu.

Step 4	Click	the Standard and Formatting toolbars share one row check box to remove the check mark and reposition the Formatting toolbar below the Standard toolbar
Step 5	Click	the Menus show recently used commands first check box to remove the check mark and show the entire set of commands for each menu
Step 6	Click	Close to close the dialog box

Working with Menus and Toolbars   OF 25

Step 7	*Observe*	the repositioned Standard and Formatting toolbars
Step 8	*Click*	Tools to view the entire set of Tools menu commands
Step 9	*Press*	the ESC key

You can return the menus and toolbars to their initial (or **default**) settings in the Customize dialog box. To reset the default menus and toolbars:

Step 1	*Open*	the Options tab in the Customize dialog box
Step 2	*Click*	the Standard and Formatting toolbars share one row check box to insert a check mark
Step 3	*Click*	the Menus show recently used commands first check box to insert a check mark
Step 4	*Click*	Reset my usage data
Step 5	*Click*	Yes to confirm you want to reset the menus and toolbars to their default settings
Step 6	*Close*	the Customize dialog box
Step 7	*Observe*	that the Tools menu and Standard toolbar are reset to their default settings

2.b Viewing, Hiding, Docking, and Floating Toolbars

> **CAUTION TIP**
>
> When you choose the Menus show recently used commands first option, it affects all the Office applications, not just the open application.
> Resetting the usage data to the initial settings does not change the location of toolbars and does not remove or add buttons to toolbars you have customized in the Customize dialog box.

Office applications have additional toolbars that you can view when you need them. You can also hide toolbars when you are not using them. You can view or hide toolbars by pointing to the Toolbars command on the View menu and clicking a toolbar name or by using a shortcut menu. A **shortcut menu** is a short list of frequently used menu commands. You view a shortcut menu by pointing to an item on the screen and clicking the right mouse button. This is called right-clicking the item. The commands on shortcut menus vary—depending on where you right-click—so that you view only the most frequently used commands for a particular task. An easy way to view or hide toolbars is with a shortcut menu. To view the shortcut menu for PowerPoint toolbars:

| Step 1 | *Right-click* | the menu bar, the Standard toolbar, or the Formatting toolbar |
| Step 2 | *Observe* | the shortcut menu and the check marks next to the names of currently visible toolbars, as shown in Figure 2-7 |

FIGURE 2-7
Toolbars Shortcut Menu

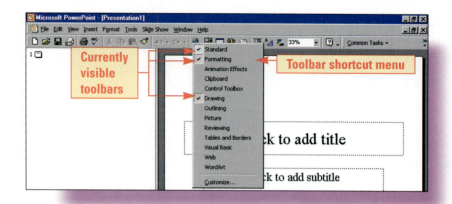

> **QUICK TIP**
>
> Some of the toolbars that appear on the toolbars list vary from Office application to application.

Step 3	Click	Tables and Borders in the shortcut menu
Step 4	Observe	that the Tables and Borders toolbar appears on your screen

The Tables and Borders toolbar, unless a previous user repositioned it, is visible in its own window near the middle of your screen. When a toolbar is visible in its own window it is called a **floating toolbar** and you can move and size it with the mouse pointer just like any window. When a toolbar appears fixed at the screen boundaries, it is called a **docked toolbar**. The menu bar and Standard and Formatting toolbars are examples of docked toolbars. In PowerPoint, the Drawing toolbar is docked above the status bar. You can dock a floating toolbar by dragging its title bar with the mouse pointer to a docking position below the title bar, above the status bar, or at the left and right boundaries of your screen. To dock the Tables and Borders toolbar below the Standard and Formatting toolbars:

Step 1	Position	the mouse pointer on the blue title bar in the Tables and Borders toolbar window
Step 2	Drag	the toolbar window slowly up until it docks below the Standard and Formatting toolbars

Similarly, you float a docked toolbar by dragging it away from its docked position toward the middle of the screen. To float the Tables and Borders toolbar:

Step 1	Position	the mouse pointer on the Tables and Borders toolbar move handle until it becomes a move pointer
Step 2	Drag	the Tables and Borders toolbar down toward the middle of the screen until it appears in its own window

Working with Menus and Toolbars

When you finish using a toolbar, you can hide it with a shortcut menu. To hide the Tables and Borders toolbar:

| Step 1 | Right-click | the Tables and Borders toolbar |
| Step 2 | Click | Tables and Borders to remove the check mark and hide the toolbar |

2.c Customizing the Menu Bar and Toolbars

Recall that you can add a button to a personalized toolbar by clicking the More Buttons list arrow on the toolbar and then selecting a button from the list of default buttons not currently visible. You can also add and delete buttons and commands on the menu bar or other toolbars with options in the Customize dialog box. To customize the menu bar:

Step 1	Right-click	any toolbar (the menu bar, Standard toolbar, or Formatting toolbar)
Step 2	Click	Customize
Step 3	Click	the Commands tab, if necessary

The dialog box on your screen should look similar to Figure 2-8.

> **QUICK TIP**
>
> Remember, the menu bar is also a toolbar. You customize the menu bar and other toolbars the same way.
>
> The Commands tab in the Customize dialog box contains a list of category names and a list of commands available for the selected category. You can view a description of a command by selecting it and clicking the Description button. When you find the command you want to add, drag it from the dialog box to the menu bar or another visible toolbar.

FIGURE 2-8
Commands Tab in the Customize Dialog Box

You add a button on the menu bar to route the active presentation to other users on the network via e-mail.

MOUSE TIP

You can add hyperlinks (the path to another document) to toolbar buttons. For more information, see online Help.

Step 4	Verify	that File is selected in the Categories: list
Step 5	Click	Routing Recipient in the Commands: list (scroll the list to view this command)
Step 6	Click	Description to view the ScreenTip
Step 7	Press	the ESC key to close the ScreenTip
Step 8	Drag	the Routing Recipient command to the right of Help on the menu bar
Step 9	Click	Close to close the dialog box and add the Routing Recipient button to the menu bar
Step 10	Position	the mouse pointer on the Routing Recipient icon to view the ScreenTip, as shown in Figure 2-9

FIGURE 2-9
Button Added to Menu Bar

You can remove a button from a toolbar just as quickly. To remove the Routing Recipient button from the menu bar:

Step 1	Open	the Customize dialog box
Step 2	Drag	the Routing Recipient button from the menu bar into the dialog box
Step 3	Close	the dialog box
Step 4	Close	the PowerPoint application and return to the Windows desktop

2.d Viewing and Customizing the Office Shortcut Bar

The **Office Shortcut Bar** is a toolbar that you can open and position on your Windows desktop to provide shortcuts to Office applications and tasks. It can contain buttons for the New Office Document and Open Office Document commands on the Start menu, shortcut buttons to create various Outlook items like the New Task button, and buttons to open Office applications installed on your computer.

You can view and use the Office Shortcut Bar as needed or you can choose to have it open each time you start your computer. To view the Office Shortcut Bar:

QUICK TIP

You can reset toolbars back to their original buttons and create new custom toolbars with options on the Tool**b**ars tab in the Customize dialog box.

You can view toolbar buttons in a larger size (for high-resolution monitors), show keyboard shortcuts in the button's ScreenTip, and add animation to menus with options in the Options tab in the Customize dialog box. **Menu animation** refers to the movement the menu makes as it opens on your screen.

Working with Menus and Toolbars

Step 1	Click	the Start button [Start] on the taskbar
Step 2	Point to	Programs
Step 3	Point to	Microsoft Office Tools
Step 4	Click	Microsoft Office Shortcut Bar
Step 5	Click	No in the Microsoft Office Shortcut Bar dialog box to not open the Office Shortcut Bar each time you start your computer

The Office Shortcut Bar may appear docked in the upper-right corner or along the right edge of your Windows desktop. Your screen may look similar to Figure 2-10.

Control-menu icon

Step 6	Right-click	the Office Shortcut Bar Control-menu icon

The Office Shortcut Bar Control-menu contains commands you can use to customize or close the Office Shortcut Bar. If your Shortcut Bar does not already contain buttons to open the individual Office applications, you may want to customize it for the Office applications you use frequently. To open the Customize dialog box:

Step 1	Click	Customize
Step 2	Click	the Buttons tab

The dialog box on your screen should look similar to Figure 2-11.

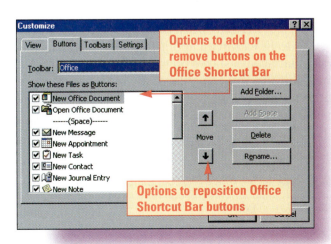

CAUTION TIP

The activities in this section assume that the Office Shortcut Bar does not open automatically when you start your computer or contain Office application buttons.

FIGURE 2-10
Office Shortcut Bar

QUICK TIP

The AutoHide command hides the Office Shortcut Bar and displays only a thin border where the Office Shortcut Bar resides. When you position the mouse pointer on the thin border, the Office Shortcut Bar appears. When you move the mouse pointer away from the border, the Office Shortcut Bar hides again.

FIGURE 2-11
Buttons Tab in the Customize Dialog Box

chapter
two

> **QUICK TIP**
>
> You can enlarge the Shortcut Bar buttons by clicking the Large Buttons check box; this inserts a check mark on the View tab in the Customize dialog box. You can place the Shortcut Bar in its own window, and then move and size the window by clicking the Auto Fit into Title Bar area check box; this removes the check mark on the View tab in the Customize dialog box.

The shortcut button for a particular application or file is visible on the Office Shortcut Bar if a check mark appears in the check box to the left of the application icon in the Show these Files as Buttons: list. To add a shortcut button that opens the Word application:

Step 1	*Scroll*	the Show these Files as Buttons: list to view the check boxes for the Office applications
Step 2	*Click*	the Microsoft Word check box to insert a check mark
Step 3	*Observe*	that a button for the Word application immediately appears on the Office Shortcut Bar

You can easily reposition a button on the Office Shortcut Bar by moving the item into the Show these Files as Buttons: list. To reposition the Word button to the right of the Open Office Document button:

Step 1	*Click*	the Microsoft Word application name to select it in the list
Step 2	*Click*	the Move up arrow until the Microsoft Word application and check box appear immediately below the Open Office Document icon and check box
Step 3	*Observe*	that the Word button on the Office Shortcut Bar is repositioned

You can also delete an application button from the Office Shortcut Bar. To remove the Word application button:

Step 1	*Click*	the Microsoft Word check box to remove the check mark
Step 2	*Move*	the Microsoft Word check box back to its original position above the Excel check box by selecting it and clicking the Move down arrow
Step 3	*Click*	OK

The Office Shortcut Bar may be in the upper-right corner of your screen and sized to fit within an application title bar. This means that Office Shortcut Bar always shows on top of the active application's title bar with small buttons. You can enlarge the buttons and place the Shortcut Bar in its own window so you can move it elsewhere on the screen. You can also hide and redisplay the Shortcut Bar as needed. To close the Office Shortcut Bar:

| Step 1 | *Right-click* | the Office Shortcut Bar Control-menu icon |
| Step 2 | *Click* | Exit |

Summary

▶ When you first start Word, Excel, or PowerPoint, you see personalized menus containing basic commands. As you use different commands, they are automatically added to the personalized menu. Commands that are not used for some time are removed from the personalized menus.

▶ When you first start Word, Excel, or PowerPoint, the Standard and Formatting toolbars share one row below the menu bar. You can reposition the Formatting toolbar to view more or fewer toolbar buttons. The remaining default toolbar buttons that are not visible on the toolbars can be added from the More Buttons list.

▶ FrontPage and Access also provide the personalized menus and toolbars options.

▶ You can turn off or reset the personalized menus and toolbars in the Options tab of the Customize dialog box.

▶ You can hide or view toolbars as you need them by using a shortcut menu.

▶ Toolbars can be docked at the top, bottom, or side of the screen or they can remain floating on the screen in their own window.

▶ You can customize toolbars by adding or deleting buttons and commands, displaying larger-sized buttons, and turning on or off the display of ScreenTips, or adding keyboard shortcut keys to ScreenTips.

▶ The menu bar is a special toolbar that can be customized just like other toolbars.

▶ The Office Shortcut Bar is a customizable toolbar you can position on the desktop and contains shortcuts for opening Office documents and applications.

Commands Review

Action	Menu Bar	Shortcut Menu	Toolbar	Keyboard
To display or hide toolbars	View, Toolbars	Right-click a toolbar, click the desired toolbar to add or remove the check mark		ALT + V, T
To customize a toolbar	View, Toolbars, Customize	Right-click a toolbar, click Customize		ALT + V, T, C

Concepts Review

Circle the correct answer.

1. **A menu is:**
   - [a] a set of icons.
   - [b] a list of commands.
   - [c] impossible to customize.
   - [d] never personalized.

2. **The Options tab in the PowerPoint Customize dialog box does not include an option for:**
   - [a] turning on or off ScreenTips for toolbar buttons.
   - [b] turning on or off Large icons for toolbar buttons.
   - [c] adding animation to menus.
   - [d] docking all toolbars.

3. **A toolbar is:**
   - [a] a list of commands.
   - [b] always floating on your screen.
   - [c] a set of icons.
   - [d] never docked on your screen.

4. **When you right-click an item on your screen, you see:**
   - [a] the Right Click toolbar.
   - [b] animated menus.
   - [c] expanded menus.
   - [d] a shortcut menu.

Circle **T** if the statement is true or **F** if the statement is false.

T F 1. The Standard and Formatting toolbars must remain on the same row.

T F 2. When updating docked personalized toolbars, some buttons may be automatically removed from view to make room for the new buttons.

T F 3. Resetting your usage data affects your toolbars regardless of their size or position.

T F 4. You cannot add animation to menus.

Skills Review

Exercise 1

1. Open the Word application.
2. Open the Options tab in the Customize dialog box and reset the usage data, have the Standard and Formatting toolbars share one row, and the menus show recently used commands first.
3. Add the Show/Hide button to the personalized Standard toolbar using the More Buttons list.

4. Add the Font color button to the personalized Formatting toolbar using the More Buttons list.

5. Open the Customize dialog box and reset your usage data in the Options tab.

6. Close the Word application.

Exercise 2

1. Open the Excel application.

2. Open the Options tab in the Customize dialog box and reset the usage data, have the Standard and Formatting toolbars share one row, and the menus show recently used commands first.

3. View the personalized Tools menu.

4. Add the AutoCorrect command to the personalized Tools menu.

5. Reset your usage data.

6. Close the Excel application.

Exercise 3

1. Open the Office Shortcut Bar. (Do not set it to automatically open when you start your computer.)

2. Customize the Office Shortcut Bar to add the Word, Excel, and PowerPoint shortcut buttons or remove them if they already appear.

3. Customize the Office Shortcut Bar to have large buttons and position it in its own window vertically at the right side of the desktop.

4. AutoFit the Office Shortcut Bar to the title bar with small buttons.

5. Remove the Word, Excel, and PowerPoint application shortcut buttons or add them back, if necessary.

6. Close the Office Shortcut Bar.

Exercise 4

1. Open the Word application.

2. Add the Clear command icon from the Edit category to the menu bar.

3. Reset the menu bar back to its default from the Toolbars tab in the Customize dialog box.

4. Close the Word application.

Exercise 5

1. Open the Excel application.

2. View the Drawing, Picture, and WordArt toolbars using a shortcut menu.

3. Dock the Picture toolbar below the Standard and Formatting toolbars.

4. Dock the WordArt toolbar at the left boundary of the screen.

5. Close the Excel application from the taskbar.

6. Open the Excel with the New Office Document on the Start menu. (*Hint:* Use the Blank Workbook icon.)

7. Float the WordArt toolbar.

8. Float the Picture toolbar.

chapter two

9. Hide the WordArt, Picture, and Drawing toolbars using a shortcut menu.

10. Close the Excel application.

Case Projects

Project 1

As secretary to the placement director for the XYZ Employment Agency, you have been using Word 97. After you install Office 2000, you decide you want the menus and toolbars to behave just like they did in Word 97. Use the Office Assistant to search for help on "personalized menus" and select the appropriate topic from the Office Assistant list. (*Hint:* You may need to view all the topics presented in the Office Assistant balloon.) Review the Help topic you select and write down the steps to make the personalized menus and toolbars behave like Word 97 menus and toolbars.

Project 2

You are the administrative assistant to the controller of the Plush Pets, Inc., a stuffed toy manufacturing company. The controller recently installed Excel 2000. She prefers to view the entire list of menu commands rather than the personalized menus and asks for your help. Use the Office assistant to search for help on "full menus" and select the appropriate topic in the Office Assistant balloon. Review the topic and write down the instructions for switching between personalized menus and full menus.

Project 3

As administrative assistant to the art director of MediaWiz Advertising, Inc. you just installed PowerPoint 2000. Now you decide you would rather view the complete Standard and Formatting toolbars rather than the personalized toolbars and want to learn a quick way to do this. Use the Office Assistant to search for help on "show all buttons" and select the appropriate topic from the Office Assistant balloon. Review the topic and write down the instructions for showing all buttons using the mouse pointer. Open an Office application and use the mouse method to show the complete Standard and Formatting toolbars. Turn the personalized toolbars back on in the Customize dialog box.

Project 4

You are the training coordinator for the information technology (IT) department at a large international health care organization, World Health International. The information technology department is planning to install Office 2000 on computers throughout the organization within the next two weeks. Your supervisor, the IT manager, asks you to prepare a short introduction to the Office 2000 personalized menus and toolbars to be presented at next Monday's staff meeting. He wants you to emphasize the advantages and disadvantages of using the personalized menus and toolbars. Write down in at least two paragraphs the advantages and disadvantages of using the personalized menus and toolbars.

Office 2000

Working With Others Using Online Collaboration Tools

Chapter Overview

In today's workplace many tasks are completed by several co-workers working together as part of a team called a workgroup. Office applications provide tools to assist workgroups in sharing information. In this chapter you learn about scheduling and participating in online meetings and conducting Web discussions with others in your workgroup.

LEARNING OBJECTIVES

- Schedule an online meeting
- Participate in Web discussions

chapter three

3.a Scheduling an Online Meeting

> **CAUTION TIP**
>
> The activities in this chapter assume you have access to directory servers and Web servers with Office Server Extensions installed, Microsoft NetMeeting, and Outlook with Exchange Server service installed. If you do not have access to the appropriate servers and software, you will be able to read but not do the hands-on activities. Your instructor will provide additional server, e-mail address, NetMeeting, and Outlook instructions as needed to complete the hands-on activities.

Many organizations assign tasks or projects to several workers who collaborate as members of a **workgroup**. Often these workgroup members do not work in the same office or some members travel frequently, making it difficult for the group to meet at one physical location. Office applications, together with Microsoft NetMeeting conferencing software, provide a way for workgroup members to participate in online real-time meetings from different physical locations—just as though everyone were in the same meeting room. In an online meeting, participants can share programs and documents, send text messages, transfer files, and illustrate ideas.

You can schedule an online meeting in advance using Outlook or you can invite others to participate in an online meeting right now by opening NetMeeting directly from Word, Excel, PowerPoint, and Access and calling others in your workgroup. To participate in an online meeting, invitees must have NetMeeting running on their computers.

Calling Others from Office Applications Using NetMeeting

Suppose you are working on an Excel workbook and want to discuss the workbook with another person in your workgroup. You know that they are running NetMeeting on their computer. You can call them while working in the workbook. To open NetMeeting and place a call from within Excel:

Step 1	Click	the Start button [Start] on the taskbar
Step 2	Click	the Open Office Document command on the Start menu
Step 3	Double-click	the *International Food Distributors* workbook located on the Data Disk
Step 4	Click	Tools
Step 5	Point to	Online Collaboration
Step 6	Click	Meet Now to open NetMeeting and the Place A Call dialog box

The directory server and list of names and calling addresses in the Place A Call dialog box on your screen will be different, but the dialog box should look similar to Figure 3-1.

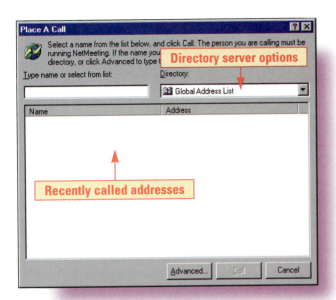

FIGURE 3-1
Place A Call Dialog Box

The person who initiates the meeting call is called the **host**. The person or persons receiving the call are called **participants**. Because you are initiating a call about the open Excel workbook, you are the host for this meeting. You can select a specific directory server and then select the participant to call from a list of persons logged onto the server or select someone from the list of frequently called NetMeeting participants. The *host* now calls a participant in the list:

| Step 1 | *Right-click* | the name of the person in the list specified by your instructor and click C̲all |

NetMeeting dials the participant. Depending on the participant's NetMeeting configuration, he or she can automatically accept the call or manually accept or ignore the call. If the NetMeeting configuration is set up to manually answer calls, an announcement appears on the participant's screen, allowing him or her to click a button to accept or decline the call.

For the activities in this chapter, the participant's NetMeeting software is configured to automatically accept incoming calls. When the call is accepted, the *International Food Distributors* workbook and the Online Meeting toolbar automatically display on the participant's screen, even if the participant does not have Excel installed. Only the host needs to have the application installed and the file available. Both the *host's* and the *participant's* screens should look similar to Figure 3-2.

The host has **control** of the *International Foods Distributors* workbook when the meeting starts, which means the host can turn on or off collaboration at any time, controlling who can edit the document. When collaboration is turned on, any one participant can control the workbook for editing. When collaboration is turned off,

chapter three

FIGURE 3-2
Host's and Participant's Screens

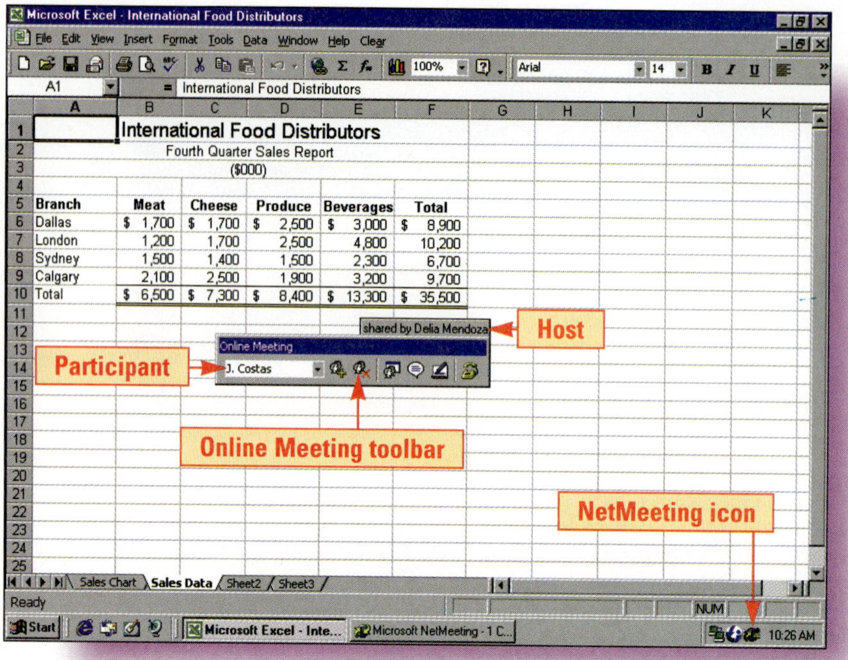

[Screenshot of Microsoft Excel – International Food Distributors showing Fourth Quarter Sales Report, with callouts labeling: Host, Participant, Online Meeting toolbar, and NetMeeting icon.]

> **QUICK TIP**
>
> Only the host of the meeting can use all the features on the Online Meeting toolbar.

only the host can edit the workbook but all participants can see it. The *host* now turns on collaboration:

| Step 1 | Click | the Allow others to edit button 🗔 on the Online Meeting toolbar |

The first time a participant wants to take control of the workbook, they double-click it. The host can regain control of the workbook at any time simply by clicking it. To regain control of the workbook after the first time they control it, a participant also clicks it. The initials of the person who currently controls the workbook appear beside the mouse pointer. The *participant* takes control of the workbook for the first time to edit it:

Step 1	Double-click	the workbook to take control and place your user initials beside the mouse pointer
Step 2	Click	Tools
Step 3	Click	Options
Step 4	Click	the View tab
Step 5	Click	the Gridlines check box to remove the check mark
Step 6	Click	OK to turn off the gridlines in the workbook

> **CAUTION TIP**
>
> When someone else controls a document during an online meeting, you cannot use your mouse pointer to access commands or edit the document until you regain control of it.

The *host* regains control of the workbook:

| Step 1 | Click | the workbook to regain control and place your initials beside the mouse pointer |
| Step 2 | Turn on | the gridlines on the View tab in the Options dialog box |

The **Whiteboard** is a tool that participants can use to illustrate their thoughts and ideas. Only the host can display the Whiteboard during an online meeting that originates from within an Office application. All participants can draw on the Whiteboard at the same time only when the host turns off collaboration. The *host* turns off collaboration:

Step 1	Click	the workbook to regain control, if necessary
Step 2	Click	the Allow others to edit button to turn off collaboration
Step 3	Click	the Display Whiteboard button on the Online Meeting toolbar

Your screen should look similar to Figure 3-3.

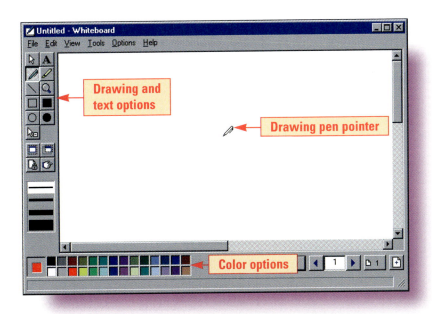

FIGURE 3-3
Whiteboard Window

> **QUICK TIP**
>
> When collaboration is turned off, meeting participants can use **Chat** to send and respond to keyed messages in real time. With a sound card and a camera attached to their computer, the host and participants in an online meeting can both hear and see one another. For more information on using Chat, audio, and video in online meetings see NetMeeting online Help.

> **QUICK TIP**
>
> The meeting host can turn off collaboration when someone else has control of the document by pressing the ESC key.

All participants, including the host, add text, draw shapes, add color, and insert additional pages in the Whiteboard window. The host can save and print Whiteboard pages. The host and participant explore using the drawing, text, and color options for the Whiteboard. First, the *host* selects a color and draws a shape:

| Step 1 | Click | Red in the color options |
| Step 2 | Draw | a shape by dragging the drawing pen pointer in the Whiteboard drawing area |

The *participant* now takes control of the drawing pen, selects a color, and draws a shape:

| Step 1 | Click | the Whiteboard to take control of the drawing pen |
| Step 2 | Click | Blue in the color options and draw a shape |

The *host* and the *participant*:

| Step 1 | Continue | to share the Whiteboard and explore the different Whiteboard options |
| Step 2 | Click | the Close button on the Whiteboard window title bar to close the Whiteboard |

Each participant can disconnect from the meeting at any time by clicking the End Meeting button on the Online Meeting toolbar. The host can also disconnect any participant by first selecting the participant from the Participants List button and then clicking the Remove Participants button on the Online Meeting toolbar. The host can also end the meeting, which disconnects all the participants. The *host* ends the meeting:

| Step 1 | Click | the End Meeting button on the Online Meeting toolbar |
| Step 2 | Close | the Excel application and workbook from the taskbar without saving changes |

Scheduling Online Meetings in Advance Using Outlook

As a host, you can schedule online meetings in advance using Outlook directly or from inside other Office applications. Suppose you are putting the finishing touches on a PowerPoint presentation and want to schedule an online meeting in advance with other workgroup members. You can do this from inside the PowerPoint application. To open a PowerPoint presentation and invite others to an online meeting:

> **MENU TIP**
>
> The host can send a copy of the active document to all participants by clicking the File menu, pointing to Send To, and clicking the Online Meeting Recipient command. All participants then receive the file as an e-mail attachment. The host can send the document to one participant by clicking the E-mail button on the Standard toolbar and attaching the document file to an e-mail message.

> **CAUTION TIP**
>
> Only the host can save and print the document during an online meeting. If a participant in control attempts to print or save the workbook, it is printed at the host's printer and saved to the host's hard disk or originating server.

Working With Others Using Online Collaboration Tools

Step 1	**Open**	the PowerPoint application and the *International Food Distributors* presentation located on the Data Disk using the Open Office Document command on the Start menu
Step 2	**Click**	T̲ools
Step 3	**Point to**	O̲nline Collaboration
Step 4	**Click**	S̲chedule Meeting

The Outlook Meeting window opens, similar to Figure 3-4.

This window provides all the options for setting up the meeting. You address the message to one or more e-mail addresses, key the subject of the meeting, and select the directory server where the meeting will be held. You also select the date and time of the meeting. The current document is selected as the Office document to be reviewed and a meeting reminder is set to be delivered to the host and attendees 15 minutes prior to the scheduled meeting.

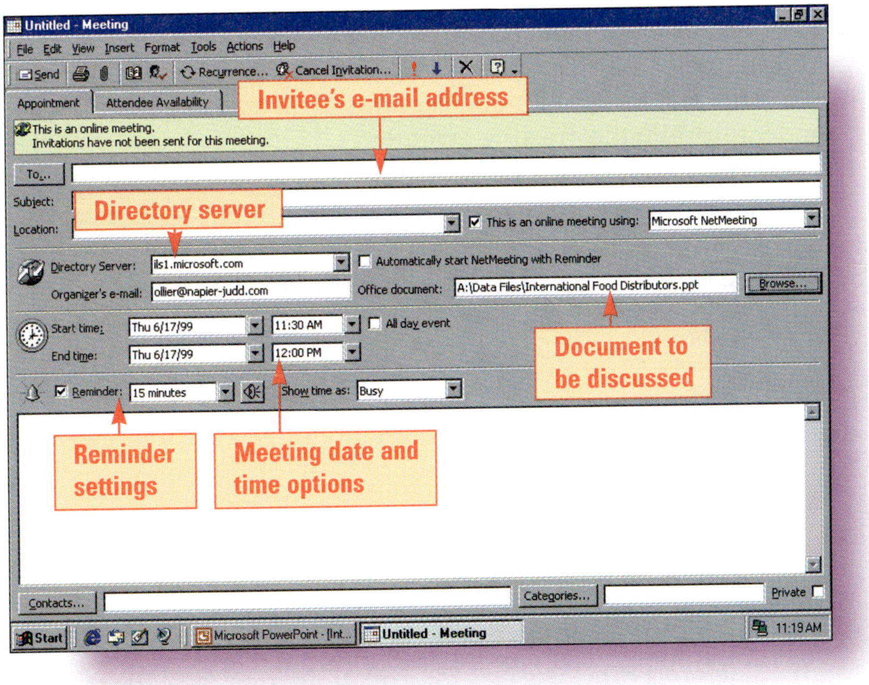

FIGURE 3-4
Outlook Meeting Window

As long as all invitees are using Outlook for their scheduling, you can determine the best time to schedule the meeting by clicking the Attendee Availability tab and inviting others from the Outlook global address book. To review the Attendee Availability tab:

Step 1	**Click**	the Attendee Availability tab

chapter
three

Step 2	*Observe*	the meeting scheduling options you can use to compare each invitee's free and busy times from their Outlook calendars and select the best meeting time
Step 3	*Click*	the Appointment tab

You send the completed meeting invitation by clicking the Send button on the Standard toolbar. Each invitee receives an e-mail message with the meeting information. They can choose to accept, decline, or tentatively accept the invitation by clicking a button inside the message window. If they accept, an Outlook appointment item is added to their calendar. Because you are the host, an appointment item is automatically added to your Outlook calendar. If invitees accept, decline, or accept tentatively, you receive an e-mail notification of their attendance choice and your meeting appointment item is updated to show who is attending and who declined.

Fifteen minutes prior to the scheduled online meeting (if Outlook is running on your computer) a meeting reminder message opens on your screen. If you are the meeting's host, you click the Start this NetMeeting button in the reminder window to begin the meeting. If you are an invited participant, you click the Join the Meeting button in the reminder window to join the meeting or you click the Dismiss this reminder to ignore the meeting invitation.

To close the message window without sending a message:

Step 1	*Click*	the Close button ⊠ on the message window title bar
Step 2	*Click*	No
Step 3	*Close*	the PowerPoint application and presentation

3.b Participating in Web Discussions

Web discussions provide a way for workgroup members to review and provide input to the same document by associating messages, called **discussion items**, with the document. Discussion items are saved in a database separate from the associated document. This enables the group to consider multiple discussion items related to the same document; it also allows the document to be edited without affecting any discussion items. Discussion items are **threaded**, which means that replies to an item appear directly under the original item. Discussion items are saved as they are entered and are available immediately when the associated document is opened.

> **QUICK TIP**
>
> For more information on scheduling meetings using Outlook, see Outlook online Help.

> **CAUTION TIP**
>
> Special software called Office Server Extensions must be installed on a Web server before discussion items can be created and stored there. For more information on Office Server Extensions software, see the documentation that accompanies Office or online Help.

Suppose you are working on a Word document and want to solicit input from others in your workgroup. Instead of sending a copy to everyone in the workgroup or routing a single copy to everyone, you decide to use the Web discussion feature. To start a Web discussion:

Step 1	Open	the Word application and the *Dallas Warehouse Audit* document located on the Data Disk using the Open Office Document command on the Start menu
Step 2	Click	Tools
Step 3	Point to	Online Collaboration
Step 4	Click	Web Discussions

After you connect to your discussion server, the Web Discussions toolbar opens docked above the status bar. See Figure 3-5.

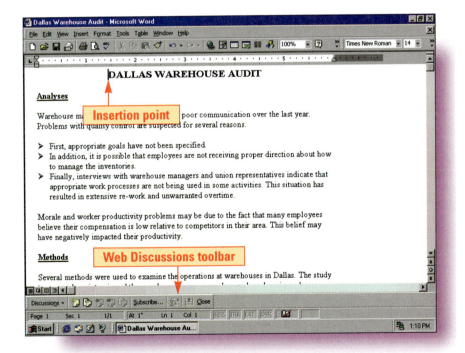

FIGURE 3-5
Document with Web Discussions Toolbar

QUICK TIP

There are two types of discussion items: an **inline discussion item** relates to a specific paragraph, picture, or table, and a **general discussion item** relates to the entire document. Word supports both inline and general discussion items. Excel and PowerPoint support only general discussion items.

First, you add a general discussion item identifying the issues to be discussed in the document. To add a general discussion item:

Step 1	Press	the CTRL + HOME keys to move the keying position (called the insertion point) to the top of the document
Step 2	Click	the Insert Discussion about the Document button on the Web Discussions toolbar

The dialog box that opens should look similar to Figure 3-6.

chapter three

FIGURE 3-6
Enter Discussion Text Dialog Box

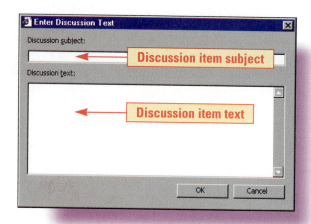

Step 3	Key	Problems in Dallas in the Discussion subject: text box
Step 4	Press	the TAB key to move the insertion point (the keying position) to the Discussion text: text box
Step 5	Key	We have only three weeks to resolve the problems in Dallas.
Step 6	Click	OK

The Discussion pane opens and contains information about the active document, the text of the discussion item, and an Action button. You use the Action button to reply to, edit, or delete a discussion item. Your screen should look similar to Figure 3-7.

FIGURE 3-7
Document with Discussion Pane

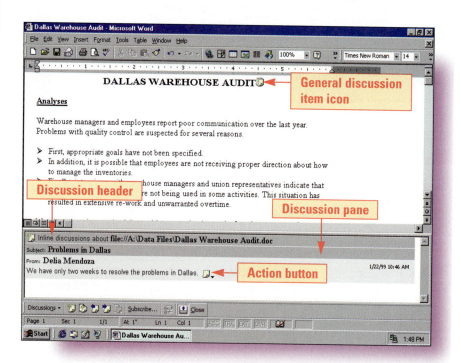

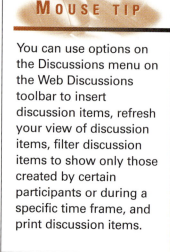

MOUSE TIP

You can use options on the Discussions menu on the Web Discussions toolbar to insert discussion items, refresh your view of discussion items, filter discussion items to show only those created by certain participants or during a specific time frame, and print discussion items.

Next you add an inline discussion item to a specific paragraph. To close the Discussion pane and add an inline discussion item:

Step 1	Click	the Show/Hide Discussion Pane button on the Web Discussions toolbar
Step 2	Click	at the end of the first bulleted item ending in "specified." to reposition the insertion point
Step 3	Click	the Insert Discussion in the Document button on the Web Discussions toolbar
Step 4	Key	Goals in the Discussion subject: text box
Step 5	Key	Doesn't Yong's group have responsibility for setting warehouse goals? in the Discussion text: text box
Step 6	Click	OK

CAUTION TIP

You can modify a document that contains threaded discussions. If you make changes in an area that is not associated with a discussion item, the inline and general discussions are not affected. If you change or delete part of the document associated with a discussion item, any inline discussions are deleted but general discussions are not affected. If you move, rename, or delete a document, all inline and general discussions are lost.

The inline discussion item icon appears at the end of the bulleted text and the Discussion pane opens. Your screen should look similar to Figure 3-8.

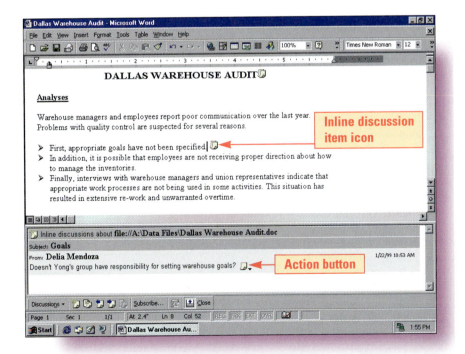

FIGURE 3-8
Inline Discussion Item

Step 7	Click	the Show/Hide Discussion Pane button on the Web Discussions toolbar to close the Discussion pane

Others in the workgroup can now open the *Dallas Warehouse Audit* document, log on to the discussion server, and review the inline and general discussion items. They can reply to existing items and create new items. They can edit or delete any discussion items they create. Now assume you are a different member of the workgroup and you just opened the *Dallas Warehouse Audit* document, logged on to the discussion server, and want to participate in the discussion. To thread a reply to the inline discussion item at the end of the bulleted list:

Step 1	Press	the CTRL + HOME keys to move the insertion point to the top of the document
Step 2	Click	the Next button twice on the Web Discussions toolbar to select the second discussion item and open the Discussion pane
Step 3	Click	the Action button in the Discussion pane
Step 4	Click	Reply
Step 5	Key	Yong's group is currently understaffed and behind schedule. in the Discussion text: text box
Step 6	Click	OK to thread your reply immediately below the original discussion item
Step 7	Close	the Discussion pane

When discussion items are no longer useful, you can delete them. To open the Discussion pane and delete the discussion items:

Step 1	Click	the Show General Discussions button on the Web Discussions toolbar to open the Discussion Pane
Step 2	Click	the Action button
Step 3	Click	Delete
Step 4	Click	Yes to confirm the deletion
Step 5	Click	the Next button on the Web Discussions toolbar
Step 6	Delete	the first inline discussion item
Step 7	Delete	the second inline action item
Step 8	Click	Close on the Web Discussions toolbar to close the discussions session
Step 9	Close	the Word application and the document without saving any changes

CAUTION TIP

Selecting and deleting the discussion item icons in a document does not remove the discussion items from the server.

QUICK TIP

Users can subscribe to an e-mail notice of changes to folders and documents stored on a server that also has the Office Server Extension software installed. When you subscribe to a folder or document, you can be notified when a new document is added to the folder, when a document is modified, renamed, moved, or deleted, or whenever a discussion item is added to or deleted from a document. You select the notification period: Within a few minutes, Once a day, or Once a week. For more information on Web Subscriptions, see online Help.

Summary

- You can work with others to complete tasks using Office applications' online collaboration tools: NetMeeting and Web Discussions.
- You can use the NetMeeting conferencing software directly from inside Office applications to host or participate in an online meeting.
- During an online meeting using NetMeeting, participants can take turns editing the current document when the meeting's host turns on collaboration.
- When collaboration is turned off, participants in a NetMeeting online meeting can use the Whiteboard.
- You can chat in real-time during an online meeting and, with a sound card and camera, both see and hear other attendees.
- You can schedule a meeting in advance, either using Outlook or from inside Office applications.
- Another way to work with others on a document is to participate in a Web discussion by associating text comments, called discussion items, with a specific document.
- Inline discussion items relate to specific paragraphs, pictures, or tables in a document. General discussion items relate to the entire document. Only the Word application supports inline discussion items.

Commands Review

Action	Menu Bar	Shortcut Menu	Toolbar	Keyboard
Schedule a meeting using NetMeeting inside Office applications	Tools, Online Collaboration, Meet Now			ALT + T, N, M
Schedule a meeting in advance using Outlook inside Office applications	Tools, Online Collaboration, Schedule Meeting			ALT + T, N, S
Participate in Web Discussions from inside Office applications	Tools, Online Collaboration, Web Discussions			ALT + T, N, W

chapter three

Concepts Review

Circle the correct answer.

1. **Workgroup members:**
   - [a] always work in the same physical location.
   - [b] never travel on business.
   - [c] always work independently of each other.
   - [d] often work in different physical locations or travel frequently.

2. **A participant in an online meeting:**
   - [a] can turn collaboration on and off.
   - [b] controls access to the Whiteboard.
   - [c] can save and print to their own hard drive or printer.
   - [d] is the person receiving the call.

3. **The first time a participant takes control of a document during an online meeting, the participant must:**
   - [a] open the Chat window.
   - [b] click the document.
   - [c] double-click the document.
   - [d] press the CTRL + HOME keys.

4. **NetMeeting participants use the Whiteboard to:**
   - [a] key real-time text messages.
   - [b] share and edit documents.
   - [c] add inline discussion items.
   - [d] illustrate their ideas and thoughts.

Circle **T** if the statement is true or **F** if the statement is false.

T T 1. To participate in an online meeting, invitees must be running NetMeeting on their computer.

T F 2. When collaboration is turned on, the host of an online meeting always maintains control of the active document.

T F 3. To gain control of a document during collaboration, participants must double-click it.

T F 4. The active document can be printed and saved to any participant's printer, hard disk, or server during an online meeting.

notes You must be connected to the appropriate directory and discussion servers and have NetMeeting and Outlook running with Exchange server to complete these exercises. Your instructor will provide the server and e-mail address information and any NetMeeting and Outlook instructions needed to complete these exercises.

Skills Review

Exercise 1

1. Open the Word application and the *Dallas Warehouse Audit* document located on the Data Disk.
2. Invite three other people to an online meeting now.
3. Take turns making changes to the document.
4. End the meeting. Close the Word application and document without saving any changes.

Exercise 2

1. Open the Excel application and the *International Food Distributors* workbook located on the Data Disk.

2. Invite four other people to an online meeting next Thursday at 2:00 PM.
3. Open Outlook and read their automatic meeting reply messages.
4. Open the Outlook appointment item created for the message and view the updated attendee information.
5. Delete the appointment item and send a message to all attendees canceling the meeting.
6. Close Outlook. Close the Excel application and workbook without saving any changes.

Exercise 3

1. Open the PowerPoint application and the *International Food Distributors* presentation located on the Data Disk.
2. Create a general Web discussion item using the text "This is an important presentation."
3. Close the Web discussion and the PowerPoint application and presentation without saving any changes.

Exercise 4

1. Open the PowerPoint application and the *International Food Distributors* presentation located on the Data Disk.
2. Reply to the general discussion item using the text "What is the project due date?"
3. Print the discussion items using a command on the Discussions menu.
4. Delete the general discussion items created for the *International Food Distributors* presentation.
5. Close the Web discussion and the PowerPoint application and presentation without saving any changes.

Case Projects

Project 1

As assistant to the accounting manager at Wilson Art Supply, you are asked to find out how to select a discussion server. Open the Word application and use the Office Assistant to search for discussion server topics using the keywords "Web discussions" and select the appropriate topic from the Office Assistant balloon. Review the topic and write down the instructions for selecting a discussion server.

Project 2

You work in the marketing department at International Hair Concepts, a company that imports professional hairdresser supplies. Your department is going to start scheduling online meetings to collaborate on Word documents and you want to be prepared for potential problems. Open the Word application and use the Office Assistant to find the "troubleshoot online meetings" topic. Write down a list of potential problems and their possible solutions.

Project 3

A co-worker at Merton Partners, a public relations firm, mentions that you can subscribe to documents and folders stored on a Web server and then be notified when changes are made to them. Using Word online Help to search for Web discussion topics; review the topic, "About subscribing to a document or folder on a Web server." Write a paragraph about how subscribing to documents and folders could help you in your work.

Project 4

The Women's Professional Softball Teams annual tournament is in two months and 30 teams from around the world will participate. The director wants to review the schedule (created in Word) at one time with the team representatives in the United States, England, France, Holland, Germany, China, Argentina, Mexico, and Australia. Write at least two paragraphs recommending an online collaboration tool and explaining why this is the best choice.

Office 2000

Introduction to the Internet and the World Wide Web

Chapter Overview

Millions of people use the Internet to shop for goods and services, listen to music, view artwork, conduct research, get stock quotes, keep up-to-date with current events, and send e-mail. More and more people are using the Internet at work and at home to view and download multimedia computer files containing graphics, sound, video, and text. In this chapter you learn about the origins of the Internet, how to connect to the Internet, how to use the Internet Explorer Web browser, and how to access pages on the World Wide Web.

Learning Objectives

- Describe the Internet and discuss its history
- Connect to the Internet
- Recognize the challenges to using the Internet
- Use Internet Explorer
- Use directories and search engines

chapter four

4.a What Is the Internet?

To understand the Internet, you must understand networks. A **network** is simply a group of two or more computers linked by cable or telephone lines. The linked computers also include a special computer called a **network server** that is used to store files and programs that everyone on the network can access. In addition to the shared files and programs, networks enable users to share equipment, such as a common network printer. See Figure 4-1.

> **CAUTION TIP**
>
> The activities in this chapter assume you are using the Internet Explorer Web browser versions 4.0 or 5.0. If you are using an earlier version of Internet Explorer or a different Web browser, your instructor may modify the following activities.

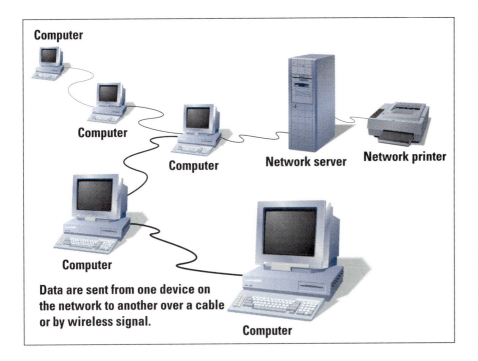

FIGURE 4-1
Computer Network

The **Internet** is a worldwide collection of computer networks that enables users to view and transfer information between computers. For example, an Internet user in California can retrieve (or **download**) files from a computer in Canada quickly and easily. In the same way, an Internet user in Australia can send (or **upload**) files to another Internet user in England. See Figure 4-2.

The Internet is not a single organization, but rather a cooperative effort by multiple organizations managing a variety of computers.

A Brief History of the Internet

The Internet originated in the late 1960s, when the United States Department of Defense developed a network of military computers called the **ARPAnet**. Quickly realizing the usefulness of such a network,

FIGURE 4-2
The Internet

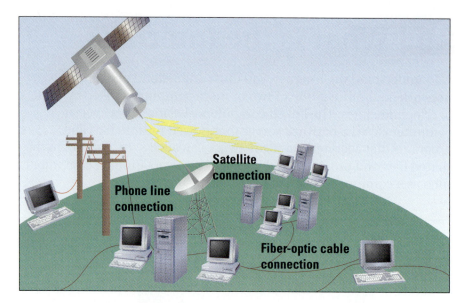

researchers at colleges and universities soon began using it to share data. In the 1980s the military portion of the early Internet became a separate network called the **MILNET**. Meanwhile the National Science Foundation began overseeing the remaining non-military portions, which it called the **NSFnet**. Thousands of other government, academic, and business computer networks began connecting to the NSFnet. By the late 1980s, the term Internet became widely used to describe this huge worldwide "network of networks."

Services Available on the Internet

You find a wide variety of services on the Internet. Table 4-1 explains just some of the options. In this chapter, you learn about using a Web browser and accessing pages on the World Wide Web. Your instructor may provide additional information on other Internet services in the list.

> **CAUTION TIP**
>
> During peak day and evening hours, millions of people are connecting to the Internet. During these hours, you may have difficulty connecting to your host computer or to other sites on the Internet.

4.b Connecting to the Internet

To connect to the Internet you need some physical communication medium connected to your computer, such as network cable or a modem. You also need a special communication program that allows your computer to communicate with computers on the Internet and a Web browser program, such as Microsoft Internet Explorer 5, that allows you to move among all the Internet resources. See Figure 4-3.

TABLE 4-1 Internet Services

Category	Name	Description
Communication	E-mail	Electronic messages sent or received from one computer to another
	Newsgroups	Electronic "bulletin boards" or discussion groups where people with common interests (such as hobbyists or members of professional associations) post messages (called **articles**) that participants around the world can read and respond to
	Mailing Lists	Similar to Newsgroups, except that participants exchange information via e-mail
	Chat	Online conversations in which participants key messages and receive responses on their screen within a few seconds
File Access	FTP	Sending (uploading) or receiving (downloading) computer files via the File Transfer Protocol (FTP) communication rules
Searching Tools	Directories	Tools that help you search for Web sites by category
	Search Engines	Tools to help you find individual files on the Internet by searching for specific words or phrases
World Wide Web (Web)	Web Site	A subset of the Internet that stores files with Web pages containing text, graphics, video, audio, and links to other pages

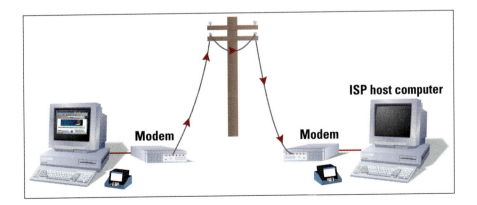

FIGURE 4-3 Internet Connection

Internet Service Providers

After setting up your computer hardware (the network cable or modem) and installing the Internet Explorer Web browser, you must make arrangements to connect to a computer on the Internet. The computer you connect to is called a **host**. Usually, you connect to a host computer via a commercial Internet Service Provider, such as America Online or another company who sells access to the Internet. An **Internet Service Provider (ISP)** maintains the host computer, provides a gateway or entrance to the Internet, and provides an electronic "mail box" with facilities for sending and receiving e-mail. See Figure 4-4.

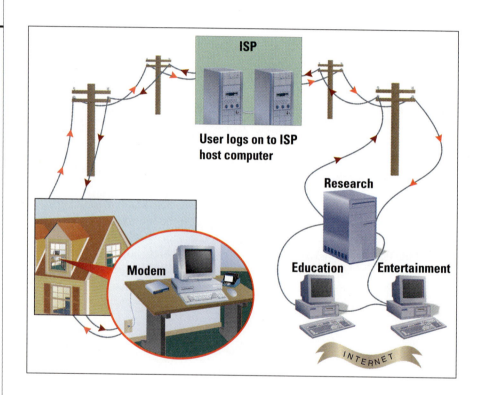

FIGURE 4-4
Internet Service Providers

Quick Tip

USENET is another network that is separate from but closely connected to the Internet. The **USENET** network is a collection of computers that maintain and exchange newsgroup articles or information shared by computer discussion groups.

Large commercial enterprises, colleges, universities, and government institutions may already have a network that is part of the Internet, through which users can connect to the Internet. Many public library systems also provide free Internet access.

Commercial ISPs usually charge a flat monthly fee for unlimited access to the Internet and e-mail services. Many commercial ISPs generally supply the communication program and browser program you need to access the Internet.

Internet Addresses

A unique Internet address or IP address that consists of a series of numbers identifies each host computer on the Internet. Computers on the Internet use these IP address numbers to communicate with each other, but you will probably need to use one only when you install dial-up networking instructions on your computer. The more important address is the host computer's descriptive address. This address specifies the individual computer within a level of organization, or **domain**, on the Internet. For example, a host computer in the math department at a university might be identified as: *raven.math.uidaho.edu* where "raven" identifies the specific computer, "math" identifies the department, "uidaho" identifies the university, and the suffix "edu" identifies that the address is for an educational institution. You'll find that the descriptive host name is much easier to use and remember than the IP address. Table 4-2 identifies the top-level domain (or highest organizational unit on the Internet) names you see as you work with Internet resources. Other top-level domain names are under consideration but not yet in use.

Top-Level Domain	Organization
.com	Commercial enterprise
.gov	Government institution
.edu	Educational institution
.mil	Military institution
.net	Computer network
.org	Other organizations

TABLE 4-2
Top-Level Domains

User Names

When you make arrangements to access the Internet via an ISP, you also set up a user name that identifies your account with the ISP. Your user name consists of a name you select and the host's descriptive name. User names can be full names, first initial and last names, nicknames, or a group of letters and numbers. For example, the user name for Beth Jackson who accesses the Internet via a commercial ISP named Decon Data Systems might be: *Beth_Jackson@decon.net* where "Beth_Jackson" is the user's name, and "decon.net" is the descriptive name for the ISP's host computer.

4.c Challenges to Using the Internet

Using the Internet to send e-mail, read and post articles to newsgroups, chat online, send and receive files, and search for information is fun and exciting. However, because people use the Internet all over the world, there is a seemingly endless source of data and information available. The sheer size of the Internet can sometimes be intimidating.

Another potential difficulty is the time it takes for messages and files to travel between computers on the Internet. Communication speeds

> **QUICK TIP**
>
> There are several commercial networks that are separate from the Internet. These commercial networks provide users with features such as online newspapers and magazines, chat groups, access to investment activities, computer games, and special-interest bulletin boards as well as Internet access. Popular commercial networks include America Online and the Microsoft Network.

can be improved by using high-speed modems and special telephone lines. Faster Internet communication via cable is also becoming more widely available.

You should also be aware that the Internet is a cooperative effort, with few widely accepted presentation standards. As a result, the presentation of information on the Internet is varied and inconsistent. Some Web sites are well-designed and easy to use, while some are not. The Internet is a dynamic environment that changes daily with new host computers and Web sites being added and existing ones being removed. This means new or different information is available constantly. Also, old or outdated information may still be available on Web sites that are not properly maintained.

Also, there may be questions about the accuracy of information you find on the Internet. Remember that the Internet is a largely unregulated environment with few, if any, controls over what information is published on the Web or contained in files at FTP sites. It is a good idea to get supporting information from another source before using any information you find on the Internet to make critical business decisions.

Another challenge to using the Internet is the lack of privacy and security for your e-mail and file transmissions. Information sent from one computer to another can travel through many computer systems and networks, where it could be intercepted, copied, or altered. When you access a page on the World Wide Web, it is possible that information such as your e-mail address, which Web pages you view, the type of computer, operating system, and browser you are using, and how you linked to that page can be captured without your knowledge. If you are concerned, you can take advantage of security software that prevents this type of information from being captured.

Certain browser and server programs on Internet computers can encrypt (or scramble) information during transmission and then decrypt (or unscramble) it at its destination. Commercial activities, such as buying an item via credit card or transferring money between bank accounts, can occur in this type of secure environment. However, be advised that much Internet activity takes place in an insecure environment. Government regulations, as well as technological methods to assure privacy and security on the Internet, continue to be developed.

4.d Using Internet Explorer

A **Web browser** is a software application that helps you access Internet resources, including Web pages stored on computers called Web servers. A **Web page** is a document that contains hyperlinks (often called links) to other pages; it can also contain audio and video clips. A **hyperlink** is text or a picture that is associated with the location (path and filename) of another page. To open the Internet Explorer Web browser:

> **QUICK TIP**
>
> Many college and university libraries have Web sites with excellent tips on how to use and evaluate information on the Internet.

> **INTERNET TIP**
>
> To change the start page for the Internet Explorer Web browser, click the Internet Options command on the View menu and then click the General tab. Define the start page by keying the URL in the Address: text box or clicking the Use Current, Use Default, or Use Blank buttons. For more information on designating a start page, see Internet Explorer online Help.

| Step 1 | **Connect** to your ISP, if necessary |
| Step 2 | **Double-click** the Internet Explorer icon 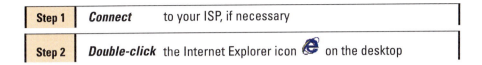 on the desktop |

When the Web browser opens, a Web page, called the **start page**, loads automatically. The start page used by the Internet Explorer Web browser can be the Microsoft default start page, a blank page, or any designated Web page. Figure 4-5 shows the home page for the publisher of this book as the start page.

MOUSE TIP

The **Address bar** contains a text box in which you key the path and filename of the Web page you want to load and a drop-down list of recently loaded Web pages and files.

The **Links bar** is a customizable bar to which you can add shortcuts to frequently loaded Web pages.

FIGURE 4-5
Internet Explorer Web Browser

QUICK TIP

As a Web page loads, the progress bar illustrates the progress of the downloading process. When you place the mouse pointer on a link in the current Web page, its URL appears in the left side of the status bar.

Loading a Web Page

Loading a Web page means that the Web browser sends a message to the computer (called a Web server) where the Web page is stored, requesting a copy of the Web page. The Web server responds by sending a copy of the Web page to your computer. In order to load a Web page, you must either know or find the page's **URL** (Uniform Resource Locator)—the path and filename of the page that is the Web page's address. One way to find the URL for a Web page is to use a search engine or directory or you might find a particular company's URL in one of the company's advertisements or on their letterheads and business cards. Examples of URLs based on an organization's name are:

South-Western Educational Publishing	www.swep.com
National Public Radio	www.npr.org
The White House	www.whitehouse.gov

QUICK TIP

When you start keying the URL of a Web page you have previously loaded, the AutoComplete feature automatically adds a suggested URL to the Address bar. You can continue by keying over the suggested URL or you can accept the suggested URL by pressing the ENTER key.

You can try to "guess" the URL based on the organization's name and top-level domain. For example, a good guess for the U.S. House of Representatives Web page is *www.house.gov*.

You can key a URL directly in the Address bar by first selecting all or part of the current URL and replacing it with the new URL. Internet Explorer adds the "http://" portion of the URL for you. To select the contents of the Address bar and key the URL for the U.S. House of Representatives:

Step 1	Click	the contents of the Address bar
Step 2	Key	www.house.gov
Step 3	Click	the Go button 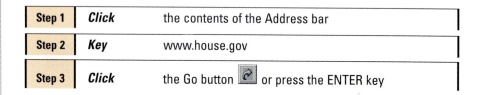 or press the ENTER key

In a few seconds, the U.S. House of Representatives page loads. Your screen should look similar to Figure 4-6.

FIGURE 4-6
U.S. House of Representatives Web Page

MENU TIP

You can key a URL in the Open dialog box by first clicking the Open command on the File menu.

You can create a favorite by clicking the Favorites command on the menu bar and then clicking Add to Favorites, by right-clicking the background (not a link) on the current Web page and clicking Add to Favorites, or by right-clicking a link on the current Web page and clicking Add to Favorites.

Creating Favorites

Web pages are constantly being updated with new information. If you like a certain Web page or find a Web page contains useful information and plan to revisit it, you may want to save its URL as a **favorite**. Suppose you want to load the U.S. House of Representatives home page frequently. You can create a favorite that saves the URL in a file on your hard disk. Then at any time, you can quickly load this Web page by clicking it in a list of favorites maintained on the F<u>a</u>vorites menu.

The URLs you choose to save as favorites are stored in the Favorites folder on your hard disk. You can specify a new or different folder and you can change the name of the Web page as it appears in your list of favorites in this dialog box. To add the U.S. House of Representatives Web page as a favorite:

Step 1	*Click*	F<u>a</u>vorites
Step 2	*Click*	<u>A</u>dd to Favorites
Step 3	*Click*	OK
Step 4	*Click*	the Home button to return to the default start page

One way to load a Web page from a favorite is to click the name of the favorite in the list of favorites on the F<u>a</u>vorites menu. To load the U.S. House of Representatives home page from the F<u>a</u>vorites menu:

Step 1	*Click*	F<u>a</u>vorites
Step 2	*Click*	the U.S. House of Representatives favorite to load the page
Step 3	*Click*	the Home button to return to the default start page

The Back and Forward buttons allow you to review recently loaded Web pages without keying the URL or using the Favorites list. To reload the U.S. House of Representatives Home page from the Back button list:

Step 1	*Click*	the Back button list arrow on the toolbar
Step 2	*Click*	United States House of Representatives

4.e Using Directories and Search Engines

Because the Web is so large, you often need to take advantage of special search tools, called search engines and directories, to find the information you need. To use some of the Web's numerous search engines and directories, you can click the Search button on the

---

QUICK TIP

Another way to load a favorite is to use the Favorites button to open the Favorites list in the **Explorer bar**, a pane that opens at the left side of your screen.

CAUTION TIP

Any Web page you load is stored in the Temporary Internet Files folder on your hard disk. Whenever you reload the Web page, Internet Explorer compares the stored page to the current Web page either each time you start the browser or each time you load the page. If the Web page on the server has been changed, a fresh Web page is downloaded. If not, the Web page is retrieved from the Temporary Internet File folder rather than downloaded. To view and change the Temporary Internet File folder options (and other Internet Explorer options), click the Internet <u>O</u>ptions command on the <u>T</u>ools menu.

chapter four

> **QUICK TIP**
>
> You can also reload pages from the History folder, which stores the Web pages you load for a specific period of time. You set the number of days to store pages on the General tab in the Options dialog box. Click the History button on the toolbar to open the History list in the Explorer bar.

Standard toolbar to open the Search list in the Explorer bar. To view the Search list:

| Step 1 | **Click** | the Search button on the toolbar |
| Step 2 | **Observe** | the search list options |

Search engines maintain an index of keywords used in Web pages that you can search. Search engine indexes are updated automatically by software called **spiders** (or **robots**). Spiders follow links between pages throughout the entire Web, adding any new Web pages to the search engine's index. You should use a search engine when you want to find specific Web pages. Some of the most popular search engines include AltaVista, HotBot, and Northern Light.

Directories use a subject-type format similar to a library card catalog. A directory provides a list of links to broad general categories of Web sites such as "Entertainment" or "Business." When you click these links, a subcategory list of links appears. For example, if you click the "Entertainment" link you might then see "Movies," "Television," and "Video Games" links. To find links to Web sites containing information about movies, you would click the "Movies" link. Unlike search engines, whose indexes are updated automatically, directories add new Web sites only when an individual or a company asks that a particular Web site be included. Some directories also provide review comments and ratings for the Web sites in their index. Most directories also provide an internal search engine that can only be used to search the directory's index, not the entire Web. You use a directory when you are looking for information on broad general topics. Popular directories include Yahoo and Magellan Internet Guide.

To search for Web pages containing "movie guides:"

Step 1	**Key**	movie guides in the search list text box
Step 2	**Click**	the Search button or press the ENTER key
Step 3	**Observe**	the search results (a list of Web pages in the search list)

> **MOUSE TIP**
>
> The Links bar provides shortcuts to various Web pages at the Microsoft Web site. You can also add shortcuts to your favorite Web pages by dragging the URL icon from the Address bar to the Links bar. You can reposition the toolbar, the Address bar, and the Links bar by dragging each one to a new location below the title bar.
>
> You can print the currently loaded Web page by clicking the Print button on the Standard toolbar or the Print command on the File menu.

The search results list consists of Web page titles as hyperlinks. To load a page from the list, simply click the hyperlink. To close the Explorer bar and search list:

| Step 1 | **Click** | the Search button on the toolbar |

Guidelines for Searching the Web

Before you begin looking for information on the Web, it is a good idea to think about what you want to accomplish, establish a time frame in which to find the information, and then develop a search strategy. As you search, keep in mind the following guidelines:

1. To find broad, general information, start with a Web directory such as Galaxy or Yahoo.
2. To find a specific Web page, start with a search engine such as Alta Vista or HotBot.
3. Become familiar with a variety of search engines and their features. Review each search engine's online Help when you use it for the first time. Many search engine features are revised frequently so remember to review them regularly.
4. Search engines use spider programs to index all the pages on the Web. However, these programs work independently of each other, so not all search engines have the same index at any point in time. Use multiple search engines for each search.
5. **Boolean operators** allow you to combine or exclude keywords when using a search engine. **Proximal operators** allow you specify that search keywords be close together in a Web page. Boolean and proximal operators are words that allow you to specify relationships among search keywords or phrases using (brackets), OR, NOT, AND, NEAR, and FOLLOWED BY. Not all search engines support Boolean and proximal operators, but use them to reduce the scope of your search when they are available. For example, if you are looking for gold or silver and don't want Web pages devoted to music, try searching by the keywords *metals* not *heavy*. To make sure the keywords are in close proximity use the NEAR or FOLLOWED BY proximal operators.
6. Use very specific keywords. The more specific the phrase, the more efficient your search is. For example, use the phrase "online classes" plus the word genealogy (*"online classes" + genealogy*) rather than simply *genealogy* to find Web pages with information about classes in how to trace your family tree.
7. Watch your spelling. Be aware how the search engine you use handles capitalization. In one search engine "pear" may match "Pear", "pEaR," or "PEAR." In another search engine, "Pear" may match only "Pear."
8. Think of related words that might return the information you need. For example, if you search for information about oil, you might also use "petroleum" and "petrochemicals."
9. Search for common variations of word usage or spelling. For example, the keywords deep sea drilling, deepsea drilling, and deep-sea drilling may all provide useful information.
10. The search returns (or **hits**) are usually listed in order of relevance. You may find that only the first 10 or 12 hits are useful. To find more relevant Web pages, try searching with different keywords.

CAUTION TIP

You get varying results when using several search engines or directories to search for information on the same topic. Also, search tools operate according to varying rules. For example, some search engines allow only a simple search on one keyword. Others allow you to refine your search by finding words within quotation marks together, by indicating proper names, or by using special operators such as "and," "or," and "not" to include or exclude search words. To save time, always begin by reviewing the search tool's online Help directions, then proceed with your search.

After you find the desired information, "let the user beware!" Because the Web is largely unregulated, anyone can put anything on a Web page. Evaluate carefully the credibility of all the information you find. Try to find out something about the author and his or her credentials, or the about validity of the origin of the information.

Summary

- A network is a group of two or more computers linked by cable or telephone lines and the Internet is a worldwide "network of networks."

- The Internet began in the late 1960s as the military Internet ARPAnet. By the 1980s the National Science Foundation assumed responsibility for the non-military portions and the term Internet became widely used.

- The World Wide Web is a subset of the Internet that uses computers called Web servers to store documents called Web pages.

- To access the Internet, your computer must have some physical communication medium, such as a cable or dial-up modem and a special communication program.

- An Internet Service Provider (or ISP) maintains a host computer on the Internet. In order to connect to the Internet, you need to connect to the host computer.

- Each host computer has an Internet address or IP address consisting of a series of numbers and a descriptive name based on the computer name and domain of the host. In addition to the host computer IP address and descriptive name, each user has a name that identifies their account at the Internet Service Provider.

- Large commercial enterprises, colleges, and universities may have a computer network on the Internet and can provide Internet access to their employees or students.

- There are many challenges to using the Internet—including the amount of available information, communication speed, the dynamic environment, lack of presentation standards, and privacy/security issues.

- You should carefully evaluate the source and author of information you get from the Internet and confirm any business-critical information from another source.

- Other external networks related to the Internet are large commercial networks, such as America Online, the Microsoft Network, and USENET.

- You use Web browsers, such as Internet Explorer, to load Web pages.

- Web pages are connected by hyperlinks, which are text or pictures associated with the path to another page.

- Directories and search engines are tools to help you find files and Web sites on the Internet.

Commands Review

Action	Menu Bar	Shortcut Menu	Toolbar	Keyboard
Load a Web page	File, Open		↻	ALT + F, O Key URL in the Address bar and press the ENTER key
Save a favorite	Favorites, Add to Favorites	Right-click hyperlink, click Add to Favorites	Drag URL icon to Links bar or Favorites command	ALT + A, A CTRL + D
Manage the Standard toolbar, Address bar, and Links bar	View, Toolbars	Right-click the Standard toolbar, click desired command	Drag the Standard toolbar, Address bar, or Links bar to the new location	ALT + V, T
Load the search, history, or favorites list in the Explorer bar	View, Explorer Bar		🔍 ⭐ 🕘	ALT + V, E

Concepts Review

Circle the correct answer.

1. **To post messages of common interest to electronic bulletin boards, use:**
   - [a] search tools.
   - [b] e-mail.
   - [c] file access.
   - [d] newsgroups.

2. **A network is:**
   - [a] the Internet.
   - [b] a group of two or more computers linked by cable or telephone wire.
   - [c] a group of two or more computer networks linked by cable or telephone lines.
   - [d] a computer that stores Web pages.

3. **The Internet began as the:**
   - [a] MILNET.
   - [b] NSFnet.
   - [c] SLIPnet.
   - [d] ARPAnet.

4. **Which of the following is not a challenge to using the Internet?**
   - [a] chat groups.
   - [b] dynamic environment and heavy usage.
   - [c] volume of information.
   - [d] security and privacy.

Circle **T** if the statement is true or **F** if the statement is false.

T F   1. An IP address is a unique identifying number for each host computer on the Internet.
T F   2. A host computer's descriptive name identifies it by name and organizational level on the Internet.
T F   3. Commercial networks that provide specially formatted features are the same as the Internet.
T F   4. USENET is the name of the military Internet.

Skills Review

Exercise 1

1. Open the Internet Explorer Web browser.
2. Open the Internet Options dialog box by clicking the Internet Options command on the View menu.
3. Review the options on the General tab in the dialog box.
4. Write down the steps to change the default start page to a blank page.
5. Close the dialog box and close the Web browser.

Exercise 2

1. Connect to your ISP and open the Internet Explorer Web browser.
2. Open the search list in the Explorer bar. Search for Web pages about "dog shows."
3. Load one of the Web pages in the search results list. Close the Explorer bar.
4. Print the Web page by clicking the <u>P</u>rint command on the <u>F</u>ile menu and close the Web browser.

Exercise 3

1. Connect to your ISP and open the Internet Explorer Web browser.
2. Load the National Public radio Web page by keying the URL, *www.npr.org*, in the Address bar.
3. Print the Web page by clicking the <u>P</u>rint command on the <u>F</u>ile menu and close the Web browser.

Exercise 4

1. Connect to your ISP and open the Internet Explorer Web browser.
2. Load the AltaVista search engine by keying the URL, *www.altavista.digital.com*, in the Address bar.
3. Save the Web page as a favorite. Search for Web pages about your city.
4. Print at least two Web pages by clicking the <u>P</u>rint command on the <u>F</u>ile menu and close your Web browser.

Case Projects

Project 1

Your supervisor asks you to prepare a fifteen-minute presentation describing the Internet Explorer toolbar buttons. Review the toolbar buttons and practice using them. Write an outline for your presentation that lists each button and describes how it is used.

Project 2

Your manager is concerned about Internet security and wants to know more about Internet Explorer security features. Click the <u>C</u>ontents and Index command on the Internet Explorer <u>H</u>elp menu to locate and review the topics about security. Write a note to your manager discussing two security topics.

Project 3

You are working for a book publisher who is creating a series of books about popular movie actors and actresses from the 1920s to the 1950s, including Humphrey Bogart and Lionel Barrymore. The research director asks you to locate a list of movies on the Web that the actors starred in. Use the Explorer bar search list and the Yahoo directory search tool to find links to "Entertainment." Close the Explorer bar and then, working from the Yahoo Web page, click "Movies" within the Entertainment category, scroll down and click the Actors and Actresses link. Search for Humphrey Bogart in the Actors and Actresses portion of the database. Link to the Web page that shows the filmography for Humphrey Bogart. Print the Web page that shows all the movies he acted in. Use the History list to return to the Actors and Actresses search page. Search for Lionel Barrymore, link to and print the filmography for him. Close the Internet Explorer Web browser.

Project 4

You are the new secretary for the Business Women's Forum. The association's president asked you to compile a list of Internet resources. Connect to your ISP, open Internet Explorer, and search for pages containing the keywords "women in business" (including the quotation marks). From the search results, click the Web page title link of your choice. Review the new Web page and its links. Create a favorite for that page. Use the Back button list to reload the search results and click a different Web page title from the list. Review the Web page and its links. Create a favorite for the Web page. Load and review at least five pages. Return to the default home page. Use the <u>G</u>o menu and the History bar to reload at least three of the pages. Print two of the pages. Delete the favorites you added, and then close Internet Explorer.

Microsoft
Excel 2000

Excel 2000

Quick Start for Excel

Chapter Overview

In this chapter, you learn about the components of the Excel workbook window. You open an existing workbook, create a new workbook, enter and revise data, and save your work. You also learn about Excel's "workhorses"–formulas and functions.

Learning Objectives

- Explore the Excel components
- Locate and open an existing workbook
- Navigate a worksheet
- Enter text, dates, and numbers
- Select cells
- Edit cell content
- Clear contents and formatting of cells
- Use Undo and Redo
- Enter formulas and functions
- Save workbooks
- Close workbooks and exit Excel

Case profile

Amy Lee runs a rapidly growing candy business called Sweet Tooth. Today, her confections are sold to retail outlets in many states. Because Sweet Tooth is growing so rapidly, the company has hired you to computerize the company records. In this chapter, you use Excel to track how many items were sold at each location.

chapter one

notes This text assumes that you have little or no knowledge of Excel. It assumes that you have read Office Chapters 1–4 of this book and that you are familiar with Windows 95 or Windows 98 concepts.

1.a Exploring the Excel Components

Spreadsheet applications, such as Excel, help you organize and analyze information, especially information involving numbers. A **spreadsheet** is a computer file specially designed to organize data into cells, which are containers that hold individual pieces of data. Cells are organized into rows and columns to create a **worksheet**. Worksheets, in turn, are collected in a file called a **workbook**.

Before you can begin to work with Excel, you must open the application. When you open the application, a new, blank workbook opens as well. To open Excel and a new, blank workbook:

Step 1	Click	the Start button on the taskbar
Step 2	Point to	Programs
Step 3	Click	Microsoft Excel

Within a few seconds, Excel starts. Your screen should look similar to Figure 1-1.

Worksheets

Each new workbook contains three worksheets, which are similar to pages in a notebook. You switch between worksheets by clicking the **tabs** near the bottom of the Excel window. Each workbook can hold as many as 255 worksheets, which you can name individually. The default names are Sheet1, Sheet2, and so on. The **current** worksheet is the worksheet that appears to be in front of the other worksheets.

Worksheets are made up of columns and rows. **Columns** run vertically up and down a worksheet. Across the top of each worksheet you see **column headings,** lettered from A to Z, AA to AZ and so on to column IV (256 in total). **Rows** run from left to right across a worksheet. On the left side of each worksheet are **row headings,** numbered from 1 to 65,536 (the maximum number of rows in a worksheet).

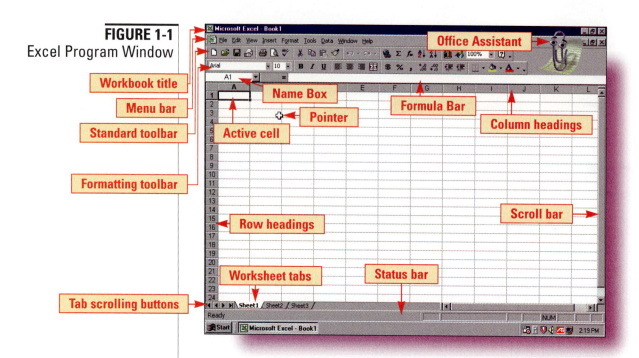

FIGURE 1-1
Excel Program Window

Cells, the intersection of rows and columns, store values. **Values** are numbers, text, hyperlinks, formulas, and functions. A **cell reference** is the column letter and row number that identifies a cell; for example, cell A1 refers to the cell at the intersection of column A and row 1. Each cell can contain as many as 32,000 characters. When you move your mouse pointer over a worksheet, it changes to a large white cross. This pointer changes shape depending on what you are doing. When you click a cell, it becomes the **active cell**, and a thick border surrounds it. Any values you enter are stored in the active cell.

Top of the Program Window

The **title bar** displays the application name as well as the current document name. The default name for the blank workbook that appears when you start Excel is Book1. On the right side of the title bar are the Minimize, Maximize/Restore, and Close buttons. The **menu bar**, located below the title bar, contains drop-down menu commands that contain groups of additional, related commands. The activities in this book instruct you to select menu bar commands with the mouse; if you prefer, however, you can press the ALT key plus the underlined letter in the menu command to open the menu, then press the underlined letter in the command on the menu. In addition, many menu commands have an associated keyboard shortcut. For example, to open a file, you could click the File menu, then click Open; you could press the ALT + F keys, then press the O key; or you could press the CTRL + O keys. The Commands Review section at the end of each chapter summarizes both the mouse and keyboard techniques to select a menu command.

QUICK TIP

Office 2000 features personalized menus and toolbars, which "learn" the commands you use most often. This means that when you first install Office 2000, only the most frequently used commands appear immediately on a short version of the menus; the remaining commands appear after a brief pause. Commands that you select move to the short menu, while those you don't use appear only on the full menu.

The **Standard toolbar**, beneath the menu bar, provides easy access to commonly used commands, such as Save, Open, Print, Copy, and Paste, as well as many other useful commands. The **Formatting toolbar**, below the Standard toolbar, provides easy access to commonly used formatting commands, such as Style, Font, Font Size, Alignment, Fill Color, and Font Color. The **Name Box**, below the Formatting toolbar, displays the current cell or cells. Use the **Formula Bar**, to the right of the Name Box, to create and edit values. The Formula Bar becomes active whenever you begin keying data into a cell. When the Formula Bar is active, the Enter, Cancel, and Edit Formula buttons appear.

Bottom of the Program Window

The **tab scrolling buttons** allow you to navigate through the tabs, or worksheets, contained in your workbook. The right- and left-pointing triangles scroll one tab to the right or left, respectively. The right- and left-pointing triangles with the vertical line jump to the first and last tabs in the notebook, respectively. Scrolling the tabs does not change your active worksheet. The **status bar** at the bottom of the Excel window indicates various items of information, such as whether NUM LOCK or CAPS LOCK is active. If you select a range of cells containing numbers, the sum of the selected cells is displayed on the status bar.

Office Assistant

The **Office Assistant**, which you can use to search for online Help topics, appears automatically when you launch Excel unless you hide it or turn it off. In this book, the Office Assistant is hidden unless you need it for a specific activity. To hide the Office Assistant, if necessary:

Step 1	*Right-click*	the Office Assistant
Step 2	*Click*	Hide

Amy, Sweet Tooth's president, would like you to review the workbook she has been using to track candy sales.

1.b Locating and Opening an Existing Workbook

When you want to edit an existing workbook, you must open the workbook from the disk where it is stored. Amy asks you to review the *Sweet Tooth 1998 Sales* workbook she created.

> **QUICK TIP**
>
> The Standard and Formatting toolbars appear on the same row when you first install Office 2000. When they are displayed in this position, only the most commonly used buttons of each toolbar are visible. All of the other default buttons appear on the More Buttons drop-down lists. As you use buttons from the More Buttons drop-down list, they move to become visible buttons on the toolbar, while the buttons you don't use move into the More Buttons drop-down list. If you arrange the Formatting toolbar below the Standard toolbar, all buttons are visible. Unless otherwise noted, the illustrations in this book show the full menus and the Formatting toolbar on its own line below the Standard toolbar.

chapter one

QUICK TIP

Press the CTRL + O keys to display the Open dialog box.

CAUTION TIP

Your system may be set up to show file extensions, which are three letters at the end of filenames that identify the file type. The Excel file extension is xls. The illustrations in this book do not show file extensions.

MENU TIP

To change the Excel default of creating three worksheets in a new workbook, select Options from the Tools menu. On the General tab, use the spinner control next to Sheets in new workbook to set the number of worksheets.

To open an existing workbook:

| Step 1 | Click | the Open button on the Standard toolbar |

The Open dialog box that appears should look similar to Figure 1-2.

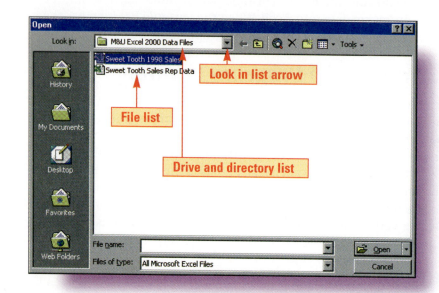

FIGURE 1-2
Open Dialog Box

Step 2	Click	the Look in: list arrow
Step 3	Switch	to the disk drive and folder where the Data Disk is stored
Step 4	Double-click	*Sweet Tooth 1998 Sales* in the file list

The *Sweet Tooth 1998 Sales* workbook opens. Amy created this workbook last year to keep track of how many items were sold to each client for the first quarter of 1998.

1.c Navigating a Worksheet

Recall that the active cell is the cell with the thick black border around it. When the pointer is over the cell you want to make active, click the cell. To activate a cell with the mouse:

| Step 1 | Point to | cell B6 |

| Step 2 | Click | cell B6 |
| Step 3 | Verify | that cell B6 is active by looking in the Name Box |

You can also use the ARROW keys and other keyboard shortcuts to move the active cell. Table 1-1 summarizes some of the keyboard shortcuts for moving around in Excel.

To Move	Press
Up one cell	UP ARROW
Down one cell	DOWN ARROW
Right one cell	TAB or RIGHT ARROW
Left one cell	SHIFT + TAB or LEFT ARROW
To the first active cell of the current row	HOME
To the last active cell of the current row	END and then ENTER
Down one page	PAGE DOWN
Up one page	PAGE UP
To cell A1	CTRL + HOME
To the last cell with data in it in a worksheet	CTRL + END or END and then HOME
To the edge of the last cell containing a value or to the edges of a worksheet	CTRL + ARROW

TABLE 1-1
Using the Keyboard to Navigate a Workbook

MOUSE TIP

You can also scroll through the worksheet by clicking the arrows to scroll one row or column at a time; drag the scroll boxes to scroll several rows or columns.

To navigate a worksheet using the keyboard:

Step 1	Press	the CTRL + HOME keys to move to cell A1
Step 2	Press	the CTRL + END keys to move to the last cell with data in it in the worksheet
Step 3	Press	the HOME key to move to the first cell in the current row
Step 4	Press	the CTRL + PAGE DOWN keys to move to Sheet2
Step 5	Press	the CTRL + PAGE UP keys to move back to Sheet1

QUICK TIP

With the IntelliMouse pointing device, you can use the scrolling wheel to scroll a worksheet. For more information on using the IntelliMouse pointing device, see online Help.

1.d Entering Text, Dates, and Numbers

You can enter numbers, letters, and symbols into the active cell. When you enter data in a cell, Excel recognizes the type of data you are entering. For example, if you enter your name in a cell, Excel knows that this is a text value and therefore cannot be used in calculations. If you enter a date in a cell, such as 1/1/99 or January 1, 1999, Excel automatically identifies it as a date value and applies a date number format that closely corresponds to the way you entered the date.

Amy gives you a copy of her records for candy sales in January, February, and March of 1999, as shown in Table 1-2.

TABLE 1-2
Sweet Tooth Sales Data

Location	January	February	March
Widgit, Inc.	45	57	52
Firehouse 451	123	97	101
Clothes Horse	36	23	28

QUICK TIP

You can also start a new workbook by pressing the CTRL + N keys, or by clicking the File menu, and then clicking New.

You enter this data in the blank worksheet. Before you do this, you need to open a new workbook. To open a new workbook:

Step 1	Click	the New button on the Standard toolbar

To enter data in a worksheet:

Step 1	Verify	that Sheet1 is the active worksheet
Step 2	Click	cell A1, if necessary
Step 3	Key	Location

MENU TIP

You can change the default behavior of the ENTER key by using the Options dialog box. On the Tools menu, click Options. On the Edit tab, locate the Move selection after Enter check box. To turn the behavior off, remove the check mark. To force the active cell in a different direction, select a new direction from the Direction: list box.

Your screen should look similar to Figure 1-3. As you enter data, the status bar displays the word "Enter." The Formula Bar displays the contents of the active cell, while the cell itself shows the results of any formula entered in the cell. In the case of numbers or text, no calculation takes place, so you see exactly what you enter. Notice that the Cancel and Enter buttons appear next to the Formula Bar. Also note that the mouse pointer changes to an I-beam pointer to indicate that you are entering a value in a cell, and a blinking **insertion point** appears in the cell to indicate where the next character that you key will go.

FIGURE 1-3
Entering Data

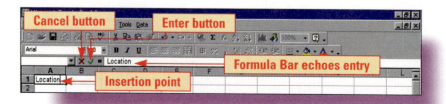

| Step 4 | Press | the ENTER key |

When you press the ENTER key, the entry is accepted and the active cell moves down one row by default.

Step 5	Click	cell B1 to activate it
Step 6	Key	January
Step 7	Press	the TAB key
Step 8	Key	February
Step 9	Press	the TAB key
Step 10	Continue	to enter the rest of the data as shown in Table 1-2

QUICK TIP

You can use any of the navigation keys you learned earlier in this chapter to complete data entry in one cell and then move to another. When you press any of the ARROW keys, the TAB key, or the SHIFT + TAB key combination, the current data entry is accepted and a new cell becomes active. To accept data and leave the active cell in place, click the Enter button on the Formula Bar. If you don't want to process the entry, press the ESC key or click the Cancel button on the Formula Bar.

When you finish, your worksheet should look similar to Figure 1-4. You cannot see some of the text in column A. You learn how to widen a column in Chapter 2.

FIGURE 1-4
Sweet Tooth Sales Data

1.e Selecting Cells

Selecting cells is one of the most fundamental skills used when working in Excel. You select cells for editing, moving, copying, and formatting. To select cells using the mouse:

| Step 1 | Click | cell A1, *but do not release* the mouse button |
| Step 2 | Drag | to cell A4 |

You have selected a range of cells. A **range** is any group of contiguous cells. To refer to a range, you specify the cells in the upper-left and lower-right corners. In this step, you selected the range A1:A4. As you

QUICK TIP

Many situations require the use of multiple, nonadjacent ranges. For example, you may need to select cells in column A and C. To select multiple ranges, select one range, press and hold the CTRL key, then select the next range from anywhere else in the workbook.

select the range, the status bar displays the sum of all cells in the selected range containing number values and the Name Box displays a running count of rows and columns in your selected range. In this example, the Name Box shows 4R x 1C, meaning four rows and one column are selected. As soon as you release the mouse button to close your selection, the Name Box displays the group's active cell reference.

Step 3	*Release*	the mouse button

The first selected cell, A1, remains unshaded to indicate that it is the active cell in the group, as shown in Figure 1-5.

FIGURE 1-5
Selecting a Range

You often want to select an entire row or column to apply the same alignment or number format over the entire row or column. To select rows and columns:

Step 1	*Click*	the row 3 heading at the left of your worksheet to select row 3
Step 2	*Click*	the column B heading at the top of your worksheet to select column B

You can also use keys to select cells. To select cells using keys:

Step 1	*Click*	cell B4 to make it the active cell
Step 2	*Press & Hold*	the SHIFT key
Step 3	*Press*	the RIGHT ARROW key twice to select cells B4 and C4
Step 4	*Press & Hold*	the SHIFT + CTRL keys
Step 5	*Press*	the UP ARROW key

| Step 6 | Release | the SHIFT + CTRL keys to select the range B1:C4 |
| Step 7 | Click | any cell in the worksheet to deselect the range |

Using the SHIFT key starts a selection that you control using only the ARROW keys. Using the CTRL key in combination with the ARROW keys causes the selection to jump in the direction you specify until it reaches the last cell containing data. If the cells in the direction you specify with an ARROW key are blank, the selection moves to the limits of the worksheet. Now that you can select cells, you're ready to continue modifying your worksheet.

QUICK TIP

While working in a selection, press the ENTER key to move the active cell down one cell. Press the TAB key to move the active cell to the right. Press SHIFT + TAB to move the active cell to the left.

1.f Editing Cell Content

Amy has given you updated data for your spreadsheet. Rather than starting a new workbook, you can edit the data in each cell in your existing workbook. To revise cell B2:

Step 1	Activate	cell B2
Step 2	Key	47 to replace the previous entry
Step 3	Press	the TAB key
Step 4	Key	55 in cell C2
Step 5	Press	the RIGHT ARROW key
Step 6	Key	60 in cell D2
Step 7	Click	the Enter button ✓ on the Formula Bar

CAUTION TIP

Although replacing cell content is the fastest way to edit a cell, be careful when taking this approach. The previous contents of the cell will be replaced with any new data you enter.

Editing in the Active Cell

Often, you need to revise only part of an entry. To edit in the active cell:

| Step 1 | Double-click | cell B4 to place the blinking insertion point in the cell |
| Step 2 | Drag | the I-beam pointer I over the value in cell B4 to select it |

MOUSE TIP

Instead of double-clicking a cell to edit its contents, you can press the F2 key.

See Figure 1-6. The value in cell B4 is **selected**, or highlighted. Anything you type will replace the selected text.

FIGURE 1-6
Editing in the Active Cell

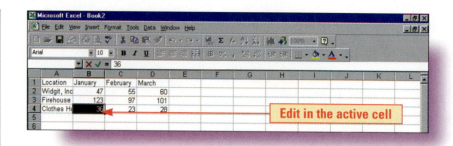

Edit in the active cell

QUICK TIP

Sometimes it's difficult to select text in a cell precisely with the mouse, especially when you're highlighting only a few characters in the middle of a long formula or text entry. The next time that you need to select a few characters, try this: Click to position the insertion point near the start of your selection. Press and hold the SHIFT key while you press the right ARROW key to move across the text. When you've selected the text, release the SHIFT key and continue your editing.

Step 3	Key	40
Step 4	Press	the ENTER key
Step 5	Use	either of the previous methods to change the contents of cell C4 to 37 and the contents of cell D4 to 38

Editing with the Formula Bar

You can edit the contents of the active cell in the Formula Bar by either moving the insertion point where you want to make changes or highlighting the text you want to change and then keying new text. To edit from the Formula Bar:

Step 1	Activate	cell B3
Step 2	Click	the I-beam pointer to the right of 1 in the Formula Bar to place the insertion point
Step 3	Press	the DELETE key to delete one character to the right
Step 4	Key	4
Step 5	Click	the Enter button ✓ on the Formula Bar
Step 6	Activate	cell C3
Step 7	Click	to the right of 7 in the Formula Bar
Step 8	Press	the BACKSPACE key to delete one character to the left
Step 9	Key	5
Step 10	Press	the TAB key to move to cell D3
Step 11	Click	to the left of the 0 in the Formula Bar
Step 12	Key	1
Step 13	Press	the DELETE key
Step 14	Press	the ENTER key

1.g Clearing Contents and Formatting of Cells

In Excel, you can clear the contents or formatting of a cell, or both, using the Clear <u>C</u>ontents, Clear <u>F</u>ormats, or Clear <u>A</u>ll commands available from the Cle<u>a</u>r command on the <u>E</u>dit menu. The <u>D</u>elete command on the <u>E</u>dit menu deletes a cell's contents and formatting, shifting the surrounding cells to replace the deleted cell. This command is generally used far less often than the Clear Contents command.

To clear values from a cell or cells:

Step 1	Select	cells A2 through A4 using any of the methods you learned earlier in this chapter
Step 2	Press	the DELETE key

The values contained in cells A2:A4 are deleted. You can also, of course, clear the contents and formatting of only the active cell.

> **QUICK TIP**
>
> When you use the DELETE key, you are actually using the Clear Contents command.

1.h Using Undo and Redo

The **Undo** command reverses your previous action or actions. Although you can undo most commands, such as formatting, moving, or data entry, certain commands, such as printing and file operations, like Save or Save As, cannot be undone. The **Redo** command reinstates the action or actions you previously undid. You can Undo and Redo one action at a time, or you can select a number of actions to Undo and Redo from a list of up to 16 previous actions. To undo the last action, click the Undo button on the Standard toolbar. The Redo button will not be active until you have used Undo. Click the Redo button to undo the last Undo command.

You realize you didn't need to delete the store locations from your worksheet. Rather than rekeying the text, use Undo. To use the Undo and Redo commands:

Step 1	Click	the Undo button 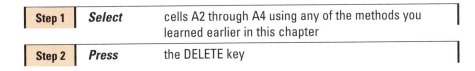 on the Standard toolbar

> **QUICK TIP**
>
> Press the CTRL + Z keys to Undo the last action. Press the CTRL + Y keys to Redo the last Undo action.

The contents of cells A2 through A4 should return to their previous values of Widgit, Inc., Firehouse 451, and Clothes Horse.

| Step 2 | Click | the Redo button on the Standard toolbar to clear the contents of cells A2:A4 again |
| Step 3 | Click | the Undo button on the Standard toolbar again to restore the values to A2:A4 |

Use the Undo list to quickly Undo several commands at once. To use the Undo list:

| Step 1 | Change | the value in cell D4 to 50 |
| Step 2 | Change | the value in cell C3 to 175 |

You have performed two actions, both data entry. The Undo list allows you to select multiple actions to Undo.

> **MENU TIP**
>
> Click the Undo command on the Edit menu to reverse your last action. Click the Redo command on the Edit menu to reverse the previous Undo action.

Step 3	Click	the Undo button list arrow on the Standard toolbar
Step 4	Move	the pointer down the list, highlighting the top two "Typing" actions
Step 5	Click	the second "Typing" action

Cell D4 returns to its previous value of 38, and cell C3 returns to its previous value of 95. The Redo list works in the same way.

1.i Entering Formulas and Functions

Spreadsheet programs would not be very useful if they didn't work with formulas and functions. A **formula** is like a recipe. When you combine ingredients in a specific way and cook the mixture for the right amount of time, a particular result comes out.

All formulas in Excel begin with the equal sign (=). Some formulas are simple, such as those that add, subtract, multiply, and divide two or more values; for example, =2+2 is a simple formula. Other formulas can be very complex and include a sequence of **functions**, or predefined formulas.

All functions require **operands**, which can be either values or references to cells containing a value, or both. Some functions require **operators** to indicate the type of calculation that will take place. Common mathematical operators include **+** for addition, **−** for subtraction, ***** for multiplication, **/** for division, and **^** for exponentiation.

Following Formula Syntax and Rules of Precedence

Formulas follow a syntax. The **syntax** is the structure, or order, of the elements (operands and operators) in a formula. It signifies that the contents of the cell will evaluate to some result.

Excel evaluates formulas using mathematical rules of precedence to determine what gets calculated first. Excel calculates a formula from left to right, first evaluating any operations between parentheses, then any exponentiation, then multiplication and division, followed by addition and subtraction. Consider the following formulas: =5+2*3 and =(5+2)*3. In the first formula, 2*3 is calculated first and then added to 5, giving a result of 11. In the second example, 5+2 is calculated first and then multiplied by 3, giving a result of 21.

Amy would like to know the total items sold at Widgit, Inc. for the first three months of 1999. To create a formula:

Step 1	Click	cell E2
Step 2	Key	=47+55+60
Step 3	Click	the Enter button ✓ on the Formula Bar

This simple mathematical formula adds 47+55+60, the total sales for Widgit, Inc., resulting in a value of 162, which is displayed in the cell. Notice that the Formula Bar displays the formula, not the calculated result, as shown in Figure 1-7.

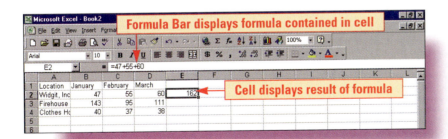

FIGURE 1-7
Formula Displayed in the Formula Bar

Adding Cell References to a Formula

The real power of formulas lies in their ability to use cell references. Using cell references allows you to quickly change values, leaving the formula intact. To replace the numerical values in cell E2 with cell references:

Step 1	Drag	to select the entry in the Formula Bar

QUICK TIP

You do not have to capitalize column references. Excel performs this task for you automatically when you enter a formula.

| Step 2 | Key | =b2+c2+d2 in the Formula Bar |
| Step 3 | Press | the ENTER key |

The result of adding cells B2, C2, and D2—162—appears in the Formula Bar and in cell E2.

| Step 4 | Change | the value in cell B2 to 55 |

When you press the ENTER key, the value in cell E2 automatically recalculates to 170 to reflect the change in the value of B2.

Using the Sum Function and AutoSum

The SUM function is one of the most commonly used functions. It is very useful for adding the values of many cells. The syntax of the SUM function is **SUM(number1**,number2,…). The terms in bold in a function's syntax are required; the terms that are not bold are optional. The terms between the parentheses are the **arguments**, values that must be supplied for the function to perform the calculation correctly. The ellipses (…) indicate you can supply as many optional arguments to the function as you like. Use the SUM function to total the number of pieces of Sweet Tooth's candy that each location sold during January, February, and March. To start keying the SUM function:

| Step 1 | Activate | Cell E3 |
| Step 2 | Key | =sum(|

Next, you need to select the range of cells to sum. To select a range of cells in a formula:

| Step 1 | Select | cells B3:D3 using the mouse |

See Figure 1-8. The range B3:D3 is the number1 argument of the SUM function.

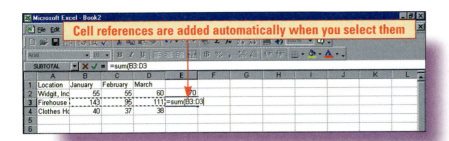

FIGURE 1-8
Using the SUM Function

Now complete the SUM function. To complete the SUM function:

| Step 1 | Click | the Enter button ✓ on the Formula Bar |

> **QUICK TIP**
>
> Need help in a hurry? Press the F1 key to bring up the Office Assistant.

If you want to sum the values in a second range, separate each argument with a comma. For example, to sum the ranges B3:D3 and B5:D5, the SUM function would be written as =SUM(B3:D3, B5:D5).

When you use the AutoSum button on the Standard toolbar, Excel inserts the SUM function and scans cells above and to the left for values to add together. If it finds any, it adds the reference as an argument. To use the AutoSum button:

| Step 1 | Activate | cell E4 |
| Step 2 | Click | the AutoSum button Σ on the Standard toolbar |

The formula =SUM(B4:D4) is inserted in cell E4. The range B4:D4 is surrounded by a flashing border.

| Step 3 | Press | the ENTER key |

The formula is accepted in cell E4. Next, you use the Min and Max functions to work with your data.

Using the Min and Max Functions

Finding the minimum and maximum values of a set of numbers are commonly performed operations. Excel uses the MIN and MAX functions to calculate these values. One way to analyze Sweet Tooth's sales data is to find these values. To use the MIN and MAX functions:

| Step 1 | Key | MIN in cell A6 |

Step 2	*Press*	the ENTER key
Step 3	*Key*	MAX in cell A7
Step 4	*Press*	the ENTER key
Step 5	*Activate*	cell B6
Step 6	*Key*	=min(
Step 7	*Select*	cells B2:D4 using the mouse
Step 8	*Press*	the ENTER key

The lowest, or minimum, value in the selected range, 37, appears as the results of the formula in cell B6.

Step 9	*Key*	=max(
Step 10	*Select*	cells B2:D4 using the mouse
Step 11	*Press*	the ENTER key

The highest, or maximum, value in the selected range, 143, appears as the results of the formula in cell B7.

1.j Saving Workbooks

The first rule of computing is: Save Your Work Often! The second rule of computing is: Follow the First Rule of Computing.

There are two distinct saving operations: Save and Save As.

Using the Save As Command

When you use the Save As command, you provide a filename and specify the disk drive and folder location where the workbook should be saved. A filename can have as many as 255 characters, including the disk drive reference and path, and can contain letters, numbers, spaces, and some special characters in any combination. If you use the Save As command on a previously saved workbook, you actually create a new copy of the workbook, and any changes you made appear only in the new copy. To save the current workbook:

> **QUICK TIP**
>
> Press the CTRL + S keys or the SHIFT + F12 keys to save your work. Press the F12 key to open the Save As dialog box.

| Step 1 | *Click* | File |

| Step 2 | Click | Save As |

Because the workbook does not have a filename yet, you can click Save instead of Save As when you save a new workbook the first time.

Step 3	Click	the Save in: list arrow
Step 4	Switch	to the disk drive and folder where you are storing your Data Files
Step 5	Drag	to select the text in the File name: box
Step 6	Key	Sweet Tooth 1999 Sales in the File name: text box

Figure 1-9 shows the Save As dialog box.

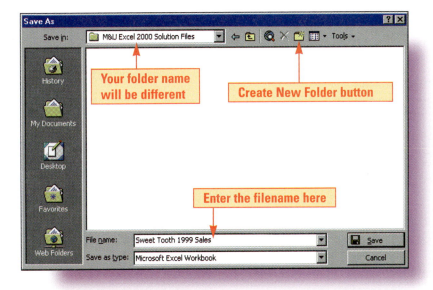

CAUTION TIP

Filenames cannot include the following special characters: the forward slash (/), the backward slash (\), the colon (:), the semicolon (;), the pipe symbol (|), the question mark (?), the less than symbol (<), the greater than symbol (>), the asterisk (*), and the quotation mark (").

FIGURE 1-9
Save As Dialog Box

QUICK TIP

 You can create a new folder in the Save As and Open dialog boxes. Click the Create New Folder button , key a new folder name, and click OK. The new folder automatically becomes the current folder.

| Step 7 | Click | Save |

The workbook is saved to your file folder as *Sweet Tooth 1999 Sales*. Notice that your title bar includes the new filename.

Using the Save Command

When you save a previously saved workbook with the Save command, no dialog box appears. Instead, the changes are saved to your current workbook and location and you go back to work. To modify your workbook and save the changes:

| Step 1 | **Change** | the value in cell B3 to 98 |
| Step 2 | **Click** | the Save button 💾 on the Standard toolbar |

No dialog box appears because you already named the workbook.

1.k Closing Workbooks and Exiting Excel

You can close individual workbooks without closing the Excel application. If you have modified the workbook you are closing, Excel prompts you to save your work. To close the *Sweet Tooth 1999 Sales* workbook:

| Step 1 | **Click** | File |
| Step 2 | **Click** | Close |

Excel displays the next open workbook, if there is one. If no workbooks are open, you see a blank workspace. The *Sweet Tooth 1998 Sales* workbook that you were using earlier appears.

| Step 3 | **Close** | the *Sweet Tooth 1998 Sales* workbook |
| Step 4 | **Click** | No to reject any changes, if prompted |

When you finish working in Excel, you should exit the program. If any workbooks that you modified remain open, Excel prompts you to save your work before closing the program. If you change your mind about exiting, click Cancel. To exit Excel:

Step 1	**Click**	File
Step 2	**Click**	Exit
Step 3	**Click**	Yes to save any edited workbooks, if necessary

---

CAUTION TIP

Computers and computer programs are not perfect. Avoid losing data from computer crashes by saving your work every 10 to 15 minutes.

MOUSE TIP

Click the Close Window button at the top of the worksheet window, just below the Excel title bar, to close the workbook.

Click the Close button on the Excel title bar to quickly exit the Excel program.

QUICK TIP

Press the CTRL + F4 or CTRL + W keys to close a workbook.

Press the ALT + F4 keys to exit the Excel program.

Summary

- A worksheet is an electronic spreadsheet. A workbook is a collection of worksheets.

- Cells are containers in worksheets for text, numerical values, and formulas that calculate data. Cells are organized into rows and columns. A cell reference identifies a particular cell through a combination of the column letter and the row number.

- You can open multiple workbooks in Excel.

- Use keyboard shortcuts like HOME, CTRL + HOME, TAB and SHIFT + TAB to navigate around a worksheet. You can also use the mouse to activate a cell or to scroll to other cells.

- By default, new workbooks are created with three worksheets.

- Enter number and text data by keying the information directly into the cell or in the Formula Bar.

- Select cells with the mouse by pressing and holding the left mouse button as you drag across cells. Select cells with the keyboard by pressing and holding the SHIFT key plus the ARROW keys, and other shortcut keys, such as the CTRL, HOME, and END keys.

- Modify data by keying data over a cell, double-clicking or pressing the F2 key and then editing directly in the cell, or clicking the cell and then using the Formula Bar to edit cell contents.

- Clear cell contents quickly by selecting ranges and pressing the DELETE key. Clear cell formatting by using the Clear command on the Edit menu.

- Use the Undo list to quickly undo as many as 16 commands at once, including formatting, data entry, editing, and deletion. The Undo command cannot be used to reverse File and Print operations, such as the Save As command.

- Formulas evaluate mathematical operations or predefined functions, returning a new value. Formulas must be preceded by an equal sign (=).

- Functions are predefined formulas that perform complex operations. They must receive valid input for all required arguments if they are to perform calculations correctly.

- Use the SUM function to sum the values of several cells. Use the AutoSum button to automatically insert the SUM formula.

chapter one

▶ Use the MIN function to find the minimum, or lowest, value in a set of numbers.

▶ Use the MAX function to find the maximum, or highest, value in a set of numbers.

▶ Use the Save command to save a new workbook or to save changes to a previously named workbook.

▶ Use the Save As command when you want to make a copy of an existing workbook.

▶ When you close a new or modified workbook, Excel reminds you to save your work.

▶ When you close the Excel application, Excel reminds you to save any unsaved workbooks.

Commands Review

Action	Menu Bar	Shortcut Menu	Toolbar	Keyboard
Open a workbook	File, Open	Right-click empty Excel workspace, click Open	📂	CTRL + O ALT + F, O
Create a new workbook	File, New	Right-click empty Excel workspace, click New	📄	CTRL + N, ALT + F, N
Save a workbook	File, Save		💾	CTRL + S, ALT + F, S
Save a workbook with a new name, location, or type	File, Save As			ALT + F, A
Edit a cell				F2
Accept a cell entry			✓	ENTER
Cancel a cell entry			✗	ESC
Use AutoSum			Σ	ALT + =
Close a workbook	File, Close		✗	CTRL + F4 ALT + F, C CTRL + W
Close multiple workbooks	Press and hold the SHIFT key, then File, Close All			SHIFT + ALT + F, C
Close Excel	File, Exit	Right-click the application icon, click Close	✗	ALT + F4 ALT + 5, X
Undo the previous action	Edit, Undo		↺	CTRL + Z ALT + E, U
Redo an undo action	Edit, Redo		↻	CTRL + Y ALT + E, R

Concepts Review

Circle the correct answer.

1. Excel worksheets contain:
   - [a] 30 rows.
   - [b] 256 rows.
   - [c] 20,000 rows.
   - [d] 65,536 rows.

2. Excel worksheets contain:
   - [a] 30 columns.
   - [b] 256 columns.
   - [c] 20,000 columns.
   - [d] 65,536 columns.

3. To cancel an entry in a cell that has not yet been accepted, press the:
   - [a] TAB key.
   - [b] ENTER key.
   - [c] ESC key.
   - [d] DELETE key.

4. The status bar displays:
   - [a] text and formulas you are entering.
   - [b] results of the formula you are entering.
   - [c] important worksheet and system information.
   - [d] the filename of your workbook.

5. To finish editing a cell:
   - [a] press the CTRL + ALT + ESC keys.
   - [b] stop keying and wait for the previous value to return.
   - [c] press the ENTER key.
   - [d] press the ESC key.

6. You can Undo or Redo as many as:
   - [a] 1 operation.
   - [b] 10 operations.
   - [c] 16 operations.
   - [d] unlimited number of operations.

7. All formulas start with:
   - [a] @.
   - [b] the keyword "Formula."
   - [c] =.
   - [d] $$.

8. To perform calculations correctly, formulas must employ the correct:
   - [a] functions.
   - [b] operands.
   - [c] operators.
   - [d] syntax.

9. Functions require the use of:
   - [a] arguments.
   - [b] documents.
   - [c] formulas.
   - [d] values.

10. An operand is:
    - [a] the same as an operator.
    - [b] a value or cell reference containing a value.
    - [c] not required in some formulas.
    - [d] a calculation performed by Excel.

Circle **T** if the statement is true or **F** if the statement is false.

T F 1. Excel can open many workbooks at once.

T F 2. Cells can contain numbers, text, or formulas.

T F 3. The formula **=(5+5)*2** gives the same result as the formula **=5+5*2**.

T F 4. The Undo command can undo any type of command in Excel.

T F 5. Skipping optional arguments in a function is acceptable.

T F 6. Changing the order of required arguments in a function is acceptable, as long as they are all there.

T F   7. Rows run vertically down the worksheet.
T F   8. The key combination of CTRL + HOME closes the Excel application and saves any open workbooks.
T F   9. By default, new workbooks contain five worksheets.
T F   10. Editing cell contents in the Formula Bar works just as well as editing directly in the cell.

Skills Review

Exercise 1

1. Create a new workbook and enter the data below on Sheet1. Enter the label TIME SHEET in cell A1. (*Hint:* Enter the dates with forward slashes and the times with colons. Use 24-hour clock times as shown in the table.)

TIME SHEET		
Date	Start Time	End Time
5/10/99	8:00	17:00
5/11/99	8:05	16:30
5/12/99	8:00	16:55

2. Save the workbook as *Time Sheet* and close it.

Exercise 2

1. Open the *Time Sheet* workbook that you created in Exercise 1.

2. Save the workbook as *Time Sheet Revised*.

3. Change the start time for 5/10/99 to 8:15.

4. Change the end time for 5/12/99 to 17:35.

5. Enter the following values in row 6:

   5/13/99   8:45   17:00

6. Save your changes and close the workbook.

Exercise 3

1. Create a new workbook and enter the data below on Sheet1. Enter the label CHECKBOOK TRANSACTIONS in cell A1.

CHECKBOOK TRANSACTIONS			
Date	Description	Expense	Income
10/12/99	Paycheck		1542.90
10/14/99	Groceries	142.57	
10/20/99	Bonus		300.00
10/21/99	House payment	842.50	

2. Save the workbook as *Checkbook Transactions* and close it.

 notes Your worksheet may display several ##### signs, indicating that the value stored in the cell is too wide for proper display. Also, trailing zeros, such as the one in 1,542.90, are dropped by default. We discuss how to fix this in the next chapter.

Exercise 4

1. Open the workbook *Checkbook Transactions* that you created in Exercise 3.

2. In cell B7, key Totals.

3. Use AutoSum in cell C7 to add all of the expense items.

4. Use AutoSum in cell D7 to add all of the income items.

5. Enter MAX in cell B9 and MIN in cell B10.

6. Find the maximum and minimum values in columns C and D and place them in cells C9 and C10.

7. Save the modified workbook as *Checkbook Transactions Revised* and close it.

Exercise 5

1. Open the workbook *Checkbook Transactions Revised* that you created in Exercise 4.

2. Change cell A1 to read "Personal Checkbook Transactions."

3. Save the file as *Personal Checkbook Transactions*.

4. Delete the four transactions found in cells A3 through D6.

5. Save and close the workbook.

Exercise 6

1. Open the workbook *Personal Checkbook Transactions* that you created in Exercise 5.

2. Enter two deposits (income) and two expense transactions using fictitious data.

3. Save the workbook as *Personal Checkbook Transactions Revised* and close it.

chapter one

Exercise 7

1. Create a new workbook and enter the data below on Sheet1. Enter the label STATE CAPITALS in cell A1.

STATE CAPITALS	
State	Capital City
Utah	Salt Lake City
Delaware	Dover
California	Sacramento
Arizona	Tempe
New York	Albany
Florida	Tallahassee
Texas	Dallas
Colorado	Denver

2. Save the workbook as *State Capitals* and close it.

Exercise 8

1. Open the *State Capitals* workbook that you created in Exercise 7.

2. Display the Web toolbar, if necessary, by clicking View, pointing to Toolbars, then clicking Web.

3. Search the Web for a list of state capitals.

4. Correct any errors you find in the workbook.

5. Save the workbook as *State Capitals Revised*.

6. Close the workbook and exit Excel.

Case Projects

Project 1

You are the office manager of a small business. One of your duties is to keep track of the office supplies inventory. Create a workbook using fictitious data for at least 20 items. Include a column for each of the following: name of item, current amount in stock, and estimated price for each item. Save your workbook as *Office Supplies Inventory*.

Project 2

As the payroll clerk at a college bookstore, you must calculate the hours worked by each student employee during the week. Create a worksheet containing fictitious employee names in column A. In columns B, C, D, E, and F, list the day names Monday through Friday, then list the number of hours that each student works each day. In column G, add up the total hours that each student is available during the week. For each student, the total hours worked should be between 10 and 25 hours per week. Save your workbook as *Employee Work Hours*.

Project 3

You are a teacher who uses Excel to record student scores. Create a workbook containing 15 fictitious student names with five assignment columns and a total column. Record data indicating each student's scores for the five assignments, then use the Total column to show each student's assignment total. Switch to Sheet2 to enter data from another class, and enter 15 more student names, five assignment columns, and a total column. Record new data and add each student's totals as you did before. Save your workbook as *Student Scores*.

Project 4

You are thinking of investing money in the stock market. Use the Internet to find the most current stock price of five companies in which you are interested. Create a new workbook to record the company name, company stock ticker symbol, opening share price, closing share price, and the date. Include a formula to calculate the net loss/gain. Save your workbook as *Stock Prices*.

Project 5

You make purchasing recommendations for computer systems to your boss. Use the Internet to obtain prices for systems offered by at least three different vendors. Create a new workbook to record the vendor name, Web address, system price, processor speed, amount of RAM, hard drive size, and monitor size. When you enter a Web address, Excel automatically formats it with blue text and underline. Save your workbook as *Computer Prices*.

Project 6

You are planning a road trip. Use the Internet to find the driving distance from your city to at least five other cities you would like to visit. (*Hint*: Search for the keywords "driving directions.") Create a new workbook to record the starting city, destination city, and driving distance. Use a formula to calculate the estimated driving time if you travel at 60 miles per hour. Calculate the minimum and maximum estimated driving times. Save your workbook as *Road Trip*.

Project 7

You must teach new employees how to use Excel. Your first lesson will cover how to open workbooks. Using the Office Assistant, find out how to open workbooks on an intranet and the World Wide Web (WWW). Use Word to create a document of at least two paragraphs explaining how to open Excel workbooks on a hard drive or from an intranet or the WWW. Save and print your document as *Open an Excel Workbook*.

Project 8

You are working on a statistics project. Over the next five days, count the number of students attending each of your classes. Create a new workbook. In row 1, enter the dates you used for your survey. In column A, enter the class names. Enter the data you collected each day for each class. Save the workbook as *Attendance Statistics*.

chapter one

Excel 2000

Formatting Worksheets

Chapter Overview

In this chapter, you become familiar with Excel's wide selection of formatting tools. Thoughtful application of formatting styles can enhance the appearance of your worksheets not only on-screen, but also in printed documents. In addition, good formatting increases the usefulness of a worksheet. Poorly formatted worksheets may provide correct calculations, but if the results are difficult to find, the worksheet will not live up to its potential. The goal of any well-designed worksheet is to provide information in a clear, easy-to-read fashion.

Learning Objectives

- Merge cells to create a worksheet title
- Work with a series to add labels
- Modify the size of columns and rows
- Change fonts and font styles
- Modify the alignment of cell contents
- Rotate text and change indents
- Apply number formats
- Apply cell borders and shading

Case profile

Sweet Tooth is growing, and Amy Lee has hired several new employees to keep up with the increase in business. You have been given the task of setting up a time sheet workbook. Employees will use the workbook to keep track of how much time they spend servicing each client throughout the month. To make the worksheet easier to use, you add formatting to emphasize important parts of the worksheet.

chapter two

2.a Merging Cells to Create a Worksheet Title

Titles provide a clear indication of what type of information can be found on the worksheet. To start your time sheet workbook:

Step 1	Start	Excel
Step 2	Key	Sweet Tooth Employee Time Sheet in cell A1
Step 3	Press	the ENTER key

Typically, the title should be centered over the area you will use, in this case cells A1:J1. To center the title:

Step 1	Select	cells A1:J1
Step 2	Click	the Merge and Center button on the Formatting toolbar to merge cells B1:J1 into cell A1
Step 3	Save	your new workbook as *Employee Time Sheet*

Your worksheet should look similar to Figure 2-1.

QUICK TIP

You can merge cells from multiple rows and columns into one large cell. Select the cells you want to use, then open the Format Cells dialog box. On the Alignment tab, click the check box next to Merge cells, then click OK.

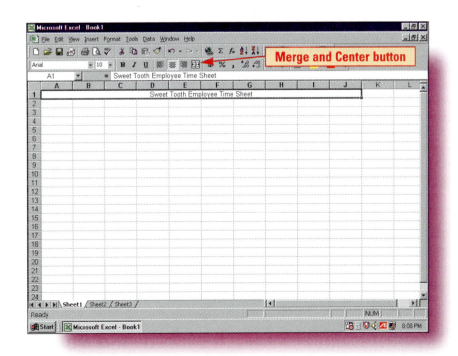

FIGURE 2-1
Using Merge and Center to Create Titles

chapter two

2.b Working with a Series to Add Labels

Sweet Tooth's employees typically service several companies each day. In the company's time sheet, you need to provide a column for each day of the week. To add a column label:

Step 1	**Activate**	cell B3
Step 2	**Key**	Monday
Step 3	**Click**	the Enter button ✓ on the Formula Bar to keep the active cell in place

Excel uses a feature called **AutoFill** to save time when you must enter a series of data. Numbers, days, months, and other series can be automatically filled in through AutoFill. To fill a series, you drag the fill handle. The **fill handle** is in the lower-right corner of the active cell. To AutoFill the days of the week:

| Step 1 | **Move** | the pointer over the fill handle, as shown in Figure 2-2, so that it changes to a thin black cross |

FIGURE 2-2
Fill Handle and Pointer

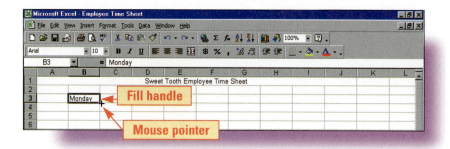

| Step 2 | **Drag** | the fill handle to cell F3 |

As you drag the fill handle, a ScreenTip appears, displaying the new values being added to each cell, as shown in Figure 2-3. When you release the mouse button, your new series of days appears in cells B3:F3. You can drag the fill handle down, left, and up as well as to the right.

MENU TIP

Point to Fill on the Edit menu to access the Fill Down, Right, Up, and Left commands.

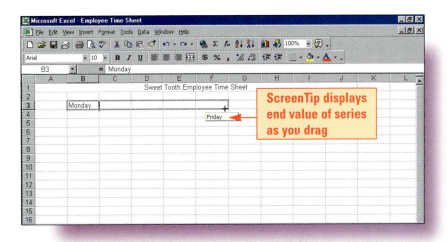

FIGURE 2-3
AutoFill Day Series

QUICK TIP

To use the Fill Down command, you can press the CTRL + D keys. To use the Fill Right command, you can press the CTRL + R keys.

To add the day of the month below the day column heads:

Step 1	*Click*	cell B4
Step 2	*Key*	1
Step 3	*Click*	the Enter button ✓ on the Formula Bar
Step 4	*Right-drag*	the fill handle to cell F4 to open a shortcut menu
Step 5	*Select*	Fill Series from the shortcut menu to fill in the dates from 1 to 5

notes

In this book, the instruction to *enter* a value or formula in a cell means to activate that cell, key the text specified, then accept the entry using the ENTER key, the ARROW keys, the TAB key, or the Enter button on the Formula Bar. Occasionally, you will be instructed to input the data using a specific method. At those times, you will be instructed to key the data, then follow specific instructions to accept the entry.

MENU TIP

To use the Series dialog box, select the range you want to fill, starting with the first cell of the series. Click Edit, then select Series from the Fill submenu.

| Step 6 | *Enter* | Total in cell G3 |
| Step 7 | *Enter* | Client in cell A3 |

The Total label creates a column in which to sum the time spent servicing each of Sweet Tooth's clients during the week. The Client label creates a column label for the client names you will add. Row

chapter
two

labels identify the contents of information stored in those rows. To add row labels:

Step 1	Enter	the clients listed below, beginning in cell A5: Widgit, Inc. Firehouse 451 Clothes Horse Mendoza Engineering Supply ZAZ Printing Jungle Planet Aquanatics Ribbon Steel Co.
Step 2	Enter	Total in cell A13
Step 3	Click	the Save button on the Standard toolbar

2.c Modifying the Size of Columns and Rows

By default, Excel columns are wide enough to display only eight characters. The number of characters in these cells exceeds this width. Because the cells next to the row labels are blank, Excel allows the full contents to spill over. When a column is too narrow to display the text value contained in a cell, Excel displays as many characters as the column width allows, hiding the rest of the characters. If a column is too narrow to display numerical values, it displays a series of # signs. One way to display the full contents of a cell is to change the column width. If a cell is selected, the **AutoFit** command automatically resizes the entire column to the width of that cell's contents. If a range is selected, AutoFit resizes the column to accommodate the cell with the longest value. To resize a column using AutoFit:

Step 1	Move	the mouse pointer to the column divider between columns A and B until the pointer changes to the horizontal resize pointer ↔
Step 2	Double-click	the column divider

The column widens to accommodate the longest entry in the column. See Figure 2-4. The AutoFit command works the same way on rows; double-click the row divider line below the row whose height you want to change.

> **MENU TIP**
>
> You can use AutoFit from the Format menu. Point to Column, then click AutoFit Selection.

> **MENU TIP**
>
> To access the Column Width dialog box, use the Format menu. Point to Column, then click Width. To open the Row Height dialog box, point to Row on the Format menu, then click Height.

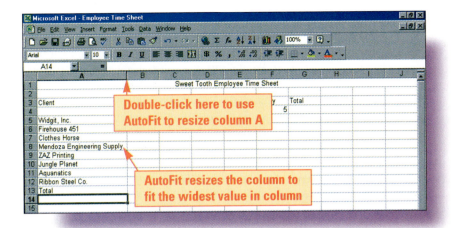

FIGURE 2-4
Using AutoFit to Resize a Column

QUICK TIP

Right-click a row heading and select <u>R</u>ow Height to adjust the row height precisely with the Row Height dialog box.

Another way to resize a column is to specify an exact width. Column width is measured in terms of how many characters can appear in the column before they spill into another column. A column 10 units wide, for example, can display 10 characters before spilling over. Excel's default width is 8.43 units. To resize columns and rows:

Step 1	*Drag*	the column headings B:G to select those columns
Step 2	*Right-click*	the selected cells
Step 3	*Click*	<u>C</u>olumn Width
Step 4	*Key*	12
Step 5	*Click*	OK to resize columns B through G
Step 6	*Deselect*	the columns by clicking cell A1
Step 7	*Drag*	the row divider between rows 3 and 4 down until the ScreenTip indicates 24.00

MOUSE TIP

Resize columns by dragging the divider line between headings, and resize rows by dragging the divider line between rows.

2.d Changing Fonts and Font Styles

MENU TIP

On the F<u>o</u>rmat menu, click C<u>e</u>lls, then click the Font tab to choose font settings.

A **font** is a set of printed characters with similar characteristics. Fonts are a combination of three factors: typeface, style, and point size. **Typeface** is the design and appearance of the font in printed form. The **style** refers to whether the font is displayed with *italic,* **bold,** <u>underlined</u>, or normal print. The **point size** refers to the print height. You can also add **effects**, such as strikethrough, superscripts, and subscripts. Some common typefaces include the following:

    Arial   Times New Roman
    `Courier New`   Book Antiqua

CAUTION TIP

To make your worksheets look as professional as possible, avoid using more than three or four font styles. Too many font styles may look comical and detract from an otherwise well-designed layout.

Changing Font and Font Size

To maintain consistency in its documents, Sweet Tooth has selected the Impact font style, set to point size 20, for worksheet titles. To change the font and font size:

Step 1	Click	the Font list arrow `Arial` on the Formatting toolbar to display the available fonts
Step 2	Click	Impact (or another font if Impact is not available)
Step 3	Click	the Font Size list arrow `10` on the Formatting toolbar
Step 4	Click	20
Step 5	Change	the font in cells A5:A12 to Garamond 12 point
Step 6	Click	cell A8
Step 7	Press	the CTRL + 1 keys to open the Format Cells dialog box
Step 8	Click	the Alignment tab
Step 9	Click	the Shrink to fit check box to select it
Step 10	Click	OK

QUICK TIP

You can use Format Painter to copy the formatting of one cell to another. Activate the cell whose formatting you want to copy, then click the Format Painter button on the Standard toolbar. Next select the cell or cells you want to apply the formatting to.

Changing Font Color

Using different font colors can enhance the visual impact of your worksheets. Sweet Tooth uses red text on its corporate logo, in its letterhead, and in worksheet titles. To change the font color:

Step 1	Click	cell A1
Step 2	Click	the Font Color list arrow on the Formatting toolbar
Step 3	Move	the pointer to the Red square (look at the ScreenTip)
Step 4	Click	the Red square to change the title color
Step 5	Select	cells B3:G3
Step 6	Select	the Blue square from the Font Color list
Step 7	Change	cells A5:A12 to Dark Red

Changing Font Style

Changing the font style to use bold, italics, or underline is another way to draw attention to or emphasize certain cells. To change the font style:

Step 1	Select	cells B4:F4
Step 2	Click	the Bold button **B** on the Formatting toolbar
Step 3	Activate	cell G3
Step 4	Press & Hold	the CTRL key while clicking cell A13
Step 5	Click	the Italic button *I* on the Formatting toolbar

2.e Modifying the Alignment of Cell Contents

Values can be aligned horizontally and vertically within a cell. By default, text values are left-aligned, and numbers, dates, and times are right-aligned. Typically, column labels are centered in the column, while row labels are left-aligned. To change the alignment of cells:

Step 1	Select	cells B3:G4
Step 2	Click	the Center button on the Formatting toolbar

The day and date labels are centered horizontally in their respective columns. Now center the labels in row 3 vertically. To center the labels vertically:

Step 1	Select	cells B3:G3
Step 2	Press	the CTRL + 1 keys to open the Format Cells dialog box
Step 3	Click	the Alignment tab
Step 4	Click	the Vertical: list arrow
Step 5	Select	Center
Step 6	Click	OK

QUICK TIP

Press CTRL + B to bold selected cells. Press CTRL + I to italicize selected cells. Press CTRL + U to underline selected cells.

QUICK TIP

When you need to make several formatting adjustments, use the Format Cells dialog box instead of the Formatting toolbar.

MENU TIP

Click the Format menu and then click Cells to open the Format Cells dialog box.

chapter two

The column labels are now centered vertically and horizontally in the cells, as shown in Figure 2-5.

FIGURE 2-5
Aligning Data Vertically and Horizontally

2.f Rotating Text and Changing Indents

In Sweet Tooth's worksheet, the data for cells B5:F12 will be entered in decimal format to denote hours and minutes worked; for example, 4 hours and 15 minutes would be recorded as 4.25 hours. The columns do not need to be 12 characters wide to accommodate this data. Instead, you can decrease the width of those columns by rotating the column labels. To rotate text:

Step 1	Verify	that cells B3:G3 are selected
Step 2	Press	the CTRL + 1 keys to open the Format Cells dialog box
Step 3	Double-click	in the Degrees spinner control box
Step 4	Key	60
Step 5	Click	OK
Step 6	Double-click	the row divider between rows 3 and 4 to AutoFit the row height
Step 7	Select	columns B:G
Step 8	Right-click	the selected cells
Step 9	Click	Column Width
Step 10	Key	7
Step 11	Click	OK
Step 12	Activate	cell A1

> **MOUSE TIP**
>
> You can change text orientation in the Format Cells dialog box by dragging the word "Text" in the Orientation box. Drag the text interactively to find a suitable orientation angle for your text.

Your worksheet should look similar to Figure 2-6.

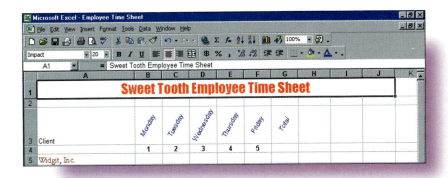

FIGURE 2-6
Rotated Text

> **QUICK TIP**
>
> To increase the Indent more, click the Increase Indent button multiple times. To decrease the Indent, click the Decrease Indent button on the Formatting toolbar.

To emphasize the break between the client names and the Total row heading, you decide to indent the Total heading in row 13. To indent text:

Step 1	*Activate*	cell A13
Step 2	*Click*	the Increase Indent button on the Formatting toolbar

2.g Applying Number Formats

As you enter numeric data, Excel attempts to identify the type of numeric format best suited to the input and automatically applies the appropriate setting. For example, if you enter **1/1/99** in a cell, Excel guesses that you are inputting a date and applies the default date number format to that cell, changing it to 1/1/1999. If you want to display the date as January 1, 1999 you can simply change the format with the Format Cells dialog box, and Excel automatically converts your entry to the desired format.

Sweet Tooth rounds each employee's time worked to the nearest five-minute increment. You need to create a list of decimal equivalencies for five-minute increments. To enter the list of five minute increments:

Step 1	*Key*	Decimal in cell I3
Step 2	*Press*	the TAB key

The text you keyed in cell I3 inherits the same formatting characteristics as the text in the rest of the list, B3:G3. If you had started in cell J3, the Extend List Format command would not have

MENU TIP

You can turn on or off the Extend List Formats feature. On the Tools menu, select Options. On the Edit tab, select or deselect the check box next to Extend list formats and formulas, according to your preferences.

extended the formatting, because two blank columns (H and I) would have separated your entry from the rest of the list.

Step 3	Enter	Time (Minutes) in cell J3
Step 4	Enter	5 in cell J4
Step 5	Enter	10 in cell J5
Step 6	Enter	15 in cell J6
Step 7	Select	cells J4:J6
Step 8	Italicize	the selection
Step 9	Drag	the fill handle to cell J14

Now you add a formula in column I to calculate the decimal equivalent. To add the formula:

Step 1	Activate	cell I4
Step 2	Key	=j4/60 to divide the time in minutes in cell J4 by the total number of minutes in an hour
Step 3	Click	the Enter button ✓ on the Formula Bar
Step 4	Drag	the fill handle to cell I14

The formula is copied, but the resulting values are a mess. Some cells display only one digit after the decimal; others display as many as six digits. See Figure 2-7. At most, your users will need two significant digits.

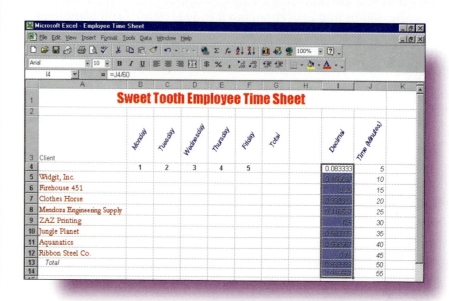

FIGURE 2-7
Decimal Equivalent of Five Minutes

Formatting Worksheets   EB 39

To adjust the decimal place:

| Step 1 | Click | the Decrease Decimal button on the Formatting toolbar |
| Step 2 | Continue | to decrease the decimal until only two digits appear after the decimal |

The main data entry area in cells B5:G13 should be formatted this way as well. This time, use the Format Cells dialog box to set the format.

Step 3	Select	cells B5:G13
Step 4	Open	the Format Cells dialog box
Step 5	Click	the Number tab
Step 6	Click	Number from the Category: list
Step 7	Verify	that Decimal places: is set to 2 (see Figure 2-8)

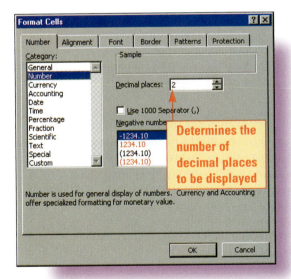

FIGURE 2-8
Number Tab of the Format Cells Dialog Box

| Step 8 | Click | OK |

Understanding how and when to apply number formats is very important. Using Excel's extensive set of number formats, you can display numerical values as times, dates, currency, percentages, fractions, and more. When you apply a numerical format to a value,

the manner in which the value is displayed may vary dramatically, but the actual value held in the cell remains the same. Table 2-1 illustrates how a common numerical value of 1054.253 would be displayed with different number formats applied.

TABLE 2-1
Comparing Number Formats

Category	Description	Default Display (Value = 1054.253)
General	No specific number format	1054.253
Number	Default of two decimal places; can also display commas for thousand separators	1054.25
Currency	Default of two decimal places, comma separators, and $, the U.S. dollar sign	$1,054.25
Accounting	Aligns currency symbol, two decimal places, and comma separators	$ 1,054.25
Date	Displays serial equivalent of date	11/19/1902
Time	Displays serial equivalent of time	11/19/1902 6:00 AM
Percentage	Multiplies value by 100 and displays result with % sign	105425%
Fraction	Displays decimal portion of value as fraction	1054 1/4
Scientific	Displays number in scientific notation	1.05E+03

> **QUICK TIP**
>
> When you activate a cell containing a date or time format, the Formula Bar displays the date or time value—not the serial, or number, value. To view the serial value of a date, you must change the cell's format to another number format.

It is important to understand how Excel deals with time and date values. In Excel, all time and date values are calculated using serial values. **Serial values** are real numbers that are converted to display a date or time. Starting with 1, which Excel displays as January 1, 1900, each day is represented by a whole-number value. Times are calculated as a decimal portion of a day. For example, Excel interprets the value 1.0 as January 1, 1900 12:00 AM. A value of .25 corresponds to 6:00 AM (25% of the day), .5 corresponds to 12:00 PM (50% of the day), and so on.

2.h Applying Cell Borders and Shading

Borders and shading are two of the more dramatic visual effects available to enhance your worksheets. Borders can be used to separate row and column labels from data. Shading can be used to emphasize important cells.

Adding Borders

Although you see gridlines on your screen, the default for printed worksheets is for no gridlines to appear. If you want only some of the gridlines to appear, you can apply a border. When applying borders to cells, Excel treats the entire selection as though it were a single cell. With one cell selected, you can apply borders to all of the cell's edges at once or to a single edge. For example, you can apply a border along the bottom edge of a cell to denote the sum line. When you select a group of cells and apply a border, however, the border is applied to the group as though the entire group was one cell. If you apply a left border to the selection, for example, only the cells on the left edge of the selection receive the border. To add a border:

Step 1	Select	cells B5:F12
Step 2	Click	the Borders list arrow on the Formatting toolbar
Step 3	Click	the All Borders button on the Borders drop-down list

> **QUICK TIP**
>
> To quickly add an outline border to selected cells, press CTRL + SHIFT + &. To remove an outline border, press CTRL + SHIFT + _ (underscore).

The All Borders command applies a border to all edges surrounding and within the selection. See Figure 2-9.

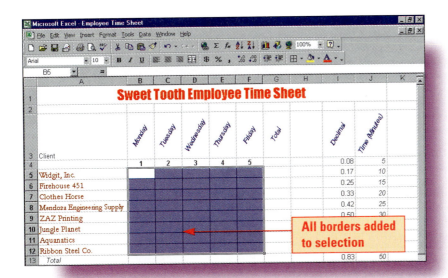

FIGURE 2-9
Adding All Borders to the Worksheet

You are not limited to the 12 choices appearing on the Borders button list. In fact, you can use the Borders tab of the Format Cells dialog box to select different line styles, change line colors, and choose additional

chapter two

border options, such as inserting diagonal lines and applying borders to only the inside of a selection. To create a custom border:

Step 1	Select	cells A13:G13
Step 2	Open	the Format Cells dialog box
Step 3	Click	the Border tab
Step 4	Select	the heavy solid line style from the Style: box
Step 5	Click	the top edge of the Border preview diagram
Step 6	Click	the bottom edge of the Border preview diagram

Your Border tab should look similar to Figure 2-10.

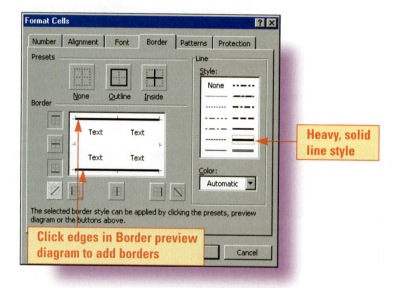

FIGURE 2-10
Creating Custom Border Settings

| Step 7 | Click | OK |

Your custom border is applied to the selection.

Adding Shading

One way you can make row 4, which contains the date numbers, stand out is to use a "reverse text" effect. To create this effect, you apply a dark fill color to the cells, then change the font color to white. To add shading to a cell:

| Step 1 | Select | cells A4:G4 |

Step 2	Click	the Fill Color list arrow on the Formatting toolbar
Step 3	Select	the Blue square from the Fill Color list
Step 4	Click	the Font Color list arrow on the Formatting toolbar
Step 5	Select	the White square from the Font Color list
Step 6	Activate	cell A1 to deselect the cells
Step 7	Click	the Save button on the Standard toolbar to save your workbook

Compare your final worksheet with Figure 2-11.

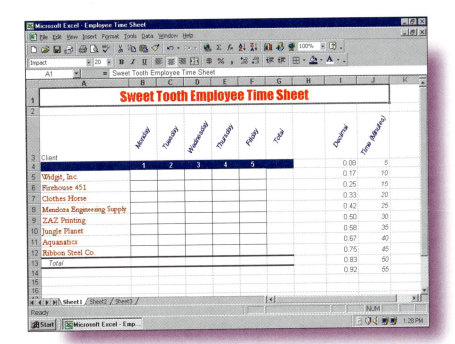

FIGURE 2-11
Finished Time Sheet

You can now distribute the *Employee Time Sheet* workbook to Sweet Tooth's different divisions. Formatting a worksheet doesn't take much time, but it can have a dramatic impact on the worksheet's appearance and legibility.

chapter
two

Summary

- Titles add visual impact and provide a guide to the worksheet's contents.

- Column and row labels aid in understanding data contained in a worksheet.

- Expand the width of a column by using AutoFit, by working with the Column Width dialog box, or by clicking and dragging column heading borders.

- Judicious use of font formats can enhance a worksheet's appearance and make it easier to read. Use Format Painter to copy formats to other cells. Use the Font tab of the Format Cells dialog box to apply several settings simultaneously.

- Expand the height of a row by using AutoFit, by working with the Row Height dialog box, or by clicking and dragging row heading borders. Row heights expand automatically with font size changes.

- Align cell contents to enhance visual clarity. The default for text is left-alignment. For numeric entries, such as currency, dates, and times, the default is right-alignment.

- Rotate text to add visual interest or to decrease the width of a column. Indent text to provide visual breaks or to indicate that a list has a certain hierarchical structure. Use the Alignment tab of the Format Cells dialog box to apply these settings.

- Use number formats to change how cells' numerical contents are displayed. Excel detects date and time entries and formats the cell accordingly.

- Borders and shading can add visual impact to worksheets. Create custom borders using the Borders tab of the Format Cells dialog box.

Commands Review

Action	Menu Bar	Shortcut Menu	Toolbar	Keyboard
Merge and center a cell			⊞	
Fill	Edit, Fill, Series	Right-click and drag fill handle		ALT + E, I, S
Fill Right	Edit, Fill, Right			CTRL + R ALT + E, I, R
Fill Down	Edit, Fill, Down			CTRL + D ALT + E, I, D
AutoFit a column	Format, Column, AutoFit		Double-click column divider	ALT + O, C, A
Change width of a column	Format, Column, Width	Right-click column heading, click Column width	Drag column divider	ALT + O, C, W
AutoFit a row	Format, Row, AutoFit		Double-click row divider	ALT + O, C, A
Change height of a row	Format, Row, Height	Right-click column heading, click Row height	Drag row divider	ALT + O, C, E
Format cells	Format, Cells	Right-click selected range, click Format Cells		CTRL + 1 ALT + O, E
Align cell contents (see Alignment tab of Format Cells dialog box)			≡ ≡ ≡	
Font Color (see Font tab of Format Cells dialog box)			A▼	
Bold (see Font tab of Format Cells dialog box)			B	CTRL + B
Italics (see Font tab of Format Cells dialog box)			I	CTRL + I
Underline (see Font tab of Format Cells dialog box)			U	CTRL + U
Increase/decrease indent (see Alignment tab of Format Cells dialog box)			≡ ≡	
Apply number formats (see Number tab of Format Cells dialog box)			$ % , .00 .00	
Add borders (see Borders tab of Format Cells dialog box)			⊞▼	
Apply outline border				CTRL + SHIFT + &
Remove outline border				CTRL + SHIFT + _
Add shading to cells (see Patterns tab of Format Cells dialog box)			◇▼	
Indent text (see Alignment tab of Format Cells dialog box)			≡ ≡	
Use Format Painter			✓	

chapter two

Concepts Review

Circle the correct answer.

1. To select multiple, nonadjacent ranges, press and hold the:
   - [a] SHIFT key.
   - [b] END key.
   - [c] ALT key.
   - [d] CTRL key.

2. To select a range using the keyboard, press and hold the:
   - [a] SHIFT key.
   - [b] END key.
   - [c] ALT key.
   - [d] CTRL key.

3. To center a title across multiple cells, use the:
   - [a] Center button.
   - [b] Merge button.
   - [c] Merge and Center button.
   - [d] Center Alignment button.

4. One reason a cell might display ###### is because:
   - [a] the text value of the cell exceeds the width of the column.
   - [b] an incorrect argument has been entered in a function.
   - [c] the numeric value of the cell exceeds the width of the column.
   - [d] the number format is not recognized.

5. Typeface refers to:
   - [a] print density.
   - [b] upright or italic print.
   - [c] print height.
   - [d] design and appearance of a font.

6. Which of these is *not* a valid method of changing the height of a row?
   - [a] Increase the font size of the contents in the row.
   - [b] Use Format, Row, Hide.
   - [c] Use Format, Row, Height.
   - [d] Drag the border between row labels.

7. Which of the following data types is *not* right-aligned by default?
   - [a] Dates
   - [b] Text
   - [c] Times
   - [d] Numbers

8. To apply multiple changes to a font, use the _____ tab of the Format Cells dialog box.
   - [a] Font
   - [b] Border
   - [c] Patterns
   - [d] Number

9. To apply custom border styles, use the _____ tab of the Format Cells dialog box.
   - [a] Font
   - [b] Border
   - [c] Patterns
   - [d] Number

Circle **T** if the statement is true or **F** if the statement is false.

T F 1. You can access the Format Cells dialog box by pressing the CTRL + 1 keys.

T F 2. You can apply a border diagonally across a cell (or cells).

T F 3. You cannot use too many fonts in a worksheet.

T F 4. Increasing the font size automatically increases the row height.

T F 5. The fill handle is found on the upper-left corner of the selection border.

T F 6. You can create an AutoFill by using the Fill command on the Edit menu.

T F 7. AutoFit resizes columns to accommodate the longest entry in the column, regardless of whether the cell is selected.

T F 8. Rotating text automatically adjusts the row height.

Skills Review

Exercise 1

1. Open the *Project Expense Log* workbook on your Data Disk.
2. Change the numeric format of column A to the MM/DD/YY date format.
3. Expand the width of column B to show the full contents of the longest entry in the column.
4. Change the number format of column C to currency style by clicking the Currency Style button on the Formatting toolbar.
5. Merge and center cell A1 across cells A1:C1.
6. Center the column labels in row 3.
7. Save your changes as *Project Expense Log Revised*.

Exercise 2

1. Open a new, blank workbook.
2. Create a title called "Calendar" at the top of your worksheet. Apply font settings so that the title stands out clearly. Center the title across columns A through G.
3. Using your knowledge of adjusting row heights and column widths, create a one-month calendar grid consisting of six rows and seven columns. Adjust row heights to 60 and column widths to 12 so that each cell is approximately square.
4. Use AutoFill to create the weekday series, starting with Sunday. Center this series vertically and horizontally.
5. Use AutoFill to create the date numbers in each cell as follows:
    a. Starting with the first Sunday as the first day of the month, Fill Series to the right.
    b. Select the first row of dates, and right-click and drag the fill handle to the fourth week of the calendar.
    c. Select Series, then enter 7 as the Step value.
    d. Add the final three dates to your calendar so that Tuesday is the 31st day of the month.
    e. Use the Alignment tab of the Format Cells dialog box to align the date number in the upper-left corner of each cell.
6. Apply shading to days on the calendar that follow the end of the month.
7. Apply shading to the column labels. Apply a border to the calendar.
8. Save your workbook as *Calendar*.

Exercise 3

1. Enter the following data in a new workbook. (Enter Employee Name in cell A1.)

Employee Name	Current Wage	Proposed Wage	Increase per Month
Mark Havlaczek	7.50	8	
Roberta Hernandez	8.25	9	
Eric Wimmer	8.25	8.85	
Micah Anderson	7.75	8.5	
Allyson Smith	9.5	10.35	
Total Increase			

2. Increase the column width to show the full contents of each cell.
3. Apply the currency format with two decimal places to cells B2:D7.
4. Create a formula in cell D2 that calculates how much *more* each employee will make per month as a result of the proposed wage increase. Assume that each employee works 168 hours per month. (*Hint:* Subtract the Current Wage from the Proposed Wage, then multiply the result by 168.)
5. Sum the amounts in column D to show the additional cost to the owner as a result of the proposed wage increases.
6. Save your workbook as *Proposed Wage Increase*.

Exercise 4

1. Open the *Proposed Wage Increase* workbook that you created in Exercise 3.
2. Use the Format Cells dialog box to format cell A1 as follows:
    a. Change the font to Times New Roman.
    b. Increase the font size to 12.
    c. Change the font color to Blue.
    d. Change the font style to Bold.
3. With cell A1 still active, click the Format Painter button on the Standard toolbar, then drag to select cells B1:D1.
4. Decrease the column widths of columns A–D to 11.
5. Turn on Wrap Text for cells A1:D1 and center the column labels.
6. Make cells A7:D7 bold and add a Gray-25% shade.
7. Clear the formatting in cells A7:C7 by pointing to Clear on the Edit menu, then clicking Formats.
8. Add a thick bottom border to cells A1:D1.
9. Indent cell A7.
10. Increase the width of column A to display the employee names correctly.
11. Save your workbook as *Proposed Wage Increase Revised*.

Exercise 5

1. Open the *Number Formatting* workbook on the Data Disk.
2. Center the column labels and apply a Light Green shade.

3. Apply the All Borders border to all cells that hold data.

4. Use the number format indicated by each column label to format the columns. Use the default settings unless otherwise directed.

   a. In the Number column, select the Use 1000 Separator (,) check box in the Number format settings.

   b. In the Date column, set the Date type to 3/14/1998. (Notice that Excel converts numbers into dates, starting with 1 equal to 1/1/1900.)

   c. In the Time column, set the Time type to 3/14/1998 1:30 PM. (If you don't have this format, set it as 3/14/98 1:30 PM.)

   d. In the Fraction column, set the Fraction type to Up to two digits (21/25). (Because many of the numbers are whole numbers, no fraction will appear in the worksheet, but the number will move to the left side of the cell to allow proper alignment of fractions when present.)

5. Use AutoFit to increase the column widths so as to fully display the numbers in each cell.

6. Save your workbook as *Number Formatting Revised*.

Exercise 6

1. Create a new workbook.

2. Enter the data as shown in the table below:

Important Dates of World War II	
Date	**Event**
9/1/1939	Germany invades Poland
6/14/40	German troops occupy Paris
7/10/40	Battle of Britain begins
6/22/1941	German troops invade Russia
12/7/1941	Japan attacks U.S. forces at Pearl Harbor, Hawaii
12/8/1941	U.S. declares war on Japan
12/11/1941	U.S. declares war on Germany and Italy
6/4/1942	Battle of Midway starts (turning point of Pacific war)
1/23/1943	Casablanca Conference decides on Cross Channel Invasion of Continental Europe
7/10/43	Allies invade Sicily
6/6/1944	D-Day Allied invasion of Western Europe commences in France
5/7/1945	Germany surrenders to Allies at Reims, France
7/16/1945	U.S. tests 1st atomic bomb in New Mexico
8/6/1945	U.S. drops atomic bomb on Hiroshima, Japan
8/9/1945	U.S. drops atomic bomb on Nagasaki, Japan
8/14/1945	Japan agrees to surrender
9/2/1945	Japan formally surrenders in Tokyo Bay

3. Merge and center the title in row 1.

4. Bold and center the labels in row 2.

5. Change the format of the Date column to the Month DD, YYYY format.

6. Format cell A1 with a black fill and white text.

7. Format the text in cell A1 as bold and increase the font size to 16 points.

8. Format row 2 with a dark gray fill and white text.

9. Save the workbook as *WWII*.

Exercise 7

1. Open the *WWII* workbook you created in Exercise 6.

2. Change the width of column B to 45.

3. Turn on wrap text with column B selected.

4. Left align cells A3:A19.

5. Italicize cells A3, A7, A13, A14, and A19.

6. Activate cell A1, then save the workbook as *WWII Revised*.

Exercise 8

1. Open the *New Computer Prices* workbook on the Data Disk.

2. Change the title in row A1 to 16 point, bold text.

3. Merge and center cell A1 across A1:G1.

4. Bold and center the labels in row 3.

5. Resize columns A-G to fit the data.

6. Format column C with Comma format.

7. Change cells E4:F6 to right aligned.

8. Save your workbook as *New Computer Prices Formatted*.

Case Projects

Project 1

You work in a large bank. You are frequently asked about the current exchange rate for U.S. dollars relative to a variety of foreign currencies. Search the Internet for a site that reports currency exchange rates. Create a new workbook to keep track of recent updates. Include the URL of the site(s) you find in your workbook, which will allow you to access these sites easily later. Record the date and currency exchange rate for converting U.S. dollars into the euro currency and the currencies of at least six countries, including those of Japan, Germany, France, and the United Kingdom. Apply currency formats displaying the appropriate currency symbol for each country (if available). Set up your workbook so that you can monitor the changes in exchange rates over time. Center and bold column labels, and italicize row labels. Save your workbook as *Foreign Currency Exchange*.

Project 2

You work for an insurance company processing accident claims. One of your tasks is to determine how many days have elapsed between the date of an accident and the date that a claim was filed. You know that Excel stores dates as numbers, so you must be able to create a formula that calculates this information. Use the Office Assistant to look up more information about how Excel keeps track of dates. Can you figure out the trick? Create a workbook with column labels for Accident Date, Claim Filed Date, and Elapsed Days. Save your workbook as *Claim Lapse Calculator*.

Project 3

You work in a warehouse run by a large furniture retailer. Your company uses a unique numbering system to track inventory in the warehouse. Inventory numbers look similar to the following: 1-234-5678. Unfortunately, it's difficult to remember the pattern of dashes when entering data in the inventory workbook. You've noticed that Excel has a custom number format option in the Format Cells dialog box, and wonder if it might be the answer to your problem. Use the Office Assistant to look up how to create a custom number format. Create a new number format and try using it to enter at least five inventory items. (*Hint:* The format should automatically supply all dashes; you should simply have to type in the numbers.) Bold and center any column headings you use, such as Part Number. Save your workbook as *Warehouse Inventory*.

Project 4

Your mom, a quilter, has come to you with an interesting project. She needs to organize her quilt pattern, but because of the number of pieces, it's very difficult to keep track of everything. You know that Excel can shade cells in different colors. That gives you an idea. Can you use shading and borders to create a fun geometrical pattern? Don't be afraid to modify column widths and row heights to achieve a more artistic pattern. Save your workbook as *Quilt*.

Project 5

You have just started a new business—a bookstore. As a small business owner, you're not sure where to turn for advice—you just know you need some. Use the Web toolbar in Excel to search the Internet for Small Business Guides. In particular, search for topics dealing with education, training, taxes, and technology. Print the home pages of at least three different sites.

Project 6

You have used the AutoFill command to automatically create series of day names, months, and all sorts of number variations. What else could you do with series fill? What about a list of color names? Use the Office Assistant to help you find out how to create a custom fill series. Create a new series using the following colors: red, orange, yellow, green, blue, and purple. Test your new fill series by entering "red" in cell A1, then AutoFilling the series to the right. Then select the values and AutoFill the series down. Save your workbook as *Color Series*.

Project 7

Use the Internet to locate a timeline showing major events of the 20th century. Create a workbook to record the date and a description of the event. Include at least one event from each decade of the 20th century. Do not include more than three events from any decade. Save your workbook as *20th Century Timeline*.

Project 8

Use the Internet to locate information about current events. Print at least one story of national importance, and one of local importance.

Excel 2000

Organizing Worksheets Effectively

Chapter Overview

Effective organization of worksheets is essential to providing timely, accurate information. Mastering the use of cell references and naming ranges helps you develop accurate formulas more quickly. You can rearrange information by inserting and deleting columns, rows, and worksheets to provide additional information. Creating outlines using the Subtotals command offers an easy way to summarize data.

Learning Objectives

- Perform single and multi-level sorts
- Copy and move data
- Rename a worksheet
- Insert, move, and delete worksheets
- Insert and delete cells, rows, and columns
- Use absolute, relative, and mixed references
- Create and use named ranges
- Freeze and unfreeze rows and columns
- Use grouping and outlines
- Check spelling in a worksheet

Case profile

For reporting and organizational purposes, Sweet Tooth divides the country into four regions: the East Coast, Mountain, West Coast, and Central. Each region is further classified into North, South, East, and West divisions. Amy Lee, the company president, has asked you to study the financial impact of paying various commission percentages to the company's sales force and to calculate the total sales for each region.

chapter three

3.a Performing Single and Multi-level Sorts

The *Sweet Tooth Sales Rep Data* workbook contains gross sales data for each salesperson employed by Sweet Tooth. You want to work with these data, but—recognizing that a lot of work has gone into creating this information—leave the original data intact. Your first task is to save a new copy of the file, enabling you to manipulate it without worrying about losing the original data. To open a file and save it with a new name:

| Step 1 | Open | the *Sweet Tooth Sales Rep Data* file on your Data Disk |
| Step 2 | Save | the file as *Sweet Tooth Sales Rep Data Revised* |

When dealing with long lists of data, such as the sales data in your workbook, it can be helpful to sort the information. Column A contains the column label, Region. This column label acts as your sort **criteria**, indicating the type of data you want to sort by. If you place the active cell in this column, Excel knows which column to sort. To sort the sales representative data:

| Step 1 | Activate | cell A4 |
| Step 2 | Click | the Sort Ascending button on the Standard toolbar |

The column is sorted in ascending order (alphabetically) by region. When Excel works with lists, it assumes that the top row of the list contains the column labels and does not sort that row. Using the Sort dialog box, you can sort by as many as three criteria. To sort on multiple columns:

| Step 1 | Click | Data |
| Step 2 | Click | Sort |

The Sort dialog box appears, as shown in Figure 3-1. When you open the Sort dialog box, Excel scans for the header row of the active list and adds the column headings to the criteria list boxes. It also assumes that the Sort by criteria is the column containing the active cell.

FIGURE 3-1
Sort Dialog Box

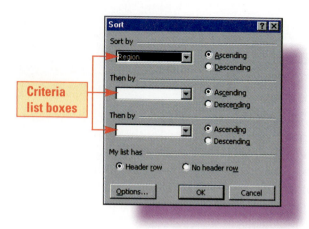

Step 3	Click	the upper Then by list arrow
Step 4	Select	Division from the list
Step 5	Click	the lower Then by list arrow
Step 6	Select	Gross Sales from the list
Step 7	Click	the Descending option button next to Gross Sales
Step 8	Click	OK

Your list is sorted by region, then alphabetically by division, then from highest to lowest by gross sales within each division.

3.b Copying and Moving Data Using Drag and Drop

In Chapter 2, you learned to copy data by using the fill handle. Another way to move and copy data is to use **drag and drop**. To drag selected cells, click the selection border using the left mouse button. Hold the left mouse button down as you *drag* the cells to a new location, then *drop* them by releasing the left mouse button. To move data using drag and drop:

Step 1	Select	cells A4:D19
Step 2	Move	the pointer over the border of your selection

The cross pointer changes to an arrow pointer ⬉. At this point, you can click the border and drag the entire range to a new location.

| Step 3 | **Drag** | the range to cells F4:I19 |

A ScreenTip and a range outline guide you in moving the cells. The data are moved from A4:D19 to F4:I19. See Figure 3-2.

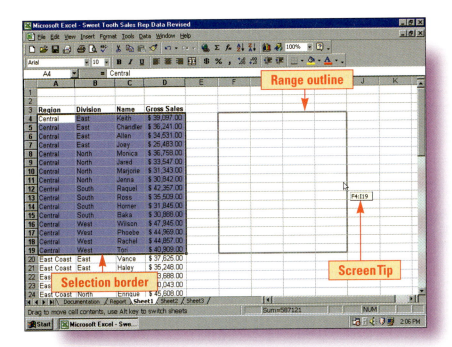

FIGURE 3-2
Dragging and Dropping the Border to Move Cells

To copy data using drag and drop, simply press the CTRL key before you start to drag a range of cells. To copy data using drag and drop:

| Step 1 | **Press & Hold** | the CTRL key |
| Step 2 | **Drag** | the border of the selected range F4:I19 to cells A4:D19 |

As you drag, the pointer changes to ▷⁺, indicating that you are creating a copy of the selected data. You realize that you copied the data by mistake. To delete the data and save your work.

Step 1	**Select**	cells F4:I19
Step 2	**Press**	the DELETE key
Step 3	**Save**	your workbook

QUICK TIP

To move data from one sheet to another using drag and drop, press and hold the ALT key as you drag the range onto the new worksheet tab. To copy data to another worksheet using drag and drop, press and hold the CTRL + ALT keys as you drag the range onto the new worksheet tab.

chapter three

3.c Renaming a Worksheet

Naming worksheet tabs simplifies the process of locating information in a workbook. To name a worksheet tab:

Step 1	Right-click	the Sheet1 tab
Step 2	Select	Rename to highlight the current tab name
Step 3	Key	Sales Report Data
Step 4	Press	the ENTER key
Step 5	Repeat	steps 1–4 to rename Sheet2 as Central Region
Step 6	Repeat	steps 1–4 to rename Sheet3 as East Coast Region

> **MOUSE TIP**
>
> You can rename a worksheet tab by double-clicking the tab.

3.d Inserting, Moving, Copying, and Deleting Worksheets

By default, Excel creates new workbooks with three worksheets. You can add or delete worksheets from your workbook at any time. Each workbook can hold a maximum of 255 worksheets. You can also change the order of worksheets as you further refine your workbook design.

Inserting a Worksheet

You need to add several new worksheets to Sweet Tooth's workbook. To add a new worksheet to a workbook:

Step 1	Right-click	the Sales Report Data worksheet tab
Step 2	Click	Insert to open the Insert dialog box
Step 3	Select	the Worksheet icon
Step 4	Click	OK

A new worksheet is inserted to the left of the selected worksheet.

| Step 5 | Repeat | steps 1–4 to insert another worksheet |

> **MOUSE TIP**
>
> You can delete a worksheet by right-clicking the tab, then clicking Delete.

> **MENU TIP**
>
> You can insert a new worksheet by selecting Worksheet from the Insert menu.

Organizing Worksheets Effectively   EB 57

| Step 6 | Rename | Sheet1 as Mountain Region |
| Step 7 | Rename | Sheet2 as West Coast Region |

When you finish, the workbook should include a total of seven worksheets.

Moving and Copying a Worksheet

You can reorganize your worksheets in any order by dragging worksheet tabs to a new location. In your workbook, the Sales Report Data should appear first, followed by each of the Region worksheets in alphabetical order. To move a worksheet:

| Step 1 | Point to | the Mountain Region tab |
| Step 2 | Press & Hold | the left mouse button |

The pointer changes to to indicate that you are moving a tab, and a small black triangle appears at the left of the tab to indicate the tab's position.

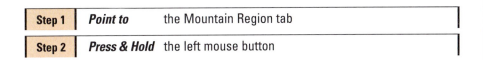

| Step 3 | Drag | the Mountain Region tab to the right of the East Coast Region tab |

As you drag, the small black triangle moves with the pointer to indicate the tab's new position, and the tabs scroll left. See Figure 3-3.

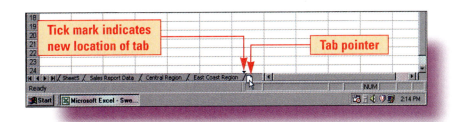

| Step 4 | Release | the mouse button |

The tab moves to the new location.
The tab scrolling buttons help you navigate when you can't see all of the tabs. The right tab scrolling button ▶ scrolls one tab to the right. The left tab scrolling button ◀ scrolls one tab to the left. The right end tab scrolling button ▶| scrolls to the tab at the extreme right, and the left end tab scrolling button |◀ scrolls to the tab to the extreme left. To

QUICK TIP

To copy a worksheet, press the CTRL key while you drag the sheet tab.

FIGURE 3-3
Moving a Sheet Tab

MOUSE TIP

To move or to copy a sheet, right-click the tab you wish to move or copy, then select Move or Copy from the shortcut menu.

chapter
three

MOUSE TIP

Drag the horizontal scroll bar resize handle at the left of the horizontal scroll bar to the right to decrease its size and view more worksheet tabs.

scroll past several tabs at once, hold the SHIFT key down when you click the right tab arrow button ▶ or the left tab arrow button ◀. Note that scrolling tabs does not change the active tab.

| Step 5 | Click | the left end tab scrolling button ◀ to scroll to the leftmost tab |
| Step 6 | Repeat | steps 1–4 to move the West Coast Region tab to the right of the Mountain Region tab |

3.e Copy and Move Data Using Cut, Copy, and Paste

You can also move and copy data using the Cut, Copy, and Paste commands. You're probably familiar with these commands from other programs, such as Microsoft Word.

Moving Data Using Cut and Paste

The Cut command removes date from the worksheet. To move data:

Step 1	Scroll	the Sales Report Data worksheet until you can see rows 52 to 67
Step 2	Select	cells A52:D67
Step 3	Click	the Cut button ✂ on the Standard toolbar

A moving, dotted border, shown in Figure 3-4, surrounds the selected area. The status bar provides instructions about how to select a destination cell. The destination can be on another worksheet or even another open workbook.

Step 4	Right-click	the right tab scrolling button ▶
Step 5	Click	West Coast Region
Step 6	Click	cell A4
Step 7	Click	the Paste button 📋 on the Standard toolbar
Step 8	Click	cell A4 to deselect the range

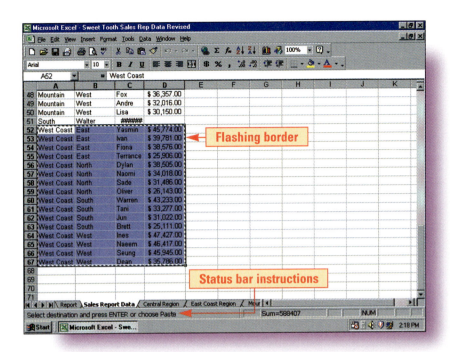

FIGURE 3-4
Dotted Border Indicating Cut or Copy Operation

CAUTION TIP

Use extreme caution when deleting worksheets. This Excel command cannot be undone. Once you've deleted a worksheet, you cannot get it back.

The Cut command in Excel works slightly differently than in other programs, such as Microsoft Word. Excel does not remove the selected text until you take one of two actions: (1) complete the move by selecting a destination and clicking Paste (or pressing the ENTER key), or (2) press the DELETE key. If you change your mind before pasting or deleting, press the ESC key to cancel the cut operation.

Copying Data Using Copy and Paste

The Copy and Paste commands enable you to create a copy of the data. Rather than using the mouse to select the cell range, you can work with the Name Box to create a selection by entering cell references. To select cells using the Name Box:

MENU TIP

Cut, Copy, and Paste are available on the Edit menu. To cut a selection, click Cut. To copy a selection, click Copy. To paste a selection, click Paste.

Step 1	Click	in the Name Box
Step 2	Key	a4:d19
Step 3	Press	the ENTER key

The desired data range is selected, and you're ready to copy it. To copy data using the Copy and Paste commands:

QUICK TIP

The shortcut keys for cut, copy, and paste are: CTRL + X to cut, CTRL + C to copy, and CTRL + V to paste.

| Step 1 | Click | the Copy button  on the Standard toolbar |

chapter three

CAUTION TIP

If the Clipboard did not appear, click the View menu, point to Toolbars, and click Clipboard.

FIGURE 3-5
The Office Clipboard

QUICK TIP

The Office Clipboard stores as many as 12 items from any Office 2000 application, including Word, Access, PowerPoint, and Excel. For example, you can use the Office Clipboard to copy several cells in Excel, copy a picture inserted in a PowerPoint slide, and then paste both items into a Word document. Items are stored in the Office Clipboard as long as any Office 2000 application remains open.

The Office Clipboard toolbar appears, similar to Figure 3-5. As you move the pointer over the clips on the Clipboard, a ScreenTip displays a portion of the contents of the clip.

| Step 2 | Click | the left end tab scrolling button |
| Step 3 | Click | the Sales Report Data tab |

Cells A52:D67 are still selected.

| Step 4 | Click | the clip on the Clipboard toolbar |

The West Coast data are pasted into the Sales Report Data worksheet. Using the Clipboard, you can copy the data by clicking the clip on the Clipboard whenever necessary.

To copy the Mountain region data:

| Step 1 | Scroll | the Sales Report Data worksheet to view rows 36 to 51 |
| Step 2 | Select | cells A36:D51 |

Notice that a data entry error appears in row 51. You will correct this error in the next section.

Step 3	Click	the Copy button on the Standard toolbar to add the clip to the Clipboard
Step 4	Click	the Mountain Region tab
Step 5	Click	cell A4
Step 6	Press	the ENTER key

When you press the ENTER key to paste a selection, it ends the Copy command in Excel. Likewise, activating a cell will stop the Copy command and gray out the Paste button on the Standard toolbar. You may want to close the Clipboard when you have finished pasting data. To close the Clipboard:

| Step 1 | Click | the Close button on the Clipboard toolbar |
| Step 2 | Click | cell A19 to deselect the range |

> **MOUSE TIP**
>
> If you need to see the Clipboard again, you can right-click any toolbar, then click Clipboard.

3.f Inserting and Deleting Cells, Rows, and Columns

As you organize worksheets, you will find many occasions when you need to insert a few cells into a list—or entire rows or columns—to add new information to a worksheet. You may also need to delete rows or columns.

Inserting and Deleting Cells

In some instances, you may need to insert extra cells without inserting an entire row or column. To insert extra cells:

Step 1	Right-click	cell A19
Step 2	Click	Insert to open the Insert dialog box
Step 3	Click	the Shift cells right option button
Step 4	Click	OK to shift all cells to the right of the selected cell to the right
Step 5	Key	M

> **QUICK TIP**
>
> Open the Insert dialog box by pressing CTRL + SHIFT + + (plus symbol key).

As you began typing "Mountain" in cell A19, Excel automatically filled the rest of the word for you. This feature is called **AutoComplete**. As you enter data in columns or rows, Excel builds a list of unique data entries, which it scans as you type. When it senses that you are duplicating an item on its list, the program fills in the rest of the entry automatically. To accept the AutoComplete entry, press the ENTER key. If you are entering a different item, continue inputting the text or data as usual.

> **MOUSE TIP**
>
> To delete cells, select the cells you want to delete, right-click them, and click Delete. The Delete dialog box that opens is similar to the Insert dialog box.

| Step 6 | Press | the ENTER key |

Don't forget to fix the Sales Report Data worksheet.

| Step 7 | *Scroll* | left to the Sales Report Data worksheet tab |
| Step 8 | *Repeat* | steps 1–6 on the Sales Report Data worksheet to correct the entry error |

Inserting and Deleting Rows and Columns

You want to insert a new row. To insert a new row:

Step 1	*Click*	the Report tab
Step 2	*Right-click*	the row 9 heading
Step 3	*Select*	Insert to insert a new row and shift row 9 to row 10

To insert columns, you use the same technique:

| Step 1 | *Right-click* | the column A heading |
| Step 2 | *Click* | Insert |

All data in the selected column and in the columns to the right are shifted to the right to make room for the new column.

You realize that you don't need the extra column. To delete columns:

Step 1	*Right-click*	the column A heading
Step 2	*Click*	Delete to delete the column from your worksheet
Step 3	*Click*	cell A1 to deselect the column
Step 4	*Save*	your workbook

MOUSE TIP

If you accidentally delete a row or column, click the Undo button to restore it.

MENU TIP

To insert a new row, or column click the Insert menu, then click Rows or Columns.

To delete rows or columns, select the row(s) or column(s), click Delete on the Edit menu.

QUICK TIP

To insert multiple rows, select the number of rows you want to insert, then right-click the row heading and click Insert.

3.g Using Absolute, Relative, and Mixed References in Formulas

Using cell references in formulas allows you to quickly update values in referenced cells. All formulas referencing those cells will automatically recalculate their results based on your changes. Excel uses three types of references: absolute, relative, and mixed references. Each of these reference types affects how a formula is copied. Amy Lee, the president of Sweet Tooth, wants you to calculate the commission for each of the company's sales people to find the total cost of the 20% sales commission.

Using Relative References in Formulas

When you copy a formula containing a **relative cell reference**, the references change relative to the cell from which the formula is being copied. If cell C1 contains the formula =A1+B1, when this formula is copied to cell D2, it changes to =B2+C2. Cell D2 is one row down and one row over from C1; cells B2 and C2 are correspondingly one row down and one row over from cells A1 and B1. To use relative cell references in a formula:

Step 1	*Activate*	the Central Region tab
Step 2	*Enter*	Planned Commission % in cell A1
Step 3	*Enter*	20% in cell A2
Step 4	*Key*	=D4*A2 in cell E4
Step 5	*Click*	the Enter button  on the Formula Bar
Step 6	*Drag*	the fill handle to cell E6 to copy the formula
Step 7	*Click*	cell E5

The formula in cell E6 is =D5*A3. Because there is no value in cell A3, the result of the formula is 0, which is displayed as a dash in the currency style number format.

Step 8	*Click*	cell E6

The error message #VALUE! appears in cell E6, because the value of cell A3 is not a numerical value. See Figure 3-6.

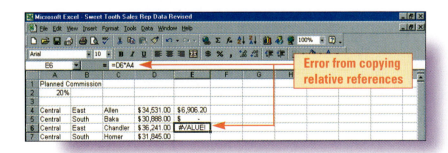

FIGURE 3-6
Errors Due to Copying Formulas with Relative References

You must fix these formulas so that they multiply the value in column D by cell A2, which contains the percentage needed for your formula.

Using Absolute and Mixed References in Formulas

Sometimes you don't want one or more of the cell references in a formula to change, no matter where you copy a formula. For example, in the formula that calculates the commission for Sweet Tooth's sales representatives, the second reference in the formula should always refer to cell A2. In such a case, you would use an **absolute cell reference**, which always refers to a specific cell. In an absolute reference, the dollar sign ($) precedes the column and row designation. In the formula you set up in cell E5, for example, an absolute reference to cell A2 would look like this: =D5***A2**.

To edit the formula and add an absolute reference:

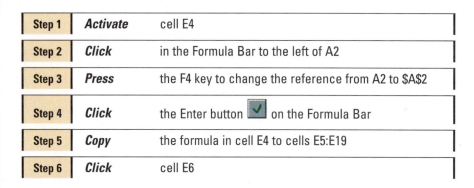

Step 1	*Activate*	cell E4
Step 2	*Click*	in the Formula Bar to the left of A2
Step 3	*Press*	the F4 key to change the reference from A2 to A2
Step 4	*Click*	the Enter button on the Formula Bar
Step 5	*Copy*	the formula in cell E4 to cells E5:E19
Step 6	*Click*	cell E6

The relative reference in the Formula Bar correctly changes to reference the cell directly to the left, while the absolute reference remains fixed on cell A2.

In addition to absolute and relative references, Excel uses mixed references. A **mixed cell reference** maintains a reference to a specific row or column. For example, suppose you need to copy the formula in cell E5 to cell G5. With a relative reference to cell D5, the formula would change to: =F5*A2. Using a mixed reference, however, you could maintain the reference to column D, but allow the row to change as you copied the formula down column G. A mixed reference would look like this: =$D5*$A$2.

> **QUICK TIP**
>
> When editing formulas, you can cycle through the four types of cell references by repeatedly pressing the F4 key.

3.h Creating and Using Named Ranges

Giving meaningful names to cells and ranges makes it easier to refer to them.

Add and Delete a Named Range

To continue preparing the report for Amy Lee, you calculate each region's total sales commissions. Using named ranges, you can easily refer to the cells containing those calculations. To name ranges:

Step 1	Select	cells E4:E19 on the Central Region sheet
Step 2	Click	the Name Box
Step 3	Key	Central
Step 4	Press	the ENTER key

Once you've named a range, it is added to the list in the Name Box. You can then use this list to select the named range. To select a named range:

Step 1	Press	the RIGHT ARROW key to move to cell F4
Step 2	Click	the Name Box list arrow
Step 3	Select	Central

You use the Define Name dialog box to add, delete and modify your named ranges. To use the Define Name dialog box to name ranges:

Step 1	Click	Insert
Step 2	Point to	Name
Step 3	Click	Define

The Define Name dialog box appears, as shown in Figure 3-7.

The cell reference in the Refers to: text box begins with an equal sign (=), because the reference is essentially a formula that calculates the range name you chose. The sheet name appears next, enclosed between single quotation marks. An exclamation point separates the sheet name from the cell references. Finally, notice that the cell

> **CAUTION TIP**
>
> When naming ranges, you can use letters, numbers, and the underscore (_) character; but you cannot use spaces. Named ranges are not case-sensitive. If you have a named range called repnames, for instance, then you try to create a new named range called REPNAMES, Excel will not create a new group, but rather selects the previously named range.

> **QUICK TIP**
>
> Press the CTRL + F3 keys to quickly open the Define Name dialog box.

FIGURE 3-7
Define Names Dialog Box

reference is an absolute reference. You can modify the cell references in the text box, select new ones from the worksheet by clicking the Collapse Dialog button, add new named ranges, or delete existing ones. To create a named range using the Define Names dialog box:

| Step 1 | Key | Commission in the Names in workbook: text box |
| Step 2 | Click | the Collapse Dialog button in the Refers to: text box |

The dialog box collapses to show only the Refers to: box, and the status bar prompts you to point to add cells to your named range.

Step 3	Select	cell A2
Step 4	Click	the Expand Dialog button in the dialog box
Step 5	Click	Add to add the new named range to the Names in workbook list
Step 6	Click	OK to close the Define Name dialog box

Using a Named Range in a Formula

You can use range names instead of cell references in formulas. In Sweet Tooth's workbook, the Report worksheet has been started for you. You create a formula using a named range to calculate the Central region's total commissions. To create a formula using a named range:

Step 1	Click	the Report tab
Step 2	Key	=sum(in cell B5
Step 3	Click	Insert

> **QUICK TIP**
>
> To delete a named range, open the Define Name dialog box, select the range name in the list, then click Delete.

Organizing Worksheets Effectively   EB 67

Step 4	Point to	<u>N</u>ame
Step 5	Click	<u>P</u>aste to open the Paste Name dialog box
Step 6	Click	Central
Step 7	Click	OK
Step 8	Click	the Enter button on the Formula Bar

Excel automatically adds the closing parenthesis for the SUM argument. Your formula should match the one shown in Figure 3-8, with the correct result appearing in cell B5.

> **QUICK TIP**
>
> Open the Paste Name dialog box quickly by pressing the F3 key.

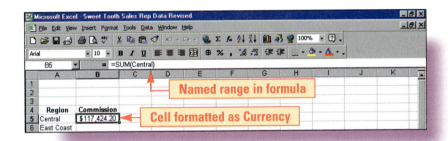

FIGURE 3-8
Using Named Ranges in Formulas

3.i Freezing and Unfreezing Rows and Columns

When working with large worksheets, it can be helpful to retain row and column headings on the screen as you scroll through your worksheet. When you need to view row or column labels while scrolling through a worksheet, use the Freeze Panes command. This command freezes the rows above, and the columns to the left of, the active cell and prevents them from scrolling off the screen. Suppose you want to see the column headings as you scroll the list on the Sales Report Data worksheet. To freeze panes:

Step 1	Click	the Sales Report Data tab
Step 2	Press	the CTRL + HOME keys to move to cell A1
Step 3	Activate	cell A4
Step 4	Click	<u>W</u>indow
Step 5	Click	<u>F</u>reeze Panes

> **QUICK TIP**
>
> You can hide a row or column temporarily. Right-click the row or column heading you want to hide, then click <u>H</u>ide. To unhide the row or column, select both row or column headings surrounding the hidden row or column. Right-click the heading and click <u>U</u>nhide.

chapter three

QUICK TIP

When you have spent time setting up a particular view of a worksheet, you may want to save the view. The View dialog box, which you open by clicking Custom Views on the View menu, can be used to save and restore named views. Click Add, key a name for your view, and click OK.

A thin, black line appears on your workbook, indicating that rows 1 through 4 are frozen. This black line will not print when you print the worksheet. These frozen rows will not scroll with the rest of your worksheet.

| Step 6 | Press & Hold | the DOWN ARROW key until your worksheet begins scrolling down |

The rows of data disappear off the screen under the column labels. When you no longer need the frozen panes, you can unfreeze them. To unfreeze panes:

| Step 1 | Click | Window |
| Step 2 | Click | Unfreeze Panes |

The panes are removed, permitting normal worksheet scrolling.

3.j Using Grouping and Outlines

Outlines offer a powerful option for viewing data in a worksheet. An **outline** allows you to view data in hierarchies, or levels. An easy way to create outlines is to use the Subtotals command. When you create subtotals, you specify at what points subtotals should be calculated. Excel automatically inserts the SUBTOTAL function at the specified points, then creates a grand total at the end. The information appearing above each subtotal is called **detail data**. Applying the Subtotals command automatically creates an outline, and a set of outline symbols appears on the left of the worksheet, providing the controls to display or hide detail data.

Using the Subtotals command, you can gather the totals requested by Amy Lee. At the same time, you can provide totals by region and for the company as a whole. To create a subtotal outline:

| Step 1 | Click | cell A4 |

Step 2	**Click**	D̲ata
Step 3	**Click**	Su̲btotals

The Subtotal dialog box appears. When the Subtotal dialog box opens, Region—the first column in the data set—is automatically selected in the A̲t each change in list. The Region column is sorted alphabetically. Whenever a new value appears in the Region column, a subtotal will be calculated. The SUM function is automatically selected in the U̲se function list. In the A̲dd subtotal in list, Gross Sales—the last column in the data set—is selected. See Figure 3-9.

FIGURE 3-9
Subtotal Dialog Box

MENU TIP

You can create an outline by clicking the D̲ata menu, pointing to Group and Outline, then clicking A̲uto Outline. Use G̲roup and U̲ngroup to create single levels of data. Note that your worksheet must be set up properly for this function to work. Use the Office Assistant to find out more about creating an outline manually.

Step 4	**Click**	OK
Step 5	**Double-click**	the column divider line between columns D and E to widen the column
Step 6	**Scroll**	the worksheet down until you can see row 72

New rows are inserted at each change in the Region column, and Excel calculates a subtotal for each region. Outline symbols showing a two-level outline appear on the left. At the bottom of the list, a grand total is calculated. See Figure 3-10.

chapter
three

FIGURE 3-10
Outline Created Using the Subtotals Command

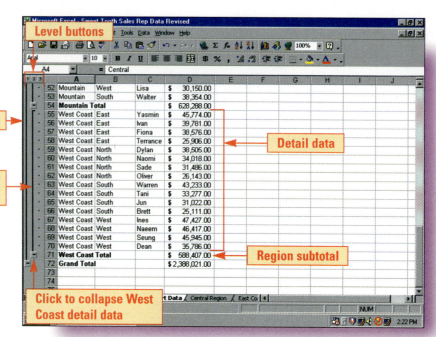

Amy has requested the totals for each region. You can hide the detail data by collapsing the outline. To collapse outline levels:

Step 1	Click	the Collapse Level button to the left of row 71 to hide the detail for the West Coast Region
Step 2	Click	the 2 Level button at the top of the outline to display only subtotals for each region
Step 3	Scroll	to the top of the worksheet to view all of the subtotals

QUICK TIP

The Collapse Level button changes to an Expand Level button .

Your outline can include up to eight levels. Anticipating that Amy might need to view each division's totals, you decide to add a third level to the outline. To add another level to an outline:

Step 1	Click	cell B20
Step 2	Click	Data
Step 3	Click	Subtotals
Step 4	Select	Division from the At each change in list
Step 5	Click	the Replace current subtotals check box to deselect it
Step 6	Click	OK

CAUTION TIP

Leaving the Replace current subtotals check box *checked* will replace your current outline with a new one. If you want to add another level of detail to an existing outline, you must remove the check mark.

Each division now has a subtotal, as shown in Figure 3-11.

Organizing Worksheets Effectively   EB 71

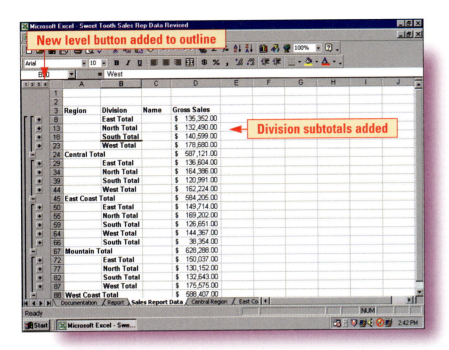

FIGURE 3-11
Adding Additional Levels to an Outline

> **MENU TIP**
>
> To run spell check from the menu bar, click Tools, then click Spelling.

3.k Checking Spelling in a Worksheet

Excel can check the spelling in your workbook. To spell check a worksheet:

Step 1	Click	the Documentation tab
Step 2	Click	the Spelling button on the Standard toolbar

The Spelling dialog box opens. Near the top of the dialog box, you will see the first misspelled word found on the worksheet. Suggested corrections appear in the Suggestion list box. See Figure 3-12.

> **notes**
>
> The dictionary that Excel uses to spell check your document does not include many proper names, so your name may be identified as the first misspelled word in this activity. If so, click Ignore to skip your first and last name, then continue the exercise.

The first word that Excel locates is part of the filename, *Revised.xls*. Because it is part of the filename, you can ignore the word by clicking the Ignore button.

> **QUICK TIP**
>
> A documentation worksheet is useful to other users. This page documents the contents of the workbook and provides other useful information, such as the creation date and date the workbook was last modified. Study the Documentation tab to familiarize yourself with the various sections.

chapter three

FIGURE 3-12
Spelling Dialog Box

CAUTION TIP

You should always proofread your worksheets for spelling errors in addition to running spell check. No spell checker is perfect, especially when dealing with specialized professions that use industry-specific vocabularies. Also, spell checkers do not find words that are spelled correctly but used incorrectly; for example, they will not flag "there" as misspelled when you should have used "their."

MOUSE TIP

To check spelling in multiple worksheets press and hold the SHIFT key, click the tabs of the sheets you want to check, then click the Spelling button. To select nonadjacent worksheets, press and hold the CTRL key as you click tabs.

| Step 3 | Click | Ignore |

Next, the spell checker finds *Reprot* next. It offers two suggested spellings. The first one is correct and is listed in the Change to: box.

| Step 4 | Click | Change |

The next misspelled word Excel locates is *comissions*. The Spelling dialog box offers only one suggested spelling, and it is the correct one.

| Step 5 | Click | Change |
| Step 6 | Click | Change to accept the suggested correction for *Paramters* |

The next misspelled word, *comission*, has been misspelled several times in the worksheet. You can quickly correct all instances of a misspelling by clicking the Change All button.

| Step 7 | Click | Change All |

When you have finished, Excel notifies you that the spelling check of the worksheet is complete.

| Step 8 | Click | OK |
| Step 9 | Save | your workbook and close it |

You are now ready to present the requested information to Amy Lee, Sweet Tooth's president.

Summary

▶ Sort data using as many as three levels of sort criteria.

▶ Drag selection borders to move data. Press the CTRL key and drag selection borders to copy data. Press the ALT key to move or copy data to another worksheet.

▶ Name worksheet tabs to make information easier to find.

▶ Insert, move, and delete worksheets to organize workbooks.

▶ Use Cut, Copy, and Paste to move or copy information.

▶ Insert and delete rows and columns as needed to organize worksheets. Insert cells by shifting them up or to the right when it is necessary to maintain surrounding information.

▶ Relative cell references change relative to the source cell when copied.

▶ Use absolute cell references to maintain links to a specific cell when copying formulas. Absolute cell references use the dollar sign ($) in front of the column and row identifiers: A1.

▶ Mixed cell references maintain links to a specific row or column when copying formulas. Mixed references use the dollar sign ($) in front of either the row or column identifier: $A1 or A$1.

▶ Create named ranges to quickly select ranges and to use the specified ranges in formulas.

▶ Freeze panes to prevent rows and/or columns from scrolling along with the worksheet.

▶ Use subtotals to create outlines automatically. Add as many as eight levels of subtotals. Use outline symbols to hide or reveal detail.

▶ Use the Spelling command to quickly spell check a worksheet or several worksheets at once.

chapter three

Commands Review

Action	Menu Bar	Shortcut Menu	Toolbar	Keyboard
Sort data	Data, Sort		A↓Z / Z↓A	ALT + D, S
Name a worksheet tab	Format, Sheet, Rename	Rename		ALT + O, H, R
Insert a worksheet	Insert, Worksheet	Insert		ALT + I, W SHIFT + F11 SHIFT + ALT + F1
Move a worksheet	Edit, Move or Copy Sheet	Move or Copy		ALT + E, M
Delete a worksheet	Edit, Delete Sheet	Delete		ALT + E, L
Cut	Edit, Cut	Cut	✂	CTRL + X ALT + E, T
Copy	Edit, Copy	Copy	📋	CTRL + C ALT + E, C
Paste	Edit, Paste	Paste	📋	CTRL + V ALT + E, P
Insert cells	Insert, Cells	Insert		ALT + I, E CTRL + SHIFT + + (plus key)
Insert rows	Insert, Rows	Insert		ALT + I, R
Insert columns	Insert, Columns	Insert		ALT + I, C
Delete rows and columns	Edit, Delete	Delete		ALT + E, D
Cycle reference type between absolute, mixed, and relative				F4
Open Define Name dialog box	Insert, Name, Define			ALT + I, N, D CTRL + F3
Open Paste Name dialog box	Insert, Name, Paste			ALT + I, N, P F3
Freeze/unfreeze pane	Window, Freeze Panes Window, Unfreeze Panes			ALT + W, F
Hide/Unhide rows or columns		Hide Unhide		
Create a named view	View, Custom Views			ALT + V, V
Open Subtotal dialog box	Data, Subtotals			ALT + D, B
Expand an outline level	Data, Group, Show detail		1 / +	ALT + D, G, S
Collapse an outline level	Data, Group, Hide detail		1 / −	ALT + D, G, H
Spelling	Tools, Spelling			ALT + T, S F7

Concepts Review

Circle the correct answer.

1. To copy a selection while dragging, press and hold the:
   - [a] SHIFT key.
   - [b] END key.
   - [c] CTRL key.
   - [d] ALT key.

2. To copy a selection to another worksheet, press and hold the:
   - [a] SHIFT + CTRL keys.
   - [b] CTRL + ALT keys.
   - [c] SHIFT + ALT keys.
   - [d] CTRL + SPACEBAR keys.

3. Which of the following formulas is an absolute reference?
   - [a] A1
   - [b] $A1
   - [c] A1
   - [d] A$1

4. Copying the formula =A1+B1 from cell C1 to cell E3 would make what change to the formula?
   - [a] =A1+B1
   - [b] =A1+C3
   - [c] =B3+C1
   - [d] =C3+D3

5. Copying the formula =$A1+B$2 from cell C1 to cell E3 would make what change to the formula?
   - [a] =$A3+D$2
   - [b] =$A1+B$2
   - [c] =$A2+E$2
   - [d] =$A3+C$2

6. Cell A1, named AMT, contains a value of $100.00. Cell B1, named TAX, contains a value of 6%. Cell C1 contains the formula =AMT*TAX. What is the result of this formula?
   - [a] none, you can't use cell names in formulas
   - [b] $106.00
   - [c] $6.00
   - [d] an error

7. Identify the type of reference for the row and column of the following cell reference: X$24.
   - [a] absolute, absolute
   - [b] absolute, relative
   - [c] relative, absolute
   - [d] relative, relative

8. You can sort data using as many as _____ levels of sort criteria.
   - [a] one
   - [b] two
   - [c] three
   - [d] four

9. You can create outlines with as many as _____ levels of detail.
   - [a] five
   - [b] six
   - [c] seven
   - [d] eight

chapter three

Circle **T** if the statement is true or **F** if the statement is false.

T F 1. You can use the F7 key to open the Paste Name dialog box.
T F 2. The freezing pane command prevents rows or columns from scrolling with the worksheet.
T F 3. Formulas containing relative references do not change when copied.
T F 4. You can use the F4 key to cycle through cell reference options when editing formulas.
T F 5. You must hold the ALT key down while selecting multiple worksheet tabs for spell checking.
T F 6. Clicking one of the Sort buttons will sort based on the column of the active cell.
T F 7. Using the Subtotals command automatically creates an outline.
T F 8. Spell check catches all spelling errors.
T F 9. Spell check checks only the current active worksheet unless you select multiple worksheets.
T F 10. Documenting a workbook is important when other users will use the workbook.

Skills Review

Exercise 1

1. Open the *Employee Time* workbook on your Data Disk.
2. Insert a new worksheet into the workbook.
3. Name the tab Revised Data.
4. Rename the Employee Time tab to Original Data.
5. Copy all of the data to the Revised Data tab (the worksheet includes data in 349 rows).
6. Save the file as *Employee Time 1*.

Exercise 2

1. Open the *Employee Time 1* workbook that you created in Exercise 1.
2. Switch to the Revised Data tab, if necessary.
3. Insert a new column at column A.
4. Move all of the data (including the column heading) under Project to the new column A.
5. Delete the empty column C.
6. Change column C to Number format with two decimal places.
7. Increase the width of column A to show the project names in full.
8. Bold and center the column labels.
9. Move the title in cell B1 to cell A1.
10. Bold the title, then merge and center it across columns A through C.
11. Delete the blank rows 2, 3, and 4 under the worksheet title.
12. Save your work as *Employee Time 2*.

Exercise 3

1. Open the *Employee Time 2* workbook that you created in Exercise 2.
2. Scroll the worksheet until row 3 is the top row you can see.
3. Activate cell A4.
4. Use freeze panes to lock the column labels in place.
5. Scroll to the bottom of the worksheet.
6. Save your work as *Employee Time 3*.

Exercise 4

1. Open the *Employee Time 3* workbook that you created in Exercise 3.
2. Unfreeze the column labels.
3. Delete all blank rows separating data (leave row 2 blank).
4. Sort the data by Project (ascending order), then by Hours (descending order).
5. Create an outline of the data by creating subtotals for each Project.
6. Collapse the outline to level 2.
7. Save your work as *Employee Time 4*.

Exercise 5

1. Open the *Employee Time 4* workbook that you created in Exercise 4.
2. Remove the subtotals from the data by opening the Subtotal dialog box, and then clicking the Remove all button.
3. Select cells C4:C328. Name this range Hours.
4. Save the workbook as *Employee Time 5*.

Exercise 6

1. Open the *Employee Time 5* workbook that you created in Exercise 5.
2. Insert a new worksheet and name it Report.
3. In cell A2, enter the row label "Number of Projects."
4. In cell A3, enter the row label "Average Hours."
5. In cell A4, enter the row label "Total Hours."
6. Widen column A so the text fits.
7. Use the Office Assistant to look up the COUNT function. Insert the COUNT function in cell B2 using the named range Hours.
8. Use the Office Assistant to look up the AVERAGE function. Insert the AVERAGE function in cell B3 to calculate the average hours spent by each employee on each of the company's projects.
9. Enter the SUM function in cell B4 to calculate the total number of hours worked.

chapter three

10. Format column B using the number style with two decimal places.

11. Save the workbook as *Employee Time 6*.

Exercise 7

1. Open the *Employee Time 6* workbook that you created in Exercise 6.

2. Check the spelling on the Report worksheet.

3. Check the spelling on the other two worksheets in the workbook.

4. Add the title Time Sheet Report to cell A1 in the Report worksheet, then merge and center it across columns A and B.

5. Insert two rows below row 1.

6. Format the Report worksheet as you see fit.

7. Save the workbook as *Employee Time 7*.

Exercise 8

1. Open the *Groceries* workbook on your Data Disk.

2. Select rows 3 through 6.

3. Click Data, point to Group and Outline, then click Group.

4. Click Data, point to Group and Outline, then click Hide Detail.

5. Activate any cell in row 9.

6. Click Data, point to Group and Outline, then click Auto Outline. Click OK when prompted to modify the existing outline.

7. Click the level 1 outline button to collapse the outline.

8. Print your worksheet.

9. Save the workbook as *Groceries with Outline*.

Case Projects

Project 1

You are an instructor at a community college who teaches working adults about Excel. Several of your students have asked you for additional resources. Use the Web toolbar to search the Internet for Excel books. Print at least three summary pages showing the title, author name, and ISBN number for each book.

Project 2

You are in charge of the accounting office at a large department store. Recently, several computational errors have occurred in various reports. In reviewing the work of junior staff members, you find that some of them are having problems understanding the difference between absolute and relative cell references. Prepare a workbook with samples of the four types of references. Use this workbook to demonstrate what happens when you move data or copy formulas containing these different types of references. Use the Office Assistant to help you brush up on your knowledge of the topic. Save the workbook as *Cell Reference Training*.

Project 3

You have just been promoted to programming director at the radio station where you work. The station manager wants to completely reorganize the way in which the station keeps track of which songs are played. Prepare a workbook that can sort songs by number of times played in a week, duration, artist, and musical classification. Be sure to format the cells so that they display the correct units. Add the titles of at least 10 songs, and create fictitious data for the number of times played and duration. Save the workbook as *Record Tracker*.

Project 4

You are a serious baseball card collector. Create a worksheet to organize your card collection by player, card manufacturer, or value. Use the Internet to locate Web sites devoted to baseball card collectors. Create a workbook containing the names, card manufacturers, card years, and values for 20 cards. Include at least three different cards for three of the players. Organize the data so that they can be sorted by player name, card manufacturer, year, or value. Save the workbook as *Baseball Card Collection*.

Project 5

You are the manager of a pizzeria. Create a worksheet with fictitious data that shows how many pizzas were sold last month. Calculate the total sales, figuring each pizza sold for $8.00. Show column headings for Overhead, Labor, Ingredients, Advertising and Profit. Calculate the amount spent in each category, figuring 15% for overhead, 30% for labor, 25% for ingredients, 10% for advertising, and the remainder for profit. Save the workbook as *Pizzeria*.

Project 6

You plan on selling your car soon and want to find out how much it is worth. Use the Web toolbar and search the Internet for used car prices. Try finding a listing for your car and two other cars built the same year. (*Hint*: Search for "Blue Book values.") Print Web pages showing the trade-in value of the cars you selected.

Project 7

Using Excel online Help, find out how to outline a list of data manually (rather than using the Subtotals command). Write a ½ page summary of the information you find out. Be sure to describe, in your own words, how to organize data to create an outline. Point out how to troubleshoot outlines that aren't working correctly. Save your work as *Manually Outlining Data.doc*.

Project 8

As an assistant to the accountant for a medium-sized accounting firm, you have been asked to ensure that the company's worksheets use consistent documentation. Create a "template" documentation page that you can copy and paste into each of the company's many Excel files, similar to the documentation sheet in the *Sweet Tooth Sales Rep Data* worksheet you used in this chapter. Be creative in your use of fonts and colors to make the documentation page easy to read and follow, and interesting to look at. Save your workbook as *Documentation Template*.

chapter three

Excel 2000

Previewing and Printing Worksheets

Chapter Overview

When you have entered all of the data on your worksheet, it's time to print a report. Excel provides many options to help you print exactly what you want. For example, you can print selections, worksheets, or entire workbooks. You can also set up headers and footers using predefined styles, or create your own custom headers and footers. Modify page break and margin settings to print sheets to fit every need.

Learning Objectives

- Preview and modify page setup options
- Insert and remove page breaks
- Print an entire workbook

Case profile

Every six months, Sweet Tooth's company president, Amy Lee, conducts a long-range planning session with her department managers. In this meeting, she reviews their accomplishments for the last six months and notes their progress toward previously set goals. Goals for the next two years are also revised and set. You have created a calendar in Excel for 1999 and 2000 that each participant in the meeting can

4.a Previewing and Modifying Page Setup Options

Previewing worksheets and setting page setup options are important tasks when it comes to printing worksheets. Because spreadsheets aren't really shaped like pages, and because *each* worksheet can hold as many as 256 columns and 65,536 rows, your poor printer may be working overtime. Before you can print calendars for next week's planning meeting, you need to preview the print job and modify the page setup options.

Setting the Print Area

The *12 Month Calendar* workbook contains a calendar you can print for Sweet Tooth's semi-annual meeting. To open and save the calendar file:

Step 1	Start	Excel
Step 2	Open	the *12 Month Calendar* workbook from your Data Disk
Step 3	Save	the workbook as *12 Month Calendar Revised*

The month titles in this calendar are formatted with the Month-YY date format. By default, Excel prints all data on the current worksheet. If you need to print only a portion of a worksheet, however, you can define a print area using the Set Print Area command. To set the print area:

Step 1	Select	cells A1:G18
Step 2	Click	File
Step 3	Point to	Print Area
Step 4	Click	Set Print Area

This action defines a print area covering the months January-99 and February-99.

Using Print Preview

You should always preview your print jobs before sending them to the printer. To preview the print area:

Step 1	Click	the Print Preview button  on the Standard toolbar

> **QUICK TIP**
>
> To print multiple ranges, select ranges using the CTRL key, then set the print area.

> **MENU TIP**
>
> Select Print Preview from the File menu to preview a document.

If your computer is attached to a color printer, your print preview appears in color; otherwise, the print preview is in black and white. See Figure 4-1. The Print Preview toolbar appears at the top of the window. The status bar indicates the number of pages in the print job.

FIGURE 4-1
Print Preview Window

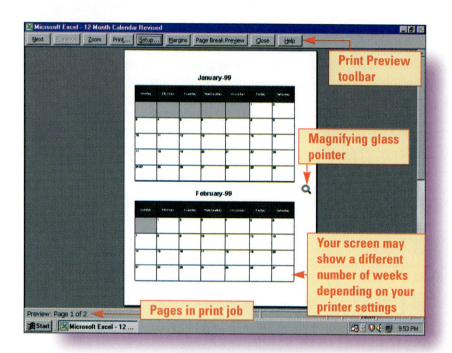

QUICK TIP

 To preview and print an entire worksheet, click the Print Preview button on the Standard toolbar before setting a print area, then click the Print button on the Print Preview toolbar.

MOUSE TIP

Drag the scroll bar in the Print Preview window to move to another page in the print job.

| Step 2 | Click | the Next button on the Print Preview toolbar to view the next page in the print job |

As you can see, page 2 of the print job contains one row (or two rows, depending on your printer) of the calendar.

Changing Page Orientation and Scale

The Page Setup dialog box provides many settings through which you can arrange the page, including scaling, orientation, and paper size settings. Scaling a document allows you to fit a report to a certain number of pages. For Sweet Tooth's meeting notes, the January and February calendars should fit on a single page. To scale a print job:

| Step 1 | Click | the Setup button on the Print Preview toolbar |
| Step 2 | Click | the Page tab, if necessary |

The Page Setup dialog box is shown in Figure 4-2.

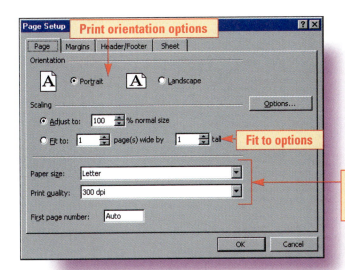

FIGURE 4-2
Page Tab of Page Setup Dialog Box

Step 3	Click	the Fit to: option button
Step 4	Verify	that the Fit to: boxes are set to 1
Step 5	Click	OK

The print job scales the print area so that it fits on a single page, which you can see by looking at the Print Preview window.

Most business documents, including letters, memos, and financial reports are printed in **portrait orientation**, or across the width of the page. In working with Excel, you may find **landscape orientation** more suitable, because it prints across the length of the page, as if you were holding the paper sideways. To change the orientation:

Step 1	Click	the Setup button on the Print Preview toolbar
Step 2	Click	the Landscape option button
Step 3	Click	OK

> **MENU TIP**
>
> You can access the Page Setup dialog box from the File menu by clicking Page Setup.

The worksheet appears in landscape orientation. You decide this print job will look better in portrait orientation.

| Step 4 | Switch | back to Portrait orientation, as shown in Figure 4-3 |

FIGURE 4-3
Portrait Orientation

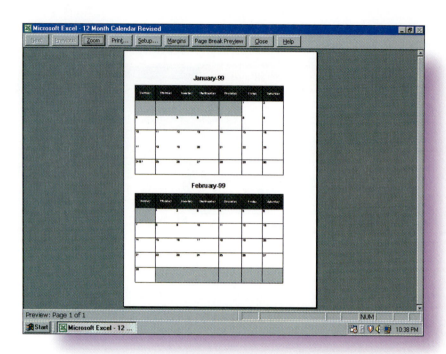

 ## Setting Page Margins and Centering

Sweet Tooth's calendar is not centered on the page, so you want to adjust its margins. To adjust the margins in print preview:

| Step 1 | *Click* | the <u>M</u>argins button on the Print Preview toolbar |

Vertical and horizontal lines appear on your preview page, indicating the left, right, top, and bottom margins, as well as the header and footer margins. Tick marks at the top indicate worksheet column widths. Your screen should look similar to Figure 4-4.

FIGURE 4-4
Adjusting Margins

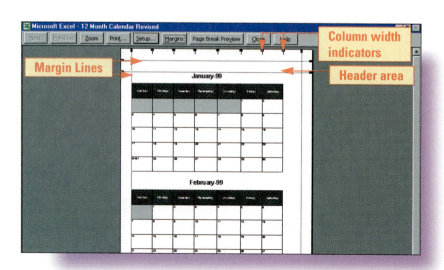

You can change the margins by clicking the line and dragging it to a new location. As you drag the margin, watch the status bar, which indicates the margin setting.

Step 2	Drag	the right margin line to the left until the status bar reads Right Margin: 1.00
Step 3	Click	the Margins button on the Print Preview toolbar

The margin lines disappear. You want to center each page of the calendar. To do this, you must use the Margins tab of the Page Setup dialog box. To center a print area on the page:

Step 1	Click	the Setup button on the Print Preview toolbar
Step 2	Click	the Margins tab

See Figure 4-5. You can use the Margins tab to set margins precisely and to specify centering options.

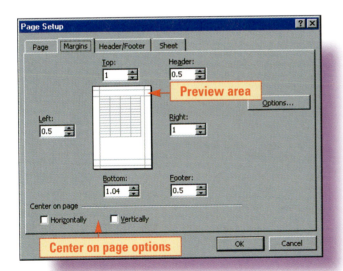

FIGURE 4-5
Margins Tab of Page Setup Dialog Box

Step 3	Click	the Horizontally check box in the Center on page section
Step 4	Click	the Vertically check box in the Center on page section
Step 5	Double-click	in the Right: margin box
Step 6	Enter	0.5
Step 7	Click	OK

Excel updates the print preview so that it now displays the months centered on the page. You add a header and footer to your print job.

Setting Up a Header and Footer

Headers and footers appear on every page of your print job. A **header** appears above the top margin of every page you print. A **footer** appears below the bottom margin of every page you print. Excel has several predefined headers and footers, using the most common options. You can also create a custom header and footer. You can specify separate font options for the header and footer. In addition to including any desired text, you can insert special codes that print the date, time, page number, filename, or sheet tab name in either the header or footer. To add a predefined header:

Step 1	Click	the Setup button on the Print Preview toolbar
Step 2	Click	the Header/Footer tab
Step 3	Click	the Header: list arrow

The Header list contains preset headers to print the current page number, filename, user name, company name, current page number, and total number of pages in the print job, as well as several variations and combinations of these elements.

| Step 4 | Click | 12 Month Calendar Revised |

This choice will print the filename as the header. The mini-preview above the Header list shows what your header will look like. To add a custom footer to your document:

| Step 1 | Click | Custom Footer |

The Footer dialog box opens. The Header and Footer dialog boxes, which look identical, contain buttons to insert special print codes. Table 4-1 lists the function of each of these buttons.

Text you enter in the left section will be left-aligned, text in the center box will be center-aligned, and text in the right section will be right-aligned.

| Step 2 | Key | *Your Name* in the Left section: box |
| Step 3 | Click | in the Right section: box |

QUICK TIP

For more information about options on this or any other tab of the Page Setup dialog box, click the question mark icon in the upper-right corner. This activates the What's This? feature. Select any setting or control in the dialog box to obtain an explanation of the control's function.

Previewing and Printing Worksheets — EB 87

To	Use	Code Inserted
Change the text font	A	
Insert a page number	#	&[Page]
Insert the total number of pages		&[Pages]
Insert the current date		&[Date]
Insert the current time		&[Time]
Insert the workbook filename		&[File]
Insert the worksheet tab name		&[Tab]

TABLE 4-1
Button Functions

> **QUICK TIP**
>
> You can control several print options on the Sheet tab of the Page Setup dialog box. To repeat rows and columns on each printed page, enter the ranges in the Print titles section. To print gridlines, select the box next to Gridlines. To print using Draft quality, which does not print gridlines or most graphics, select the box next to Draft quality. To print row and column headings, select the box next to Row and column headings.

Step 4	Click	the Date button
Step 5	Click	in the Center section: box
Step 6	Click	the Page Number button
Step 7	Press	the SPACEBAR
Step 8	Key	of
Step 9	Press	the SPACEBAR
Step 10	Click	the Total Pages button (see Figure 4-6)

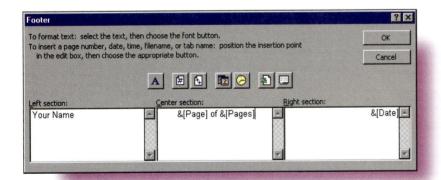

FIGURE 4-6
Header/Footer Dialog Box

| Step 11 | Click | OK |

Your footer appears in the Footer list box, and the mini-preview below the Footer list box shows what the footer will look like.

| Step 12 | Click | OK to apply the header and footer |

Now print the print area you set earlier. To print a print area:

| Step 1 | Click | the Print button on the Print Preview toolbar |
| Step 2 | Click | OK to print the print area and return to Normal view |

Clearing a Print Area

The January and February calendars print. When the Print dialog box closes, Print Preview closes as well and you return to the worksheet. You can now clear the print area. To clear the print area and restore the print scale:

Step 1	Click	File
Step 2	Point to	Print Area
Step 3	Click	Clear Print Area
Step 4	Open	the Page setup dialog box
Step 5	Click	the Page tab
Step 6	Click	the Adjust to: option button
Step 7	Key	100 in the Adjust to: box
Step 8	Click	OK
Step 9	Press	the CTRL + HOME keys

4.b Inserting and Removing Page Breaks

When printing multiple page print jobs, you may need to adjust the position of page breaks so that information appears on the correct page. To do this, you use Page Break Preview mode. For Sweet Tooth's meeting, you would like to print all the calendars for 1999 two to a page. To change the worksheet view to Page Break Preview:

| Step 1 | Click | View |

| Step 2 | Click | Page Break Preview |

The Welcome to Page Break Preview dialog box might appear, containing instructions for adjusting page breaks.

| Step 3 | Click | OK to close the Welcome to Page Break Preview dialog box if it appears on your screen |

See Figure 4-7. Dashed blue lines represent Excel's automatic page breaks. A light gray page number indicates the order in which pages will print. You can drag the page break to a new location to change how pages are printed.

CAUTION TIP

You must set page breaks separately for each worksheet in your workbook.

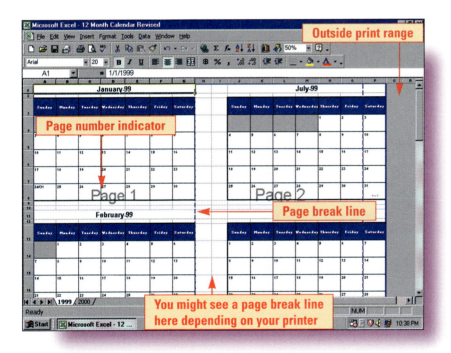

FIGURE 4-7
Page Break Preview Mode

MOUSE TIP

You can insert or remove page breaks by right-clicking in the Page Break Preview window. Select Insert Page Break to insert additional page breaks above and to the left of the active cell. Right-click a cell to the right of a vertical page break or below a horizontal page break and then select Remove Page Break to remove page breaks. You can also select Reset All Page Breaks to return to Excel's default page breaks.

| Step 4 | Scroll | the worksheet to view rows 16–24 |
| Step 5 | Drag | the first horizontal page break between rows 20 and 21 |

The dashed blue line changes to a solid blue line, representing a manually adjusted page break. Notice that the page break between columns G and H automatically shifted.

| Step 6 | Drag | the dashed blue page break line between columns I and J to columns H and I |

MENU TIP

The dotted black page break lines can be turned on and off using the Options dialog box. Click the Tools menu, click Options, then click the View tab. In the Window options group, click the Page brea<u>k</u>s check box to turn this option on or off.

QUICK TIP

When you are printing multiple worksheets, remember that you must check the page breaks on every page.

CAUTION TIP

Be careful when you click the Print button on the Standard toolbar. It will immediately send the print job to the printer using the current page setup options. You may not be aware of the current print area, or even which printer will receive the job.

| Step 7 | *Scroll* | the worksheet to verify that the other page break appears between rows 40 and 41 |

Your calendar will now print as two months per page.

| Step 8 | *Click* | the Print Preview button 🔍 on the Standard toolbar |
| Step 9 | *Click* | the Close button on the Print Preview toolbar |

To return to Normal view:

| Step 1 | *Click* | View |
| Step 2 | *Click* | Normal |

Returning to Normal worksheet view, you see dotted black lines indicating the page break settings. Because Sweet Tooth's meeting will cover long-range planning for two years, you need to print calendars from both tabs of the workbook. Until now, you have been working with areas on only one worksheet. In the next section, you learn how to print multiple worksheets.

4.c Printing an Entire Workbook

As noted earlier, you can print an area of a worksheet, an entire worksheet, or an entire workbook. You have already learned how to print a named range, how to clear the print area, and how to set page breaks for an entire worksheet. You still need to print all the months from both worksheets for the planning meeting, however. Before you can print the year 2000 calendars, you should check the page breaks on that worksheet.

To print the entire workbook:

| Step 1 | *Click* | File |
| Step 2 | *Click* | Print |

The Print dialog box opens, as shown in Figure 4-8.

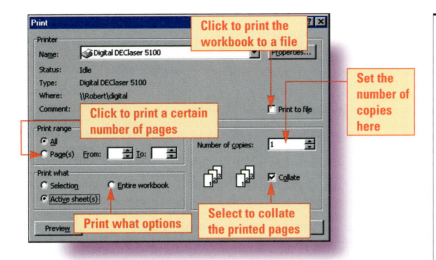

FIGURE 4-8
Print Dialog Box

Step 3	Click	the Entire workbook option button in the Print what section
Step 4	Click	the up spin arrow in the Number of copies: box, to change it to 2
Step 5	Click	Preview at the bottom of the dialog box
Step 6	Verify	that the pages will print as desired
Step 7	Verify	that your instructor wants you to print two copies of all 12 pages

notes Because you're not really going into a meeting, your instructor probably doesn't want to print two copies of all 12 pages. At this point, you can change the Number of copies back to 1, click the Page(s) option button, key 1 in the From: box, click in the To: box, and key 2. Excel will then print one copy of the first two pages of the workbook. Alternatively, you can click the Print to file check box, then click OK to open the Print To File dialog box. Key a filename in the File name: box, verify the drive and directory location, then click OK. If you print the workbook to a file, skip to step 10.

Step 8	Click	the Print button on the Print Preview toolbar
Step 9	Save	your workbook
Step 10	Close	the *12 Month Calendar Revised* workbook

You're all set for the meeting!

MENU TIP

You can print a selected area or a worksheet without setting the print area. If you want to print a worksheet, click Print on the File menu, then click the Active sheet(s) option button in the Print what group. If you want to print a selection, select the area you want to print, then click Print on the File menu. Click the Selection option button in the Print what group, then click OK.

QUICK TIP

The Collate check box in the Print dialog box organizes the order of your print job. When the Collate option is checked, Excel prints a complete copy of the document before starting the next copy.

Summary

- Preview worksheets and print options before printing. Zoom in on a print preview to see more detail.
- Use the Page Setup dialog box to specify the print options.
- Use the Page tab to set the print job's orientation and scaling options.
- Use the Margins tab to adjust margin settings and select page centering options.
- Use the Header/Footer tab to add a header and/or footer to a print report.
- Use the Sheet tab to select print areas, select draft quality, and toggle gridline and row and column heading printing.
- Work in Page Break view to manually adjust page breaks.
- Print selected areas by selecting File, Print area, then Set Print Area.
- Print a workbook by clearing print areas. Select Entire Workbook from the Print dialog box.

Commands Review

Action	Menu Bar	Shortcut Menu	Toolbar	Keyboard
Preview the printed workbook	File, Print Preview			ALT + F, V
Display Page Setup dialog box	File, Page Setup			ALT + F, U
View page breaks	View, Page Break Preview			ALT + V, P
View normal worksheet	View, Normal			ALT + V, N
Print	File, Print			CTRL + P ALT + F, P

Concepts Review

Circle the correct answer.

1. To select multiple ranges for printing, press and hold the _____ key while selecting areas.
   - [a] SHIFT
   - [b] END
   - [c] CTRL
   - [d] ALT

2. To set centering options for a print report, use the _____ tab of the Page Setup dialog box.
   - [a] Page
   - [b] Margins
   - [c] Header/Footer
   - [d] Sheet

3. To set a page to print in landscape orientation, use the _____ tab of the Page Setup dialog box.
   - [a] Page
   - [b] Margins
   - [c] Header/Footer
   - [d] Sheet

4. What does the print formula &[Page] do when you include it in a header or footer?
   - [a] Prints &[Page] on every page.
   - [b] Prints the total page count on every page.
   - [c] Prints the current page number on each page.
   - [d] Prints a box where you can write in the page number by hand.

5. In Normal view, page breaks are indicated by a:
   - [a] heavy blue line.
   - [b] heavy black line.
   - [c] dotted black line.
   - [d] thin blue line.

6. In Page Break Preview view, default page breaks are indicated by a:
   - [a] dotted blue line.
   - [b] heavy black line.
   - [c] solid blue line.
   - [d] thin blue line.

7. You just printed a named range, January. Now you need to print the entire worksheet. When you switch to Print Preview, however, all you see is the January range. What should you do?
   - [a] Close Print Preview, then try opening Print Preview again to see whether the problem goes away.
   - [b] Click the Print button and hope it prints correctly.
   - [c] Clear the print area.
   - [d] Click the Margins button on the Print Preview toolbar and widen the margins.

8. You set up page breaks on Sheet1 of a workbook and select Entire workbook from the Print dialog box. Sheet2 doesn't print correctly. What should you do?
   - [a] Click the Print button again to see whether the problem goes away.
   - [b] Check to see whether the printer is working properly.
   - [c] Clear the print area.
   - [d] Use Page Break Preview mode to check page breaks for both worksheets.

9. To set collating options for a print job, you use the:
   - [a] Page Setup dialog box.
   - [b] Page Break Preview.
   - [c] Print dialog box.
   - [d] Options button in the Page Setup dialog box.

10. When you manually adjust page break lines, what is displayed?
    - [a] dotted blue line
    - [b] heavy black line
    - [c] solid blue line
    - [d] thin blue line

Circle **T** if the statement is true or **F** if the statement is false.

T F 1. You should always preview before you print.
T **F** 2. Clicking the Print button on the Standard toolbar displays the Print dialog box.
T **F** 3. The dotted black page preview lines cannot be turned off.
T **F** 4. To center a print area on a page, you must drag it in the Print Preview window until it looks centered.
T **F** 5. Once you change page break locations, you can't undo them.
T F 6. You can see page breaks only in Page Break Preview mode.
T F 7. You can scroll in a zoomed Print Preview window using the ARROW keys.
T F 8. Headers and footers must use the same font.
T F 9. You can set margins in the Print Preview window or by pressing the Margin tab of the Page Setup dialog box.
T **F** 10. You need to set footer options for each page in your printed report.

Skills Review

Exercise 1

1. Open the file *24 Month Calendar* from your Data Disk.
2. Set the view to Page Break preview.
3. Select the January-00, February-00, and March-00 calendars.
4. Set the print area with these ranges selected.
5. Print preview your report.
6. Give this multiple selection the name Qtr1_2000 in the Name Box for printing later.
7. Print the report if instructed to do so.
8. Change the view to Normal view.
9. Activate cell A1.
10. Save the workbook as *24 Month Calendar Revised 1*.

Exercise 2

1. Open the *24 Month Calendar Revised 1* workbook that you created in Exercise 1.
2. Insert the filename as the header.
3. Modify the header by clicking Custom Header; select the text in the center section, then change the text to 16 point, bold.
4. Set the May-99 calendar as the print area using the Name Box to select the range.

5. Center the print area vertically and horizontally.

6. Preview your print job.

7. Print the report if instructed to do so.

8. Save the workbook as *24 Month Calendar Revised 2*.

Exercise 3

1. Open the *24 Month Calendar Revised 2* workbook that you created in Exercise 2.

2. Set up a named range covering all months of 2000. Name this range Year2000.

3. Set this area as the print area.

4. Use the Fit to option to print all of the calendars on one page.

5. Set the print options to center the calendars vertically and horizontally.

6. Print the report if instructed to do so.

7. Save the workbook as *24 Month Calendar Revised 3*.

Exercise 4

1. Open the *24 Month Calendar Revised 3* workbook that you created in Exercise 3.

2. Set July99 as the print area.

3. Set the page orientation to landscape.

4. Scale to 125%.

5. Print the report if instructed to do so.

6. Save the workbook as *24 Month Calendar Revised 4*.

Exercise 5

1. You will be distributing the *24 Month Calendar Revised* to all employees in your company. Write a step-by-step description explaining how to print the January-99 calendar only. Save the document as *Printing a Calendar*. Include the following instructions:

    a. Explain how to add "1999" as the header for the printed report.

    b. Explain how to print the calendar in landscape orientation.

2. Print your document or e-mail it to a classmate. Have your classmate follow your directions *exactly* and print the report. See how well he or she was able to follow your instructions.

3. Save your document as *Printing a Calendar.doc*.

Exercise 6

1. Open the *Sweet Tooth Q2 1998 Sales* workbook on your Data Disk.

2. Set print options to print the worksheet centered horizontally and vertically using Portrait orientation.

3. Print the worksheet.

chapter four

4. Set print options to print the worksheet centered horizontally but not vertically using Landscape orientation.

5. Print the worksheet.

6. Save the workbook as *Sweet Tooth Q2 1998 Sales Revised*.

Exercise 7

1. Open the *Sweet Tooth Q2 1998 Sales Revised* workbook you created in Exercise 6.

2. Change the print options to print gridlines and row and column headings.

3. Create a custom footer displaying the filename on the left, date in the center, and time on the right.

4. Print the worksheet.

5. Save the workbook as *Sweet Tooth Q2 1998 Sales Revised 2*.

Exercise 8

1. Open the *Sweet Tooth Q2 1998 Sales Revised 2* workbook you created in Exercise 7.

2. Set the print scale to 150%.

3. Set the print quality to Draft quality on the Sheet tab.

4. Print the worksheet.

5. Save the workbook as *Sweet Tooth Q2 1998 Sales Revised 3*.

Case Projects

Project 1

Your job is to train employees in the use of Excel. Search the Internet for Excel tips to include in your weekly "Excel Training Letter." Select one tip and create a Word document of at least two paragraphs describing it. Provide the URL of any sites that you used as references for your tip. Save the document as *Excel Training Letter.doc*.

Project 2

As part of your job, you track inventory at a used car dealership. You must record the number of cars sold by type per month. Create a worksheet providing data on at least four different makes of cars. Enter fictitious data for sales of each make of car for a period of four months. Sort the list by make of car, and then print it. Rearrange the data to display the months in order, then print the list again. (*Hint:* Add an index column in front of the month column with the number of each month next to the month name—for example, January=1, February=2, and so on.) Save the workbook as *Car Sales*.

Project 3

You're an office manager for a busy construction company. You have a lot of names, phone numbers, and addresses to manage. Create a worksheet containing the following column headings: Last Name, First Name, Address, City, State, Zip, Phone number. Enter fictitious data for 20 people. Your data should use at least four but not more than six states. Sort the list by state, then move the records for each state to separate worksheets (insert new worksheets as necessary). Be sure to copy the column headings and name tabs. Print the entire workbook. Save the workbook as *Phone List*.

Project 4

You are a travel agent. To stay competitive, you use the Internet to find out about your competitors' offers. Use the Web toolbar to locate at least three Web sites offering five- to seven-night packages to Cancun, Mexico. Print pages showing information about each of these packages.

Project 5

You are interested in increasing your productivity while using Excel. Using Office Assistant, search for the topic "keyboard shortcuts." Print one of the pages containing keyboard shortcuts for any of the shortcut key categories. Instructions for printing are included on each page in the Help file.

Project 6

As manager of a growing software company, you want to begin selling your products over the Internet. Use the Web toolbar to search for information regarding secure transactions over the Internet. (*Hint:* Search for the Secure Sockets Layer [SSL] protocol.) Write a two-paragraph document in Word describing what SSL is and how it works. Save your document as *Secure Transactions.doc*.

Project 7

In order to be better organized, you decide to create a day planner. Create a worksheet that breaks the day into 1-hour segments starting from when you get up in the morning to when you go to bed at night. Fill in the planner with your usual schedule for seven days. Print the worksheet(s). Save the workbook as *Day Planner*.

Project 8

You are the accounts manager of a graphic design company. Create a list of 10 clients who owe your company money. Use fictitious client names and amounts due (between $500 and $2,000). Add a column indicating how many days the account is overdue. Sort the list by the number of days the account is overdue. Print the worksheet. Save the workbook as *Overdue Accounts*.

chapter four

Excel 2000

Creating Charts

Chapter Overview

As more information becomes available to us, the skills of analyzing and summarizing information are even more vital today than they were in past years. Charts offer a great way to summarize and present data, providing a colorful, graphic link to numerical data collected in worksheets. Creating such an explicit relationship helps other people analyze trends, spot inconsistencies in business performance, and evaluate market share.

Learning Objectives

- Use Chart Wizard to create a chart
- Format and modify a chart
- Preview and print charts
- Work with embedded charts

Case profile

Each quarter, Sweet Tooth's regional managers meet with the company president, Amy Lee, to review sales figures and set goals for the next quarter. You have collected data from each of the region offices and are now ready to compile a report for the meeting. You decide to use charts to show the company's final sales figures.

chapter five

5.a Using Chart Wizard to Create a Chart

A chart provides a graphical interface to numerical data contained in a worksheet. Almost anyone can appreciate and understand the colorful simplicity of a chart. The data found in the *Sweet Tooth Sales Rep Data Q1 1999* workbook represents Sweet Tooth's sales for the first quarter. Your job is to create and format a chart for use in tomorrow's sales meeting. To open the workbook and save it with a new name:

Step 1	*Start*	Excel
Step 2	*Open*	the *Sweet Tooth Sales Rep Data Q1 1999* workbook from your Data Disk
Step 3	*Save*	the workbook as *Sweet Tooth Sales Rep Data Q1 1999 Revised*

Excel's Chart Wizard walks you step-by-step through a series of four dialog box boxes to quickly create a chart. You can create charts as separate workbook sheets called **chart sheets**, or you can place them directly on the worksheet page as **embedded charts**. One type of chart, called a column chart, helps you compare values across categories. To create a chart using the Chart Wizard:

Step 1	*Activate*	cell A5 on the Summary worksheet
Step 2	*Click*	the Chart Wizard button on the Standard toolbar

See Figure 5-1. In step 1, you select the type of chart you want to create from the list of chart types on the left side of the dialog box. Clicking a chart type on the left displays chart subtypes on the right side of the dialog box. A description of the chart subtype is given beneath the preview window. You decide to create three-dimensional charts, which provide an interesting visual alternative to two-dimensional charts.

Step 3	*Verify*	that Column is selected in the Chart type: list
Step 4	*Click*	the Clustered column with a 3-D visual effect from the Chart sub-type: box
Step 5	*Click*	Next >

> **QUICK TIP**
>
> Chart Wizard automatically detects the extents of a range of data when you activate any cell within the range.

> **QUICK TIP**
>
> The fastest way to create a chart is to use the shortcut key, F11. This shortcut key creates a default two-dimensional column chart on a separate chart sheet. Pressing the ALT + F1 keys creates a default chart as well.

FIGURE 5-1
Step 1 of the Chart Wizard

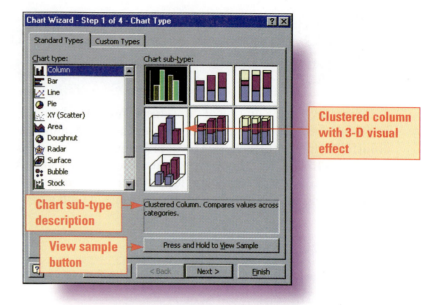

> **QUICK TIP**
>
> The default is for the data to be plotted with the row labels along the *x*-axis. If the chart doesn't communicate the information you expected, try clicking the Series in Rows option button in step 2 of the Chart Wizard. This option will change the chart so that the column labels are plotted along the *x*-axis.

In step 2, you select or modify the chart's source data. A preview of the selected data appears at the top of the Data Range tab. Notice the moving, dotted line border around the range in the worksheet in the background.

| Step 6 | *Click* | Next > |

Step 3 of the Chart Wizard appears with the Titles tab on top. See Figure 5-2. In this step, you enter chart options such as titles, legends, and data labels. Each type of chart produces different tabs here.

FIGURE 5-2
Step 3 of the Chart Wizard

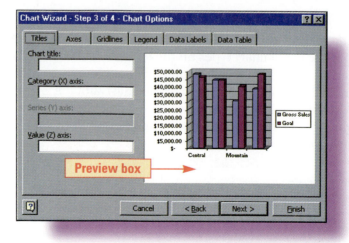

> **MOUSE TIP**
>
> Change your mind while using the Chart Wizard? Step backward at any time by clicking <Back. Make any changes, then click Next> to continue. The wizard leaves all other settings intact.

Step 7	Click	in the Chart title: box
Step 8	Key	Gross Sales by Region
Step 9	Press	the TAB key to move to the Category (X) axis: box
Step 10	Key	Region Name
Step 11	Click	the Legend tab
Step 12	Click	the Bottom option button
Step 13	Click	Next >

See Figure 5-3. In step 4 of the Chart Wizard, you specify the location of the new chart. You can create the chart as a new sheet or as an object in another worksheet.

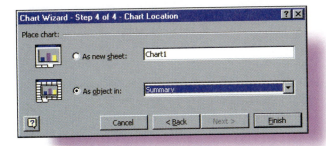

FIGURE 5-3
Step 4 of the Chart Wizard

Step 14	Click	the As new sheet: option button
Step 15	Key	Gross Sales by Region Chart in the As new sheet: box
Step 16	Click	Finish

The chart appears on a new worksheet in your workbook. See Figure 5-4.

When you create a chart, the Chart toolbar appears, and the Chart menu replaces the Data menu in the menu bar. The Chart menu and Chart toolbar contain chart-specific tools to aid in the creation and modification of charts and the elements that make up the chart, called **chart objects**. To enhance the chart even more for Sweet Tooth's meeting, you can modify the formatting of individual chart objects.

MOUSE TIP

You can change the chart to a different type any time. Right-click the chart you want to change, then click Chart Type. Select a new chart type and subtype, then click OK.

FIGURE 5-4
Chart Created with Chart Wizard

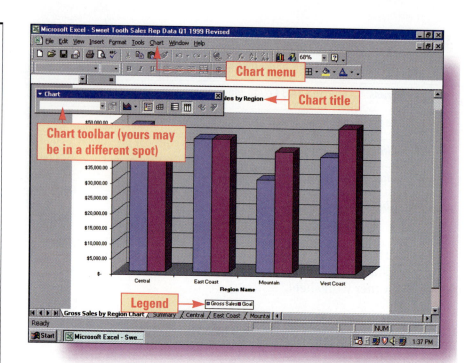

MOUSE TIP

You can change the location of a chart by right-clicking the chart and clicking Location.

5.b Formatting and Modifying a Chart

Every element of a chart, such as the title, legend, and plot area, is considered an object. An **object** is a graphical element added to a worksheet that you can manipulate, by moving, resizing or reformatting. Some of the more important chart objects are defined here. The **legend** is a key used to identify the colors assigned to categories in a chart. **Tick marks** are small marks on the edges of the chart that delineate the scale or separate the data categories. **Data points** represent the numerical data in your worksheet. In the current chart type, the data points are represented by horizontal bars. Data points, however, can also be represented by bars, columns, pie slices, and a variety of other shapes and marks. A **data series** represents all related data points in a set. On Sweet Tooth's chart, the Gross Sales bars are a data series, as are the Goal bars. The **plot area** of a chart is the area including only the chart itself. **Data labels** identify the data points with the category name, the data values, or the percentages.

Each chart object can be formatted by double-clicking the object, or right-clicking the object, then clicking Format *object* (*object* is the name of the object you selected, such as legend). The Format dialog box displays options unique to each object.

MENU TIP

Do you use a certain type of chart most of the time? You can change the default chart type. First, create a chart. From the Chart menu, click Chart Type. Choose the type of chart and the subtype that you use most often, then click Set as default chart at the bottom of the dialog box.

Changing Chart Fonts

You can change font settings for all text on the chart simultaneously, or you can select individual text objects and then customize their font settings. For Sweet Tooth's chart, the title should stand out from the other elements of the chart. To change fonts for individual objects:

Step 1	Move	the pointer over the Chart Title object at the top of the chart to see the ScreenTip
Step 2	Double-click	the Chart Title object

Double-clicking any chart object opens the Format dialog box for that object.

Step 3	Click	the Font tab in the Format Chart Title dialog box
Step 4	Select	Impact from the Font: list
Step 5	Select	20 from the Size: list
Step 6	Click	the Color: list arrow
Step 7	Click	Red
Step 8	Click	the Patterns tab
Step 9	Click	the Automatic option button in the Border group
Step 10	Click	OK
Step 11	Press	the ESC key to deselect the Chart Title object

The chart title is now formatted with your selections. Next, you learn to format the Legend object.

Formatting the Axes

You can modify both axes of the chart. The **category axis**, sometimes called the *x*-axis, is the axis along which you normally plot categories of data. The **value axis** is the axis along which you plot values associated with various categories of data. The value axis is the *y*-axis in two-dimensional charts, but the *z*-axis in three-dimensional charts. In bar charts in Excel, the category axis serves as the vertical axis and the value axis represents the horizontal axis.

Excel gives you full control over the scale of the axes, the number format, and the appearance of the axis labels. You decide to modify

MOUSE TIP

You can quickly format Chart Area fonts. For example, suppose all text on the chart should be bold. Click the Chart Area to select it, then click the Bold button on the Formatting toolbar.

QUICK TIP

You can change a title by editing the title text in the object box. Click a title once to select it, then move the pointer over the title text. The pointer changes to an insertion pointer. Click anywhere in the title to begin editing the text.

QUICK TIP

When a chart object is selected, you can cycle to other chart objects by pressing the ARROW keys. The UP and DOWN ARROW keys cycle through major chart objects such as Chart Title, Data Series, Plot Area, and Chart Area. The LEFT and RIGHT ARROW keys cycle through minor chart objects, such as Legend, Value Axis, and individual data points.

the number format of the value axis by dropping the decimal amount. To modify the value axis scale:

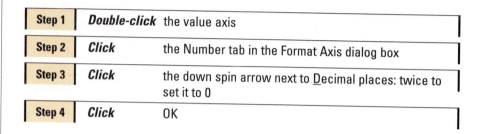

Step 1	*Double-click*	the value axis
Step 2	*Click*	the Number tab in the Format Axis dialog box
Step 3	*Click*	the down spin arrow next to Decimal places: twice to set it to 0
Step 4	*Click*	OK

Your screen should look similar to Figure 5-5.

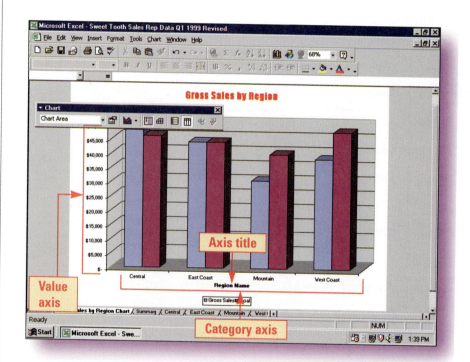

FIGURE 5-5
Changing Value Scale Options

MOUSE TIP

Data labels show the exact values of data points on a chart. You can add data labels by right-clicking the data series, then clicking the Data Labels tab. Select an option button, then click OK.

Adding a Data Table to a Chart

A **data table** displays the actual data used to create the chart. Sometimes you may find it helpful to show this information on the chart worksheet. To add a data table to the chart:

| Step 1 | *Click* | the Data Table button 🔳 on the Chart toolbar |

The data table is added beneath the value axis, as shown in Figure 5-6.

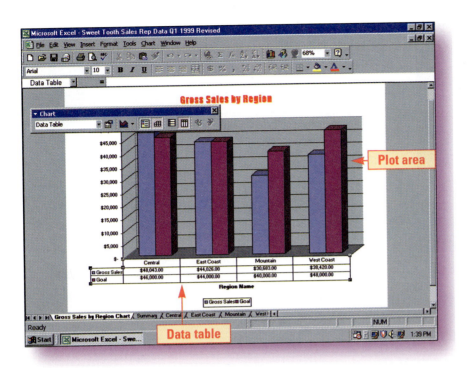

FIGURE 5-6
Adding a Data Table to a Chart

MOUSE TIP

Some types of charts allow you to do interesting things with the data points. For example, you can drag a "slice" of a pie chart away from the rest of the "pie" by clicking the slice once to select the data series. Click the slice again to select the individual point, then drag the slice to its new location.

| Step 2 | **Save** | your workbook |

The Gross Sales by Region chart is complete. In the next section, you print the chart for your upcoming meeting.

5.c Previewing and Printing Charts

Before you print your chart for the meeting, you should preview it in Print Preview to make sure that everything looks the way you expected. You can preview a chart, change print setup options, and print the chart from the Print Preview window. To change chart printing options:

| Step 1 | **Click** | the Print Preview button on the Standard toolbar |

The chart appears in print preview. If your default printer is a color printer, the preview will show the chart in color; otherwise, you will see a black-and-white preview of your chart. Your screen should look similar to Figure 5-7.

FIGURE 5-7
Previewing the Chart

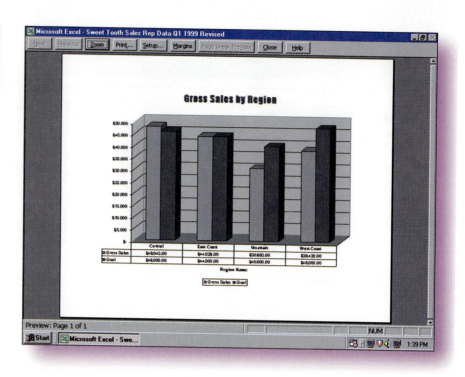

MOUSE TIP

Embedded charts are objects that "float" above your worksheet. This means that they can cover up data you may want to print. You can move or resize an embedded chart. To move an embedded chart, move the pointer over the chart then drag the chart to a new location. To resize an embedded chart, click the chart once to select it, then drag one of the black resize handles to make the chart larger or smaller.

Step 2	Click	the Setup button on the Print Preview toolbar
Step 3	Click	the Chart tab
Step 4	Click	the Scale to fit page option button

This option scales the chart until either the height or the width of the chart hits a page margin. The Use full page option scales the chart until both the height and the width touch the page margins on all sides.

Step 5	Click	OK
Step 6	Click	the Print button on the Print Preview toolbar
Step 7	Click	OK
Step 8	Save	your workbook

5.d Working with Embedded Charts

An embedded chart appears in a worksheet rather than on a chart sheet by itself. Because an embedded chart "floats" over the data on a worksheet, it may cover data that you need to see. You can move an embedded chart by dragging it to a new location. In addition, you can resize the chart by clicking the size control handles and stretching the chart as desired. As with chart sheet charts, you can modify all chart objects.

The embedded chart on the West Coast worksheet has already been created for you. You decide to reposition the chart. To reposition the embedded chart:

Step 1	Click	the right end tab scroll button
Step 2	Click	the West Coast worksheet tab
Step 3	Move	the pointer over the chart until you see the Chart Area ScreenTip
Step 4	Drag	the chart to the right side of the data until it is approximately in the range D2:J19

To resize the embedded chart:

| Step 1 | Move | the pointer over the lower-right resize handle |

The pointer changes to a two-headed sizing pointer.

| Step 2 | Press & Hold | the CTRL key |
| Step 3 | Drag | the handle to shrink the chart until it approximately fills the range D3:J17 |

Using the CTRL key resizes the chart uniformly from the center.

| Step 4 | Click | the worksheet outside the chart object to deselect the chart object |

The chart is deselected and you can edit the worksheet again.

| Step 5 | Save | your workbook and close it |

With your printed chart in hand, you're ready for the sales meeting.

> **QUICK TIP**
>
> You can print an embedded chart by itself or with the data on the worksheet. To print an embedded chart by itself, select the chart by clicking it once, then click the Print Preview button on the Standard toolbar.

> **MOUSE TIP**
>
> To resize the chart proportionally from the edge, press and hold the SHIFT key while dragging a resize handle.

> **QUICK TIP**
>
> To delete an embedded chart, select the chart, then press the DELETE key. To delete a chart sheet, right-click the chart sheet tab, then click Delete.

Summary

- Use the Chart Wizard to create a chart. Create a new default chart by pressing the F11 key.
- Charts can be placed on a separate chart tab, or they can be embedded on a worksheet. You can move and resize embedded worksheets as you like. Chart locations can be changed at any time.
- Charts contain many types of objects, including titles, legends, data tables, and plot areas. Each of these objects can be formatted independently.
- Change formatting elements for all chart objects at any time by using the Format dialog box.
- Add a data table to a chart to show the actual data used to create the chart.
- Preview charts before printing them so you can set print options. Embedded charts can be printed separately or as part of the active worksheet.

Commands Review

Action	Menu Bar	Shortcut Menu	Toolbar	Keyboard
Use the Chart Wizard	Insert, Chart			ALT + I, H
Create a default chart				F11 ALT + F1
Format a selected chart object	Format, Selected (chart object name)	Right-click chart object, click Format (chart object name)		ALT + O, E CTRL + 1
Change chart type	Chart, Chart Type	Chart Type		ALT C + T
Change chart options	Chart, Chart Options	Chart Options		ALT C + O
Show Chart toolbar	View, Toolbars, Chart			ALT + V, T
Add a data table to a chart				

Concepts Review

Circle the correct answer.

1. **A data label:**
   [a] displays the name of a chart object when the pointer is over that object.
   [b] displays the actual data used to create a chart.
   [c] is a key used to identify patterns, colors, or symbols associated with data points on a chart.
   [d] supplies information about a data point.

2. **A legend:**
   [a] displays the name of a chart object when the pointer is over that object.
   [b] displays the actual data used to create a chart.
   [c] is a key used to identify patterns, colors, or symbols associated with data points on a chart.
   [d] can show the value of a data point on a chart.

3. **To create a default chart, select the data range, then press the:**
   [a] CTRL + 1 keys.
   [b] F4 key.
   [c] F11 key.
   [d] CTRL + C keys.

4. **A data point:**
   [a] represents a series of data.
   [b] represents a single value.
   [c] can be shown as a pie slice, column, bar, or other graphical representation.
   [d] both b and c.

5. **Which of the following does *not* bring up the Format (chart object) properties dialog box?**
   [a] Double-click (chart object)
   [b] Right-click (chart object), select Format (chart object)
   [c] Select object, click Edit, click Format (chart object)
   [d] Click the Chart Objects list arrow on the Chart toolbar to select the chart object, then click the Format (chart object) button on the Chart toolbar

6. **The F11 shortcut key allows you to:**
   [a] create an embedded chart.
   [b] choose whether to use the Chart Wizard.
   [c] create only a chart sheet chart.
   [d] create either an embedded chart or a chart sheet chart.

7. **The Chart Wizard allows you to:**
   [a] create either an embedded chart or a chart sheet chart.
   [b] create only an embedded chart.
   [c] create only a chart sheet chart.
   [d] change the data values used to create the chart.

8. **If you change your mind while using the Chart Wizard, click:**
   [a] Cancel and start over.
   [b] Finish, delete the chart, and start over.
   [c] Next >.
   [d] < Back.

9. **To change the location of a chart, right-click the chart and select:**
   [a] Chart Type.
   [b] Source Data.
   [c] Chart Options.
   [d] Location.

Circle **T** if the statement is true or **F** if the statement is false.

T F 1. Charts make data easier to understand.

T F 2. Embedded charts cannot be moved on the worksheet.

T F 3. A data point is a graphical means of displaying numerical data. *see p. 102*

T F 4. You cannot change the default chart style created when you press the F11 key.

T F 5. The Format (chart object) dialog box is the same no matter which object is selected.

T F 6. Once you create a chart on a chart sheet, you cannot change it into an embedded chart.

T F 7. A data table cannot be displayed on the same worksheet as a chart.

T F 8. Chart objects can be moved and modified.

T F 9. You cannot print an embedded chart by itself.

Skills Review

Exercise 1

1. Open the workbook *Sales Data* on your Data Disk.
2. Using the data on the Summary tab, create a new Clustered Column chart with a three-dimensional effect.
3. Title the chart "Sales by Region."
4. Insert the chart on a new chart sheet called "Sales by Region Chart."
5. Print the Sales by Region Chart.
6. Save the workbook as *Sales Data Revised*.

Exercise 2

1. Open the *Sales Data Revised* workbook that you created in Exercise 1.
2. Using the embedded chart on the West Coast tab, find two other types of charts that present the data in a clear manner. *bar chart, column chart*
3. Find two types of charts that make it more difficult to understand the data. *area chart, radar, line, scatter*
4. Using Microsoft Word, write at least two paragraphs describing why certain types of charts worked well to illustrate the data and why others did not. Try to discern from the chart type description what type of information is needed for each type of chart and why your data did or did not work.
5. Save the document as *Chart Types.doc*. and print it.

Exercise 3

1. Open the *Exports by Country* workbook on your Data Disk.
2. Activate cell A2.
3. Create a line with markers chart using the Chart Wizard.
4. Title the chart "Exports by Country."
5. Add "1999" to the Category (X) axis.
6. Create the chart as an object on Sheet1.
7. Preview and print your chart as part of the worksheet (move the chart or change the paper orientation if necessary).
8. Save the workbook as *Exports by Country Chart*.

Exercise 4

1. Open the *Exports by Country Chart* workbook that you created in Exercise 3.
2. Add the following data to row 5: Japan, $6,438,945.00, $2,345,743.00, $5,098,7
3. Select the chart and use the Range Finder to add Japan's data to the chart.
4. Save the workbook as *Exports by Country Chart Revised* and print the worksheet.

[Sticky note: select & drag the highlighted boxes in the data ranges]

Exercise 5

1. Open the *Expenses* workbook on your Data Disk.
2. Activate cell A2.
3. Create a Bar of Pie type chart using the Chart Wizard (in the Pie chart type category). This type of chart uses a selected number of values from the bottom of a list of values to create a "breakout" section. In this case, the breakout section is the category Taxes.
4. Title the chart "Expenses."
5. Show the percentage data labels.
6. Create the chart as an embedded chart.
7. Save the workbook as *Expenses Chart* and print worksheet.

Exercise 6

1. Open the *Computer Comparison* workbook on your Data Disk.
2. Create a new chart, using the Line – Column on 2 Axes custom type of chart. (*Hint:* Click the Custom Types tab in step 1 of the Chart Wizard.)
3. Title the chart Computer Price/Speed Comparison.
4. Title the *x*-axis "System."
5. Title the *y*-axis "Price."
6. Title the secondary *y*-axis "Speed."
7. Create the chart as a new sheet.
8. Save the workbook as *Computer Comparison Chart* and print the chart sheet.

Exercise 7

1. Open the *Computer Comparison Chart* that you created in Exercise 6.
2. Show the data table on the chart.
3. Click the PII-450 data point to select it (select the individual point, not the series). Drag the data point handle at the top-middle of the data point down until the value reads $3,110.00.
4. Modify the value of the PII-400a data point to become $2,700.00 by dragging the data point handle.
5. Print the chart and save the workbook as *Computer Comparison Chart Revised*.

Exercise 8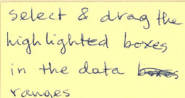

1. Open the *Class Attendance* workbook located on your Data Disk.
2. Create a new chart with the Chart Wizard.
3. Use the Custom Types tab to select the Colored Lines chart type.

4. Title the chart "Class Attendance."

5. Put the chart on a new sheet called "Attendance Chart."

6. Change the area fill of the Plot Area and the Chart Area to Automatic (white).

7. Print the chart and save your workbook as *Class Attendance with Chart*.

Case Projects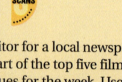

Project 1

As the entertainment editor for a local newspaper, you publish a weekly chart of the top five films based on their box office revenues for the week. Use the Web toolbar to search the Internet for information on the top five movies from the last week. Create a worksheet listing each of the titles and showing how much each film grossed in the last week. Add another column to show total revenues to date for each film. Create a chart that best illustrates the data. Save the workbook as *Box Office*.

Project 2

Use the Office Assistant to find out how to add a text box to a chart. Create a Word document and use your own words to describe step by step how to accomplish this task. Save the document as *Adding a Text Box to a Chart.doc*.

Project 3

As the owner of a mall-based cookie store, you want to track your cookie sales by type and month to determine which cookies are best-sellers and what the best time of the year is for cookie sales. Create a worksheet with 10 types of cookies (examples: chocolate chip, oatmeal, walnut, peanut butter). Include fictitious data for cookie sales for each type of cookie during the past 12 months. Create charts showing overall cookie sales by month and overall cookie sales by type. Save the workbook as *Cookie Sales*.

Project 4

Use the Web toolbar to search the Internet for different types of charts. Look for charts showing sales volume, stock prices, or percentages of sales by category. Print Web pages containing at least three different chart types.

Project 5

Stock price charts are usually displayed using a high-low-close style chart, which requires three columns of data. Use the Web toolbar to search the Internet for stock prices for three companies whose products you use. Locate price histories for the last five days for each stock, including the high, low, and closing prices for each day. Create a High Low Close chart (stock category) for each company, showing the price plotted against the date. Save the workbook as *High Low Close*.

Project 6

Create a worksheet showing one month's expenses for at least 10 expense categories in your household (estimate your family's expenses or supply fictitious data). Create a three-dimensional pie chart, and separate the largest expense from the pie. Use data labels to display the percentage of each expense. Save the workbook as *Family Expenses*.

Project 7

As the weather editor of a local newspaper, your job is to create a chart of the 5-day forecasts for your city. Using the Internet, locate a site that provides a 5-day forecast for your area. Enter the data on a new worksheet and create a chart showing the high and low temperatures for each day. Save the workbook as *Temperature Forecast*.

Project 8

You are interested in finding out how the government spends its budget. Using the Internet, find a site that shows where the government spends taxes. Create a new workbook and pie chart showing the information you find. Include at least 5 categories. Print the chart and save your workbook as *Government Spending*.

Excel 2000

Integrating Excel with Office Applications and the Internet

Chapter Overview

You can create reports in Word using Excel data or enhance PowerPoint presentations with Excel data and charts. In addition, you can create Access tables from existing Excel lists or query Access databases from Excel to analyze data. You can paste or link workbook data to documents created in other programs. You also can embed workbooks within other documents to share Excel's functionality with other programs.

Learning Objectives

- Integrate Excel with Word and PowerPoint
- Integrate Excel with Access
- Import data from other applications
- Send a workbook via e-mail
- Integrate Excel with the Internet

Case profile

You are responsible not only for gathering data produced by the various departments of Sweet Tooth, but also for distributing the data to company officers and department managers. For example, you periodically write memos to regional managers, distribute reports to management, and prepare presentations for potential investors. By integrating Excel-based data into other Office documents, you can save both yourself and your co-workers a lot of time and ensure accurate data.

integration

EX.a Integrating Excel with Word and PowerPoint

There are several ways to integrate Excel data with other types of files, such as Word documents and PowerPoint presentations. First, you can insert an Excel file (the **source file**) in a Word document or PowerPoint presentation (the **target file**). Second, you can embed an Excel object in a Word document or PowerPoint presentation. Third, you can create a link between an Excel workbook and a Word document or PowerPoint presentation.

When you insert Excel data in a Word document, you place the data in a Word table that can be edited using Word's Table editing commands. When you **insert** Excel data in a PowerPoint presentation, the data is inserted as a graphic object, similar to a picture of the data, which cannot be edited. All links to the original data are lost. Thus, if you modify the data in the target file, the original Excel workbook will not be updated. Likewise, if you update the Excel workbook, the target file will not be updated. Because you can use the Copy and Paste commands to insert Excel data into the target file, this method is very fast.

Embedding an Excel file in a target file creates a link between the target application and Excel. When you double-click an embedded worksheet to edit it, the target application's menu bar and toolbars are replaced with the Excel menu bar and toolbars. Using an embedded worksheet is like opening a window in the target application to the Excel application. Although you can use the familiar Excel menu bar and toolbars to edit the data, you are not actually altering the original data. That is, your changes are not reflected in the original Excel workbook. When you do not need to maintain a link to the original data, but do want access to Excel's features to format and edit data, use this method.

When you **link** an Excel worksheet to a target file, you create a reference to the original Excel worksheet. As with embedded files, double-clicking a linked file to edit the data opens the original file. Because the workbook is linked to the target file, any changes you make in Excel will be reflected in your target file. Linking files saves hard drive space because you do not create a second copy of the data in the target file. If having up-to-date data in the target file is essential, linking is your best option.

Embedding Excel Data in a Word Document

You need to send a memo to the management personnel at Sweet Tooth showing the preliminary sales totals for 1999. You wrote the memo in Word, and you collected the data in Excel. You want to

> **QUICK TIP**
>
> To find out more about linking or embedding data, use the Office Assistant.

embed the Excel data, so the managers can change the data if necessary. To embed Excel data in a Word document:

Step 1	Start	Word
Step 2	Open	the *Memo to East Division Manager.doc* file on your Data Disk
Step 3	Save	the Word document as *Memo to East Division Manager with Embedded Data.doc*
Step 4	Key	your name, replacing *Your Name* on the From line
Step 5	Press	the CTRL + END keys to move to the end of the document
Step 6	Start	Excel
Step 7	Open	the *Mountain Region Sales* workbook on your Data Disk
Step 8	Click	the East Division worksheet tab
Step 9	Select	cells A1:F9
Step 10	Click	the Copy button on the Standard toolbar
Step 11	Click	the Word taskbar button
Step 12	Click	Edit
Step 13	Click	Paste Special

The Paste Special dialog box opens in Word.

Step 14	Click	Microsoft Excel Worksheet Object in the As: list
Step 15	Verify	that the Paste: option button is selected
Step 16	Click	OK

> **QUICK TIP**
>
> You can press and hold the ALT key, then press the TAB key to cycle through open programs. When you release the ALT + TAB keys, you switch to the selected program.

The worksheet is embedded in the document as an object. You can drag the object in Word to reposition it, just as you would manipulate drawing objects in Excel. To move the embedded object:

Step 1	Drag	the embedded worksheet object below the last line of the memo and center it on the page

integration

When a worksheet is embedded in the target file, you must change it from within the Word target file. To edit the embedded Excel object in the Word document:

| Step 1 | **Double-click** | the embedded worksheet object |

Your screen should look similar to Figure EX-1.

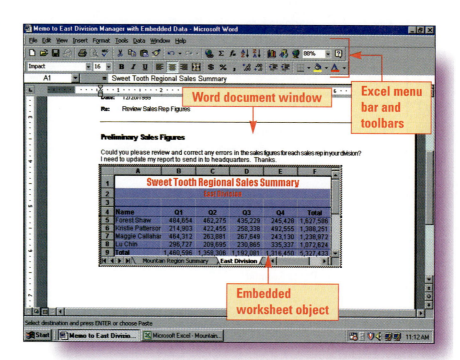

FIGURE EX-1
Embedded Worksheet Object

Step 2	**Select**	the range B5:F9
Step 3	**Click**	the Currency Style button $ on the Formatting toolbar
Step 4	**Resize**	columns B:F to fit
Step 5	**Activate**	cell A1
Step 6	**Click**	anywhere in the Word document to deselect the object
Step 7	**Drag**	the embedded worksheet object so that it is centered horizontally on the page
Step 8	**Deselect**	the embedded worksheet object by clicking elsewhere in the Word document

---

MOUSE TIP

Note that the Standard and Formatting toolbars may appear in the same row. If they do, then you can use the More Buttons button to access additional buttons.

Your document should look similar to Figure EX-2.

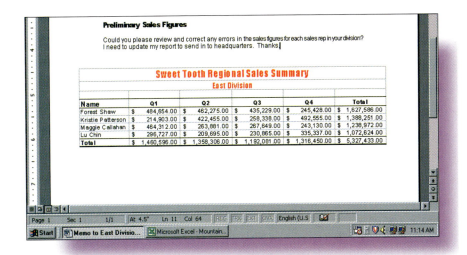

FIGURE EX-2
Embedded Worksheet Object after Formatting

Step 9	**Save & Close**	the Word document
Step 10	**Exit**	Word
Step 11	**Close**	the *Mountain Region Sales* workbook

QUICK TIP

To embed data in a file, press the CTRL key and drag the data from one file window to another.

Linking an Excel Chart to a PowerPoint Presentation

You are working on a PowerPoint presentation showing sales data for the South Region. You want to include a chart showing this year's data in the presentation. You know that the chart will be updated later, so you decide to link it to the presentation. You will then be able to update the chart right before your presentation. To add a link to the data:

Step 1	**Open**	the *South Division Summary* workbook on your Data Disk (in Excel)
Step 2	**Save**	the workbook as *South Division Summary Revised*
Step 3	**Click**	the Summary Chart worksheet tab
Step 4	**Start**	PowerPoint
Step 5	**Open**	the *South Summary.ppt* file on your Data Disk
Step 6	**Click**	the Excel taskbar button
Step 7	**Click**	the Copy button on the Standard toolbar

integration

Step 8	Click	the PowerPoint taskbar button
Step 9	Drag	the scroll bar down to move to slide 2 in the presentation
Step 10	Click	Edit
Step 11	Click	Paste Special
Step 12	Click	the Paste link option button

The dialog box on your screen should look similar to Figure EX-3.

FIGURE EX-3
Paste Special Dialog Box

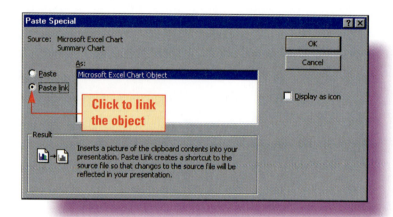

| Step 13 | Click | OK |

The chart is now linked to the PowerPoint presentation, but you need to resize it so it fits on the page. To resize the chart object:

| Step 1 | Press & Hold | the CTRL key |

When you press and hold the CTRL key while you resize an object, the object resizes proportionally toward or from the center of the object.

Step 2	Drag	a corner resize handle until the object fits nicely in the slide
Step 3	Move	the object so it is visually centered in the slide
Step 4	Click	anywhere in the PowerPoint window to deselect the object
Step 5	Save	the presentation as *South Summary Presentation.ppt*

> **MOUSE TIP**
>
> Right-drag a selection from Excel to Word to create a linked object.

Your screen should look similar to Figure EX-4.

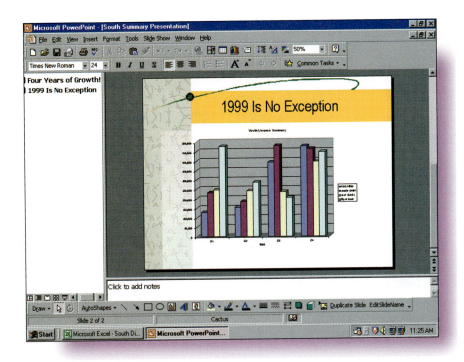

FIGURE EX-4
Adding Linked Excel Data to a PowerPoint slide

The chart is now linked to the PowerPoint presentation. When an Excel chart is linked to a target file, double-clicking the Excel object takes you directly to Excel. As you edit the linked data, the target file updates automatically. To modify the chart object:

| Step 1 | *Double-click* | the linked chart object |

Excel becomes the active program, and the workbook containing the chart object appears in the active window.

Step 2	*Maximize*	the Excel workbook window, if necessary
Step 3	*Right-click*	the Windows taskbar
Step 4	*Click*	Tile Windows Vertically so you can see both program windows at the same time
Step 5	*Click*	in the Excel window to make it active

integration

Your screen should look similar to Figure EX-5.

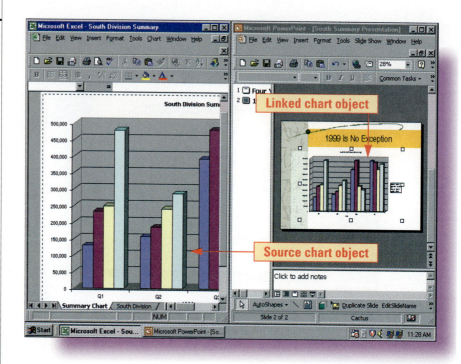

FIGURE EX-5
Viewing PowerPoint and Excel at the Same Time

CAUTION TIP

If you move or rename a workbook that has been linked to other files, the link must be corrected in order to update the data. However, the most recently updated data (before the link was broken) is displayed until you update the link. For more information about breaking and reestablishing links in a PowerPoint presentation, use the Office Assistant in PowerPoint.

Step 6	*Select*	the Chart Title object
Step 7	*Press*	the DELETE key to delete the Chart Title object

Notice that the linked chart is automatically adjusted in the presentation.

Step 8	*Maximize*	the PowerPoint program window
Step 9	*Save & Close*	the PowerPoint presentation
Step 10	*Exit*	PowerPoint
Step 11	*Maximize*	the Excel program window
Step 12	*Save & Close*	the workbook

EX.b Integrating Excel with Access

Although Excel can store a large volume of data in list form, a database application—such as Access—is better suited to holding large amounts of this type of data. As your Excel lists grow in size, you can export them to create Access tables.

Exporting Excel Data to an Access Database

You can use existing lists of Excel data to build data tables in Access. The *Sales Rep Data* workbook contains a variety of information about the sales for each of Sweet Tooth's divisions. You think it would be a good idea to store the data in a database rather than in Excel. Before you import Excel-based data into Access, however, you should prepare the information. To prepare the Excel data:

| Step 1 | Open | the *Sales Rep Data* workbook on your Data Disk |
| Step 2 | Save | the workbook as *Sales Rep Data to Import* |

You should delete any worksheet titles and blank rows that appear above the data to be imported into Access.

| Step 3 | Delete | rows 1–4 |
| Step 4 | Verify | that the column headings appear in the first row of the worksheet you'll be importing |

The column headings become the field names in the database.

| Step 5 | Activate | cell A1 |
| Step 6 | Save & Close | the workbook |

Now, you're ready to start Access and create a new database. To create a new database:

| Step 1 | Start | Access |
| Step 2 | Click | the Blank Access database option button in the Access startup dialog box |

> **QUICK TIP**
>
> Even though databases store large amounts of data efficiently, Excel still offers advantages when it comes to performing calculations on that information. As a result, you may prefer to import data from Access databases to Excel to perform more complex calculations and create charts.

integration

Step 3	Click	OK
Step 4	Select	the folder containing your Data Files
Step 5	Drag	to select the name in the File name: box
Step 6	Key	Sales Rep Data in the File name: box
Step 7	Click	Create

Once the database has been created, you can import data from an Excel file. To import data:

Step 1	Click	File
Step 2	Point to	Get External Data
Step 3	Click	Import
Step 4	Click	the Files of type: list arrow in the Import dialog box
Step 5	Click	Microsoft Excel
Step 6	Click	Sales Rep Data to Import
Step 7	Click	Import

The Import Spreadsheet Wizard opens. The first row of data in the workbook contains the column headings.

| Step 8 | Click | the First Row Contains Column Headings check box |

Notice, in the bottom half of the dialog box, that the column headings from the worksheet become the field headings for the new Access table. Below those headings, you see how the data will be divided into records (horizontally) and fields (vertically).

Step 9	Click	Next >
Step 10	Click	Next > to accept the default of creating the database in new table
Step 11	Click	Next > to accept the default and let Access index the table

When you are working with a database, a primary key is used to uniquely identify each record in a table and to speed up data retrieval in large databases. Access adds a primary key by default in Step 4 of the Wizard.

Step 12	Click	Next >
Step 13	Key	Sales Report Data in the Import to Table: box to name the new Access table
Step 14	Click	Finish
Step 15	Click	OK to close the alert box that appears

The new table appears in the Database window.

Step 16	Double-click	the Sales Report Data table icon

Your screen should look similar to Figure EX-6.

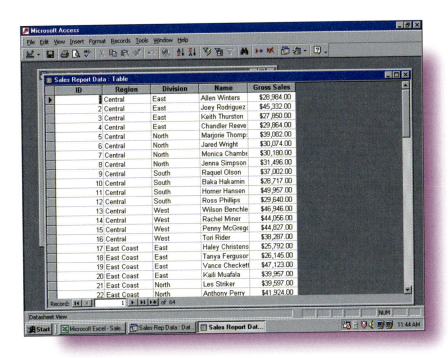

FIGURE EX-6
Access Table Created Using an Excel List

Step 17	Close	Access

Querying Data from an Access Database

A query is a method of extracting information from a database. You can use Excel to query data stored in Access and search for records meeting certain criteria. Then, you can import only those records that meet your criteria into Excel so as to create charts, develop PivotTable reports, or perform statistical analysis. To query a database, you use Microsoft Query in Excel. To query the database:

Step 1	**Start**	a new workbook in Excel
Step 2	**Click**	<u>D</u>ata
Step 3	**Point to**	Get External <u>D</u>ata

notes You might need to install Microsoft Query. If an alert box appears, insert the CD and click Yes to install it. If you are working in a lab or on a network, see your instructor.

Step 4	**Click**	<u>N</u>ew Database Query
Step 5	**Click**	MS Access Database* in the Choose Data Source dialog box
Step 6	**Verify**	that the <u>U</u>se the Query Wizard to create/edit queries check box has a check mark in it
Step 7	**Click**	OK
Step 8	**Click**	Sales Rep Data.mdb in the Database N<u>a</u>me list in the Select Database dialog box

This file is the Access database that you created in the previous activity.

| Step 9 | **Click** | OK |

Once you have selected a database source, the Query Wizard starts. In Step 1 of the wizard, you select which columns you want included in your query. If you omit a column, the data in that column will not be extracted from the database. To add columns to your query:

Step 1	**Click**	the + next to Sales Report Data to see which columns are available in your table, Sales Report Data
Step 2	**Verify**	that Sales Report Data is selected
Step 3	**Click**	the > button to add the entire table to the <u>C</u>olumns in your query: box
Step 4	**Click**	<u>N</u>ext >

QUICK TIP

For more information about using Microsoft Query, click the question mark icon in the Microsoft Query dialog box, then click Help with this feature.

Step 2 of the Query Wizard enables you to set query filters. Filters allow you to view only records meeting criteria you define. For this query, you want to extract only the records of sales representatives who work in the West Coast Region whose gross sales exceed $35,000. To set query filters:

Step 1	Click	Gross Sales in the Column to filter: list
Step 2	Click	the list arrow in the active box
Step 3	Click	is greater than from the list of operators
Step 4	Key	35000 in the value box on the right
Step 5	Verify	that the And option button is selected

At this point, your query will extract all records for which the value in the Gross Sales column is greater than $35,000. See Figure EX-7.

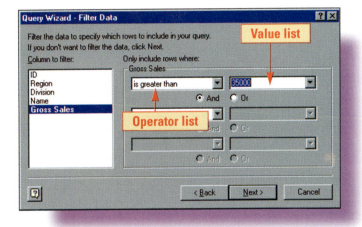

FIGURE EX-7
Step 2 of the Query Wizard

Step 6	Click	Region in the Column to filter: list
Step 7	Click	equals from the operator list
Step 8	Click	the value list arrow
Step 9	Click	West Coast

Because the And option button was selected before you chose this second filter, the query will extract all records where the value in the Gross Sales column is greater than $35,000 *and* where the region equals West Coast.

| Step 10 | Click | Next > |

The third step of the Query Wizard allows you to define a sort order for the records. To set the sort order:

Step 1	Click	the Sort by list arrow
Step 2	Click	Gross Sales
Step 3	Click	the Descending option button
Step 4	Click	Next >

The final step of the Query Wizard allows you to specify where the data should appear. You want to create a new list in Excel. To specify the output option of your query results:

| Step 1 | Verify | that the Return Data to Microsoft Excel option button is selected |
| Step 2 | Click | Finish |

The Returning External Data to Microsoft Excel dialog box opens. You need to select a location where the data will be placed. Cell A1 (the default) will work just fine.

| Step 3 | Click | OK |
| Step 4 | Save | the workbook as *Database Query* |

The query returns the results shown in Figure EX-8.

QUICK TIP

If you will reuse this query to update data at a later time, you can save it by clicking the Save Query button in the last step of the Query Wizard.

FIGURE EX-8
Results of Database Query

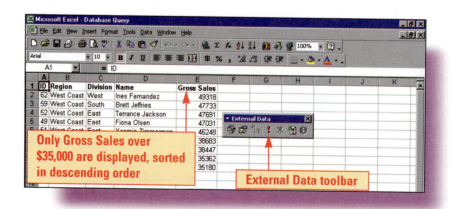

MOUSE TIP

The External Data toolbar appears after you run a query. Using this toolbar, you can refresh the data source, modify the query to extract other records, or modify the data range properties.

| Step 5 | Close | the workbook |

EX.c Importing Data from Other Applications

A commonly used method of exchanging data involves **comma-separated**, or **tab-delimited**, text files. These files can be created in any text editor and use commas or tabs to separate columns of data. You can import such a file into an open workbook, or you can create a new workbook using the text file. You have located an old document containing financial data dating from early in Sweet Tooth's history. This file uses tabs to separate information into columns. To import data from a delimited file into Excel:

Step 1	Start	a new workbook
Step 2	Click	Data
Step 3	Point to	Get External Data
Step 4	Click	Import Text File

> **QUICK TIP**
>
> Virtually any character can be used as a delimiter, including commas, semicolons, or even spaces, so Excel permits you to specify a character in the Other box. If the data is not divided into columns automatically, you need to specify a character other than a tab.

The Import Text File dialog box opens. Note that the Files of type: box at the bottom of the dialog box specifies Text Files.

Step 5	Select	Monthly Cash Flow from the Data Disk
Step 6	Click	Import

Step 1 of the Text Import Wizard appears. This wizard walks you through three steps to help you import and properly separate the text file into columns of data. Because Sweet Tooth's file is delimited, you can leave the settings at their defaults.

Step 7	Click	Next > to go to Step 2
Step 8	Click	Next > to accept the default choice of tabs as delimiters
Step 9	Click	Finish to accept the default settings for specifying how columns of data are formatted
Step 10	Click	OK in the Import Data dialog box

Once you have imported the data, you can format and rearrange the data as necessary. Because Sweet Tooth's file is a plain text file, it cannot

carry formulas with it; thus all totals and subtotals are included as values only. Upon reviewing the information, you notice that the totals in the workbook are not correct. You decide to correct the totals by replacing them with functions. To replace values with functions:

Step 1	Activate	cell B10
Step 2	Click	the AutoSum button on the Standard toolbar
Step 3	Press	the ENTER key
Step 4	Repeat	steps 1–3 to sum the total expenses in cells B14:B29 in cell B30
Step 5	Enter	=b10-b30 in cell B33
Step 6	Save	the workbook as *Old Monthly Cash Flow*
Step 7	Close	the workbook

QUICK TIP

Address book data is frequently exported as a comma delimited file. You can import the data into Excel to create and sort an address list.

EX.d Sending a Workbook via E-mail

notes The steps in this section describe how to send workbooks via e-mail using Microsoft Outlook as the mail client. Depending on your particular mail client, the process you follow may differ somewhat.

Using Excel's built-in e-mail capabilities, you can quickly send a worksheet or an entire workbook to a colleague. You can transmit a single worksheet as an HTML formatted mail message—an option that allows the recipient to see all the formatting of the original message. The recipient can select the data in his or her message and drag it into Excel. When you need to send an entire workbook, you can transmit it as an attachment. Attachments accompany a regular e-mail message and allow you to send any type of document or program.

When several colleagues need to review a workbook in a certain order, you can set up a routing slip to control the order of delivery. The routing slip accompanies the workbook transmission and contains the e-mail addresses and order in which you'd like the workbook to be reviewed. As each person finishes with the workbook, he or she can send it to the next person on the list.

Sending a Worksheet as HTML Mail

HTML mail allows you to send a Web page as the body of an e-mail message. Microsoft Outlook can receive and display HTML mail. To test this method, you send the Mountain Region Summary worksheet in the *Mountain Region Sales* workbook to yourself. To send a worksheet as part of a message:

Step 1	Open	the *Mountain Region Sales* workbook on your Data Disk
Step 2	Click	the E-mail button on the Standard toolbar

A dialog box opens, asking whether you want to send the entire workbook as an attachment or only the current worksheet as the message body. You want to send the current worksheet as the message body.

Step 3	Click	the Send the current sheet as the message body option button
Step 4	Click	OK

A messaging toolbar appears above the worksheet, as shown in Figure EX-9.

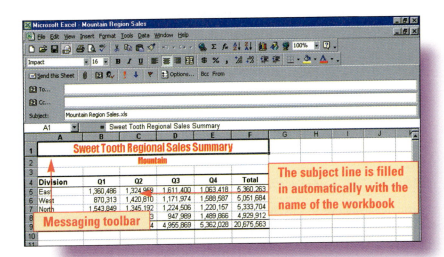

FIGURE EX-9
Sending a Worksheet as Part of a Message

Step 5	Enter	your own e-mail address in the To box
Step 6	Click	Send this Sheet

> **CAUTION TIP**
>
> While most newer e-mail clients can properly display HTML mail, many older clients cannot. If this is the case with your system, you should be able to send the message but may not be able to view it properly when you receive it.

> **MENU TIP**
>
> You can send a worksheet by clicking the File menu, pointing to Send to, then clicking Mail recipient.
>
> To send the entire workbook as an attachment, point to Send to on the File menu, then click Mail Recipient (as Attachment). When you send a workbook as an attachment, the recipient can then open the file in Excel.

QUICK TIP

If you want to use the Address Book to fill in e-mail addresses, click the To button or the Address Book button on the messaging toolbar. You can also use the shortcut keys, CTRL + SHIFT + B. Change your mind about sending a worksheet? To turn off the messaging toolbar without sending the message, click the E-mail button on the Standard toolbar again.

The message is sent to your e-mail program's Outbox. You need to start your e-mail program, connect to your ISP, and send the message. After a few minutes, use your e-mail program to check for new messages.

| Step 7 | **Send** | the e-mail message |
| Step 8 | **Download** | the new message |

If your e-mail program can display HTML mail, your message should look similar to Figure EX-10.

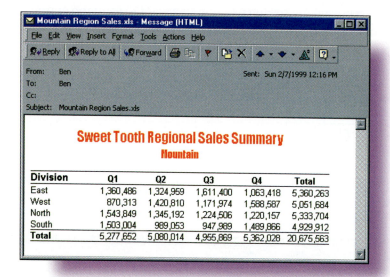

FIGURE EX-10
Viewing HTML Mail

| Step 9 | **Close** | the e-mail message |
| Step 10 | **Click** | the Excel taskbar button, if necessary |

Routing a Workbook

To successfully complete this activity, you will need the e-mail addresses of two classmates. To route a workbook:

Step 1	**Click**	File
Step 2	**Point to**	Send to
Step 3	**Click**	Routing Recipient

The Routing Slip dialog box opens, as shown in Figure EX-11.

Integrating Excel with Office Applications and the Internet   EX 19

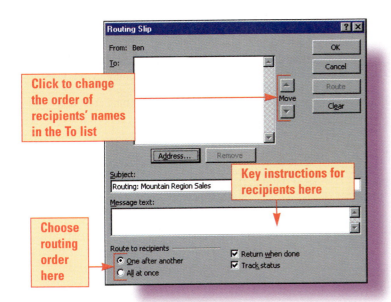

FIGURE EX-11
Routing Slip Dialog Box

| Step 4 | Click | Address |

The Address Book opens, allowing you to select the recipients to whom you want to send the workbook.

Step 5	Scroll	the Name list until you find the first person whose address should be added to the recipient list
Step 6	Double-click	the name to add it to the Message Recipients: list
Step 7	Repeat	Steps 5 and 6 to add the second person's address
Step 8	Click	OK

The Routing Slip dialog box appears again. You want to route the workbook to the recipients in the order shown, so leave the settings at their defaults.

| Step 9 | Click | Route |
| Step 10 | Save | the workbook as *Mountain Region Sales Final* and close it |

The e-mail message and attached workbook are sent to your e-mail client's Outbox. You may need to send the message by clicking the Send button in your e-mail program. After each recipient modifies the workbook, he or she can send the revised workbook to the next recipient.

CAUTION TIP

If you have not added your classmates' addresses to the Address Book, you won't be able to select their names until you do so. Click the New Contact button, then fill in the First and Last name boxes, along with the E-mail address.

integration

QUICK TIP

If the order in which the workbook is received is important, you can change the order by selecting a name in the To box and clicking the Move buttons to transfer the name up or down in the list. You can also add a short, instructional message in the Message text box. The Route to recipients group allows you to send the workbook to one person at a time on the list or to everyone on the list simultaneously.

To send a workbook to the next recipient on a routing slip:

Step 1	Open	the e-mail message containing the routed workbook
Step 2	Open	the attached workbook from your e-mail message
Step 3	Click	File
Step 4	Point to	Send to
Step 5	Click	Next Routing Recipient

A dialog box informs you that the document has a routing slip. You want to send the workbook using the routing slip, so leave the default setting intact.

Step 6	Click	OK
Step 7	Close	the workbook in Excel without saving changes
Step 8	Close	the e-mail message
Step 9	Send	the message from your e-mail program and download new messages

When the last person on the list routes the workbook, it returns to the person who originated the routing slip, along with a message informing the sender that the document has completed its routing and is being returned. You can then open this workbook and save it as a new workbook or replace the original workbook with the final version.

| Step 10 | Close | the e-mail program |

EX.e Integrating Excel with the Internet

As business becomes increasingly Web-centered, you undoubtedly will gain a greater appreciation of Excel's wide variety of tools, which enable you to easily publish your workbooks to the Internet. When you save workbooks as Web pages, you can save either individual sheets or entire workbooks. Interactive Web pages allow users to modify data, sort lists, add subtotals, and update charts on the Web page itself. You can also use Excel to open and edit existing Web pages.

Saving Excel Workbooks as Web Pages

Sometimes, you want users to be able to view data, but not to interactively change the data. Saving a workbook as a Web page is nearly as simple as saving any workbook. A few additional options exist when you save Web pages, however. When you **publish** a workbook (or Web page) to a Web server, any hyperlinks in the document are automatically adjusted to match the file structure on the Web server. For Sweet Tooth, you want to publish the data from the *South Division Summary* workbook, including the chart. To save your workbook as a Web page:

Step 1	Open	the *South Division Summary* workbook on your Data Disk
Step 2	Click	File
Step 3	Click	Save as Web Page
Step 4	Key	South Division Summary Web Page in the File name: box
Step 5	Change	the Save in: drive and directory to your Data Files folder

When you save a workbook or worksheet as a Web page, the Save As dialog box includes a few additional options.

| Step 6 | Click | Save to save the workbook as a Web page |
| Step 7 | Close | the workbook |

Now try viewing your Web page. To view your Web page:

Step 1	Open	your Internet browser
Step 2	Click	File
Step 3	Click	Open
Step 4	Click	Browse
Step 5	Locate	the folder where you are storing your Data Files
Step 6	Click	South Division Summary Web Page
Step 7	Click	Open
Step 8	Click	OK

MENU TIP

You can preview any workbook as a Web page by clicking the File menu, then Web page preview. Your browser will open, along with an HTML preview version of your workbook.

QUICK TIP

If you have access to a Web server, you can click Publish and immediately publish your workbook to the server.

Your Web browser opens, with the South Division Summary page displayed. At the bottom of the Web page, you notice hyperlink "tabs" that enable you to navigate between worksheets.

To navigate the Web page:

| Step 1 | *Click* | the Summary Chart tab |

Your screen should look similar to Figure EX-12.

FIGURE EX-12
Workbook Saved as Web Page

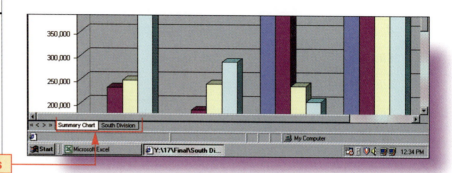

Hyperlink tabs

| Step 2 | *Click* | the Excel taskbar button |

Creating an Interactive Web Page

When you saved the *South Division Summary* workbook as a Web page, the chart and data pages presented static images of the data. Sometimes, however, you want to encourage users to interact with the data. Interactive Web pages enable users to change data, update charts, and rearrange PivotCharts.

To add interactivity to a Web page:

Step 1	*Open*	the *Sweet Tooth Sales to Stores* workbook on your Data Disk
Step 2	*Click*	File
Step 3	*Click*	Save as Web Page
Step 4	*Change*	the Save in: folder to your Data Files folder

CAUTION TIP

When you save a workbook as a Web page, a new folder is created with "_files" added to the end of the filename. If you copy the Web page file to another disk or folder, this folder must be copied with it. If you do not copy the folder to the same disk or folder as the Web page, the Web page will not function correctly.

When you save an entire workbook, you cannot add interactivity. Instead, you save the worksheet or chart which you want to be interactive.

Step 5	Click	the Selection: Chart option button

This option button changes to reflect the top worksheet.

Step 6	Click	the Add interactivity check box
Step 7	Click	Change Title
Step 8	Key	Sweet Tooth Sales to Stores

This title will appear centered in your Web page above the PivotChart.

Step 9	Click	OK
Step 10	Drag	to select the text in the File name: box
Step 11	Key	Sales to Stores Interactive Web Page in the File name: box
Step 12	Click	Save

Now you can switch to your browser and open the new Web page to test it.

To open the Web page and modify the PivotChart:

Step 1	Click	the browser taskbar button
Step 2	Open	the *Sales to Stores Interactive Web Page* file in your Data Files folder
Step 3	Scroll	to the bottom of the Web page

Your screen should look similar to Figure EX-13. You can modify the table in the Web page by changing filter options on the existing field button.

FIGURE EX-13
An Interactive PivotTable Web Page

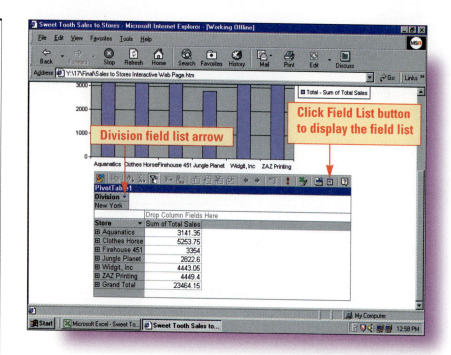

MOUSE TIP

 You can modify the table in the Web page by dragging new field buttons onto the chart from the PivotTable Field List.

QUICK TIP

 There are two ways to insert HTML data from an interactive Web page. You can either use the Copy and Paste buttons on the toolbar directly above the table or click the Export to Excel button on that toolbar.

Step 4	Click	the field list arrow on the Division button
Step 5	Click	the check box next to (All)
Step 6	Click	OK

Notice that the chart is updated to include sales to all regions.

| Step 7 | Click | the Excel taskbar button |
| Step 8 | Close | the workbook without saving any changes |

Importing a Table from a Web Page

> **notes**
> The following steps can be carried out only with Microsoft Internet Explorer 4.01 or higher. If you do not have Internet Explorer 4.01 or later installed on your computer, read through this section, but you may not be able to follow all of the steps on your computer.

You can import data from any table published on a Web page. This option can prove very useful when you need to track types of data that are frequently displayed in tables, such as stock tables. The Central Region manager has published her region's sales summary as a Web page. You can drag this table from the Web page to create a new workbook using the same data. To open your Web browser and the Central Region manager's Web page:

Step 1	Start	a new workbook in Excel
Step 2	Tile	the Excel and browser windows so that you can see them both at the same time
Step 3	Open	the *Central Region Sales.htm* file in your Internet browser

Your screen should look similar to Figure EX-14.

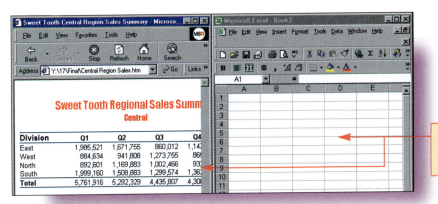

FIGURE EX-14
Web Page with an Excel Table

To copy the data to Excel:

Step 1	Select	the table in the browser by dragging across the data, starting from the left of the title and moving to the right of the bottom corner of the table
Step 2	Drag	the selected table from your browser to Excel
Step 3	Drop	the cells into cell A1 of your workbook
Step 4	Activate	cell B9 to see that the formula remained intact
Step 5	Save	the workbook as *Central Region Sales Download* and close it
Step 6	Right-click	the Windows taskbar
Step 7	Click	Undo Tile to restore Excel and the browser to full screen size
Step 8	Close	the Internet browser

Because formulas remain intact throughout the copying process, this process can be a very effective method of distributing data to a wide range of people on a company intranet or on the Internet.

integration

Summary

- Paste Excel data into a Word document to use Word's table tools.
- Embed Excel data to use Excel's functionality without providing for data to be updated from the source. Link Excel documents when data must be kept up-to-date.
- Embed or link charts and data to PowerPoint slides to enhance presentations.
- Use Excel lists to create tables in Access. Query Access databases from Excel to create charts, reports, and statistical analysis.
- Import data from different types of files using the Import Text Wizard.
- Send worksheets or workbooks to others without leaving Excel. E-mail worksheets as HTML mail, or send workbooks as e-mail attachments. Route workbooks to several colleagues when others should review a workbook and then return it to you.
- Save Excel workbooks, worksheets, and charts as Web pages. Add interactivity to enable users to manipulate data and modify charts.

Commands Review

Action	Menu Bar	Shortcut Menu	Toolbar	Keyboard
Insert a copy of Excel data in a Word document	Insert, File			ALT + I, L
Place Excel data in a Word document as a Word table	Edit, Copy Edit, Paste	Right-click selected data, Copy Right-click insertion point, Paste		ALT + E, C ALT + E, P CTRL + C CTRL + V
Embed Excel data in a Word document or PowerPoint slide	Insert, Object Edit, Copy Edit, Paste Special, Paste			ALT + I, O ALT + E, C ALT + E, S, P
Link Excel data in a Word document or PowerPoint slide	Edit, Copy Edit, Paste Special, Paste link	Right-click Excel range, Copy		ALT + E, C ALT + E, S ALT + L
Send worksheet as e-mail message	File, Send To, Mail Recipient			ALT + F, D, M
Send workbook as e-mail attachment	File, Send To, Mail Recipient (as Attachment)			ALT + F, D, A
Route a workbook	File, Send To, Routing Recipient			ALT + F, D, R
Route a workbook to next recipient	File, Send To, Next Routing Recipient			ALT + F, D, N
Preview Excel worksheet as a Web page	File, Web Page Preview			ALT + F, B
Publish Excel worksheet or chart	File, Save as Web Page			ALT + F, G

Concepts Review

Circle the correct answer.

1. **To embed worksheet data in a Word document:**
   - [a] use Copy and Paste.
   - [b] use Copy and Paste Special.
   - [c] press the CTRL key and drag a selection from Excel to Word.
   - [d] both b and c.

2. **Integrating Excel with other applications:**
   - [a] is difficult and creates outdated copies of data.
   - [b] is unnecessary because Excel can format a worksheet any way you want.
   - [c] increases your productivity and enhances your options for presenting data.
   - [d] none of the above.

3. **Embedding an Excel file in Word or PowerPoint:**
   - [a] creates a link to the Excel application and the source data.
   - [b] creates a link to the Excel application but not the source data.
   - [c] makes a copy of the Excel data using a Word table structure.
   - [d] makes a picture object of the data that can be only resized or moved.

4. **When creating a Word document with integrated Excel data that might change later, you should use:**
   - [a] embedded data.
   - [b] linked data.
   - [c] inserted data.
   - [d] none of the above.

5. **If you need to keep a "snapshot" of Excel data in another document at a given time, you should:**
   - [a] use embedded data.
   - [b] use linked data.
   - [c] use a screenshot.
   - [d] insert the data using the Copy and Paste commands.

6. **Text files can use which of the following characters as delimiters?**
   - [a] comma
   - [b] tab
   - [c] semicolon
   - [d] all of the above

7. **When Excel lists become very large, a better option may be to:**
   - [a] remove infrequently used records.
   - [b] create a second workbook and move half the records there.
   - [c] convert the worksheet to an Access database.
   - [d] condense the data by abbreviating names and other information.

8. **You can output the results of a query to:**
   - [a] the Microsoft Query window.
   - [b] an Excel worksheet.
   - [c] the Excel Query dialog box.
   - [d] all of the above.

9. **Routing a workbook is a good choice when you need to:**
   - [a] send a workbook to several colleagues and have it returned to you.
   - [b] send a workbook as the body of a message.
   - [c] save a workbook as a Web page.
   - [d] send a workbook to a colleague but don't need it returned.

10. **Which application is best suited to storing large lists of data?**
    - [a] Excel
    - [b] Word
    - [c] PowerPoint
    - [d] Access

Circle **T** if the statement is true or **F** if the statement is false.

T F 1. Inserting and embedding data create copies of the data that are not linked to the source data.

T F 2. Linking Excel data to a Word document requires more disk space than embedding because it creates an additional copy of the Excel workbook.

T F 3. You cannot create a simultaneous link to the same data in both a Word document and a PowerPoint presentation.

T F 4. The Paste Special dialog box can be used to embed or link data.

T F 5. Right-click and drag from Excel to a Word document to create a linked object.

T F 6. When editing embedded or linked Excel data in a Word document, you can access the Excel menu and toolbars.

T F 7. Sending a workbook as an e-mail attachment and routing a workbook are identical operations.

T F 8. A routing slip contains the e-mail addresses and order in which a workbook is sent to others.

T F 9. Interactive Web pages enable users to interact with the Web page's data.

T F 10. Learning to use the right software for the job can save time and effort.

Skills Review

Exercise 1

1. Open a new, blank worksheet.
2. Use Microsoft Query (<u>D</u>ata, Get External <u>D</u>ata, <u>N</u>ew Database Query) to query the *Excel List.mdb* database on your Data Disk.
3. Create a query to extract records from the Mountain or Central regions where the gross sales exceed $40,000.
4. Sort the results by gross sales in descending order.
5. Output the results to Excel.
6. Create a chart on a new sheet listing the top 10 sales representatives and their gross sales totals.
7. Add a title to your chart that describes its contents.
8. Print the chart.
9. Save the workbook as *Extract 1*.

Exercise 2

1. Open the *Extract 1* workbook that you created in the Exercise 1.
2. Save the workbook as *Extract 1 Modified*.
3. Open the *Top 10 Sales Representatives.ppt* presentation on your Data Disk using PowerPoint.
4. Save the presentation as *Top 15.ppt*.
5. Link the Top 10 Chart to the first slide in the presentation by using Copy and Paste Special, then selecting Paste <u>l</u>ink.

6. Resize and reposition the chart as necessary.
7. Click the Excel application button on the taskbar.
8. Modify the Chart Source Data to include the top 15 representatives.
9. Rename the tab as Top 15.
10. Remove the chart title.
11. Click the PowerPoint application button on the taskbar.
12. Rename the Slide title as "Top 15 Sales Representatives."
13. Print the slide from PowerPoint.
14. Close the PowerPoint application.
15. Close the workbook.

Exercise 3

1. Open the *Warehouse Inventory* workbook on your Data Disk.
2. Save the workbook as *Warehouse Inventory Modified*.
3. Sort the list by Part No.
4. Select the range A4:F16 and click the Copy button on the Standard toolbar.
5. Open the Word application.
6. Open the *Letter to Warehouse Division Manager.doc* on your Data Disk.
7. Save the Word document as *Letter with Data.doc*.
8. Insert a blank line between the first and second paragraphs of the letter.
9. Use Paste Special from the Edit menu to embed the data.
10. Reposition the embedded object as necessary.
11. Double-click the embedded object to make the following modifications:
    a. Change the price of item 1020 to $29.95.
    b. Change the quantity of item 3001 to 500.
    c. Center column E.
    d. Turn off display of gridlines using the Options dialog box from the Tools menu.
12. Print and save the letter.

Exercise 4

1. Open the *Letter with Data.doc* that you created in Exercise 4, and delete the embedded object.

2. In the Excel file *Warehouse Inventory Modified*, copy the range A4:F16.

3. In Word, use Paste Special to create a linked object in the document.

4. Double-click the link object to edit the data as follows:

   a. Center column E.

   b. Change the price of item 1020 to $35.95.

   c. Change the quantity of item 3001 to 750.

   d. Select the range A5:A16 and left-justify the range.

5. Save the workbook.

6. Save the Word document as *Letter with Linked Data.doc* and print it.

7. Close the workbook and the Word document.

Exercise 5

1. Open the *Work Files Manager* workbook on your Data Disk.

2. Add hyperlinks to each of the bevel objects pointing to the corresponding files on your Data Disk.

3. Save the file as *Work Files Manager Revised*.

4. Save the file as a Web page by clicking Save as Web Page on the File menu. In the Save As dialog box, do the following:

   a. Change the Web page title to Work Files Manager.

   b. Change the filename to *Work Files Manager*.

   c. Click the Save button.

5. Open your Internet browser.

6. Open the *Work Files Manager.htm* file that you just saved by clicking the File menu. Select Open, then click the Browse button and locate your file.

7. Test the hyperlinks, then print the Web page and close your browser and any files you opened.

Exercise 6

1. Use the *Month Calendar* template on your Data Disk to create a new calendar workbook. (*Hint:* In the Open dialog box, select All Microsoft Excel files in the Files of type: box.)

2. Enter the correct dates for the current month.

3. Modify the calendar title in cell A1 to display the current month.

4. Modify the cell shading to correspond to the current month.

5. Select the calendar area.

6. Save the calendar as a Web page with interactivity. Name the Web page *Calendar Web Page.htm*.

7. Print the workbook, then close it.

Exercise 7

1. Open the *Calendar Web Page.htm* file in your browser.
2. Add at least five appointments to the calendar.
3. Click the Export to Excel button in the browser to create a copy of the appointments.
4. Save the workbook as an Excel workbook named *Calendar Export* and print it.
5. In the browser window, click the Copy button on the toolbar directly above the table.
6. In a new Excel workbook, click the Paste button.
7. Save the workbook as *Calendar Copy* and print it.
8. Close the browser.
9. In Excel, click the Open button, select the HTML file *Calendar Web Page*, click the list arrow next to Open, then click Open in Microsoft Excel.
10. Save the workbook as an Excel file named *Final Calendar* and print it. (*Hint:* In the Save As dialog box, click the Save as type: list arrow and select Microsoft Excel Workbook.)
11. Close all open workbooks.

Exercise 8

1. Open the *Extract 1* workbook that you created in Exercise 1.
2. Send the chart as the body of an e-mail message to a classmate.
3. You should receive a similar message from a classmate. Print the e-mail message if your e-mail program is capable of displaying HTML mail.
4. Close the workbook without saving changes.

Case Projects

Project 1

As a mortgage officer, you want to provide the best possible service to your clients. One tool that you find helpful is a mortgage loan calculator, which calculates the monthly payment for a loan at a given percentage. (*Hint:* Use Excel Help to find out how to use the PMT functions.) Use Excel to create an interactive Web page where visitors to your site can input a loan amount, term in months, and interest rate and then calculate a monthly payment and total interest. Save the workbook as *MLC* and the Web page as *MLC.htm*.

Project 2

You are a busy stockbroker. In an effort to drum up investment business, you decide to send a letter to your clients showing the recent results of several stocks that have been performing well lately. Use the Internet to research two or three companies that might pique your clients' interest. Create a workbook to record high/low/close prices for each stock over the last week. Save the workbook as *Stock Prices*. Create a chart for each stock and link the charts to your letter. Print the letter and save the document as *Stock Letter*.

Project 3

You are the assistant to the president of a large advertising company. One of your responsibilities is to prepare a monthly report showing the amounts collected from your five largest clients. Create a workbook with fictitious data for 10 clients over the last three months. Sort the data by totals for the quarter to find your five largest clients. Create a chart of the data for these clients. Save the workbook as *Client Data*. Working in PowerPoint, create a new slide show. Link the chart from your workbook to the first slide. Link the data, including all 10 clients, to the second slide. Save the presentation as *Clients.ppt*.

Project 4

You are the personnel director for a large firm. You have been keeping a list of employee data, including first and last names, ages, phone extensions, and departments in an Excel workbook. Because the list keeps growing larger, you decide to maintain this information in an Access database. Create a workbook containing data for 20 fictitious employees. Save the workbook as *Personnel Data*. In Access, create a new, blank database and import the data from this newly created workbook.

Project 5

Use the Internet to locate a table of data displaying current stock prices for Microsoft (stock symbol: MSFT). Select the table in your browser and drag it into a new Excel workbook. Save the workbook as *Imported Stock Price*.

Project 6

As an investment advisor for a small mutual fund that caters to first-time investors, you want to help your clients see how ups and downs in the stock market have affected their investments. Create a worksheet with an initial investment of 250 shares purchased at a price of $40 per share. Create a formula to calculate the value of the investment. Save the workbook as *Investment*. Next, save the workbook as an interactive Web page called *Investment Interactive*. Test your Web page in a browser by changing the price of the shares (the calculated value of the investment should change).

Project 7

As a travel broker, you want to encourage your existing clients to travel more often. This month, you are featuring a special on travel to Europe. Create an advertisement in Excel using travel-oriented clip art objects. Use the Internet to look up the current exchange rate between U.S. dollars and the euro. Include this information as part of your advertisement. Save the worksheet as a Web page (not interactive) called *Travel to Europe*.

Project 8

You and a colleague work together to record NFL football scores for the local newspaper. Prepare a workbook including two team names, column labels for four quarters, plus a total column. Add a formula in the total column that will sum the total number of points scored by each team. Save the workbook as *NFL Score*. Route the workbook to your colleague, who will then fill in the score (using fictitious data or by looking up the score of a recent NFL game on the Internet) and return the workbook to you. Save the final workbook as *NFL Score Final*.

Chapter Overview

Excel features a rich set of drawing tools that you can use to enhance worksheets or create diagrams. Start with AutoShapes, lines, text boxes, WordArt, and clip art. Set your creativity loose as you apply shadows, line styles, fill effects, and 3-D effects, including lighting and surface type, to create an endless variety of custom drawing objects.

Learning Objectives

- ▶ Use clip art and AutoShapes
- ▶ Add and modify text and line objects
- ▶ Add shadow and 3-D effects to objects
- ▶ Modify stack order and group objects
- ▶ Create WordArt

Case profile

Sweet Tooth's central office uses a computer network to help company employees communicate and share data. You have been asked to draw a network diagram, illustrating how each of the central office computers and peripherals is connected to the company server. Also, you are responsible for creating a summary page, using last quarter's sales data, to include in the company's quarterly newsletter.

chapter

QUICK TIP

C To delete clip art or an AutoShape object, click it to select it, then press the DELETE key.

6.a Using Clip Art and AutoShapes

Excel's drawing tools help you create a variety of useful diagrams and enhance charts. Instead of drawing complex graphics, such as a computer or a person riding a bicycle, you can insert clip art. **Clip art** is ready-made graphics you can insert in a worksheet. Office 2000 uses a program called **Clip Gallery** to index clip art, making it easier to find the graphic you want to use. **AutoShapes** are simple outlined shapes, such as squares, circles, arrows, and banners, that you can insert in your worksheet. Another special AutoShape, called a connector line, helps you create diagrams.

Inserting Clip Art Objects

Using clip art, you create a network diagram for Sweet Tooth's central office. A network diagram is useful as a map showing how computers on the network communicate with one another. To open the data file used in this chapter:

Step 1	**Start**	Excel
Step 2	**Open**	the *Sweet Tooth Computer Equipment Inventory* workbook on your Data Disk

This workbook contains information about the computer equipment used in Sweet Tooth's central office.

Step 3	**Edit**	cell A1 to read "Central Office Computer Equipment Diagram"
Step 4	**Save**	the file as *Sweet Tooth Computer Equipment Diagram*

This file has been zoomed out to 75% to view more of the worksheet area. Several objects have already been inserted in this worksheet, but a printer is missing from the diagram. You insert a printer using the Clip Gallery. To open the Clip Gallery:

Step 1	**Click**	the Drawing button on the Standard toolbar

The Drawing toolbar appears. (If it disappears, click the Drawing button again.) The Drawing toolbar might appear along the bottom of the Excel window or in the middle of the screen.

MOUSE TIP

C To zoom a worksheet, click the Zoom list arrow `100%` on the Standard toolbar. Percentages less than 100% zoom out to display more of the worksheet. Percentages greater than 100% zoom in to display less of the worksheet.

| Step 2 | **Click** | the Insert Clip Art button  on the Drawing toolbar |

The Clip Gallery opens, displaying the Insert ClipArt dialog box.

| Step 3 | **Click** | the Maximize button  to maximize the Insert ClipArt dialog box |

Your screen should look similar to Figure 6-1.

MENU TIP

You can insert clip art from the Insert menu. Point to Picture, then click Clip Art to open the Insert ClipArt dialog box.

FIGURE 6-1
Clip Gallery

INTERNET TIP

To access thousands more clips, click the Clips Online button at the top of the Clip Gallery. This opens your browser and brings you to Microsoft's Clip Gallery Live Web site.

The Clip Gallery indexes clip art by allowing you to add categories and keyword information to a graphic file. Its categories display related clips. For example, the Networking category displays clip art of several computers and computer peripherals, such as printers, scanners, and a CD-ROM drive. All of the clips in the *Sweet Tooth Computer Equipment Diagram* worksheet came from the Networking category. You can search for graphics by keyword, or you can browse categories by clicking a category button.

To search for a printer clip:

Step 1	**Click**	in the Search for clips: box
Step 2	**Key**	printer
Step 3	**Press**	the ENTER key

QUICK TIP

Create your own clip art category by clicking the New Category button in the Insert ClipArt dialog box. Enter a name for your new category. Right-click the clip you want to add to your new category, then select Clip Properties. On the Categories tab, click the check box next to your new category.

All clips with the keyword "printer" are displayed. The yellow clip is perfect for your diagram. To insert the clip:

| Step 1 | **Move** | the pointer over the clip |

The clip appears to pop up, and a ScreenTip displays the clip name, file size, and graphic file type. See Figure 6-2.

FIGURE 6-2
Using the ScreenTip to See a Clip Name

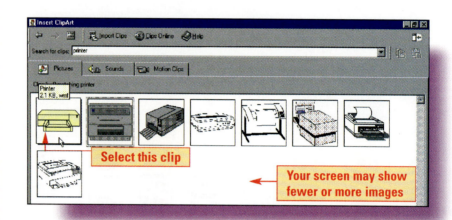

QUICK TIP

You can also drag a clip onto a worksheet. If the Clip Gallery window is maximized, start dragging the clip. The Clip Gallery shrinks to a smaller window, allowing you to drop the clip on your worksheet. The Clip Gallery window remains open, and its icon appears in the taskbar until you close it.

| Step 2 | **Click** | the yellow printer clip |

A pop-up menu of icons appears.

| Step 3 | **Click** | the Insert clip icon (the top icon) |
| Step 4 | **Click** | the Close button 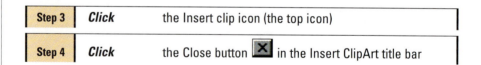 in the Insert ClipArt title bar |

The Clip Gallery closes and the worksheet appears. The printer clip art image appears in the upper-left corner of the worksheet.

Next, you need to resize the clips and move the printer clip into position.

Scaling and Moving Objects

You can reposition and resize drawing objects. The clips are too large for the area on your worksheet. To resize the objects:

| Step 1 | **Press & Hold** | the SHIFT key |

Now you can select multiple objects for editing.

| Step 2 | **Click** | each of the clips on the worksheet (a total of six) |

Selection handles appear around the objects to show that they are selected.

| Step 3 | **Right-click** | one of the objects |
| Step 4 | **Click** | Format AutoShape |

The Format AutoShape dialog box opens.

| Step 5 | **Click** | the Size tab |

The dialog box on your screen should look similar to Figure 6-3.

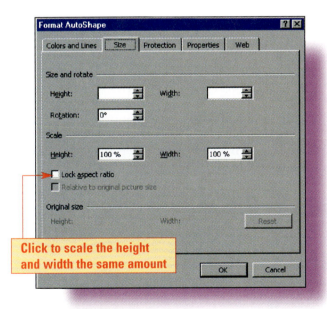

| Step 6 | **Click** | the Lock aspect ratio check box |

When you modify the height or width of an object with the lock aspect ratio turned on, the object scales an equal amount in the other direction.

| Step 7 | **Double-click** | the entry in the Height: box in the Scale section |
| Step 8 | **Key** | 65 in the Height: box |

MENU TIP

To open the Format AutoShape dialog box, click Format, then click AutoShape.

QUICK TIP

To open the Format AutoShape dialog box, select an object or objects for editing, then press the CTRL + 1 keys.

FIGURE 6-3
Size Tab of the Format AutoShape Dialog Box

MOUSE TIP

If you need to remove an object from a multiple object selection, press and hold the SHIFT key, then click the object that you want to remove.

chapter six

MOUSE TIP

Move an AutoShape with text by dragging its border.

QUICK TIP

Resize an object by dragging any of the resize handles. Press and hold the CTRL key to resize the object from the center.

Step 9 | **Press** | the TAB key

Notice that the Width: box automatically adjusts to 65%.

Step 10 | **Click** | OK

All of the objects are scaled to 65% of their original size.

Step 11 | **Press** | the ESC key to deselect the drawing objects

Now you must move the printer object above its description in cells G26:H26. To move an object:

Step 1 | **Move** | the mouse pointer over the printer clip

The mouse pointer changes to a move object pointer.

Step 2 | **Drag** | the clip above row 26 in columns G and H

See Figure 6-4. As you insert drawing objects in a worksheet, Excel names the objects to keep track of them. The Name Box displays the name of the selected clip. Next, you add connector lines to the diagram.

FIGURE 6-4
Printer Clip Repositioned

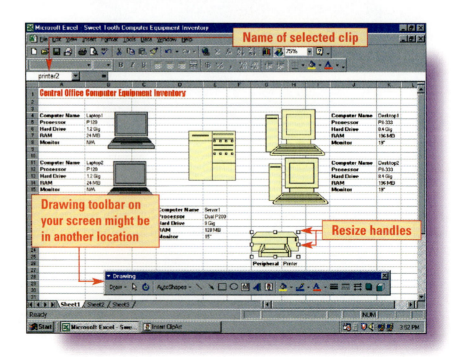

MOUSE TIP

To move an object in a straight line or in 15-degree increments, press and hold the SHIFT key while dragging the object.

Drawing in Excel   EL 7

Inserting AutoShapes

To diagram Sweet Tooth's network properly, you must connect the clips using connector lines. A **connector line** is a special type of AutoShape, which automatically snaps to connection points on an object. Connection lines, unlike line objects, stay attached to an object even when the object is moved. Other categories of AutoShapes include arrows, callouts, stars and banners, and flowchart symbols. To add connector lines:

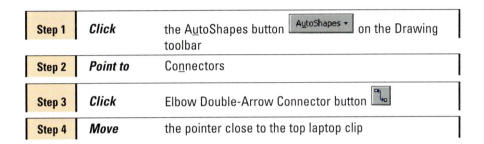

MENU TIP

You can use the AutoShapes toolbar to insert AutoShapes. To display the AutoShapes toolbar, click the Insert menu, point to Picture, then click AutoShapes.

As you move the pointer near a clip, the pointer changes to the connection pointer ⊕ and blue connection points surround the edges of the clip. See Figure 6-5.

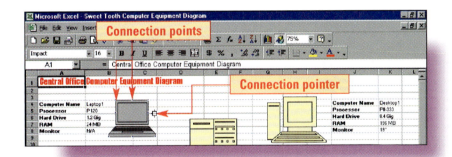

FIGURE 6-5
Using Connection Points

Step 5	Click	the middle-right connection point on the first laptop clip
Step 6	Move	the pointer to the server clip
Step 7	Click	the middle-left connection point on the server clip

Your screen should look similar to Figure 6-6. When a connector line is attached, a red square appears at the end of the line. When a connector line is unattached, a green square is displayed. You can drag the yellow adjustment handle to change the position of the line.

FIGURE 6-6
Completed Connector Line

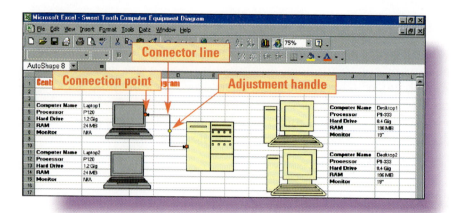

| Step 8 | *Repeat* | steps 1–7 to attach each of the clips to the server clip |

Refer to Figure 6-7 as you draw your lines.

FIGURE 6-7
Final Diagram

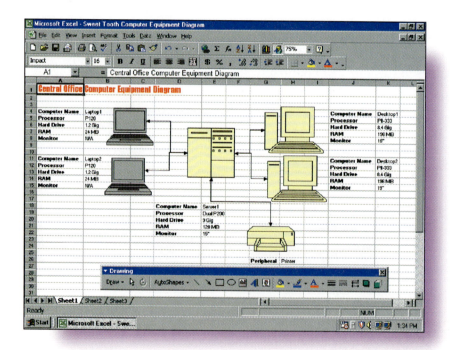

QUICK TIP

You can copy objects by using either the Copy and Paste commands on the Edit menu or the Copy and Paste buttons on the Standard toolbar. You can also make a copy by pressing and holding the CTRL key as you drag an object.

| Step 9 | *Press* | the ESC key to deselect the connector line |

Now that you have finished drawing your diagram, you should print a copy. To print the network diagram:

| Step 1 | *Click* | the Print Preview button on the Standard toolbar |

The print options in this file have already been set to fit a single page using landscape orientation.

Step 2	Click	Print on the Print Preview toolbar
Step 3	Click	OK
Step 4	Save & Close	your workbook

Your next assignment is to create a page for Sweet Tooth's company newsletter containing sales information from the first quarter of 1999.

6.b Adding and Modifying Text and Line Objects

You can add other objects, such as lines and text boxes, to enhance a worksheet or chart. Text can also be added to most AutoShapes.

Every quarter, Sweet Tooth sends a newsletter out to each employee. You are responsible for developing the page that shows the final sales figures for each region and division. You decide to use Excel's drawing tools to create a more interesting newsletter page. To open the workbook:

| Step 1 | Open | the *Sweet Tooth Q1 Results* workbook on your Data Disk |
| Step 2 | Save | the workbook as *Sweet Tooth Q1 Results Newsletter* |

This file contains the data and several drawing objects that you modify to create the newsletter page.

Adding Text to AutoShape Objects

You can add AutoShape objects to a worksheet or chart, then include informative text as part of the object. For Sweet Tooth's newsletter, you would like to highlight the accomplishments of the Central Region by using an AutoShape with text. To insert an AutoShape:

| Step 1 | Click | the AutoShapes button [AutoShapes ▼] on the Drawing toolbar |
| Step 2 | Point to | Stars and Banners |

> **MENU TIP**
>
> You may find it difficult to draw on top of cells while the gridlines remain on. You can turn gridlines on or off by clicking Options on the Tools menu. On the View tab in the Options dialog box, click the Gridlines check box in the Window options group to select it.

> **QUICK TIP**
>
> To change an AutoShape to another AutoShape, select the shape in the worksheet and click the Draw button on the Drawing toolbar. Point to Change AutoShape and select a new AutoShape.

| Step 3 | Click | the Vertical Scroll button |
| Step 4 | Drag | from cell A7 to cell A11, as shown in Figure 6-8 |

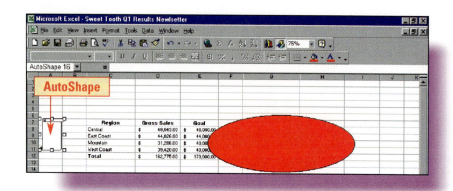

FIGURE 6-8
Creating an AutoShape

MOUSE TIP

Many AutoShapes have an object handle that lets you modify certain characteristics unique to that particular AutoShape. For example, the scroll adjustment handle lets you change the size of the scroll. Select the scroll object, then drag the yellow diamond-shaped handle down to increase the size of the scroll or up to decrease the size of the scroll.

Step 5	Right-click	the AutoShape
Step 6	Click	Add Text
Step 7	Key	Highest Gross <ENTER> Sales Region!

Press the ENTER key between "Gross" and "Sales."

| Step 8 | Press | the ESC key to accept the text entry |

Using the Format AutoShape dialog box, you can change the formatting of an AutoShape object.

Modifying a Text Object

You would like the size of the scroll to match the size of the text more closely. One way to do this is to resize the object by dragging the resize handles. In addition, text objects can be resized to fit automatically. To resize a text object:

| Step 1 | Double-click | the Vertical Scroll object border |

The Format AutoShape dialog box opens.

QUICK TIP

To change font and alignment settings for text added to AutoShapes, select the object, then open the Format AutoShape dialog box.

| Step 2 | Click | the Alignment tab |
| Step 3 | Click | the Horizontal: list arrow |

Drawing in Excel **EL 11**

Step 4	Click	Center
Step 5	Click	the A̲utomatic size check box
Step 6	Click	OK
Step 7	Press	the ESC key to deselect the object

The text is centered horizontally in the scroll, and the scroll is resized to fit the text.

Inserting and Modifying Line Objects

You can use lines to indicate relationships between cells or as borderlines between different areas of a worksheet. Lines can appear in different styles, such as dashed, dotted, or solid. In addition, you can set different line thicknesses and choose from among six arrowheads for each end of the line. You decide to draw a line from the scroll object to the Central Region name. To draw a line:

| Step 1 | Click | the Arrow button on the Drawing toolbar |

The Arrow tool draws a line with an arrow style already selected.

| Step 2 | Drag | just right of the scroll object (cell B8) to the left of the text "Central" in cell C8 |

You have added an arrow line object. To modify a line object:

Step 1	Verify	that the arrow line object is selected
Step 2	Click	the Line Color list arrow  on the Drawing toolbar
Step 3	Click	the Blue square
Step 4	Click	the Line Style button ≡ on the Drawing toolbar
Step 5	Click	3 pt
Step 6	Press	the ESC key to deselect the object

Next, you add special effects to objects in your worksheet.

> **QUICK TIP**
>
> Text boxes are useful when you want to add informative text. You can insert text boxes by clicking the Text Box button 🅰 on the Drawing toolbar.

> **MOUSE TIP**
>
> You can add or change arrowheads on either end of a line object. Select the line, then click the Arrow Style button ⇶ on the Drawing toolbar to select one of the arrow styles.

chapter
six

6.c Adding Shadow and 3-D Effects to Objects

You can add several effects to drawing objects, such as a shadow and three-dimensional (3-D) effects. You apply these effects to other drawing objects in your newsletter.

Adding Shadow to an Object

Adding a shadow makes a drawing object appear to float over the page. This option can create a dramatic effect when used in conjunction with text boxes and other objects. You decide to add a shadow to the scroll object. To add a shadow effect:

Step 1	**Press & Hold**	the SHIFT key
Step 2	**Click**	the scroll object

The selection box around the object consists of a series of dotted lines. By pressing the SHIFT key at the same time that you click an object with text in it, you select the entire object. If you click the center of the object without pressing the SHIFT key, the selection box is made up of slanted lines; you can then type in the selection box, but the object is not selected.

Step 3	**Click**	the Shadow button on the Drawing toolbar
Step 4	**Click**	the Shadow Style 6 button

Another way to add visual interest to drawing objects is to add a 3-D effect. In the next section, you use this effect to modify the sun object on the worksheet.

Creating and Modifying 3-D Shapes

Adding a 3-D effect to drawing objects gives the illusion of depth. You can then specify the depth, perspective, lighting, and surface qualities of this 3-D effect. You would like the sun object to appear as if it were three-dimensional. To create a 3-D object:

Step 1	**Click**	the sun object located in cell C17 to select it

---

MOUSE TIP

You can change the fill color of an object by clicking the Fill Color list arrow on the Drawing toolbar. To make an object transparent, click No Fill.

QUICK TIP

You can modify shadow settings, such as the shadow color and position, by displaying the Shadow Settings toolbar. To display the Shadow Settings toolbar, click the Shadow button on the Drawing toolbar, then click Shadow Settings.

Drawing in Excel **EL 13**

Step 2	**Click**	the Zoom list arrow `100%` on the Standard toolbar
Step 3	**Click**	Selection

This option zooms the worksheet to the selected object or area.

Step 4	**Click**	the 3-D button on the Drawing toolbar
Step 5	**Click**	the 3-D Style 1 button

> **MOUSE TIP**
>
> To rotate an object, select it, click the Free Rotate button on the Drawing toolbar, then drag a selection handle.

Your screen should look similar to Figure 6-9.

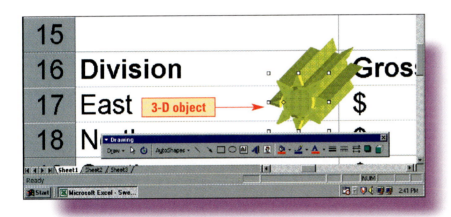

FIGURE 6-9
3-D Effect Applied to an Object

> **MOUSE TIP**
>
> Change the 3-D projection color by clicking the 3-D Color list arrow on the 3-D Settings toolbar.

To modify 3-D settings such as object tilt, lighting, surface, depth, and direction, you use the 3-D Settings toolbar. To modify 3-D settings:

Step 1	**Click**	the 3-D button on the Drawing toolbar
Step 2	**Click**	3-D Settings

The 3-D Settings toolbar appears.

Step 3	**Click**	the Depth button on the 3-D Settings toolbar
Step 4	**Drag**	to select the number in the Custom: box
Step 5	**Key**	24 in the Custom: box
Step 6	**Click**	the Depth button to accept the changes

MOUSE TIP

Sometimes it is useful to flip an object horizontally or vertically. To flip an object, select it, then click the D<u>r</u>aw button on the Drawing toolbar. Point to Rotate or Flip, then click Flip <u>H</u>orizontal or Flip <u>V</u>ertical, depending on which way you want the object to turn.

You have reduced the sun's 3-D depth. You can also control the lighting direction and brightness.

| Step 7 | *Click* | the Lighting button on the 3-D Settings toolbar |

The lighting palette shows the currently selected light as an indented button.

| Step 8 | *Click* | the upper-left corner light |

The object displays new shading to reflect the new light source direction.

Another factor that influences your lighting choice is the surface. Table 6-1 describes each of the 3-D surface settings.

TABLE 6-1
3-D Surface Settings Descriptions

3-D Surface Setting	Description
Wireframe	Draws an outline of the object's edges. Because there are no surfaces with this setting, the lighting selection has no effect on the object.
Matte	All surfaces have a uniform, nonreflective surface. Matte is the default surface.
Plastic	All surfaces have a dull reflective quality.
Metal	All surfaces have a shiny reflective quality.

QUICK TIP

You may have to experiment with some of the 3-D settings, such as lighting and surface, to achieve the look you want.

| Step 9 | *Click* | the Close button in the title bar of the 3-D Settings toolbar |

Figure 6-10 shows the finished 3-D sun object.

FIGURE 6-10
Modified 3-D Object

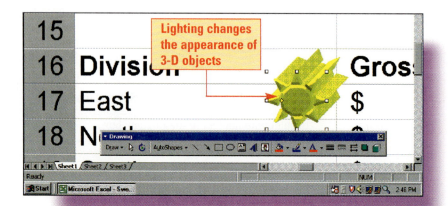

MOUSE TIP

To toggle the 3-D settings on and off, click the 3-D On/Off button on the Drawing toolbar.

Step 10	Click	the Zoom list arrow 100% on the Standard toolbar
Step 11	Click	75%
Step 12	Press	the ESC key to deselect the sun object
Step 13	Press	the CTRL + HOME keys to move the active cell to A1 and scroll the worksheet up

Next, you modify the stack order of the oval object on your worksheet to display the object underneath it.

6.d Modifying Stack Order and Grouping Objects

As you add drawing objects to a worksheet, the new objects are stacked on top of previously inserted drawing objects. You can modify the **stack order** to make one object appear in front of or behind other objects, regardless of the order in which you inserted them in the worksheet or chart. You can also group objects to create a larger object. This option is useful when you must move several objects but want to maintain certain spacing, or when you need to apply formatting to several objects simultaneously.

Modifying a Shape's Stack Order

In your worksheet, an oval AutoShape has been inserted on top of a bevel AutoShape object you can't see. You want to move the oval behind the bevel by changing the oval's stack order. To change an object's stack order:

Step 1	Right-click	the red oval shape
Step 2	Point to	O<u>r</u>der
Step 3	Click	Send to Bac<u>k</u>

The oval moves to the back, and the bevel shape that was previously positioned behind the oval appears.

You want both of the shapes to stay together. To do this, you need to create a group.

> **QUICK TIP**
>
> The direction settings determine the direction of the 3-D effect. You can also set the type of projection. **Perspective projection** uses a vanishing point to provide the illusion of the object becoming smaller as it moves farther away. **Parallel projection** maintains the same size for both ends of the object.

> **MENU TIP**
>
> To change the order of an object, click the D<u>r</u>aw button on the Drawing toolbar and point to O<u>r</u>der. Then click the desired order option.

Grouping Shapes

When an arrangement of shapes should stay together, you can create a group. A **group** consists of two or more objects that behave as a single object during moving, copying, formatting, and resizing operations. To create a new group:

Step 1	Verify	that the oval shape is still selected
Step 2	Press & Hold	the SHIFT key
Step 3	Click	the bevel shape
Step 4	Right-click	the oval shape
Step 5	Point to	Grouping
Step 6	Click	Group

One set of selection handles appears around the outer edges of the new group. You decide to line up this group with the right edge of the values in column I. To move the group:

Step 1	Drag	the group to the right
Step 2	Drop	the group when its right edge lines up with the gridline separating columns I and J

Your screen should look similar to Figure 6-11.

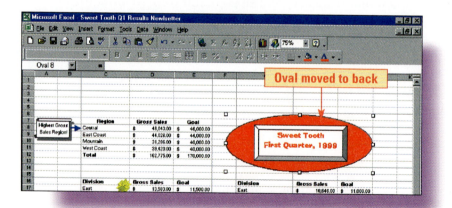

FIGURE 6-11
Repositioned Grouped Object

Step 3	Press	the ESC key to deselect the group

The only thing missing is a logo that will draw attention to your newsletter page. In the next section, you learn to use WordArt.

MENU TIP

To create a group of objects, click the Draw button on the Drawing toolbar, then click Group.

QUICK TIP

To modify one object in a group, you must ungroup the objects. Select the group, then click the Draw button on the Drawing toolbar. Click Ungroup, then select and modify the desired object. Click the Draw button again and click Regroup to recreate the group. You do not have to reselect all of the objects in the original group.

6.e Creating WordArt

Your newsletter page needs a strong logo to catch the reader's eye. WordArt is perfect for this application. **WordArt** is a special type of text object to which you can add custom fills and apply a variety of interesting shapes. Using any of 30 preset styles, you can modify WordArt settings to create an endless variety of WordArt objects. A **WordArt style** is a preset combination of shape, color fill, alignment, and character spacing settings. To create a WordArt title:

| Step 1 | Click | the Insert WordArt button on the Drawing toolbar |

The WordArt Gallery appears, as shown in Figure 6-12.

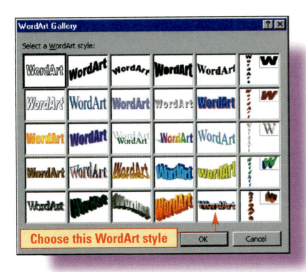

FIGURE 6-12
WordArt Gallery

> **MOUSE TIP**
>
> You can see the name of each button on the WordArt toolbar by moving the pointer over it.

| Step 2 | Click | the WordArt style located one cell to the left of the lower-right corner |
| Step 3 | Click | OK |

The Edit WordArt Text dialog box opens.

| Step 4 | Key | Another Record Quarter! |
| Step 5 | Click | OK |

The WordArt object appears on your worksheet, along with the WordArt toolbar. The WordArt toolbar includes tools to modify

> **MOUSE TIP**
>
> You can copy formatting attributes from one object to another by using Format Painter. Select the source object, then click the Format Painter button on the Standard toolbar. Next, click the object you want to format.

chapter six

MOUSE TIP

Drag the yellow adjustment handle to modify the WordArt shape. For example, a WordArt object with a curved style uses this handle to control the amount of curve. A WordArt object with a straight style uses the handle to slant the text.

WordArt settings, such as style, shape, text height, alignment, and character spacing. To change the shape of a WordArt object:

Step 1	Click	the WordArt Shape button on the WordArt toolbar
Step 2	Click	the Arch Up (Curve) button
Step 3	Move	the pointer over the WordArt object
Step 4	Drag	the object to center it visually at the top of your worksheet
Step 5	Press	the ESC key to deselect the WordArt object

Your worksheet should look similar to Figure 6-13.

FIGURE 6-13
Final Newsletter Page

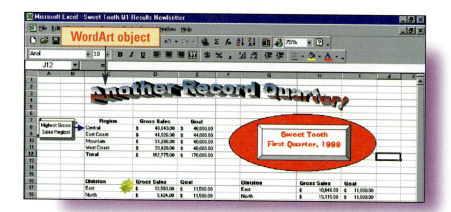

With your newsletter page nearly complete, you preview it and make any adjustments. To preview and print the newsletter page:

| Step 1 | Click | the Print Preview button on the Standard toolbar |

Satisfied with the object's placement, you print the worksheet.

Step 2	Click	the Print button on the Print Preview toolbar
Step 3	Click	OK
Step 4	Save & Close	your workbook

Your newsletter report is sure to be a big success!

QUICK TIP

If you have trouble centering a WordArt object visually, try using Print Preview to see how your page will look when printed.

Summary

- Use the Microsoft Clip Gallery to insert clip art symbols. Locate clip art by opening a category or by searching for keywords.
- Scale objects by dragging their resize handles or by using the Size tab of the Format AutoShape dialog box.
- Connect objects using connector lines. Connector lines automatically route around objects and stay attached when you move either connected object. Choose from a variety of connector styles, including straight, elbow, and curved.
- AutoShapes include a variety of shapes, such as arrows, callouts, stars and banners, and flowchart symbols.
- Transform one AutoShape into another AutoShape by using the Change AutoShape command on the Draw menu on the Drawing toolbar.
- Fit AutoShapes to text using the Alignment tab of the Format AutoShape dialog box.
- Line objects can use a variety of styles, weights, and arrowhead styles.
- Objects can be copied, rotated, and flipped. Press the CTRL key while dragging an object, or use the Copy and Paste buttons to copy an object.
- Add color fill to an object by using the Colors and Lines tab of the Format AutoShape dialog box.
- Add shadows to drawing objects to make them appear as if they are floating over the page.
- Create 3-D objects for visual interest with different lighting, surface, and depth effects.
- Objects are assigned an order (back to front) with the newest objects appearing at the front or on top of other objects. You can change the order to display objects in any order you prefer.
- Objects can be grouped to maintain alignment or to apply formatting.
- WordArt objects enable you to add interesting text effects to titles. In addition to applying different text styles and color fills, you can modify the shape of WordArt objects.

chapter six

Commands Review

Action	Menu Bar	Shortcut Menu	Toolbar	Keyboard
View Drawing toolbar	View, Toolbars, Drawing		[icon]	ALT + V, T
Open Insert ClipArt dialog box	Insert, Picture, Clip Art		[icon]	ALT + I, P, C
Open Format AutoShape dialog box	Format, AutoShape	Format AutoShape		ALT + O, O CTRL + 1
View AutoShapes toolbar	Insert, Picture, AutoShape			ALT + I, P, A
Insert AutoShapes			AutoShapes ▾	
Insert Text box			[icon]	
Change AutoShape			Draw ▾, then Change AutoShape	
Insert line object			[icon]	
Insert arrow object			[icon]	
Change line color			[icon]	
Change line style			[icon]	
Change dash style			[icon]	
Change arrow style			[icon]	
Deselect objects				ESC
Rotate objects			[icon]	
Flip objects			Draw ▾, then Rotate or Flip	
Insert WordArt	Insert, Picture, WordArt		[icon]	ALT + I, P, W
Add or modify color fill			[icon]	
Add shadow to an object			[icon]	
Create 3-D objects			[icon]	
View 3-D Drawing toolbar			3-D [icon], 3-D Settings	
Change stack order		Order	Draw ▾, then Order	
Group objects		Grouping, Group	Draw ▾, then Group	
Ungroup objects		Grouping, Ungroup	Draw ▾, then Ungroup	
Zoom	View, Zoom		100% ▾	ALT + V, Z

Concepts Review

Circle the correct answer.

1. **To select multiple objects for editing, press and hold the _____ key while selecting objects.**
   - [a] SHIFT
   - [b] END
   - [c] CTRL
   - [d] ALT

2. **To move an object in a straight line (or in 15-degree increments), press and hold the _____ key while dragging the object.**
   - [a] SHIFT
   - [b] END
   - [c] CTRL
   - [d] ALT

3. **To deselect an object, press the _____ key.**
   - [a] SHIFT
   - [b] ESC
   - [c] CTRL
   - [d] ALT

4. **Connection lines are more useful than line objects when diagramming because:**
   - [a] you can't change the arrow style of a line object.
   - [b] connection lines stay attached even when objects are moved.
   - [c] once a line object is drawn, you cannot reposition it.
   - [d] both b and c.

5. **WordArt is:**
   - [a] a text box with special formatting applied.
   - [b] an AutoShape object with text added.
   - [c] a special type of text object that uses fills and shapes.
   - [d] text in a cell with special formatting applied.

6. **Which of the following is not a property of lines?**
   - [a] line style
   - [b] dash style
   - [c] arrow style
   - [d] bold, italics, and normal style

7. **Which of the following is *not* a valid method of copying objects?**
   - [a] Press CTRL while dragging an object.
   - [b] Use Copy and Paste from the Edit menu.
   - [c] Use the Copy and Paste buttons on the Standard toolbar.
   - [d] All are valid.

8. **WordArt styles do *not* include:**
   - [a] line style settings.
   - [b] shape.
   - [c] color fill.
   - [d] alignment.

9. **After you add text to an AutoShape:**
   - [a] you cannot reformat the text.
   - [b] you must reformat the text to fit the size of the AutoShape.
   - [c] you can automatically adjust the size of the AutoShape to fit the text.
   - [d] the text stays in the same cell even if you move the AutoShape.

10. **Which of the following is *not* a 3-D setting?**
    - [a] depth
    - [b] lighting
    - [c] shape
    - [d] surface

Circle **T** if the statement is true or **F** if the statement is false.

T **F** 1. You must turn off gridlines before using drawing tools.
T **F** 2. AutoShapes cannot be resized.
T F 3. When adding connector lines, tiny blue connection points appear when the pointer is moved close to an object.
T **F** 4. A green handle on a connector indicates that the connector is attached to a connection point.
T F 5. A red handle on a connector indicates that the connector is attached to a connection point.
perspective **T** F 6. Parallel projection is used when a 3-D projection should disappear in the distance.
T **F** 7. You can modify the width of a line object, but you cannot change it from a solid line to a dashed line.
T F 8. You can change an object's stack order regardless of the order in which it was inserted into the drawing.
CTRL T **F** 9. The SHIFT key is used to copy objects when you use the drag-and-drop method.
SHIFT T **F** 10. The ALT key constrains rotation and movement angles to 15-degree increments.

Skills Review

Exercise 1

1. Start a new workbook.
2. Create the following shapes using AutoShapes:
   a. Rectangle
   b. Oval
   c. Triangle
   d. Cross
   e. Star
3. Change all of the objects to 3-D objects.
4. Change the lighting to upper-left corner.
5. Change the depth of all the shapes to 72 pt.
6. Change the 3-D color of the oval and triangle shape to turquoise.
7. Change the surface of the rectangle and cross object to wireframe.
8. Delete the star by clicking it to select it, and then pressing the DELETE key.
9. Use the Curved Connector AutoShape to connect the four objects together.
10. Save the workbook as *3-D Objects* and print it.

Exercise 2

1. Start a new workbook.
2. Open the Insert ClipArt dialog box.
3. Search for clips using the keywords related to picnicking. (*Hint:* Try food, picnic, and basket).

4. Using the ScreenTips to read the clip descriptions, insert the Seniors clip.

5. Change the fill color of the Seniors clip to Light Green.

6. Return to the Insert ClipArt dialog box and click the All Categories button (or press the ALT + HOME keys) to view the categories.

7. Scroll the category list and click the Food & Dining category.

8. Insert four clips of food that are likely to be found at a picnic. Place them around the clip you previously inserted. (If you don't have any additional food images in your Clip Gallery, use any other images you like.)

9. Use the Straight Arrow Connector to connect the Seniors clip in the middle with the four clips around it.

10. Save the file as *Picnic* and print it.

Exercise 3

1. Open the *Computer Price Chart* workbook on your Data Disk.

2. Display the Drawing toolbar, if necessary.

3. Add a Rectangular Callout AutoShape over the PII-266a system with the text "Biggest Price Drop!"

4. With the callout object selected, click the center alignment button on the Formatting toolbar to center the text.

5. Change the fill color to white.

6. Use the Format AutoShape dialog box to automatically size the callout shape to fit the text.

7. Add Shadow Style 6 to the callout.

8. Draw an arrow line from the callout to the Now price of the PII-266a system.

9. Save the workbook as *Computer Price Chart Revised* and print it.

Exercise 4

1. Open the *Business Transactions* workbook on your Data Disk.

2. Zoom in on the worksheet, if necessary.

3. Draw a line between the Total Income in cell C22 and cell E16.

4. Draw a line between the Total Distributions in cell K15 and cell F17.

5. Draw a line between the Total Expenses in cell D42 and cell F18.

6. Change the line style of all lines to 3pt.

7. Change the line color to lavender.

8. Change the arrow style to Arrow Style 7.

9. Zoom the worksheet to 50% if you changed it earlier.

10. Save the workbook as *Business Transactions Revised* and print it.

Exercise 5

1. Start a new workbook.

2. Create a new WordArt object using the style in the upper-left corner, with the text "WordArt Practice."

3. Click the Edit Text button on the WordArt toolbar.

4. Change the text to "Changing Text Even More." Press the ENTER key between each word.

5. Change the shape to Button (Pour).

6. Resize the WordArt object using the resize handle so that the shape is nearly a circle. An outline of the object shape will help you in this task.

7. Change the fill color to Dark Blue.

8. Save your file as *WordArt* and print it.

Exercise 6

1. Create a new workbook, if necessary.

2. Click the Insert ClipArt button on the Drawing toolbar.

3. Use Clip Art Help to read the What's new in Clip Gallery? section.

4. Find out how to create a new category and how to add clips to a category.

5. Create a new category called "My Favorites."

6. Search for a clip of George Washington.

7. Add the clip to your new category.

8. Delete the new My Favorites category. (*Hint:* Click the All Categories button, right-click the My Favorites category that you added, then click Delete Category.)

Exercise 7

1. Create a new workbook.

2. Using the Rectangle button on the Drawing toolbar, draw a box representing a house.

3. Add a brick pattern to the house.

4. Using more rectangles, add windows with a light blue fill color to the house.

5. Add a door with a window and a doorknob.

6. Using a triangle AutoShape, add a roof with a brown fill color.

7. Add a rectangle for a tree trunk with dark red fill color.

8. Using the Explosion 2 AutoShape, create the top of the tree with a green fill color.

9. Print your drawing and save the workbook as *House Drawing*.

Exercise 8

1. Create a new workbook.

2. Using lines and text boxes or callout AutoShapes, create a map providing driving directions to a notable location in your city, for example, your school, city hall, a state park, or a museum.

3. Print your worksheet and save the workbook as *Driving Directions*.

Case Projects

Project 1

You work for a mortgage company that is seeking ways to promote its low interest rates on home loans. Open the *Interest* workbook on your Data Disk. Using WordArt, AutoShapes with text, and clip art, create a newsletter-type document in Excel advertising a 6.9% interest rate. Target your newsletter toward first-time home buyers. Try searching for clip art associated with homes, saving money, and families. Save your workbook as *Interest Advertisement* and print it.

Project 2

You own a successful restaurant. You train your employees using a four-step system to serve clients. The steps are as follows: (1) Greet Customers; (2) Take the Order; (3) Prepare the Order; and (4) Collect the Amount Due. Using WordArt and curved connector lines, create a flowchart that you can use in training meetings to emphasize this system. You may need to resize the WordArt objects to fit on-screen. Print your worksheet, then save your workbook as *Serve System*.

Project 3

As the owner of a small beauty supply shop, you want to create a flier announcing a Valentine's Day sale on scissors and blow dryers. Be sure to mention that scissors are discounted 25% and blow dryers are discounted 30%. Use appropriate WordArt and clip art to advertise the sale. Save your workbook as *Beauty Supply Sale* and print it.

Project 4

You own a café. Unfortunately, dessert sales have dropped off in the last month. You decide to provide incentives to servers who sell a certain amount of desserts. Use one column to indicate the servers' target numbers. Use another column to hold the bonus associated with each of the target numbers. Using clip art and WordArt, create an ad to promote your sales incentive program. Save your workbook as *Dessert* and print it.

Project 5

Use the Web toolbar to browse the Internet for online shopping sites that make good use of graphics. Print three examples of effective graphics that make you want to buy from that site. Print three examples of sites from which you wouldn't make a purchase because of the graphics used to promote these stores.

Project 6

Use the Web toolbar to search the Internet for articles about reducing graphic file sizes for use in Web pages. Search for topics such as color bit depth, compression, and dithering. Write a three-paragraph summary of your findings. Include URLs for the sites you found. Save the document as *Web Graphics.doc*.

Project 7

You work for an interior design company creating layouts of office furniture. Use the Clip Gallery to insert clip art of office furniture. (*Hint:* Design an office space using the Office Layout category or search for the keyword *furniture*.) Save the workbook as *Office Layout* and print it.

Project 8

You work as a technical support engineer. Each day you receive calls from customers who are having problems opening Excel workbooks. To make it easier for you to do your job, create a trouble-shooting flowchart of questions you can ask to determine the source of the problem. Each question should have a Yes or No answer. If the answer is Yes, you ask the next question on your list; if the answer is No, include steps to solve the problem. Place each question and each solution set in its own text box, then connect the boxes using connectors. (If you like, you can use shapes from the Flowchart AutoShapes palette.) Save the workbook as *Troubleshooting*.

chapter six

Excel 2000

Using Worksheet Functions

Chapter Overview

Functions provide much of Excel's real calculating power. With more than 300 functions covering everything from engineering to statistical computations, from text searching to date and time functions, Excel can handle a wide variety of calculating needs.

Selected functions are described in detail, and the activities are intended to help you use the functions in actual business situations. Use of the Paste Function and Formula Palette is covered in depth. The chapter also reviews the use of natural language formulas.

Learning Objectives

- Use worksheet functions
- Use Paste Function and the Formula Palette
- Create natural language formulas
- Use date and time functions
- Use financial functions
- Use logical functions
- Use statistical functions
- Use engineering functions
- Use lookup and reference functions
- Use text functions

Case profile

As the central office manager for Sweet Tooth, you have many different responsibilities. Not only do you keep track of employee and client data, but you also must track sales data, analyze sales statistics, and manage company assets. Learning more about Excel's specialized functions will help you use your time more effectively.

chapter seven

7.a Using Worksheet Functions

Earlier, we referred to functions and formulas as Excel's "workhorses." Functions are predefined formulas that perform calculations by using specific values, called arguments, supplied in a particular order. You've already learned how useful the SUM, MAX, MIN, and AVG functions can be.

In addition, you've learned that functions must follow a specific structure called a syntax. Functions are written as **function name** (**required arguments,** optional arguments), where the elements in bold are required arguments. Each function has its own unique required and optional arguments. Given the more than 300 functions available, it's nearly impossible to remember all of the details about every function's syntax—let alone remember all the functions that are available. In fact, Excel provides so many functions that we could easily spend an entire book talking about them. Relax—we have only one chapter to dedicate to functions, so we'll do our best to highlight the most useful ones. Remember, the Office Assistant is always available to provide you with detailed help about functions whenever you need it.

notes If a particular function is not immediately available, you may need to install the Analysis ToolPak.
In such a case, Excel usually prompts you.
Once the feature is installed, you enable it by selecting Add-Ins from the Tools menu. Click the Analysis ToolPak check box, then click OK.

7.b Using Paste Function and the Formula Palette

To help you enter functions, you can use a command called **Paste Function**. Paste Function acts like a Function Wizard. First, you select a function from one of the many function categories. Next, Paste Function pastes the selected function in the active cell. It then displays the Formula Palette to help you enter values or cell references for each of the required arguments in the correct order.

chapter seven

Using Paste Function

Your first task of the day is to retrieve some information from the *Function Reference* workbook. Specifically, you need to find out how many employees are currently employed at Sweet Tooth, and the average age of those employees. To locate this information, you use Paste Function and the Formula Palette to insert the AVERAGE and COUNT functions. To use Paste Function to enter the COUNT function:

Step 1	*Open*	the *Function Reference* workbook on your Data Disk
Step 2	*Save*	the file as *Function Reference Revised*
Step 3	*Activate*	cell F5 on the Employee Data worksheet
Step 4	*Click*	the Paste Function button on the Standard toolbar

An equal sign (=) appears in the Formula Bar, and the Paste Function dialog box opens. Function categories are displayed on the left, and functions belonging to each category are on the right. The Most Recently Used category lists functions you've used recently—a great convenience when you need to reuse functions frequently. The All category provides an alphabetical list of all available functions. This category is helpful when you know the name of a function, but can't remember to which category it belongs.

> **MENU TIP**
>
> To open the Paste Function dialog box using a menu command, select Function from the Insert menu.

Step 5	*Click*	Statistical in the Function category: list
Step 6	*Scroll*	down the Function name: list until you see COUNT
Step 7	*Click*	COUNT in the Function name: list

When you select a function, the function's syntax and an explanation of the function appear at the bottom of the dialog box, as illustrated in Figure 7-1.

The COUNT function counts either the number of cells in a range that contains numbers or the number of number values supplied as arguments to the count function. For example, the formula =COUNT(10,20,30,40,50) produces a result of 5, because five numerical values are supplied as arguments. If cells A1, B1, C1, D1, E1, and F1 held the values 10, 20, 30, 40, 50, and Hello, respectively, and you used the formula =COUNT(a1:f1), the result would also be 5, because the value in F1 is not a numerical value.

Step 8	*Click*	OK

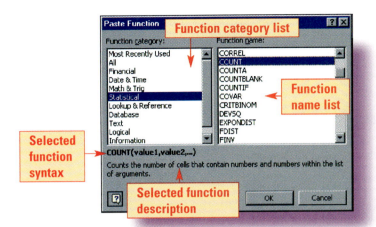

FIGURE 7-1
Paste Function Dialog Box

 Throughout this book we capitalize the names of functions to distinguish them from other text. Function names are not case-sensitive, so =count, =Count, and =COUNT are all valid ways to enter the function name.

Entering Functions using the Formula Palette

The Formula Palette appears. Your screen should look similar to Figure 7-2. The **Formula Palette** assists you in building the formula. It displays the function's required and optional arguments, an explanation of each of the arguments, and a running result of the function as you supply and modify arguments to it. If you have not provided all of the required arguments to a given function, the formula result will be blank.

MOUSE TIP

Click the Equal button on the Formula Bar to edit formulas using the Formula Palette.

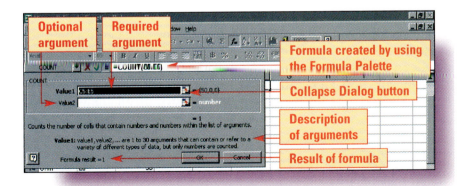

FIGURE 7-2
Building a Function with the Formula Palette

Excel automatically scans horizontally and vertically for a range of values. In this case, it finds a value in row 5 and selects the range

C5:E5. Use the Collapse Dialog button for the Value1 box to select the correct range. To enter arguments using the Formula Palette:

Step 1	Click	the Collapse Dialog button 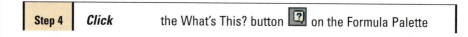 in the Value1 box
Step 2	Select	cells C5:C68
Step 3	Click	the Expand Dialog button

Look just below the Formula Bar for the Expand Dialog button. The result =64 now appears at the bottom of the Formula Palette. The What's This? button in the lower-left corner of the Formula Palette gives you quick access to the Office Assistant and online Help about the function that you are currently using.

Step 4	Click	the What's This? button on the Formula Palette

The Office Assistant appears, displaying two options.

Step 5	Click	Help with this feature in the Office Assistant dialog balloon

The Office Assistant displays help for the Formula Palette. You can also look up help for the selected function.

Step 6	Click	Help on selected function in the Office Assistant dialog balloon

The Microsoft Excel Help window appears, providing information about the COUNT function currently displayed. The information includes a description of the function, the function's syntax, tips on how to use the function, and examples of its application. The Office Assistant is a valuable resource when you're working with unfamiliar functions.

Step 7	Click	the Close button in the Help window title bar
Step 8	Click	OK on the Formula Palette

In the Formula Bar, you see the complete formula, =COUNT(C5:C68), and the result, 64, is displayed in cell F5. This result means that Sweet Tooth has 64 sales representatives.

Next, you need to add the AVERAGE function to cell G5 to calculate the average age of Sweet Tooth's employees. To enter the AVERAGE function using Paste Function:

Step 1	*Activate*	cell G5
Step 2	*Click*	the Paste Function button on the Standard toolbar
Step 3	*Click*	AVERAGE from the Statistical function category
Step 4	*Click*	OK

The Formula Palette opens, with the cell reference F5 selected. You can enter a range directly in the Number1 argument box.

Step 5	*Key*	C5:C68
Step 6	*Click*	OK

The formula calculates the average age and displays it in cell F6. You decide to reformat this cell to display two decimal places.

Step 7	*Click*	the Decrease Decimal button on the Formatting toolbar four times

Spend some time browsing through the Paste Function dialog box to familiarize yourself with the functions available in Excel. Before you move to the next section, you need to take care of some "housekeeping" tasks. To hide the Office Assistant and save the workbook:

Step 1	*Right-click*	the Office Assistant
Step 2	*Click*	Hide
Step 3	*Save*	the workbook

One of your many duties at Sweet Tooth is to calculate the net profit or loss each month by subtracting expenses from income. In the next section, you learn how to construct natural language formulas that can make this task a piece of cake.

chapter seven

7.c Creating Natural Language Formulas

Previously in this book, you learned about using range names in formulas. This type of reference entry is called **natural language**. In addition to working with named ranges, you can also use column and row labels in formulas. By default, Excel 2000 does not let you use labels in formulas. You can change this default, however. To enable natural language references:

| Step 1 | Click | Tools |
| Step 2 | Click | Options |

The Options dialog box opens.

Step 3	Click	the Calculation tab
Step 4	Click	the Accept labels in formulas check box to select it, if necessary
Step 5	Click	OK

Now you can create formulas using labels. To create natural language formulas using labels:

| Step 1 | Click | the Income Expense worksheet tab |
| Step 2 | Enter | =January Income-January Expense in cell D5 |

This natural language formula locates the intersection of the row label January and the column label Income (cell B5), and the intersection of the row label January and the column label Expense (cell C5). The result of the formula, $4,692.30, is displayed in cell D5. You can create absolute references using labels by inserting the $ symbol in front of the label in a formula. Because the formula you created in cell D5 contains relative references, you can copy it to the other cells in column D and it will still work correctly.

| Step 3 | Activate | cell D5 |
| Step 4 | Drag | the fill handle down to cell D16 |

Next, you enter a formula to sum the Income column.

Step 5	Enter	=SUM(Income) in cell B17
Step 6	Activate	cell B17
Step 7	Drag	the fill handle to cell D17
Step 8	Click	cell D17

Note that the formula in the Formula Bar uses Net as the argument for the SUM function in cell D17. Because Income was a relative reference, Excel adjusted the reference in the copied formulas to access the correct data for each column.

The numbers in parentheses are negative numbers. The Accounting format uses parentheses to display negative numbers.

Natural language can make your formulas easier to understand, though it may not save any keystrokes. It is especially helpful when you are working with large worksheets. Using row and column labels in formulas can be big time savers, because you do not have to name ranges to use them.

Next, you use date and time functions to set up Sweet Tooth's work schedule for 1999.

7.d Using Date and Time Functions

When you enter a date or time value in Excel, the program stores the value as a numeric value called a serial value. For example, the serial value 1 represents the date January 1, 1900, the serial value 2 represents the date January 2, 1900, and so on. Time values are stored as decimal fractions, because hours, minutes, and seconds are considered fractions of a day. For example, 12:00 AM is stored as 0, but 12:00 PM is stored as .5 because it represents half of a day.

When you enter a value that Excel recognizes as a date or time format, the serial value is calculated automatically. The serial date, however, does not display in the cell or in the Formula bar. The only way to view the serial value is to change the format of the cell to a general number format. This consideration is important when you need to find out how many days have elapsed between two dates. For example, suppose you create a formula in cell C1 to subtract the date 1/1/1999 in cell A1 from the date 6/30/1998 in cell B1. Because Excel is subtracting one date from another, it assumes that the answer should be returned in date format. The answer, 7/3/1900, may not seem to make sense. Actually it does—if you remember that dates are stored as serial values. Changing the format of cell C1 to general number format gives you the expected result, 185, which is the number of days between June 30, 1998, and January 1, 1999. The date 7/3/1900 is 185 days after 1/1/1900, which is the date from which Excel begins calculating dates.

Excel supplies 19 functions to handle a variety of date and time conversions. Table 7-1 describes the functions covered in this section.

TABLE 7-1
Common Time and Date Functions

Function Name	Function Purpose
TODAY	Returns the serial number of today's date
NOW	Returns the serial number of the current date and time
NETWORKDAYS	Returns the number of whole workdays between two dates
WEEKDAY	Converts a serial number to a day of the week

> **CAUTION TIP**
>
> Dates before January 1, 1900, are not converted to serial values. Thus you can't use such dates in Excel as part of your calculations.

At the beginning of each year, you must figure out the official work schedule for Sweet Tooth. Date and time functions turn this job into an easy task.

TODAY Function

The **TODAY** function retrieves the current date from your system, calculates the serial number value, then displays the number using a date format. This function is very useful when the current date should appear on a worksheet whenever the workbook is being viewed or edited. The TODAY function has the following syntax:

=TODAY()

The TODAY function has no required arguments, but it does need the open and close parentheses. To use the TODAY function:

Step 1	Click	the Work Schedule tab
Step 2	Enter	=TODAY() in cell A5

The current date is displayed.

NOW Function

Similar to the TODAY function, the **NOW** function returns the current date and time from your system. The NOW function has the following syntax:

=NOW()

The NOW function requires no arguments. It simply gathers the system time and date and then displays this information. The time is updated every time the worksheet is recalculated. To use the NOW function:

| Step 1 | Key | =NOW() in cell B5 |
| Step 2 | Click | the Enter button  on the Formula Bar |

The current time and date are displayed. You decide to change the format of this cell to general number format to check the serial value of this time and date.

Step 3	Press	the CTRL + 1 keys to open the Format Cells dialog box
Step 4	Click	General in the Category: list on the Number tab
Step 5	Click	OK

Note the decimal equivalent of the hours, minutes, and seconds.

| Step 6 | Press | the F9 key |

Pressing the F9 key recalculates the worksheet. As part of the recalculation, the NOW function is updated to the most current second. Use Undo to return the format to the MM/DD/YYYY HH:MM format.

| Step 7 | Click | the Undo button on the Standard toolbar |

NETWORKDAYS Function

You need to figure out how many workdays are contained in each month for 1999, using the list of holidays supplied in cells A9:A21. To perform this task, you can use the **NETWORKDAYS** function. This function returns the number of workdays between two dates, skipping weekends and optional holidays, and is particularly useful for setting up work schedules and project deadlines. The NETWORKDAYS function has the following syntax:

=**NETWORKDAYS(start_date,end_date**,holidays)

The optional holidays argument can be a range of cells containing dates. To use the NETWORKDAYS function:

| Step 1 | Activate | cell H9 |

Step 2	Click	the Paste Function button ƒx on the Standard toolbar
Step 3	Double-click	the NETWORKDAYS function from the Date & Time category

Double-clicking a function name has the same effect as clicking the function name to select it, then clicking the OK button. The Formula Palette opens.

Step 4	Key	F9 in the Start_date argument box
Step 5	Press	the TAB key
Step 6	Key	G9 in the End_date argument box
Step 7	Press	the TAB key
Step 8	Click	the Collapse Dialog button in the Holidays argument box
Step 9	Select	cells A9:A21
Step 10	Click	the Expand Dialog button

Because you'll be copying this formula to other cells, the holiday range should use absolute references.

Step 11	Click	to the left of the colon (:) in the Holidays argument box
Step 12	Press	the F4 key
Step 13	Press	the RIGHT ARROW key
Step 14	Press	the F4 key

Both references in the range address are absolute references.

Step 15	Click	OK

The value returned in cell H9 is the number of workdays in January 1999. Next, you copy this formula to the other cells in column H.

Step 16	Copy	the formula in cell H9 to cells H10:H20

WEEKDAY Function

The **WEEKDAY** function returns a numerical value representing the day of the week from a given date. The WEEKDAY function has the following syntax:

=**WEEKDAY(serial_number,**return_type)

The serial_number argument can be a date or serial number entered directly in the formula or located in another cell. You have three options for the return_type argument. Option 1 is to number the days from 1 (Sunday) to 7 (Saturday); this option is the default setting and will be supplied automatically if you omit this argument. Option 2 is to number the days from 1 (Monday) to 7 (Sunday). Option 3 is to number the days from 0 (Monday) to 6 (Sunday). To use the WEEKDAY function:

| Step 1 | Enter | =WEEKDAY(A9) in cell B9 |

In this formula, you omitted the optional return_type argument. As a result, Excel assumes option 1, which is the Sunday to Saturday type of calendar, where Sunday is the first day of the week and Saturday the seventh. The value returned in cell B9 should be 6, which is the serial number for Friday. The WEEKDAY function becomes even more useful when you nest it within an IF function to display the actual day of the week instead of a number. You learn about the IF function and nesting functions later in this chapter.

| Step 2 | Copy | the formula in cell B9 to cells B10:B21 |
| Step 3 | Activate | cell A1 |

Your screen should look similar to Figure 7-3.

| Step 4 | Save | your workbook |

In the next section, you use financial functions to help Sweet Tooth's president, Amy Lee, make several important business decisions regarding loans, investments, and taxes.

QUICK TIP

Use the Office Assistant to learn about the more than 60 math and trigonometry functions available in Excel. For example, the ROMAN function converts Arabic numerals to their Roman numeral equivalents. The RAND function generates random numbers between 0 and 1. The RANDBETWEEN function generates random whole numbers ranging between any two numbers you provide. Several functions—such as ROUND, EVEN, ODD, and INT—are used to round numbers. The SORT function finds the square root of a number.

FIGURE 7-3
Using Date and Time Functions

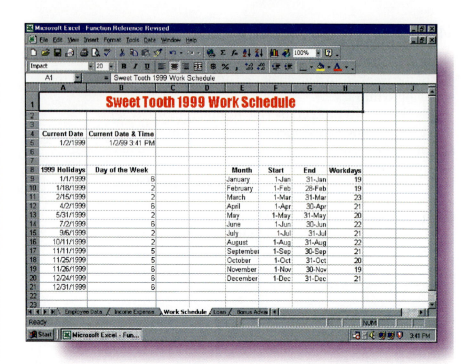

 ## 7.e Using Financial Functions

The financial functions category contains more than 50 functions, making it one of the largest categories of functions offered by Excel. Financial functions are used to calculate values for all types of investments and loans, as well as to calculate depreciation of assets using a variety of depreciation methods. Table 7-2 describes the financial functions covered in this section.

TABLE 7-2
Common Financial Functions

Function Name	Function Purpose
CUMIPMT	Returns the cumulative interest paid on a loan between two periods
FV	Returns the future value of an investment
SLN	Returns the straight-line depreciation of an asset for one period

Many financial functions use similar arguments, as shown in Table 7-3.

TABLE 7-3
Common Arguments for Financial Functions

Argument	Definition
FV (future value)	Value of an investment or loan after all payments have been made
NPER (number of periods)	Total number of payments or periods of an investment
PMT (payment)	Amount paid periodically to an investment or loan
PV (present value)	Value of an investment or loan at the beginning of the investment period
RATE (rate)	Interest rate or discount rate for a loan or investment
TYPE (type)	Interval at which payments are made during the payment period, such as the beginning of a month (0) or the end of the month (1)

CUMIPMT Function

The **CUMIPMT** function is used to calculate the amount of interest paid on a loan between a start and an end period, or payment. The loan worksheet provides the information you need to supply to the CUMIPMT function. Sweet Tooth needs to find the range of acceptable interest rates for the loan to buy new cars. The company needs to borrow $125,000, and wants to pay it back over 36 months. Because Amy has asked about the amount of interest paid over the life of the loan, the start period is 1, and the end period is 36, covering all payments on the loan. Column F gives the values for the Type argument, which specifies when the payment will be made. In this case, the payments will be made at the end of each month. The CUMIPMT function has the following syntax:

=**CUMIPMT(rate,nper,pv,start_period,end_period,type)**

The start_period and end_period arguments are numerical arguments representing the number of the payment. Refer to Table 7-3 for an explanation of the other arguments.

Sweet Tooth is thinking about buying several new cars that regional managers can use for business travel. Amy Lee has asked you to calculate how much interest will be paid over the term of the auto loan given different rates of interest. To calculate the cumulative interest on a loan:

Step 1	Click	the Loan worksheet tab
Step 2	Activate	cell G5
Step 3	Click	the Paste Function button f_x on the Standard toolbar
Step 4	Double-click	the CUMIPMT function from the Financial category
Step 5	Drag	the Formula Palette to the bottom of the worksheet

CAUTION TIP

When using the CUMIPMT and other financial functions, it is very important that the rate and nper arguments "agree." Typically, the interest rate is stated as a yearly interest rate. For example, a loan at 8.5% means that you are paying 8.5% interest on your loan over the course of the entire year—not monthly. Because you usually make payments on a loan monthly, the nper argument is most likely expressed in months. For a three-year loan, the number of periods, or payments, is 36. To calculate the interest correctly, you must show the interest rate in months, not years. Using a mathematical formula, you can divide the interest rate by 12 to bring it into agreement with the number of periods, or payments, on the loan.

QUICK TIP

The IPMT and PPMT functions are related to the CUMIPMT function. IPMT calculates the interest portion of a given payment on a loan. The PPMT function calculates the principal portion of a given payment on a loan.

| Step 6 | *Scroll* | the worksheet down so that row 4 is the top visible row |
| Step 7 | *Key* | A5/12 in the Rate argument box |

The interest rate must be expressed in terms of months, rather than years, to agree with the monthly payments in the nper argument.

| Step 8 | *Press* | the TAB key |

The rest of the arguments match the column labels.

Step 9	*Key*	B5 in the Nper argument box
Step 10	*Press*	the TAB key
Step 11	*Key*	C5 in the Pv argument box
Step 12	*Press*	the TAB key
Step 13	*Key*	D5 in the Start_period argument box
Step 14	*Press*	the TAB key
Step 15	*Key*	E5 in the End_period argument box
Step 16	*Press*	the TAB key
Step 17	*Key*	F5 in the Type argument box

Compare your screen with Figure 7-4.

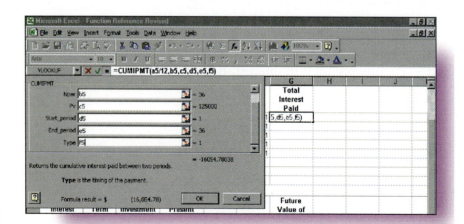

FIGURE 7-4
Function Palette with the CUMIPMT Function

| Step 18 | *Click* | OK |

The total interest paid is calculated at $(16,054.78). This value is displayed as a negative value, as it represents an expense to the company.

| Step 19 | Copy | the formula in cell G5 to cells G6:G9 |

Using this information, the company knows what it can afford while shopping for interest rates.

FV Function

The **FV** function calculates the future value of an investment based on a fixed periodic payment and a constant interest rate. Sweet Tooth invests a portion of its cash assets in CDs (certificates of deposit, not music compact discs). To calculate the future value of that investment, you can use the FV function. The FV function has the following syntax:

=**FV(rate,nper,**pmt,pv,type**)**

To use this function, you must include either the amount to be invested each period (pmt) or the present value (pv) of the investment.

The accounting department has asked you to calculate the future value of two CDs. One is a 24-month CD, with an interest rate of 4%, and a planned investment of $1,000 per month. The other is a 60-month CD at 6.75%, given a present value of $25,000. To use the FV function:

Step 1	Activate	cell G15
Step 2	Click	the Paste Function button *fx* on the Standard toolbar
Step 3	Double-click	the FV function from the Financial category
Step 4	Key	A15/12 in the Rate argument box

> **QUICK TIP**
>
> The PV function returns the present value of an investment given the future value.

The interest rate must be expressed in terms of months, rather than years, to agree with the monthly payments in the nper argument.

Step 5	Press	the TAB key
Step 6	Key	B15 in the Nper argument box
Step 7	Press	the TAB key
Step 8	Key	C15 in the Pmt argument box

Both the payment (pmt) and present value (pv) arguments are shown as negative numbers in the worksheet, because they represent cash paid out from the company. The final calculation will show the future value as a positive number, representing the cash that the company receives back.

| Step 9 | Click | OK |

You don't need to provide the present value (pv) because you supplied the payment argument. Skipping the type argument causes Excel to use the default setting of 0, indicating that payments will be made at the beginning of the month. The future value of this investment will be $24,942.89. With a small modification, this same formula can be used to calculate the future value of the other investment.

Step 10	Copy	the formula in cell G15 to cell G16
Step 11	Activate	cell G16
Step 12	Press	the F2 key

Next, edit the reference to cell C16 using Range Finder.

Step 13	Drag	the purple Range Finder box from cell C16 to cell D16
Step 14	Press	the LEFT ARROW key four times to place the cursor in front of D16 in the formula
Step 15	Key	, (a comma)

A blank space is inserted where the payment argument would be. Your screen should look similar to Figure 7-5.

FIGURE 7-5
Modifying the FV Function

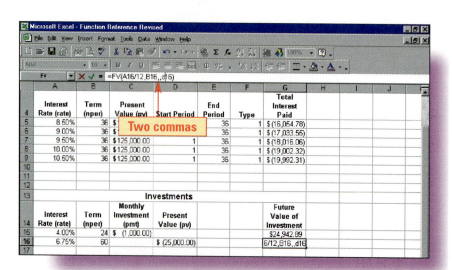

| Step 16 | Press | the ENTER key |

The future value of this investment is calculated at $35,002.87.

SLN Function

Because business assets, such as computer equipment, furniture, automobiles, and buildings, remain useful for a number of years, the expense of purchasing these items is spread out over a number of years for taxation purposes. This expense is called depreciation. Several methods can be used to calculate depreciation, and several functions are available to apply each method of depreciation. Each of the depreciation functions uses the same three arguments: cost, salvage, and life. The **cost** is the initial cost of the asset. The **salvage** is the asset's value at the end of the depreciation period. The **life** is the number of periods over which the asset is being depreciated.

Typically, assets are depreciated over a number of years, so one year represents one period of depreciation. Some depreciation functions allow an optional argument, month, which indicates the number of months that the asset was owned in the first year.

The depreciation method called the straight-line method is the simplest to understand. With this accounting method, the depreciation amount remains the same for all years of the asset's life. The **SLN** function returns the straight-line depreciation of an asset for one period. The SLN function has the following syntax:

=SLN(cost,salvage,life)

Sweet Tooth bought a computer valued at $3,000 last year. The life of the asset is five years, with the salvage (or resale) value being $0. Calculate the yearly depreciation for this asset, using the SLN function. To use the SLN function:

| Step 1 | Scroll | the worksheet to view rows 19–21 |
| Step 2 | Enter | =SLN(a21,b21,c21) in cell D21 |

The depreciation amount using this method is calculated at $600.00 per year. See Figure 7-6.

> **QUICK TIP**
>
> You can use information functions, such as the INFO function, to retrieve information about the computer on which you are working. For example, the formula =INFO("osversion") finds information about your operating system. The formula =INFO("release") indicates which version of Excel you are currently using. Use the Office Assistant to find out more about information you can access using the INFO function and to learn about other useful information functions.

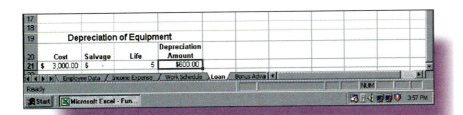

FIGURE 7-6
Using the SLN Function

> **Step 3** | **Save** | your workbook

In the next section, you learn about a very important category of functions, logical functions. You use these functions to determine bonuses for Sweet Tooth's sales staff based on the amount of sales generated by each sales representative.

7.f Using Logical Functions

Logical functions are used to test data using a true/false type of evaluation. Another way to think of true/false evaluation is as a yes/no choice. For example, suppose you are testing the value of a cell to find out whether the value is greater than 100. The answer is either yes (true), the value is greater than 100, or no (false), the value is not greater than 100. Although logical testing seems simplistic because only two outcomes are possible, you can build extremely complex tests by nesting logical functions.

Table 7-4 describes the logical functions covered in this section.

TABLE 7-4
Common Logical Functions

Function Name	Function Purpose
IF	Returns one value if a condition you specify evaluates to TRUE and another value if it evaluates to FALSE
AND	Returns TRUE only if all of its arguments are true; returns FALSE if one or more arguments is false
OR	Returns TRUE if at least one of its arguments is true; returns FALSE only if all of its arguments are false
NOT	Returns TRUE if its argument is false; returns FALSE if its argument is true
TRUE	Assigns the logical value TRUE to a cell
FALSE	Assigns the logical value FALSE to a cell

IF Function

The **IF** function is used to evaluate whether a given statement is true. If the statement is true, the function performs one operation; otherwise it does something else. The IF function has the following syntax:

=IF(logical_test,value_if_true,value_if_false)

The first part of the statement identifies the logical test. The second part of the statement indicates what will happen if the logical test is true. The last part of the statement identifies what will happen if the logical test is false. For example, bonuses are paid to Sweet Tooth's sales representatives based on the amount of sales that each salesperson generates. If a sales representative generates sales of $10,000 or more, he or she earns a bonus of $500; otherwise, the bonus is 0.

The logical test in this case determines whether the sales amount is greater than or equal to $10,000. If the sales amount is greater than or equal to $10,000, then the logical test returns TRUE. If it is less than $10,000, the logical test returns FALSE. Sometimes it's easier to create logical functions by writing them in statement form:

If sales are greater than or equal to 10,000, **then** the bonus is 500, **else** (otherwise) the result is 0.

Translate your sentence into something resembling function syntax:

=IF(sales>=10000, then bonus is 500, else bonus is 0)

Finally, create your formula using named ranges, cell references, or values. To use the IF function:

Step 1	Click	the Bonus Advancement tab
Step 2	Activate	cell C5
Step 3	Click	the Paste Function button f_x on the Standard toolbar
Step 4	Double-click	the IF function in the Logical category
Step 5	Key	B5>=10000 in the Logical_test argument box
Step 6	Press	the TAB key to move to the Value_if_true argument box
Step 7	Key	500
Step 8	Press	the TAB key to move to the Value_if_false argument box
Step 9	Key	0
Step 10	Click	OK

Because the value in cell B5 ($15,500) is greater than 10000, the value of cell C5 evaluates to 500.

Step 11	Click	cell B5
Step 12	Key	9000
Step 13	Press	the TAB key

The value of C5 evaluates to 0 (displayed as a dash in accounting format), because the value in cell B5 ($9,000) is less than 10,000.

AND Function

Sweet Tooth pays another bonus if the amount of sales generated exceeds $20,000. This scheme classifies the sales representatives into three categories: those who sold less than $10,000; those who sold at least $10,000 but less than $20,000; and those who sold $20,000 or

> **QUICK TIP**
>
> The #NUM! error occurs when you use an unacceptable argument in a function requiring a numeric argument. This error also arises if a formula produces a number too large (greater than $1*10^{307}$) or too small (less than $-1*10^{307}$) to be represented in Excel.

chapter seven

more. To figure out these bonuses, we need to set up a new condition to test whether the sales amount is greater than or equal to 10,000 *and* less than 20,000. To accomplish this task, you will nest the AND function inside the IF function. **Nested functions** are functions that replace one of the arguments of another function.

The AND function is used to test multiple conditions. If any of the tested conditions returns FALSE, the AND operation returns FALSE. The AND function has the following syntax:

=**AND(logical1**,logical2,…)

You can supply as many as 30 arguments to be evaluated. All arguments must evaluate to true if the AND function is to return a value of TRUE.

When you create a nested formula, it's easiest to build from the inside out. That is, you figure out the nested formula first, then set that formula in its place within the other formula. In this case, you need to construct an AND statement:

Sales is greater than or equal to 10,000 AND Sales is less than 20,000
In function syntax, you write this condition as follows:

AND(Sales>=10000,Sales<20000)

This formula is inserted as the logical test for the IF function:

If Sales is greater than 10,000 **AND** less than 20,000,
then bonus is 500, **else** bonus is 0.

In function syntax, you write the following:

IF(AND(Sales>=10000,Sales<20000), 500, 0)

To modify the formula and use the AND function:

| Step 1 | *Click* | the Edit Formula button = on the Formula Bar |

The Formula Palette opens with the Logical_test argument selected.

| Step 2 | *Click* | the Function box list arrow on the Formula Bar |

See Figure 7-7. The Function box displays a list of the most recently used functions. You can use this box to help build nested functions. Any function you select here will replace the Logical_test argument, because it is selected in the Formula Palette.

| Step 3 | *Click* | More Functions |

The Paste Function dialog box opens.

| Step 4 | *Double-click* | the AND function in the Logical category |

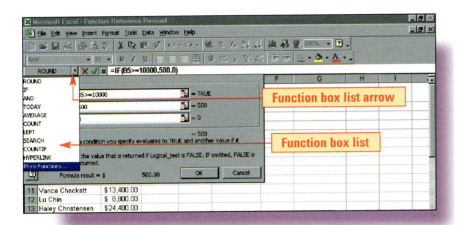

FIGURE 7-7
Function Box List

The Formula Palette changes to the AND function. Notice that the Formula Bar indicates your nested formula: =IF(**AND**(),500,0). The bold AND indicates the current formula being constructed. You can move the Formula Palette to view the worksheet more clearly.

Step 5	*Drag*	the Formula Palette to the middle of the worksheet
Step 6	*Key*	B5>=10000

The Formula Palette displays the results of the Logical1 condition as you type. This test evaluates to FALSE because cell B5 contains less than 10,000.

Step 7	*Press*	the TAB key to move to the Logical2 argument box
Step 8	*Key*	B5<20000

The result of the Logical2 condition is true because the value in cell B5 is less than 20,000. The entire AND function returns FALSE, however, because one of the conditions returned FALSE.

Step 9	*Click*	OK

The bonus calculated in cell C5 is 0, because the value of cell B5, 9,000, is less than 10,000.

Step 10	*Click*	cell B5
Step 11	*Key*	11000

chapter seven

| Step 12 | Press | the TAB key |

The bonus calculated in cell C5 is 500, because the value of cell B5, 11,000, is greater than 10,000. This formula works better than the first one, but can you spot the problem? What happens if the sales are greater than $20,000?

Step 13	Click	cell B5
Step 14	Key	22000
Step 15	Press	the TAB key

Using this formula, sales people who generate $20,000 or more in sales would receive the same bonus as those who generated less than $10,000 in sales, $0. Not exactly fair. To correct this situation, you can nest an IF statement as the ELSE argument of the original IF statement. The condition argument returns true only if the value in cell B5 is between 10,000 and 20,000. Thus values higher than 20,000 and lower than 10,000 are passed to the else condition. Using another IF statement, you can evaluate these values. Before you become confused, figure out the second IF statement on its own:

If sales are greater than or equal to $20,000, **then** the employee receives a bonus of $1,000, **else** the employee receives no bonus.

In formula syntax, you would write the following:

=IF(sales>=20000,1000,0)

Finally, combine this condition with the original statement:

=IF(AND(sales>=10000,sales<20000), then bonus is 500, else **IF(sales>=20000, *then* bonus is 1000, *else* bonus is 0))**

The second IF statement is evaluated only when the value of sales is greater than 20,000 or less than 10,000, and determines the correct bonus. To modify the formula:

Step 1	Click	the Edit Formula button = on the Formula Bar
Step 2	Double-click	the Value_if_false argument box to select the value
Step 3	Click	the Function box list arrow on the Formula Bar
Step 4	Click	IF
Step 5	Key	b5>=20000
Step 6	Press	the TAB key
Step 7	Key	1000
Step 8	Press	the TAB key

Step 9	Key	0
Step 10	Click	OK

The bonus in cell C5 is correctly calculated as $1,000.00.

Step 11	Enter	5000 in cell B5

The bonus recalculates as 0.

Step 12	Enter	15500 in cell B5

The bonus recalculates as $500.

Step 13	Activate	cell C5
Step 14	Copy	the formula in cell C5 to cells C6:C68
Step 15	Activate	cell C5
Step 16	Save	your workbook

Your worksheet should look similar to Figure 7-8.

QUICK TIP

If you paste a cell over another cell referred to by a formula in another cell, the #REF! error occurs. Undo the paste action to fix the error.

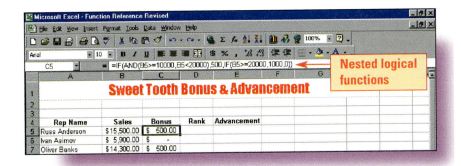

FIGURE 7-8
Nesting IF and AND Functions to Evaluate Multiple Conditions

OR, NOT, TRUE, and FALSE Functions

The logical functions, OR and NOT, are also commonly nested within IF formulas. The **OR** function, like the AND function, is used to test multiple criteria. The OR function has the following syntax:

=**OR**(**logical1,** logical2, …)

Unlike with the AND function, where all conditions must be satisfied to return TRUE, only one of the criteria in an OR statement must be satisfied to return TRUE.

The **NOT** function indicates whether a condition is *not* true. Basically, it returns the opposite of its argument's value. The NOT function has the following syntax:

=NOT(logical)

Two other logical functions, **TRUE** and **FALSE,** are used to assign a logical value to a cell. To find out more about any of these functions and to see examples of how to use them, use the Office Assistant. In the next section, you use statistical functions to analyze the sales data on the Bonus Advancement tab.

7.g Using Statistical Functions

Statistical functions are the single largest category of functions offered by Excel, encompassing nearly 80 functions. You've already used some statistical functions, such as AVERAGE, COUNT, MIN, and MAX. Many of the formulas are used with complex statistical models that are beyond the scope of this book. In this section, you learn about two useful statistical functions, described in Table 7-5.

TABLE 7-5
Common Statistical Functions

Function Name	Function Purpose
RANK	Returns the rank of a number in a list of numbers
PERCENTILE	Returns the percentile value of a range

RANK Function

Advancement in Sweet Tooth is determined in large measure by the sales generated by each employee. The RANK function can be used to rank employees based on the total sales generated by each employee. Another way to evaluate employee performance is to identify those employees who are in the top 10%, or 90th percentile, of all employees based on total sales generated. This value is calculated using the PERCENTILE function.

The **RANK** function is used to determine a given value's rank in a list of values. The RANK function has the following syntax:

=RANK(number,ref,order)

The number argument is the number whose rank you want to find in the list of values supplied as the ref argument, which identifies a range of values. The optional argument, order, determines the sort order of the list. If order is set to 0 (zero) or omitted, the number is ranked as if ref were a list sorted in descending order. If order is set to any other nonzero value, the number is ranked as if ref were a list sorted in ascending order.

Note that RANK assigns duplicate numbers the same rank. For example, if you were evaluating team scores in a tournament, and two teams tied for second, Excel would assign both values a rank of 2nd.

The next ranking value would be assigned a rank of 4th, not 3rd, as two values occupy the rank of 2nd.

To use the RANK function:

| Step 1 | Enter | =RANK(b5,b5:b68) in cell D5 |

The value 27 is returned in cell D5, because the value of cell B5 (15500) ranks twenty-seventh in the list of values found in cell B5:B68.

| Step 2 | Copy | the formula from cell D5 to cells D6:D68 |

PERCENTILE Function

The **PERCENTILE** function returns the *K*th percentile of values in a range, where *K* is a percentage value between 0 and 1. For example, suppose you want to identify employees who are in the top 10%, or 90th percentile. In this case, *K* equals 0.9, or 90%. The PERCENTILE function has the following syntax:

=**PERCENTILE(array,k)**

The array argument is either an **array**, a list of values, or a range of data that defines relative standing.

At Sweet Tooth, advancement is considered for those employees who rank in the top 10% for two consecutive quarters. To use the PERCENTILE function:

| Step 1 | Enter | =PERCENTILE(b5:b68,.9) in cell E5 |

This formula calculates the 90th percentile to be $23,040.00. Thus any sales representative who had sales totaling $23,040 (or more) is in the top 10% of all sales people.

To make this formula more useful, you can nest it with an IF function to identify whether the employee is a candidate for advancement. First, consider the statement of this function:

If sales are greater than the 90th percentile, **then** consider advancing the employee, **else** don't consider advancing the employee.

Next, write the formula:

IF(sales>90th percentile, then "Yes", else "No")

Instead of using the Formula Palette, you'll edit this formula in the Formula Bar. To edit the formula in the Formula Bar:

| Step 1 | Activate | cell E5 |
| Step 2 | Click | the Formula Bar in front of the "P" in PERCENTILE |

Step 3	Key	IF(b5>
Step 4	Press	the END key to move to the end of the formula
Step 5	Key	,"Yes","No")
Step 6	Click	the Enter button ✓ on the Formula Bar

This formula compares the sales amount in cell B5 ($15,500) against the 90th percentile ($23,040) for all sales. If the value in cell B5 is greater than this 90th percentile value, the formula returns the text string "Yes" in cell E5. Otherwise, it returns the text string "No." Before you can copy this formula, you must make one other modification.

The nested PERCENTILE formula contains a relative reference to the range B5:B68. This reference needs to be absolute.

Step 7	Click	the Formula Bar to the left of the colon between B5 and B68
Step 8	Press	the F4 key
Step 9	Press	the RIGHT ARROW key
Step 10	Press	the F4 key
Step 11	Click	the Enter button ✓ on the Formula Bar
Step 12	Copy	the formula in cell E5 to cells E6:E68
Step 13	Activate	cell E5
Step 14	Press	the ESC key to end the Paste command, if necessary
Step 15	Save	your workbook

Your screen should look similar to Figure 7-9.

FIGURE 7-9
Combining Statistical and Logical Functions

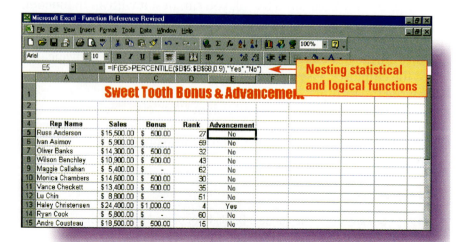

In the next section, you use an engineering function to help Sweet Tooth's shipping department solve a problem converting distances when shipping goods overseas.

7.h Using Engineering Functions

notes The engineering functions are available only if you have installed and enabled the Analysis ToolPak Add-In. See the note at the beginning of the chapter for information on how to enable the Analysis ToolPak Add-In.

Excel provides more than 39 functions in the engineering category. Many of these functions perform complex engineering calculations that are beyond the scope of this book. To find out more about the functions in the engineering category, use the Office Assistant. Table 7-6 describes the engineering function covered in this section.

Function Name	Function Purpose
CONVERT	Converts a number from one measurement system to another

TABLE 7-6
Common Engineering Function

CONVERT Function

The **CONVERT** function is used to convert measurements from one unit to another unit. The shipping department at Sweet Tooth sends goods to locations around the country and around the world. As a result, members of this department are constantly converting miles to kilometers. Excel can perform this conversion for you using the CONVERT function. The CONVERT function has the following syntax:

=CONVERT(number,from_unit,to_unit)

The from_unit and to_unit arguments are string arguments and must belong to the same measurement group or category. A **string** is a value treated as text. To indicate that a value is a string, you enclose it in quotes. The CONVERT function can work with the following measurement groups: weight and mass, distance, time, pressure, force, energy, power, magnetism, temperature, and liquid measure. In the example above, miles (using the unit abbreviation "mi") and meters (using the unit abbreviation "m") are both units of measurement belonging to the distance group. Because the distance group does not contain a unit abbreviation for kilometers, you have to convert miles to meters, then divide the result by 1,000 to display the distance in kilometers. To find out more about the unit abbreviations for each group, use the Office Assistant. To use the CONVERT function:

Step 1	Click	the Shipping worksheet tab
Step 2	Activate	cell D5
Step 3	Click	the Paste Function button on the Standard toolbar
Step 4	Double-click	the CONVERT function in the Engineering function category
Step 5	Key	C5 in the Number argument box
Step 6	Press	the TAB key
Step 7	Key	"mi" in the From_unit box

This argument must be a string, which is why you use the quotation marks.

| Step 8 | Press | the TAB key |
| Step 9 | Key | "m" in the To_unit box |

The unit abbreviations are case-sensitive.

| Step 10 | Click | OK |

The formula calculates the distance between Los Angeles, California, and Hong Kong, China, to be 11,651,651 meters. Now modify this formula to display the result in kilometers.

Step 11	Press	the F2 key
Step 12	Key	/1000
Step 13	Click	the Enter button on the Formula Bar

The correct result, 11,652, displays in cell D5.

| Step 14 | Copy | the formula in cell D5 to cells D6:D9 |

> **QUICK TIP**
>
> The #NAME? error can occur for a number of reasons. For example, using a named range that does not exist or misspelling a named range or function name can cause this error. Likewise, failing to enclose a text string in quotes for arguments requiring quoted text will create such an error. For example, you must enclose the from_unit and to_unit arguments of the CONVERT function in quotes.

To convert kilometers to miles, you need to multiply the kilometers value by 1,000 (to provide a value in meters), then convert from meters to miles.

| Step 15 | Enter | =CONVERT(D10*1000,"m","mi") in cell C10 |

The number argument calculates the meters by multiplying the value of cell D10 by 1,000, then converts from meters to miles.

Step 16	Copy	the formula in cell C10 to cells C11:C12
Step 17	Activate	cell C12
Step 18	Press	the ESC key to end the Copy command, if necessary
Step 19	Save	your workbook

Your worksheet should look similar to Figure 7-10.

> **QUICK TIP**
>
> The #DIV/0! error occurs when a formula attempts to divide by 0 (zero).

FIGURE 7-10
Using the CONVERT Function

In the next section, you use lookup and reference functions to help Sweet Tooth's Warehouse division look up information about items in the company's warehouse.

7.i Using Lookup and Reference Functions

Lookup functions are a special class of functions that can be used to locate information in a workbook. Excel provides more than 15 lookup and reference functions. To find out more about functions not covered

chapter seven

in this section, use the Office Assistant. Table 7-7 lists the functions covered in this section.

TABLE 7-7
Common Lookup and Reference Functions

Function Name	Function Purpose
VLOOKUP	Searches for a value in the leftmost column of a table, then returns a value in the same row from a column you specify in the table
HLOOKUP	Searches for a value in the top row of a table, then returns a value in the same column from a row you specify in the table

Many of the lookup functions require an array argument. In simple terms, an **array** is an arrangement or list of items. In fact, any of the lists you've used in this book could be described as an array.

The Warehouse worksheet contains two sets of data. Both sets hold the same information, but they are organized in different ways. Both lists can be considered arrays. Although the lists of data here are quite short, real warehouse lists might contain hundreds or thousands of entries, making it difficult to locate information quickly. The HLOOKUP and VLOOKUP functions were designed for this type of situation.

VLOOKUP Function

The manager of Sweet Tooth's Warehouse division would like to be able to input a Part No. in either cell A5 or H5 and then look up the rest of the data associated with that Part No. automatically. The **VLOOKUP** function searches for a value in the leftmost column of an array, then returns a value from the same row in the column you specify. The VLOOKUP function has the following syntax:

=**VLOOKUP(lookup_value,table_array,col_index_num**,range_lookup)

In the warehouse example, the lookup_value is the Part No. you will input in cell A5. The table_array is the list set up in cells A13:D16. When VLOOKUP finds a match of the Part No., it retrieves the value located in the same row as the function and in the column number in the array specified as the col_index_num argument. By default, VLOOKUP will search for an exact match. This option works the same way as setting the optional range_lookup argument to TRUE. Using the default range_lookup setting also requires your data to be sorted in ascending order. If range_lookup is set to FALSE, the data does not have to be sorted, and VLOOKUP does not have to find an exact match.

To use the VLOOKUP function:

Step 1	*Click*	the Warehouse worksheet tab
Step 2	*Activate*	cell B5

Using Worksheet Functions **EI 57**

Step 3	**Click**	the Paste Function button *fx* on the Standard toolbar
Step 4	**Double-click**	the VLOOKUP function in the Lookup & Reference function category
Step 5	**Key**	A5 in the Lookup_value argument box
Step 6	**Press**	the TAB key
Step 7	**Select**	cells A13:D16

The Formula Palette automatically collapses when you start your selection and expands when you release the mouse button.

| Step 8 | **Press** | the TAB key |

You want to retrieve the value located in the second column of the array, the Description.

Step 9	**Key**	2 in the Col_index_num box
Step 10	**Press**	the TAB key
Step 11	**Enter**	FALSE in the Range_lookup box
Step 12	**Click**	OK

Cell B5 displays the #N/A error because cell A5 does not contain a value to look up.

| Step 13 | **Enter** | 11-a-1407 in cell A5 |

Cell B5 displays the correct product description, 5 Gallon Sprinkles. Now finish adding VLOOKUP formulas to the remaining cells.

| Step 14 | **Enter** | =VLOOKUP(a5,a13:d16,3,false) in cell C5 |
| Step 15 | **Enter** | =VLOOKUP(a5,a13:d16,4,false) in cell D5 |

Now look up another Part No.

| Step 16 | **Enter** | 11-a-1404 in cell A5 |

The information is retrieved from the list and displayed in cells B5:D5.

> **QUICK TIP**
>
> The #N/A! error occurs when a value is not available to a function or formula.

chapter seven

HLOOKUP Function

The HLOOKUP function works similarly to the VLOOKUP function, but searches for values in a row rather than a column. When it finds a match, the HLOOKUP function retrieves data located in a specified row of the column where the match was found. The HLOOKUP function has the following syntax:

=**HLOOKUP(lookup_value,table_array,row_index_num**,range_lookup)

To use the HLOOKUP function:

Step 1 *Enter* =HLOOKUP(h5,h12:k15,2,false) in cell H6

When a match of cell H5 is found in the first row of the list, HLOOKUP will retrieve value in the second row of the list. For now, the resulting value is #N/A because cell H5 does not contain a value.

Step 2 *Enter* =HLOOKUP(h5,h12:k15,3,false) in cell H7

Step 3 *Enter* =HLOOKUP(h5,h12:k15,4,false) in cell H8

Step 4 *Enter* 11-a-1405 in cell H5

The information for Part No. 11-A-1405 is retrieved and displayed in cells H6:H8. See Figure 7-11.

QUICK TIP

The #VALUE! error occurs when you use the wrong type of argument or operand. For example, entering "hello" as the range_lookup argument in the VLOOKUP function would produce this error. Supply the correct type of argument required by the function to fix this error.

FIGURE 7-11
Using the VLOOKUP and HLOOKUP Functions

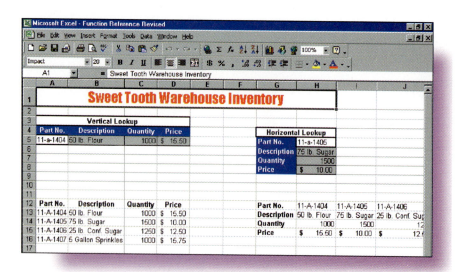

Your next task is to prepare lists of employee names and computer usernames for all the employees at Sweet Tooth. Text functions help you accomplish both of these tasks quickly.

7.j Using Text Functions

Excel provides 23 functions devoted to working with text. Text strings typically contain an assortment of characters, including the letters, numbers, and punctuation. In fact, you can use text functions on any type of value in a worksheet, including numerical values, dates, and times, though the use of dates and times will cause the text function to return serial values. Table 7-8 lists the text functions covered in this section.

Function Name	Function Purpose
CONCATENATE	Joins several text items into one text item
PROPER	Capitalizes the first letter in each word of a text value
UPPER	Converts text to uppercase
LEFT	Extracts a certain number of characters starting from the left of a text string
FIND	Finds one text value within another
MID	Extracts a certain number of characters starting from a given position within a text string

TABLE 7-8
Common Text Functions

CONCATENATE Function

You want to create a list of the full names of all employees at Sweet Tooth. You already have a list of employee names with the first and last names in separate columns. Rather than laboriously reentering the first and last names as one entry, you can use the CONCATENATE function to join the text in the First Name column with the text in the Last Name column. The CONCATENATE function has the following syntax:

=**CONCATENATE(text1,text2,…)**

You can join as many as 30 text items in a single text item using the CONCATENATE function. To use the CONCATENATE function:

> **QUICK TIP**
>
> You can use the ampersand, &, instead of the CONCATENATE function, for example, =B5&" "&A5.

Step 1	Click	the right tab scroll arrow ▶, if necessary
Step 2	Click	the Employee Name List worksheet tab
Step 3	Enter	=CONCATENATE(B5," ",A5) in cell D5

Make sure you press the SPACEBAR between the quotation marks in the formula. This formula joins the contents of cell B5 with a space and then with the contents of cell A5.

| Step 4 | Copy | the formula in cell D5 to cells D6:D68 |

QUICK TIP

If you need to use the value returned by a text function as text, you can use Copy, Paste Special to paste values instead of formulas. Select the cell containing the text formula, then click the Copy button on the Standard toolbar. Select the cell to which you want to paste, right-click, and select Paste Special. Click the Values option button in the Paste Special dialog box, then click OK.

PROPER Function

The **PROPER** function capitalizes the first letter in each word of a text string. The PROPER function has the following syntax:

=**PROPER(text)**

The text argument can be either text enclosed in quotation marks or a cell reference containing text. To use the PROPER function:

Step 1	Enter	=PROPER(d5) in cell E5

The text value "Russ Anderson" is returned in cell E5.

UPPER Function

The **UPPER** function converts text to uppercase. The UPPER function has the following syntax:

=**UPPER(text)**

To use the UPPER function:

Step 1	Enter	=UPPER(d5) in cell F5

The text value "RUSS ANDERSON" is returned in cell E5.

Step 2	Copy	the formulas in cells E5:F5 to cells E5:F68
Step 3	Activate	cell A1
Step 4	Press	the ESC key to end the Paste command, if necessary

Extracting Text Using the LEFT, FIND, and MID Functions

Many of the text functions return a numerical value indicating the number of characters in a text string or the starting position of a certain character within a text string. You can then use this numerical value in a variety of ways to edit the text string using other text functions.

Every employee at Sweet Tooth is assigned a username to access the company network. This username is derived by combining the first letter of the employee's first name with the first four letters of the employee's last name. This painstaking task can be performed automatically with a formula using several nested text functions.

To better understand each text function, you create several separate formulas, then nest the formulas to create the final formula. First, you need to get the first letter of the employee's first name. The **LEFT** function is used to retrieve a certain number of characters from a text string, starting from the left and moving to the right. The LEFT function has the following syntax:

=**LEFT**(**text**,num_chars)

The text argument can be a quoted string or a cell reference. The optional num_chars argument defaults to 1 if you omit this argument. You would include a value for this argument if you need to retrieve more than one character from the text string. To use the LEFT function:

Step 1	Click	the right tab scroll arrow ▶, if necessary
Step 2	Click	the Username worksheet tab
Step 3	Enter	=LEFT(a5,1) in cell C5

You could have omitted the 1 in this case. The formula correctly returns the value "r" in cell C5. Next, you need to get the first four characters of the employee's last name. The **MID** function is used to extract text from the middle of a text string. This operation is exactly what you need, but you need to know the starting point—in other words, the beginning of the last name—in each string to make the function work.

To find the starting point, which is a numerical value, you can use the FIND function to search for the space character between first and last names. The **FIND** function finds one text value within another. FIND is case-sensitive and returns the number of the starting position of the text for which you are searching. The FIND function has the following syntax:

=**FIND**(**find_text,within_text**,start_number)

The find_text argument is the text value for which you are searching, and within_text specifies a text value in which to search. The optional argument, start_number, allows you to specify a character number from which to start the search. This option is useful if you want to skip a certain portion of a text value. To use the FIND function:

| Step 1 | Enter | =FIND(" ",a5) in cell D5 |

The formula returns a value of 5 in cell D5. You can use this value with the MID function to extract the first four letters of the last name. The MID function has the following syntax:

=**MID**(**text,start_num,num_chars**)

chapter
seven

The start_num argument is the starting position in the text string you want to extract. You don't want to extract the space, so you add 1 to the value returned by the FIND function. The num_chars argument is the number of characters to extract. In this case, you want to extract four characters. To use the MID function:

| Step 1 | Enter | =MID(a5,d5+1,4) in cell E5 |

The start_num argument in this formula is yet another example of a nested formula, which adds the value of cell D5 to 1, providing the starting position of the first letter of the employee's last name. The formula correctly returns the value "ande" in cell E5.

The final step in creating the formula is to combine these three formulas, using the CONCATENATE function to create the username. Instead of the CONCATENATE function, you decide to use the shortcut & sign. To create the username formula:

| Step 1 | Key | =LEFT(a5,1)& in cell B5 |

You should still be in entry mode in cell B5. The & indicates that you will join the results of the LEFT function to the remainder of the formula. Next, you nest the FIND function in the MID function as the start_num argument.

| Step 2 | Key | MID(a5,FIND(" ",a5)+1,4) |

The FIND function returns a numerical value that is added to 1 to provide the starting position for the MID function.

| Step 3 | Press | the ENTER key |

The new username, "rande," appears in cell B5. Now copy the formula to create the other usernames.

Step 4	Copy	the formula in cell B5 to cells B6:B68
Step 5	Delete	the formulas in cells C5:E5
Step 6	Activate	cell B5

> **QUICK TIP**
>
> Because database functions require the use of several terms unique to database structures, Chapter 13 examines this function category in more detail.

Your worksheet should look similar to Figure 7-12.

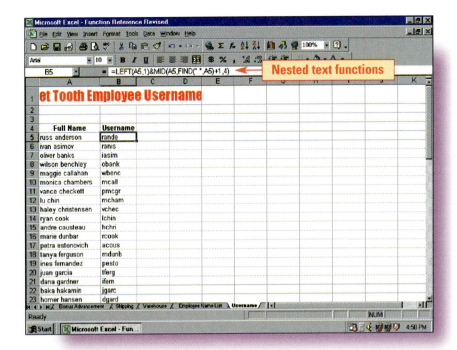

FIGURE 7-12
Nesting Text Functions

Before you print the workbook, change the window options so that the formulas appear in this worksheet instead of the calculated values.

Step 7	*Click*	Tools
Step 8	*Click*	Options
Step 9	*Click*	the View tab
Step 10	*Click*	the Formulas check box to select it
Step 11	*Click*	OK
Step 12	*Double-Click*	the columns divider line between columns B and C, if necessary

Your worksheet should look similar to Figure 7-13.

FIGURE 7-13
Displaying Worksheet Formulas

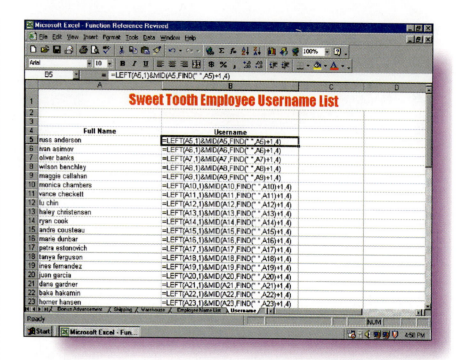

Step 13	*Click*	File
Step 14	*Click*	Print
Step 15	*Click*	the Entire workbook option button

This workbook is fifteen printed pages, but the last two pages are blank.

Step 16	*Enter*	1 in the From: box
Step 17	*Enter*	13 in the To: box
Step 18	*Click*	Preview
Step 19	*Click*	the Print button on the Print Preview toolbar
Step 20	*Save*	your workbook and close it

Excel's built-in functions have a wide variety of uses. To find out more about functions, use the Office Assistant.

Summary

▶ Paste Function and the Formula Palette act as a function wizard, providing helpful information to guide you through the construction of complex formulas.

▶ Use column and row labels to create natural language formulas and functions.

▶ Use a variety of functions to perform calculations.

▶ Nest functions to create more powerful formulas.

▶ Date and time functions, including TODAY, NOW, NETWORKDAYS, and WEEKDAY, allow you to perform calculations using dates.

▶ Financial functions, including CUMIPMT, FV, and SLN, allow you to calculate values for investments and loans and to calculate depreciation of assets.

▶ Logical functions, including IF, AND, OR, NOT, TRUE, and FALSE, test data using a true/false evaluation. The calculated result depends on the result of the test.

▶ Statistical functions, including RANK and PERCENTILE, calculate various statistics on sets of data.

▶ Engineering functions, including CONVERT, perform engineering calculations.

▶ Lookup functions, including VLOOKUP and HLOOKUP, search for a value in a row or column, then return another value in the table or array depending on the arguments supplied.

▶ Text functions, including CONCATENATE, PROPER, UPPER, LEFT, FIND, and MID, allow you to manipulate text values.

Commands Review

Action	Menu Bar	Shortcut Menu	Toolbar	Keyboard
Paste Function	Insert, Function		f_x	ALT + I, F
Open the Formula Palette			=	
Create a nested formula in the Formula Palette			VLOOKUP ▼	

chapter seven

Concepts Review

Circle the correct answer.

1. Which of the following does *not* use the correct syntax?
   [a] =SUM(A1:B4)
   [b] =SUM(Sales)
   [c] =COUNT(Income:Expense)
   [d] ==COUNT(A1:B4)

2. The #VALUE! error occurs when:
   [a] you use the wrong type of argument or operand.
   [b] a formula attempts to divide by 0.
   [c] a formula is entered incorrectly.
   [d] a moved cell is pasted onto a cell reference used in a formula.

3. The #NUM! error occurs when:
   [a] you use the wrong type of argument or operand.
   [b] a formula attempts to divide by 0.
   [c] a number cannot be represented in Excel.
   [d] a moved cell is pasted onto a cell reference used in a formula.

4. The MID function extracts text from a string starting:
   [a] from the right and working left.
   [b] at a given point within the string and working right.
   [c] from the left and working right.
   [d] at a given point within the string and working left.

5. The NOW function returns the current:
   [a] date and time.
   [b] date.
   [c] time.
   [d] status.

6. The CUMIPMT function returns the:
   [a] cumulative interest paid on a loan between two periods.
   [b] cumulative depreciation of an asset.
   [c] depreciation of an asset using straight-line depreciation.
   [d] depreciation of an asset using double-declining balance.

7. The proper syntax for an IF formula is:
   [a] =IF(condition,value_if_false,value_if_true)
   [b] =IF(condition,value_if_true,value_if_false)
   [c] =IF(value_if_true,value_if_false,condition)
   [d] =IF(value_if_false,value_if_true,condition)

8. The RANK function returns the:
   [a] maximum value in a list of arguments.
   [b] *K*th percentile of values in a range.
   [c] minimum value in a list of arguments.
   [d] rank of a number from a list of numbers.

9. The proper syntax for the CONVERT function is:
   [a] =CONVERT(from_unit,to_unit,number)
   [b] =CONVERT(to_unit,from_unit,number
   [c] =CONVERT(number,from_unit,to_unit)
   [d] =CONVERT(number,to_unit,from_unit)

10. The VLOOKUP function:
    [a] searches for a specific value in the leftmost column of a table or an array.
    [b] searches for a specific value in the topmost row of a table or an array.
    [c] returns the relative position of an item in a table or an array that matches a specific value.
    [d] returns a value or the reference to a value from within a table or an array.

Circle **T** if the statement is true or **F** if the statement is false.

T F   1. The Formula Palette displays the results of the formula as you add values for each of the arguments.

T F   2. Row and column labels can be used in formulas just like named ranges.

T F   3. Excel calculates dates previous to 1/1/1900 using negative numbers.

T F   4. The serial value 0.5 is recognized by Excel as 12:00 PM.

T F   5. The NETWORKDAYS function automatically skips all weekends.

T F   6. The WEEKDAY function returns a day of the week from a date, such as "Monday" or "Tuesday."

T F   7. Instead of using the CONCATENATE function, you can insert an & (ampersand).

T F   8. A good way to create a logical formula is to write it out in statement form first.

T F   9. The from_unit and to_unit arguments are not case-sensitive when you are using the CONVERT function.

T F   10. The value returned by the PERCENTILE function is the same as the percentage scored on a test.

notes   For all Skills Review Exercises below, include a worksheet title and other column or row headings as required. Bold and center column headings and bold row headings.

Skills Review

Exercise 1

1. Create a new workbook.
2. Create a table containing tax rates for the following income levels: 0–12,000 = 12%; $12,001–$18,000 = 15%; $18,001–$30,000 = 21%; $30,001–$42,000 = 28%; >$42,000 = 39%.
3. Create a formula using the VLOOKUP function to multiply a given income by the proper tax percentage.
4. Save the workbook as *Choose Tax* and print it.

Exercise 2

1. Create a new workbook.
2. Using the values 100, 121, 135, 117, 143, 122, 125, 118, 111, and 135, use statistical functions to perform the following tasks: find the average value; find the 50th percentile; count the number of items; determine the minimum value; determine the maximum value.
3. Create a bar chart of the statistical values.
4. Save the workbook as *Test Scores* and print it.

Exercise 3

1. Create a new workbook.
2. Create a formula(s) using nested IF statements and the WEEKDAY function that returns the day of the week in text form given any date since January 1, 1900.
3. Save the workbook as *Day Finder* and print it.

chapter seven

Exercise 4

1. Create a new workbook.
2. Enter "The Quick Brown Fox" in cell A2.
3. In cell A3, enter "Jumps Over The Lazy Dog."
4. Use a text function to join the two strings together in cell C2. (*Hint:* Remember to add a space.)
5. Use a text function to copy the string in cell C2 to cell C3, then convert the string in cell C3 to uppercase.
6. Use a text function to find the character position of the letter "Q" in cell A2.
7. Save the workbook as *Text Practice* and print it.

Exercise 5

1. Open the *Class Finder* workbook.
2. On the Student Locator worksheet, create formulas to look up a student's schedule on the Student Schedules worksheet. Return each of the teacher names by period (the colomns), given a student name in cell A2.
3. Save the workbook as *Class Finder Revised* and print it.

Exercise 6

1. Create a new workbook.
2. Use the SLN function to calculate the straight-line depreciation for each year of the machine's life for an office machine costing $25,000, with a useful life of 10 years and a salvage value of $1,000.
3. Using the Office Assistant, look up help on the DB and DDB functions, which calculate depreciation using fixed-declining balance and double-declining balance methods of depreciation, respectively.

    a. Calculate the depreciation for each year of the machine's life using the DDB function.

    b. Calculate the depreciation for each year of the machine's life using the DB function.
4. Save the workbook as *Depreciation Calculator* and print it.

Exercise 7

1. Create a new workbook.
2. Enter the following numbers in column A: 1900, 1941, 1999, 2000, 2010.
3. Use the ROMAN function in column B to convert the numbers to ROMAN numerals.
4. Save the workbook as *Roman Conversion* and print it.

Exercise 8

1. Create a new workbook.
2. Use the Office Assistant to look up the RAND and RANDBETWEEN functions (Math & Trig category).
3. Using the RAND function, generate five random numbers in column A.
4. Using the RANDBETWEEN function, generate five random numbers between 1 and 100 in column B.
5. In column C, create a formula to generate whole numbers between 1 and 100 using the RAND and ROUND functions.
6. Save the workbook as *Random Numbers* and print it.

Case Projects

Project 1

You are the personnel manager of a large bookstore. Each employee is given one week (5 days) of vacation after he or she has been employed for at least 6 months (180 days). After that time, one day of holiday is added for every 45 days the employee has worked. Create a new workbook that will calculate the number of holidays an employee has earned by subtracting the employee's hire date from today's date. Save the workbook as *Holiday Calculator* and print it.

Project 2

Create a workbook with five dates, using column A for the year, column B for the month (use number 1–12), and column C for the day. Create your own data. In column D, use the Paste Function button and the Formula Palette to insert the DATE Function to combine these entries into an Excel date. Save the workbook as *Date* and print it.

Project 3

Use the Web toolbar to search the Internet for an online encyclopedia. Locate an article defining depreciation. Print the Web page.

Project 4

You are a college entrance administrator. To gain admittance to your school, a prospective student must score in the 80th percentile on the school's entrance exam. In a new workbook, generate a list of 100 random test scores between 30 and 100. Then copy and paste the values over the formulas in the scores column to keep them from changing. (*Hint:* Use Copy, Paste Special.) Name the range of data, "Scores." Use statistical formulas to find the median test score (use the Office Assistant to learn about the MEDIAN function), the 80th percentile of the scores, and the average test score. Use an IF function with the PERCENTILE function to display "Yes" if the score is higher than the 80th percentile, or "No" if the score is lower than the 80th percentile. Save the workbook as *College Entrance Exam Scores* and print it.

Project 5

As owner of a catering business, you must order the appropriate quantity of ingredients for each recipe for a given number of people. Use the Web toolbar to search the Internet for three of your favorite recipes. Save or print the Web page(s) containing the recipes. Create a worksheet that recalculates how much of each ingredient is needed given the number of people to feed. Save the workbook as *Ingredient Calculator* and print it.

Project 6

Use the Office Assistant to find help about nesting functions. Find out what the limit of nested levels is. Print this page for future reference.

Project 7

You work as a lab technician in a bio-engineering firm. You need to convert temperatures from Fahrenheit to Celsius and to Kelvin. Create a worksheet with 10 Fahrenheit temperatures in column A. In column B, use the CONVERT function to convert the temperatures to Celsius. In column C, convert from Celsius to Kelvin degrees. Save the workbook as *Temperature Conversion* and print it.

Project 8

You are considering a loan for $8,000 to buy a car. The loan will be paid back in 36 months at an interest rate of 6.5%. Calculate the monthly payment using the PMT function. Then, calculate the amount of interest and principal for each payment of the loan using the IPMT and PPMT functions. Save the workbook as *Car Loan Payments* and print it.

chapter seven

Excel 2000

Formatting Worksheets with Styles and Custom Formats

Chapter Overview

Excel provides several ways to format cells automatically. You can create conditional number formats to change font colors by using value comparison operators. With conditional formatting, you can apply cell formats based on comparisons of cell values or logical formula results. You can also define cell format styles that allow you to easily apply borders, shading, and font settings. To quickly format selected areas, you can use the AutoFormat feature.

Learning Objectives

- Create custom number formats
- Use conditional formatting
- Apply AutoFormats
- Define, apply, and remove styles

Case profile

To make Sweet Tooth's company workbooks have a more consistent appearance, you decide to investigate creating custom number formats and styles. You learn about conditional formatting, which helps you identify data in lists that meet certain conditions. You also learn about Autoformat. Using the tools, you solve data entry problems for the warehouse department and you streamline the personnel department's procedure for identifying employees ready for advancement.

chapter eight

8.a Creating Custom Number Formats

You already know how to apply number formats such as currency, percentage, and accounting styles. You can also set up custom number styles to format values such as ZIP codes and telephone numbers to make data entry easier. Next, you explore how number formats modify the display of a value without changing the value itself. Then you create a new number format to be used by Sweet Tooth's warehouse.

Applying Number Formats

Number format styles, such as currency and percentage styles, don't change the value entered in the cell; they add special formatting and symbols, such as monetary symbols, comma separators, and so on. The formatting styles that change the appearance of a numeric entry most dramatically are the time and date formats. The *Sweet Tooth Warehouse Receiving Log* contains data from the Warehouse division noting the time and the date that shipments were received, as well as the item number, quantity, and cost of the item. To examine number formats in the worksheet:

Step 1	**Start**	Excel
Step 2	**Open**	the *Sweet Tooth Warehouse Receiving Log* workbook on your Data Disk
Step 3	**Save**	the workbook as *Sweet Tooth Warehouse Receiving Log Revised*

The columns in this worksheet are formatted with different formats. See Figure 8-1.

Step 4	**Click**	cell I5

In the Formula Bar, you see the actual value entered in the cell, without the extra formatting that makes this value appear as a phone number.

FIGURE 8-1
Number Formats

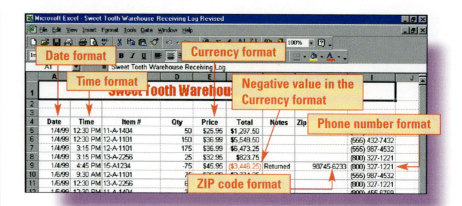

| Step 5 | **Press** | the CTRL + 1 keys to open the Format Cells dialog box |

This cell is formatted as a Phone Number in the Special category.

| Step 6 | **Click** | Accounting in the Category: list on the Number tab |

The sample window displays the value with the accounting format applied.

| Step 7 | **Click** | the Symbol: list arrow |
| Step 8 | **Click** | $ |

A dollar sign appears as part of the format. As you can see, Excel offers quite a variety of ways to format numbers.

| Step 9 | **Click** | Cancel |

Creating Custom Number Formats

You are not limited to only the number formats provided by Excel. You can create number formats to meet your own special needs. At Sweet Tooth's warehouse, each item receives a special sorting code made up of a mixture of letters and numbers to make it easier to locate specific items.

On the Warehouse Receiving Log, you can see an example of the number format that the warehouse department would like to apply in the Item # column. These entries are text values and therefore are not recognized as numbers. Correct entries use the ##-A-#### format, where # represents a significant digit. Each character must be entered by hand. As shown in Figure 8-2, the log includes several incorrect entries.

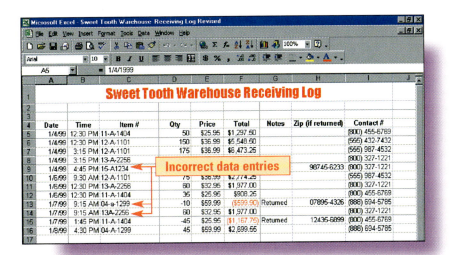

QUICK TIP

Significant digits on the left of a decimal point start with the number farthest to the left that is not a zero. Significant digits to the right of the decimal point do not include ending zeros.

FIGURE 8-2
Incorrect Entries in the Warehouse Receiving Log

As part of an effort to reduce data entry errors, you can create a custom numeric format that corresponds to the company's existing system. To create a custom number format:

Step 1	Click	cell C5
Step 2	Key	11404 in cell C5, replacing the previous entry

This value is the numerical portion of the item number.

Step 3	Click	the Enter button ✓ on the Formula Bar
Step 4	Press	the CTRL + 1 keys to open the Format Cells dialog box
Step 5	Click	the Number tab, if necessary
Step 6	Click	Custom in the Category: list

Figure 8-3 shows the Custom category of the Number tab. The formats listed in the Type: list can serve as starting points for your own custom format.

FIGURE 8-3
Creating a Custom Number Format

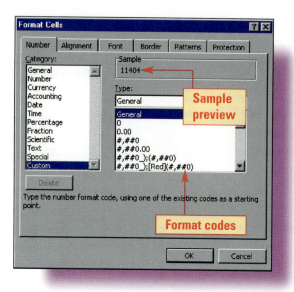

The formats listed in the Type: list use codes to specify formats. Table 8-1 describes these codes.

TABLE 8-1
Custom Number Format Codes

Format Code	Use
#	Displays significant digits, but not insignificant zeros
0	Displays insignificant zeros if a number has fewer digits than the number of zeros specified in the format
?	Adds spaces for insignificant zeros to line up decimals; also used for fraction formats with varying numbers of digits
,	Thousands separator
*	Repeats the next character in the format code to fill any blank spaces in a cell
"text"	Inserts any text within the quotes as part of the number format
\	Displays a single character as part of the number format
_	Inserts a space character in the number format
;	Separates sections of a custom number format; each format can have four sections to format positive, negative, zero, and text values
<=, <, >=, >, <>, =	Conditional operators that apply the custom format only if a numerical value meets the specified condition
[Color]	Use one of eight colors (Black, Blue, Cyan, Green, Magenta, Red, White, and Yellow) to display values; colors must be listed first in a section
@	Used as the last entry in a custom number format to display text; if this symbol is omitted from the custom format, any text entered will not be displayed

For each custom number format you define, you can specify four separate formats, in the following order: positive numbers, negative numbers, zero values, then text. Each section is separated by a semicolon. If you omit the negative and zero value formats from the style definition, those values display in the same way as the positive number format. If you omit the text style from the style definition, text entered in the cell is stored but not displayed.

| Step 7 | **Double-click** | in the Type: box to select the previous entry |
| Step 8 | **Key** | [Blue]000000 |

This format uses two codes. The first code sets the color of the number to blue. The color code must be listed first in each section. Because the warehouse system requires each entry to have six digits, the 0 code is used to insert as many as six zeros to fill out the entry. In the Sample window, you can see that a 0 has been inserted in front of the five-digit number entered in cell C5.

| Step 9 | **Click** | OK |

Figure 8-4 shows the formatting applied to cell C5.

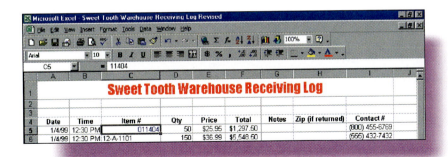

FIGURE 8-4
Applying a Simple Custom Format

Modifying Custom Number Formats

The number format you created earlier is a good first step, but needs some additional elements to be more useful to the warehouse personnel. To modify a custom format:

| Step 1 | **Open** | the Format Cells dialog box |

Notice your new format has been added to the Type: list and is highlighted. When you modify this entry, you actually create a new format that will be added to the list when you click OK.

> **QUICK TIP**
>
> You can delete any formats that you have previously created by clicking the Delete button. You cannot delete any of the standard custom number formats that come with Excel.

QUICK TIP

Before defining a custom number format, you should always enter a numerical value in a nonimportant cell, then open the Format Cells dialog box with that cell active. The Sample window on the Number tab then displays the results of your formula as you create it.

The formatting codes allow you to insert text, spaces, or other symbols. To insert text or another character in a format, enclose it in quotation marks.

| Step 2 | Click | between the second and third 0 in the Type: box |
| Step 3 | Key | "-A-" (include the quotation marks) |

The Sample window displays the results of your new format. This format will work very well for Sweet Tooth's warehouse. Warehouse personnel, however, have made one other request. When they can't locate an Item #, the warehouse employees like to add a note to "Locate Item #: *Employee Name*," where *Employee Name* is the name of the person who is in charge of looking up and creating new item numbers. If the Item # column is formatted with a custom number format, any non-numeric entry will not be displayed unless you define a text section in the number format code.

| Step 4 | Press | the END key to move to the end of the line |
| Step 5 | Key | ;;; |

The first semicolon ends the positive number section, while the second and third semicolons skip the negative and zero value sections.

| Step 6 | Key | [Green]"Lookup: "@ |

The [Green] code changes the font color to green when the user enters text in the cell. The text string "Lookup: " is inserted automatically, reducing the amount of data entry that the warehouse workers must perform. The @ symbol is the format code to display text entered in the cell. Thus the warehouse employees can simply enter the name of the employee who is in charge of locating the Item #. Your screen should now look similar to Figure 8-5.

| Step 7 | Click | OK |

Notice that the entry in cell C5 is formatted correctly using the positive number code.

| Step 8 | Enter | Gina in cell C5, replacing the previous entry |

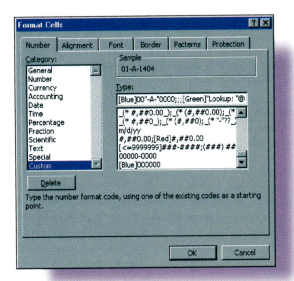

FIGURE 8-5
Custom Number Format

The entry in cell C5 changes to "Lookup: Gina"—exactly what the warehouse wanted. Use Format Painter to copy the formatting from cell C5 to the other cells in the Item # column.

Step 9	**Activate**	cell C5
Step 10	**Click**	the Format Painter button on the Standard toolbar
Step 11	**Select**	cells C6:C16

Because the previous entries were text entries (not just the numbers), the format code handles each entry as text. Gina, the Sweet Tooth employee at the warehouse, will correct these entries when you send the workbook back to her.

Creating Conditional Number Formats

Custom number formats can also test numeric entries to see whether they meet one of two conditions. A **conditional number format** applies formatting to a number based on whether the cell value meets a given criteria. When the warehouse receives a shipment of more than 100 units of a given item, employees would like to call attention to the entry. Using a conditional number format, they can highlight the number with one of the eight color codes. They would also like to highlight *negative* shipments—that is, goods returned to the manufacturer because they don't meet Sweet Tooth's standards. Thus the worksheet should test for the following conditions: (1) Is the numeric value < 0? and (2) Is the numeric value > 100? To create a conditional number format:

Step 1	Select	cells D5:D16
Step 2	Open	the Format Cells dialog box
Step 3	Click	the Custom category
Step 4	Double-click	the Type: box
Step 5	Key	[Magenta][<0]-#;[Red][>100];[Black]

Your dialog box should look similar to Figure 8-6.

FIGURE 8-6
Conditional Number Format

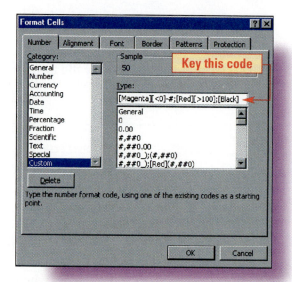

Technically, custom number formats can test for only two conditions. In this example, however, you've gained three formats for the price of two, because a third condition—the numbers between 0 and 100—is implied. This code changes the font color for numeric entries less than 0 to magenta and displays the negative sign; entries greater than 100 are colored red; everything else is colored black.

Step 6	Click	OK
Step 7	Activate	cell A1
Step 8	Save	your workbook

The personnel department just called. Members of this department would like to streamline the process of identifying sales representatives who are ready to be promoted. In the next section, you learn about conditional formatting, which can test more than numeric entries, and apply additional formatting to the cell itself, such as borders and shading.

8.b Using Conditional Formatting

In the previous activity, you set up a conditional number format to change the font color depending on the numerical value of a cell. A conditional number format can test only whether the numerical value of the cell meets one of two conditions and alters the display of the number only by changing the font color or inserting additional characters, as defined in the custom number code. More advanced conditional formatting can be applied at the cell level. When you apply **conditional formatting** to a cell, you can test for as many as three conditions by using cell-to-cell comparisons or a logical function; you can then apply shading and borders to the cell itself, in addition to changing the font style and color. Conditional formatting can apply as many as three different formatting styles based on either a comparison of the cell value to another value or the results of a logical function. To apply conditional formatting:

| Step 1 | Open | the *Sweet Tooth Employee Sales Data Q2* file on your Data Disk |
| Step 2 | Save | the workbook as *Sweet Tooth Employee Sales Data Q2 Revised* |

To identify the sales representatives who are ready to be promoted, you decide to use conditional formatting to identify employees whose combined sales for Q1 and Q2 are equal to or greater than $6,000. The Source Data tab contains the required data. To apply a conditional format:

Step 1	Select	cells C2:C65
Step 2	Click	F<u>o</u>rmat
Step 3	Click	Con<u>d</u>itional Formatting

chapter eight

The Conditional Formatting dialog box opens, as shown in Figure 8-7. This dialog box expands to accommodate as many as three conditions. You add a second condition later.

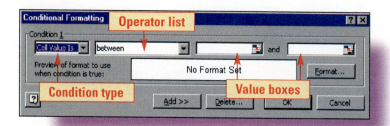

FIGURE 8-7
Conditional Formatting Dialog Box

The list box on the left allows you to change the type of condition used as the testing mechanism. The Cell Value Is type compares the value of the currently selected cell (or cells) to a value or the value of another cell (or cells). Values can be either numeric or text. The Formula Is type allows you to create a formula to be used as the test condition. Its only limitation is that the formula must evaluate to a logical TRUE or FALSE.

Step 4	Click	the Type list arrow (the list arrow on the left)
Step 5	Click	Formula Is
Step 6	Press	the TAB key

You want to add the Q1 and Q2 figures and see whether that total is equal to or greater than $6,000. Because the sum of the two numbers must be either equal to or greater than $6,000 (TRUE) or less than $6,000 (FALSE), this test will make a valid condition formula.

| Step 7 | Key | =SUM(d2:e2)>=6000 in the formula box |

Now you set the format for the cell when the condition evaluates to TRUE.

| Step 8 | Click | Format in the Conditional Formatting dialog box |

A modified Format Cells dialog box opens. You can set cell fill colors and a limited set of border, and font options. Some font options, such as the font type and size, cannot be changed.

Step 9	*Click*	the Color: list arrow on the Font tab
Step 10	*Click*	the Blue square
Step 11	*Click*	the Patterns tab
Step 12	*Click*	the Light Yellow square
Step 13	*Click*	OK

The Conditional Formatting dialog box, shows a preview of the cell formatting when the formula evaluates to TRUE. See Figure 8-8.

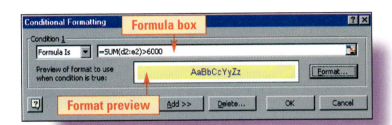

FIGURE 8-8
First Condition

| Step 14 | *Click* | OK |
| Step 15 | *Click* | cell C2 |

The names of employees to be considered for advancement are highlighted on your worksheet.

The personnel department is equally concerned with helping employees who are struggling to achieve a certain level of sales. Sweet Tooth has established additional training programs to help these employees. The company needs a way to identify the eligible employees for this training. By adding another level of conditional formatting, you can identify these employees on the worksheet. First, you need to find the cells that have conditional formatting applied. One way to do this is with the Go To dialog box. To find conditionally formatted cells using the Go To command:

| Step 1 | *Click* | Edit |
| Step 2 | *Click* | Go To |

The Go To dialog box, shown in Figure 8-9, displays a list of all named ranges in the workbook. You are looking for cells with special formatting.

FIGURE 8-9
Go To Dialog Box

Step 3	**Click**	Special

The Go To Special dialog box appears. This dialog box provides a wide variety of options for which to search, as shown in Figure 8-10.

FIGURE 8-10
Go To Special Dialog Box

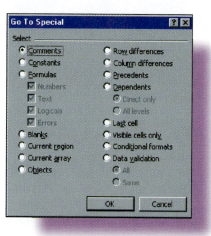

Step 4	**Click**	the Conditional formats option button
Step 5	**Click**	the Same option button

This suboption locates cells with the same conditional formatting as the currently selected cell.

Step 6	**Click**	OK

The cells are selected. Now you want to identify employees whose Q1 and Q2 sales are less than $3,000. To add another level of conditional formatting:

Step 1	Click	Format
Step 2	Click	Con̲ditional Formatting
Step 3	Click	A̲dd >>

A new condition group is added to the dialog box.

Step 4	Click	the Type list arrow in the Condition 2 section
Step 5	Click	Formula Is
Step 6	Press	the TAB key
Step 7	Key	=SUM(d2:e2)<3000 in the formula box
Step 8	Click	F̲ormat in the Condition 2 section
Step 9	Click	the Patterns tab, if necessary
Step 10	Click	the Pale Blue square
Step 11	Click	OK
Step 12	Click	OK
Step 13	Activate	cell C2

The names of the employees who satisfy the second condition are highlighted in the list. (You may need to scroll down the column to see a name formatted with the second condition.) Your screen should look similar to Figure 8-11.

| Step 14 | Save | the workbook |

So far, you've concentrated on formatting individual cells. But how do you format groups of cells or an entire worksheet? In the next section you learn about AutoFormats, which are used to apply multiple cell formats to a selected range. This option is very helpful as you prepare the final second-quarter summary report.

FIGURE 8-11
Second Condition for Formatting Added

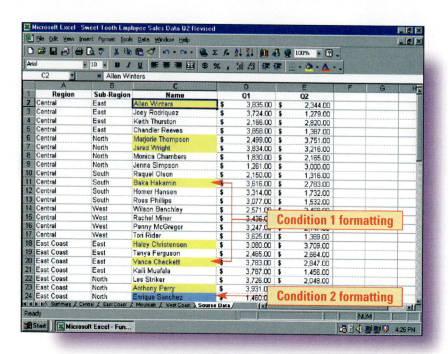

8.c Applying AutoFormats

Amy Lee, Sweet Tooth's president, has asked you to prepare a second-quarter sales summary report. You have already prepared the tables of data; now you want to give the tables a more professional appearance. One way to accomplish this goal is by using AutoFormats. **AutoFormats** apply a variety of settings, such as border lines, cell shading, and font styles to different portions of a selected range. Although you can't define your own AutoFormats, you can control which portions of an AutoFormat are applied to the range. To apply an AutoFormat:

Step 1	Click	the Mountain worksheet tab
Step 2	Select	cells A4:D9
Step 3	Click	F_ormat
Step 4	Click	AutoFormat

The AutoFormat dialog box appears. The O_ptions button extends the dialog box, providing access to additional setting options. For example, you may want to apply only the border and shading options of an AutoFormat style, leaving your number format, font, and alignment settings intact.

Formatting Worksheets with Styles and Custom Formats   EI 85

| Step 5 | **Click** | <u>O</u>ptions |

See Figure 8-12. You can scroll down to see sample images of 17 different styles that you can apply to the selected area.

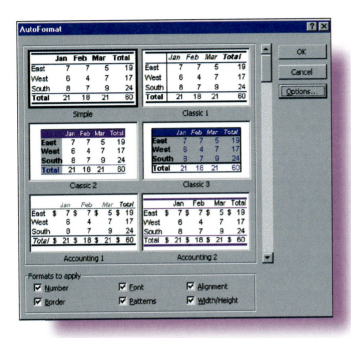

FIGURE 8-12
AutoFormat Dialog Box with Options Displayed

CAUTION TIP

Generally speaking, the AutoFormat previews provide a good example of acceptable "minimum" table structures using five columns and five rows. Some AutoFormats and AutoFormat options may apply formatting unpredictably if your data table does not include this minimum number of columns and rows. If the formatting is applied incorrectly, click the Undo button immediately after you apply the AutoFormat. Try another AutoFormat style, or modify your table to contain at least five rows and five columns.

| Step 6 | **Click** | Classic 3 |

This option is a good choice because it emphasizes the Total row.

| Step 7 | **Click** | OK |
| Step 8 | **Click** | cell A1 to deselect the range (see Figure 8-13) |

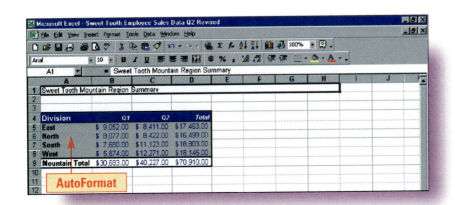

FIGURE 8-13
AutoFormat Applied

chapter
eight

Step 9	Click	the West Coast worksheet tab
Step 10	Press & Hold	the CTRL key
Step 11	Click	the East Coast and the Central worksheet tabs
Step 12	Release	the CTRL key
Step 13	Select	cells A4:D9
Step 14	Click	F̲ormat
Step 15	Click	A̲utoFormat
Step 16	Click	the Classic 3 AutoFormat
Step 17	Click	OK
Step 18	Right-click	the West Coast worksheet tab
Step 19	Click	U̲ngroup Sheets

In addition to AutoFormats, you can create your own custom style formats. For example, you can create custom styles for worksheet titles, column labels, row labels, and data. Using these styles, you can quickly add borders, cell shading, font and number formats, and alignment settings. To save time when formatting Sweet Tooth's worksheets, you decide to create several styles that you can quickly apply to other worksheets.

8.d Defining, Applying, and Removing Styles

You can quickly create custom styles to format a variety of style settings. A **style** is a set of formats saved under a name. Styles can include a number format, alignment settings, font type, cell borders, and cell patterns.

Defining and Applying a New Style

You consistently use the same settings for worksheet titles at Sweet Tooth: Impact font, size 20, and red font color. This collection of settings represents a perfect candidate for a style. To create a style:

| Step 1 | Click | cell A1, if necessary |

| Step 2 | Click | F_ormat |
| Step 3 | Click | S_tyle |

The Style dialog box appears, displaying the settings for the Normal style as shown in Figure 8-14. The Normal style is the default style applied when you add text, numeric values, or formulas to a cell.

QUICK TIP

Open the Style dialog box by pressing the ALT + ' (apostrophe) keys.

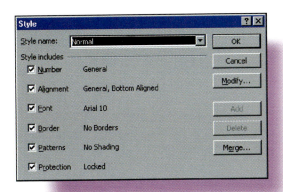

FIGURE 8-14
Style Dialog Box

| Step 4 | Click | the S_tyle name: list arrow |

As you can see, special settings are already provided for the currency, comma, and percent styles.

| Step 5 | Click | Normal |

You can type a new style name in the S_tyle name: box to create a new style, then modify the settings as necessary.

| Step 6 | Key | Worksheet Title in the S_tyle name: box |

The Worksheet Title style is automatically added to the list.

| Step 7 | Click | M_odify |

The Format Cells dialog box, with which you're already familiar, appears.

| Step 8 | Click | the Font tab |

chapter eight

Step 9	Select	Impact from the Font: list
Step 10	Select	20 from the Size: list
Step 11	Select	the Red square from the Color: list
Step 12	Click	the Alignment tab
Step 13	Click	the Horizontal: list arrow
Step 14	Click	Center
Step 15	Click	OK
Step 16	Click	Add in the Style dialog box
Step 17	Click	OK to apply the style to the active cell

Now apply this style to the other titles in the workbook. To apply the style:

Step 1	Click	the left end tab scrolling button
Step 2	Click	the Summary worksheet tab
Step 3	Press & Hold	the SHIFT key
Step 4	Click	the Mountain worksheet tab

With the group of worksheets selected, you have to apply the style only once and all titles will be formatted correctly.

Step 5	Verify	that cell A1 is the active cell
Step 6	Click	Format
Step 7	Click	Style to open the Style dialog box
Step 8	Click	the Style name: list arrow
Step 9	Click	Worksheet Title
Step 10	Click	OK to apply the style
Step 11	Right-click	the Summary worksheet tab
Step 12	Click	Ungroup Sheets

The Worksheet Title style is applied to the titles on each of the worksheets you selected.

> **QUICK TIP**
>
> To remove a style, select the style name in the Style dialog box, then click the Delete button.

Creating a Style from a Previously Formatted Cell

You can also create a style—including font settings, alignment, cell shading and borders—from the formatting previously applied to a cell. To create a style based on a formatted cell:

Step 1	Activate	cell A4 on the Summary worksheet
Step 2	Open	the Style dialog box
Step 3	Key	Column Label
Step 4	Click	OK

Now you can apply the format to other cells.

Step 5	Select	cells B4:D4
Step 6	Open	the Style dialog box
Step 7	Click	the Style name: list arrow
Step 8	Click	Column Label
Step 9	Click	OK

Modifying a Style

An additional benefit of using styles to format cells comes when you decide to modify the style settings. All cells with that style are automatically updated when you modify the underlying style. On reviewing your style for Sweet Tooth's column labels, you decide that the vertical orientation of the text should be set to Center. To modify a style:

Step 1	Click	cell A4
Step 2	Open	the Style dialog box
Step 3	Verify	that Column Label is listed in the Style name: box
Step 4	Click	Modify
Step 5	Click	the Alignment tab, if necessary
Step 6	Click	Center from the Vertical: list
Step 7	Click	the Font tab

chapter eight

Step 8	**Select**	MS Sans Serif from the Font: list
Step 9	**Select**	12 from the Size: list
Step 10	**Click**	the Border tab
Step 11	**Click**	the Color: list arrow
Step 12	**Click**	Dark Teal (fourth from the right in the top row)
Step 13	**Click**	the left, right and bottom borders in the Border preview window to place borders on the sides and bottom
Step 14	**Click**	OK
Step 15	**Click**	OK
Step 16	**Activate**	cell A1

The style is automatically updated throughout the entire workbook. See Figure 8-15.

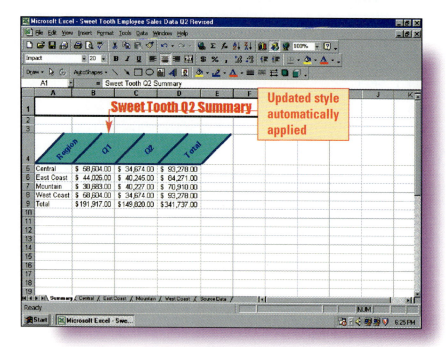

FIGURE 8-15
Modifying Styles

Step 17	**Save**	the workbook

After setting up these styles, you would like to use them in other workbooks you've created. As noted earlier, you need to merge styles in the Style dialog box to make the styles accessible to other workbooks.

Merging Styles from Other Workbooks

Styles are saved with the workbook you created them in. If you want to copy a style created in another workbook, you can merge them. To merge styles from another workbook, both the **source** (the workbook containing the styles you've defined) and the **target** (the workbook to which you want to add the style) must be open. You want to merge the two new styles you just created with the Warehouse Receiving Log. The *Sweet Tooth Warehouse Receiving Log Revised* workbook should still be open. To merge styles:

> **QUICK TIP**
>
> You can switch between open workbooks by pressing the CTRL + F6 keys.

Step 1	*Click*	Window
Step 2	*Click*	Sweet Tooth Warehouse Receiving Log Revised to switch to that workbook
Step 3	*Select*	cells A4:I4
Step 4	*Open*	the Style dialog box
Step 5	*Click*	Merge

The Merge Styles dialog box lists open worksheets from which you can merge styles. See Figure 8-16.

FIGURE 8-16
Merge Style Dialog Box

Step 6	*Click*	Sweet Tooth Employee Sales Data Q2 Revised
Step 7	*Click*	OK

The styles are merged and displayed in the Style name: list.

Step 8	*Click*	the Style name: list arrow
Step 9	*Click*	Column Label
Step 10	*Click*	OK

Mouse Tip

You can copy styles from workbook to workbook by using Format Painter. Open both workbooks (the source and the target). In the source workbook, select a cell with the formatting style you want to copy and click Format Painter. Switch to the target workbook, then click to apply the formatting to another cell. The style is automatically transferred to the Style list of the target workbook.

Quick Tip

You can copy styles from workbook to workbook using Copy and Paste. Open both workbooks, copy the cell in the source workbook containing the desired style, then paste it into the target workbook.

The style is applied to the column headings. Your final task is to print the worksheets you've modified, then save and close the open workbooks. To print the modified worksheets and save and close the open workbooks:

Step 1	Click	cell A1
Step 2	Print	the Warehouse Receiving Log worksheet
Step 3	Save	the workbook
Step 4	Close	the *Sweet Tooth Warehouse Receiving Log Revised* workbook

The *Sweet Tooth Employee Sales Data Q2 Revised* workbook is now the active workbook.

Step 5	Print	the Summary worksheet of the *Sweet Tooth Employee Sales Data Q2 Revised* workbook
Step 6	Click	the Mountain worksheet tab
Step 7	Print	the Mountain worksheet
Step 8	Click	the Source Data worksheet tab
Step 9	Print	the Source Data worksheet
Step 10	Save	the workbook
Step 11	Close	the workbook

After sending a copy of the workbooks to Sweet Tooth's warehouse and personnel departments, you receive several calls from grateful employees thanking you for making their jobs so much easier.

Summary

- Number formats change the manner in which numerical values are displayed; they do not change the underlying values.
- Create custom number formats to display additional characters, text, comma styles, and decimal options.
- Create a custom conditional number format to display numerical values in different colors based on a conditional value operator.
- Apply conditional formatting to cells. Use cell value comparisons or logical formula evaluations to determine which formatting should be applied to a cell. Assign as many as three conditions with which to test a cell.
- Use AutoFormats to apply 17 preset formatting styles and give your data a more professional-looking appearance.
- Create a custom cell format style. Selectively turn on or off style options such as font format, border style, and fill color. Merge styles from other workbooks.

Commands Review

Action	Menu Bar	Shortcut Menu	Toolbar	Keyboard
Format cells	Format, Cells	Format Cells		CTRL + 1 ALT + O, E
Apply conditional formatting	Format, Conditional Formatting			ALT + O, D
Apply AutoFormat	Format, AutoFormat			ALT + O, A
Create/apply styles	Format, Style			AL + O, S ALT + ' (right apostrophe)

Concepts Review

Circle the correct answer.

1. The @ symbol in a custom number format code:
   - [a] displays an @ symbol in the cell.
   - [b] acts as a repeat code; the character following will be repeated to fill a cell.
   - [c] allows display of text in a cell formatted with a number format.
   - [d] displays nonsignificant 0s.

2. What font color is applied to a value of 100 when the cell is formatted using the following custom number format code: [Green][<100];[Red][>100]?
   - [a] Red
   - [b] Green
   - [c] Yellow
   - [d] none of the above

3. Given a value of 9995551234, what is displayed when the cell is formatted using the following custom number format code: (###) ###-####?
   - [a] 9995551234
   - [b] 999 555 1234
   - [c] (999) 555-1234
   - [d] (###) ###-####

4. Which code below would display the value 1234 as ===A123 4?
   - [a] A### #
   - [b] *=A### #
   - [c] *A### #=
   - [d] [Red]A### #

5. The fourth section of a custom number format specifies settings for:
   - [a] positive numbers.
   - [b] text.
   - [c] negative numbers.
   - [d] zeros.

6. Conditional formatting (*not* conditional number format) can check a maximum of _____ conditions.
   - [a] one
   - [b] two
   - [c] three
   - [d] four

7. Given values of A1=10, A2=15, and A3=20, which of the following is a valid formula to use in a conditional format located in cell A4?
   - [a] =sum(a1:a3)
   - [b] =count(a1:a3)
   - [c] =average(a1:a3)>10
   - [d] =average(a1:a3)

8. The * code in a number format:
   - [a] repeats the next character after it.
   - [b] indicates where a space should go.
   - [c] identifies text strings.
   - [d] indents the number.

9. To use a style in another workbook:
   - [a] open the source and target workbooks, then click the Merge button in the Styles dialog box.
   - [b] open the source and target workbooks, then use Format Painter to copy the formatting.
   - [c] open the source and target workbooks, then use Copy and Paste to copy the formatting.
   - [d] all of the above.

10. Which of the following is *not* a valid option for a style setting?
    - [a] cell borders
    - [b] cell shading
    - [c] number format
    - [d] fill effects

Circle **T** if the statement is true or **F** if the statement is false.

T **F** 1. Changing a cell's number format alters the actual value of the cell.

T **F** 2. Setting up a custom conditional number format is the same as applying a conditional format to a cell.

T F 3. The shortcut keys ALT + ' are used to open the Style dialog box.

T F 4. You can turn parts of an AutoFormat on and off.

T F 5. You can create your own cell styles.

T **F** 6. You can create your own AutoFormats.

T F 7. You can merge styles created in other workbooks.

T **F** 8. A value of 100 displays in red given a custom number format code of [Blue]#;[Red]#.

T **F** 9. A format code can have only two sections, one for positive numbers and one for negative numbers.

T **F** 10. You can set all font options, including font size, when setting conditional formatting options. p.79

Skills Review

Exercise 1

1. Open the *Warehouse* file on your Data Disk.

2. Create a custom number format to display the Part No. as shown, using only numerical entries. All part numbers start with the letter *A* and end with the letter *B*.

3. Create a custom number format to display the Storage location as shown, using only numerical entries.

4. Reenter the data in cells A2 and B2 as the numerical values 1240 and 1125, respectively, to test your number format.

5. Enter four other 4-digit numbers in each column and apply the correct number format to each column.

6. Print the worksheet.

7. Save the workbook as *Warehouse Numbers*.

Exercise 2

1. Open the *Semi-Annual Results* file on your Data Disk.

2. Select cells A4:D9

3. Open the AutoFormat dialog box remove the style by applying the None style.

4. Change the numeric format to Accounting with two decimal places and the dollar sign.

5. Deselect the cells.

6. Print the worksheet.

7. Save the workbook as *Semi-Annual Results Revised*.

Exercise 3

1. Open the *Semi-Annual Results Revised* file that you created in Exercise 2.
2. Apply a conditional format to cell D5 that does the following:
    a. Formats any cell with a value less than 100 with a red italic font.
    b. Formats any cell with a value equal to or greater than 100 with a yellow cell fill.
3. Use Format Painter to format cells D6:D9 with the same format as cell D5.
4. Deselect the cells.
5. Print the worksheet.
6. Save the workbook as *Semi-Annual Results Formatted*.

Exercise 4

1. Open the *Goal* file on your Data Disk.
2. In cell F10, create a formula to count the number of contributors in cells A13:A20. (*Hint:* COUNT counts only numerical values. Use the Office Assistant to look up information about the COUNTA function, which counts nonblank cells.)
3. In cell F9, create a formula to display the same value as cell B21.
4. Apply a conditional format to cell F9 that does the following:
    a. If the value of cell B21 is equal to or greater than $1,000 **or** the number of contributors in cell F10 exceeds 7, the cell should be colored red with white font. (*Hint:* The bold **or** in this sentence *is* your hint!)
    b. If the value of cell B21 is equal to or greater than $750, the font color should be red.
5. Add a new contributor, Mrs. Gardner, who gave $125.
6. Add two other contributors, Ms. Olson and Mr. Young, who contribute enough to push the total over $1,000.00.
7. Save the workbook as *Goal Achieved* and print the worksheet.

Exercise 5

1. Create a new workbook.
2. Enter "Title" in cell A1.
3. Change the Font style to Times New Roman, font size 16, and color blue.
4. Fill the cell with Light-Turquoise color.
5. Create a new style "Title" based on cell A1.
6. Enter "Column Heading" in cell A2.
7. Rotate the text 45 degrees.
8. Change the alignment to center horizontally and vertically.
9. Add a left and right dashed style border.
10. Create a new style "Column Heading" based on cell A3.
11. Save the workbook as *Cell Styles* and print the worksheet.

Exercise 6

1. Open the *Apply Styles* file on your Data Disk.
2. Open the *Cell Styles* workbook that you created in Exercise 5.
3. Merge the styles from *Cell Styles* into *Apply Styles*.
4. Format the worksheet title with the Title style.
5. Format the column headings with the Column Heading style.
6. Save the *Apply Styles* workbook as *Apply Styles Revised* and print the worksheet.
7. Close both workbooks.

Exercise 7

1. Open the *Semi-Annual Results Formatted* workbook you created in Exercise 3.
2. Insert two columns between C and D.
3. Use the AutoFill handle to add the labels Q3 and Q4 to columns D and E.
4. Add values between $25 and $100 to cells D5:E9, then sum the totals in row 9.
5. Double-click each formula in column F and use Range Finder to correct the formulas to properly sum columns B:E.
6. Apply the 3D Effects 1 AutoFormat to the data.
7. Use the Go To dialog box, Special option to highlight all cells with conditioned formatting applied.
8. Change the conditional formatting of Condition 1 to less than 200.
9. Change the conditional formatting of Condition 2 to greater than or equal to 200.
10. Save the workbook as *Semi-Annual Results Formatted 2*.

Exercise 8

1. Create a new workbook.
2. Enter five different times in column A.
3. Enter five different dates in column B.
4. Select the values in column A.
5. Create a new time format that inserts the text string "Time:" in front of the time format. (*Hint:* Look at the custom number formats for illustrations of custom date and time formats.)
6. Select the values in column B.
7. Create a new time format that inserts the text string "Date:" in front of the time format. (*Hint:* Look at the custom number formats for illustrations of custom date and time formats.)
8. Save the workbook as *Custom Date and Time* and print the worksheet.

chapter eight

Case Projects

Project 1

You are the manager of a bookstore. As part of your job, you use Excel to keep track of your inventory and to signal when you are over- and under-stocked on any titles. Use the Internet to search for the current top 10 best-seller list. Create a worksheet listing those titles. Generate random numbers of books in stock for each title (between 1 and 20). (*Hint:* Use the RANDBETWEEN function, which is available only if you have access to the Analysis ToolPak Add-In. You can also generate the random numbers by manipulating the results of the RAND function using multiply and divide, and nesting this result within the ROUND function.) Use conditional formatting to highlight cells in red if the number of books is 5 or less; highlight cells in yellow if the number of books is between 6 and 10; highlight cells in green if the number of books is 11 or greater. Save the workbook as *Book Inventory*.

Project 2

You are in charge of keeping track of donations to a local charity. Create a workbook with five fictitious donors and amounts between $50 and $1,000. Use column headings and widen columns to fit the data as necessary. Create and apply a number format that inserts the text "Gift:" in front of the gift amount, displays a $ symbol in front of the amount, and uses a decimal and two zeros after the decimal. Apply a conditional format that highlights donations exceeding $500 with red text and a border around the cell. Save the workbook as *Donations*.

Project 3

You are a busy salesperson who is constantly visiting clients in your car and who therefore depends on a cellular phone. You want to see if your usage in the last year warrants changing your cellular calling plan. Create a worksheet with columns for local and long-distance minutes. Randomly generate numbers for each month between 0 and 400 for local airtime, and numbers between 0 and 150 for long-distance air time. Use conditional formatting to identify total airtimes exceeding 500 minutes for any given month. Copy the values, then use Paste Special to paste only the values (not the formulas) in the same cells. Save the workbook as *Cell Phone*.

Project 4

You've decided to change your cellular phone plan. Use the Web toolbar and search the Internet for cellular phone rates. Print Web pages showing rates from at least three cellular phone companies.

Project 5

Use the Web toolbar to search the Internet for online shopping stores. Find similar products from at least three different stores. Print a page for each product that shows the product number used by each company to identify the product. In a new worksheet, create custom formats to properly format other items from each company. Save the workbook as *Store Formats*.

Project 6

You are the assistant account manager of a new firm. As the firm has not agreed on a formatting style for its electronic files, including Excel workbooks, the board of directors has asked you to create sample styles for worksheet titles, column and row headings, data, and total columns. Create at least three different styles on separate worksheets, using sample data. Be sure to include borders, cell fills, font colors, and various alignment settings in each your styles. Save the workbook as *Sample Styles*.

Project 7

You work for a retail company that uses a special inventory numbering system. If the inventory number is less than 1000, the inventory number is entered: "A-0999-B"; if the inventory number is greater than or equal to 1000, the inventory number is entered: "C-1001-D." Create a new workbook with a custom number format that will allow you to enter just the numerical portion of the entry. Add 20 inventory numbers between 0 and 1000. Save the workbook as *Part Numbers*.

Project 8

You are interested in learning about breaking news stories. Radio has long been a good source for learning about the latest developments. Many radio stations now "broadcast" over the Internet, allowing you to listen to radio broadcasts from across the country and around the world. Search for the topic "Internet radio," then locate a news oriented radio station that broadcasts on the Internet and listen to a few minutes of the broadcast (your computer must have a sound card, speakers and Internet connection). Write a one-paragraph summary of the story you listened to. Save the document as *News Report.doc*.

Excel 2000

Summarizing Data with Data Maps, PivotTables, and PivotCharts

Chapter Overview

LEARNING **O**BJECTIVES

- Use data map
- Use data analysis
- Create PivotTable reports
- Modify a PivotTable report
- Format a PivotTable report
- Create PivotChart Reports

Excel provides many ways to analyze and summarize data. In addition to charts, you can use Microsoft Map to create map charts that display data by geographic location. Data analysis tools help you to prepare reports based on selected data, using a variety of statistical calculations. Using PivotTables and PivotCharts, you can prepare data reports by dragging and dropping report fields. PivotTables are very powerful, allowing you to quickly reorganize data as necessary.

Case profile

The Sweet Tooth warehouse needs to know which items are the best-sellers to keep in stock. Shipping needs to know which stores are buying the most so that it can prepare orders accordingly. Marketing wants to know which stores are buying the most and which divisions are generating the most sales. Personnel wants to know which sales representatives are ready to be promoted based on their sales. Data maps, data analysis tools, and PivotTables make short work of all these requests.

chapter nine

9.a Using Data Map

Data maps are a special kind of chart that display information using geographical maps. They can be a nice way to illustrate data in different areas of the country or around the world. By default, Microsoft Map is not installed when you install Excel. Instead, you must install this feature before you can use it.

notes We assume that Microsoft Map is installed. If it is not, when you click the Map button, alert boxes instruct you how to install the feature.

Adding Microsoft Map to the Toolbar

To successfully complete this activity, the Map button must be added to a toolbar. If the Map button already appears on the Standard toolbar on your computer, you can skip to the next section, "Creating a Data Map." If the Map button is not on the Standard toolbar on your screen, you need to add it manually. To add the Map button to your Standard toolbar:

| Step 1 | **Click** | the More Buttons button on the Standard toolbar |

notes If the Standard and Formatting toolbars on your screen appear on one line, the More Buttons button looks like .

| Step 2 | **Point to** | Add or Remove Buttons |
| Step 3 | **Click** | Customize |

The Customize dialog box opens.

Step 4	**Click**	the Commands tab
Step 5	**Click**	Insert in the Categories list
Step 6	**Scroll**	down until you see Map in the Commands list

| Step 7 | Drag | the Map button from the Commands list to the Standard toolbar |

A vertical place marker guides the placement of the button.

| Step 8 | Drop | the button between the Drawing toolbar button and the Zoom box 100% |
| Step 9 | Click | Close in the Customize dialog box |

Throughout the remainder of this book, we refer to Microsoft Map as Map.

Creating a Data Map

Data maps are a special type of chart that permit you to view data in association with a geographic map. You have been asked to prepare a map highlighting each of the areas around the country where Sweet Tooth operates. In addition, you want to show the relative ranking of each division, according to the total sales generated for 1999. The *Data Map* file on your Data Disk contains sales information for all four quarters of 1999. To create a data map:

| Step 1 | Open | the *Data Map* file on your Data Disk |
| Step 2 | Save | the file as *Data Map Revised* |

This worksheet contains a summary report of the 1999 sales data. To work with Map, you changed the division names to state names. Each division (state) has been ranked using the RANK function.

| Step 3 | Select | cells A1:C17 |
| Step 4 | Click | the Map button on the Standard toolbar |

The pointer changes to the cross pointer +.

| Step 5 | Drag | from approximately cell D4 to cell J22 |

The Multiple Maps Available dialog box appears, prompting you to select a map. If Map can't determine which map to use from your data, it displays a more extensive list of maps.

> **MENU TIP**
>
> You can insert a data map by clicking Object on the Insert menu. On the Create New tab, click Microsoft Map in the Object type list and click OK.

| Step 6 | **Select** | United States (AK & HI Inset) |
| Step 7 | **Click** | OK |

The map and the Microsoft Map Control dialog box appear, as shown in Figure 9-1. Notice that the menu bar and toolbar have changed to provide controls for working with maps. In addition, the title bar indicates that you are working with Microsoft Map. On your map, you can see several states shaded with various shades of gray. According to the legend, the darkest shade indicates states with the highest sales, while the lightest shade indicates states with the lowest sales.

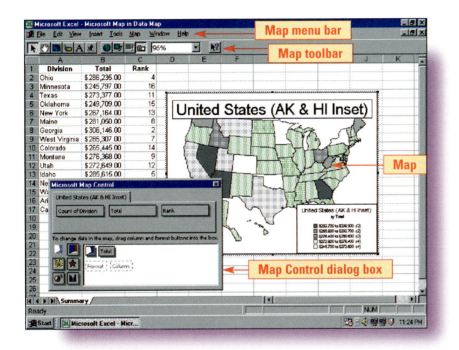

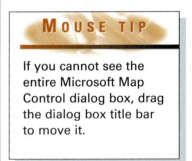

FIGURE 9-1
Microsoft Map

MOUSE TIP

If you cannot see the entire Microsoft Map Control dialog box, drag the dialog box title bar to move it.

While you are working in Map, you cannot modify your worksheet. To exit map:

| Step 1 | **Click** | cell A1 |

When you click anywhere outside the map, Map closes and the box surrounding the map object disappears. A map can be manipulated just like any other drawing or clip art object. That is, you can move the object around your worksheet by dragging it or resize it by dragging the resize handles. To move the map:

| Step 1 | **Drag** | the map up to row 2 |

chapter nine

Notice the resize handles around the object. You want to add more information to the map, so you need to reopen it for editing. To reopen Map:

| Step 1 | **Double-click** | the map object |

Map reopens, displaying the Map toolbar, menu, and Map Control dialog box. You can now edit the map.

Formatting a Data Map

You can modify or delete a map's title, add road and city markers, modify the legend scale and appearance, add labels, reposition the map, and zoom in on it. You want to make several modifications to the map object. First, you would like to edit the map's title to better describe the information it illustrates. To edit the title:

| Step 1 | **Double-click** | the title object in the map |

The Edit Text Object dialog box opens with the current title text selected.

Step 2	**Key**	1999 Ranking by Total Sales
Step 3	**Click**	OK
Step 4	**Right-click**	the title object
Step 5	**Click**	Format Font
Step 6	**Select**	Impact in the Font: list
Step 7	**Select**	14 in the Size: list
Step 8	**Select**	Red in the Color: list
Step 9	**Click**	OK
Step 10	**Drag**	the title to reposition it at the top center of the Map window
Step 11	**Press**	the ESC key to deselect the title object

Next, you would like to display a label indicating each state's rank in terms of sales. You can create labels from map features, such as state names, country names, or ocean names, and you can create labels from data in your worksheet. To add labels to a map:

| Step 1 | **Click** | the Map Labels button on the Map toolbar |

When Map detects changes to the data or when you open a previously saved map, you are prompted to refresh the map.

| Step 2 | Click | OK |

The Map Labels dialog box opens.

Step 3	Click	the Values from option button
Step 4	Click	the list arrow in the text box next to Values from:
Step 5	Select	Rank
Step 6	Click	OK
Step 7	Move	the pointer over the state of California

As you move across any of the gray-shaded states, a label appears, indicating the state's sales rank, as calculated from column C in the worksheet.

| Step 8 | Click | on the state of California to pin the label on the map |

Your screen should look similar to Figure 9-2.

CAUTION TIP

One drawback to using data maps is that data labels are not automatically updated, unlike other types of charts. If your data changes, make sure that Map is closed (that is, deselect the map), right-click the map, point to Microsoft Map Object, then click Refresh Data. Delete the existing labels based on the changed data and relabel the chart as necessary. Map informs you if it detects changed data in your workbook whenever you try to reenter Map. Click OK to update the map.

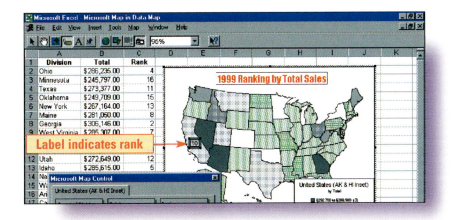

FIGURE 9-2
Adding Labels to a Map

| Step 9 | Repeat | steps 7 and 8 to pin labels to the other 15 states in the data list (in shades of gray on the map) |

The map legend currently shows five categories or levels. You would like to reduce that number to four to provide more contrast between

the various categories. To modify the number of value categories in the legend:

| Step 1 | **Double-click** | the Legend object |

The Format Properties dialog box opens.

Step 2	**Click**	the Value Shading Options tab
Step 3	**Click**	the Number of value ranges list arrow
Step 4	**Click**	4 (you may need to scroll up)
Step 5	**Click**	OK

The map is updated to reflect the new setting. Now you want to focus on a particular area of the map. You can zoom in, zoom out, and reposition the map inside the Map window as necessary. To reposition the map:

| Step 1 | **Click** | the Center Map button on the Map toolbar |
| Step 2 | **Click** | the southern tip of Nevada |

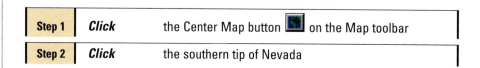

The map shifts to the right to center the point you clicked in the Map window.

| Step 3 | **Click** | the Zoom Percentage of Map list arrow on the Map toolbar |
| Step 4 | **Click** | 250% |

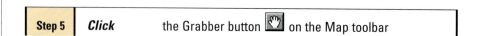

The map zooms in on California, Nevada, Arizona, Utah, and Colorado. The Grabber tool helps you pan, or reposition, the map in the Map window.

| Step 5 | **Click** | the Grabber button on the Map toolbar |

The pointer changes to a hand pointer when you position it over the map.

| Step 6 | **Drag** | the map to the left |

The map is redrawn to show Colorado, Oklahoma, and a portion of Texas. To restore the map to its normal setting, use the Display Entire tool.

| Step 7 | Click | the Display Entire button  on the Map toolbar |

The map is redrawn with its original settings. You can add other details, such as major cities, to the map. You can also change the default fill color to another color of your liking. To change map features:

| Step 1 | Right-click | the Map object |
| Step 2 | Click | Features |

The Map Features dialog box opens. As you can see in the dialog box, the United States (AK & HI Inset) is selected and has a check in the Visible column.

| Step 3 | Click | the Custom: option button in the Fill Color group |

Any changes you make to the fill color apply to the selected item in the list.

| Step 4 | Click | the list arrow below Custom: |
| Step 5 | Select | Teal from the Custom: color list |

Now you add major cities to the map display.

| Step 6 | Click | the check box next to US Major Cities (AK & HI Inset) |
| Step 7 | Click | the Custom: option button |

The default symbol for cities is the square shown below the Custom option button. You would like to show a star for major cities, rather than the default square.

| Step 8 | Click | the button with the square symbol on it |

The Symbol dialog box opens, allowing you to select a custom symbol.

| Step 9 | Click | the black star symbol |

Your dialog box should look similar to Figure 9-3.

FIGURE 9-3
Symbol Dialog Box

| Step 10 | Click | OK to close the Symbol dialog box |
| Step 11 | Click | OK to close the Map Features dialog box |

The map is redrawn with the new color and city symbol you chose. You need to reposition some of the data labels, however. To reposition data labels:

| Step 1 | Click | the Select Objects button on the Map toolbar |
| Step 2 | Drag | any label covering a star away from the star |

Your finished map should look similar to Figure 9-4. Your last task is to preview and print the map.

Unlike with embedded charts, you cannot print a Map object by itself. For now, save the map so that you can print it later. To close Map and save the workbook:

| Step 1 | Click | cell A1 to close Map |
| Step 2 | Save | the workbook |

Your next task is to analyze the sales data using Excel's data analysis tools. Statistical reports are important for several departments at

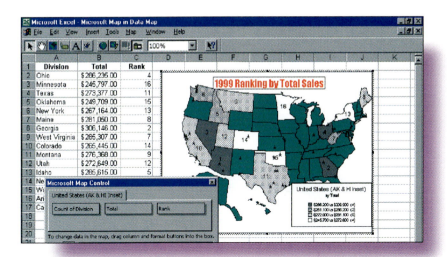

FIGURE 9-4
Modified Map

Sweet Tooth, allowing employees to analyze the company's growth and plan for the future.

9.b Using Data Analysis

Data analysis tools comprise a set of statistical analysis tool used to quickly generate reports based on a given set of data. Excel offers nearly 20 such analysis tools. In this section, you learn about the descriptive statistics and the rank and percentile tools. These tools generate statistics using several of the statistical functions with which you are already familiar.

The **descriptive statistics** tool creates a table of statistical data based on a range of numerical data. Statistics generated include Sum, Count, Minimum, Maximum, Range, Median, Mean, and Standard Deviation. By analyzing these types of statistics generated over a certain period of time, Amy Lee, Sweet Tooth's president, can spot trends in the growth of the company. This information can be very helpful when Amy must make decisions about Sweet Tooth's future. To generate a descriptive statistics report:

Step 1	*Click*	<u>T</u>ools
Step 2	*Click*	<u>D</u>ata Analysis

The Data Analysis dialog box opens.

Step 3	**Click**	Descriptive Statistics in the Analysis Tools list
Step 4	**Click**	OK

The Descriptive Statistics dialog box opens, as shown in Figure 9-5. Use this dialog box to select the input range and set output options for the statistical report.

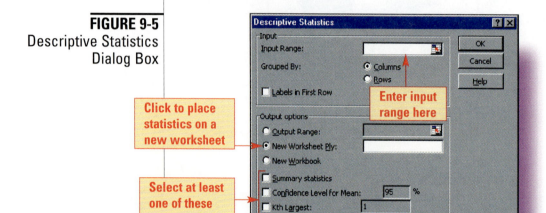

FIGURE 9-5
Descriptive Statistics Dialog Box

Step 5	**Click**	the Collapse Dialog button next to Input Range:
Step 6	**Drag**	to select cells B1:B17 as the input range
Step 7	**Click**	the Expand Dialog button
Step 8	**Click**	the check box next to Labels in First Row
Step 9	**Click**	in the box next to New Worksheet Ply:
Step 10	**Key**	Statistics

The statistical report will generate on a new worksheet named Statistics in your workbook.

Step 11	**Click**	the check box next to Summary statistics
Step 12	**Click**	OK

A new worksheet named Statistics is inserted in your workbook.

Step 13	**Resize**	both columns to fit
Step 14	**Click**	cell A1 to deselect the cells

See Figure 9-6. Notice that many of the statistics in this report could be derived from statistical functions you already know, such as SUM, MIN, MAX, and COUNT.

QUICK TIP

To find out more about any of the other descriptive statistics generated, use the Office Assistant.

FIGURE 9-6
Report Generated Using Descriptive Statistics Analysis Tool

The **rank and percentile** tool creates a ranking table that sorts values in order from largest to smallest and provides a percentage based on each item's ranking. You can use this type of table to analyze the relative standing of values in a data set. To generate a rank and percentile report:

Step 1	**Click**	the Summary worksheet tab
Step 2	**Click**	Tools
Step 3	**Click**	Data Analysis
Step 4	**Click**	Rank and Percentile (you may have to scroll down)
Step 5	**Click**	OK

The Rank and Percentile dialog box opens.

Step 6	**Click**	the Collapse Dialog button  next to Input Range:

CAUTION TIP

When you use data analysis tools, you do not actually insert formulas in the reports. Creating these reports is like taking a snapshot of the data at a given point in time. Having such a fixed reference point is important when you need to evaluate statistical trends over a period of time. If the source data changes, you must create a new statistical report.

QUICK TIP

To find out more about the other data analysis tools, use the Office Assistant.

Step 7	Drag	to select cells B1:B17
Step 8	Click	the Expand Dialog button
Step 9	Click	the check box next to Labels in First Row to select it
Step 10	Enter	Rank & Percentile in the New Worksheet Ply: box
Step 11	Click	OK

A new worksheet named Rank & Percentile is created.

| Step 12 | Click | cell A1 to deselect the selected cells |

A new worksheet named Rank & Percentile is inserted in your workbook. See Figure 9-7.

FIGURE 9-7
Report Generated Using Rank & Percentile Analysis Tool

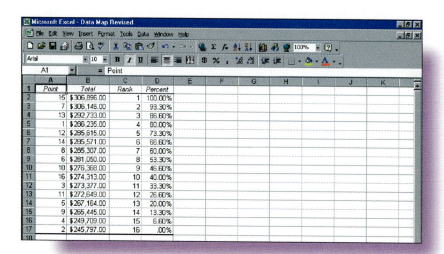

The rank and percentile report includes four columns of information. The Point column identifies the original position, or order, of the data "point" in the source data (the Summary worksheet). The Total column displays the actual values, or points, from the raw data. The totals for the points are sorted in descending order, from highest to lowest, and are ranked in the Rank column from first to last. The final column, Percent, gives the percentage of each item in terms of its rank.

Now you must print the reports and the data map you created in the first section for Amy Lee to review. To print the data map and statistical reports:

| Step 1 | Click | File |

Step 2	Click	Print
Step 3	Click	the Entire workbook option button
Step 4	Click	Preview
Step 5	Click	Next twice to preview the other pages
Step 6	Click	the Print button on the Print Preview toolbar
Step 7	Save	the workbook
Step 8	Close	the workbook

9.c Creating PivotTable Reports

Excel is often used to maintain lists of data. You've already learned how to sort lists and create outlines using lists. **PivotTables** are a special kind of table that you create to summarize unsorted data. Using PivotTables, you can quickly rearrange how data are displayed and select different data sets to use.

You receive requests for data from Sweet Tooth's many departments every day. Rather than maintaining separate lists of data for each department, which increases the chance of introducing errors in your data lists, you can maintain a single list of data. Then, using PivotTable reports, you can quickly display the exact data requested. The *Sweet Tooth Sales to Stores* workbook contains a portion of the sales data for the company's Central and East Coast Regions. To respond to the many requests for the data, you will create PivotTables. To create PivotTables:

| Step 1 | Open | the *Sweet Tooth Sales to Stores* workbook on your Data Disk |
| Step 2 | Save | the workbook as *Sweet Tooth Sales to Stores Revised* |

As you can see in Figure 9-8, this workbook includes several columns of data.

Before you move on, take a moment to examine the worksheet. Column D uses a custom number format to add the text "A-" in front of the numeric entry. Column F uses the VLOOKUP function to locate the price of an item by matching the Item # in column D to the data

chapter
nine

FIGURE 9-8
Source Data List

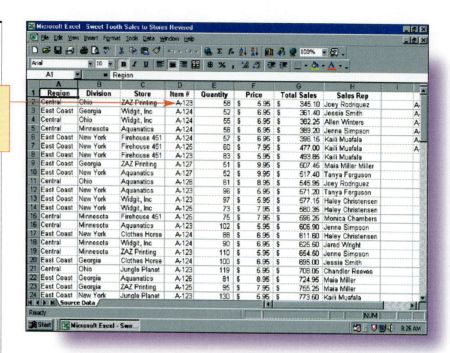

Custom number format changes value so it displays with "A-" in front of it

table in cells J1:K7, which has been named "Price Chart" to make it easier to reference. The nested CONCATENATE function is used to create a text string using the numeric value in column D. As a result, VLOOKUP can find a match in column J, which doesn't use the custom number format.

Sorting allows you to readily retrieve certain information for lists. For example, you can easily sort the list by Region and Division, then add subtotals to generate a summary of sales by Division. Suppose that you were asked to generate a report identifying how many units of Item # A-123 were sold to Widgit, Inc. Or perhaps you want to find the quantity of each item sold to stores in Georgia. With PivotTable reports, the information is a quick drag and drop away.

Step 3	*Enter*	A1:H97 in the Name Box to select the range
Step 4	*Click*	Data
Step 5	*Click*	PivotTable and PivotChart Report

The PivotTable and PivotChart Wizard guides you through three steps to create your PivotTable or PivotChart report. In Step 1 of the PivotTable and PivotChart Wizard, you select the source of your data and the type of report you wish to create. Because you're using data in the current workbook and creating a PivotTable, you leave the settings in this step at their defaults. See Figure 9-9.

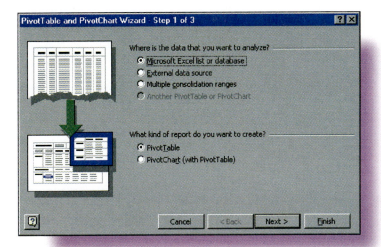

FIGURE 9-9
Step 1 of PivotTable and PivotChart Wizard

| Step 6 | **Click** | Next > |

Step 2 of the Wizard lets you specify the data to use in your report, as shown in Figure 9-10. You've already selected the range, so accept the range indicated in this step.

QUICK TIP

If you are using data from another workbook or a database, click Browse in Step 2 of the PivotTable and PivotChart Wizard to locate the file.

FIGURE 9-10
Step 2 of PivotTable and PivotChart Wizard

| Step 7 | **Click** | Next > |

In Step 3 of the Wizard, you can specify the destination of your report as either a new worksheet or an existing worksheet, as shown in Figure 9-11. Leave the settings for Step 3 at the defaults to insert the report on a new sheet.

chapter nine

FIGURE 9-11
Step 3 of PivotTable and PivotChart Wizard

> **QUICK TIP**
>
> The Layout button lets you select a layout for your data, but you can also make this selection directly on the worksheet. The Options button lets you set format and data options for your report.

| Step 8 | Click | Finish |

A new worksheet containing an empty PivotTable is inserted in your workbook and the PivotTable toolbar appears. Your screen should look similar to Figure 9-12. Notice that the buttons on the PivotTable toolbar match the column labels of your worksheet. You create the actual report by dragging field buttons from the PivotTable toolbar to different areas of the PivotTable.

FIGURE 9-12
Empty PivotTable

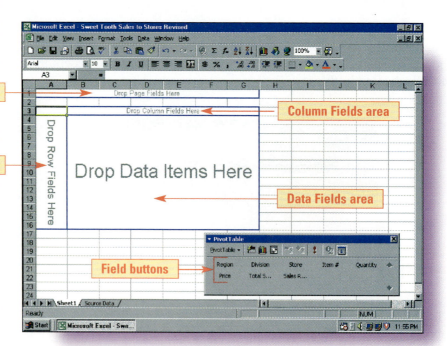

You want to find the quantity of each item sold to each store located in Georgia.

To create this report:

Step 1	*Drag*	the Division button on the PivotTable toolbar to the Drop Page Fields Here area at the top of the worksheet

The Page Fields area is used when you need to limit the data displayed in the report. Cell A1 displays the Division button. Cell B1 contains a filter list arrow that allows you to filter the data displayed in the report. This list includes each unique name found in the Division column (column B) of the Source Data tab. For Sweet Tooth's report, you will limit the display of data to only Georgia, one of the company divisions, after you've added the other fields to the report.

Your report should include the names of the stores to which the items were sold. Add this field to the row area of the PivotTable report.

Step 2	*Drag*	the Store button on the PivotTable toolbar to the Drop Row Fields Here area at the left of the worksheet

The Store button appears in cell A4 with a filter list arrow. This list includes each unique name found in the Store column (column C) of the Source Data tab. When the report is complete, you can use this filter to display data for all stores or only a selected group of stores.

Your next step is to add the Item # field to the report. You add this information to the column field area.

Step 3	*Drag*	the Item # button on the PivotTable toolbar to the Drop Column Fields Here area in rows 3 and 4 of the worksheet

The Item # button appears in cell B3 with a filter list arrow. This list includes each unique name found in the Item # column (column D) of the Source Data tab. As with the other buttons in your report, you can filter the Item #s displayed in your report by using the filter list arrow.

The last item needed in your report is the quantity of items sold to each store. This data is found in the Quantity column (column E) of the Source Data tab. Add the Quantity field to the data area of the report.

Step 4	*Drag*	the Quantity button on the PivotTable toolbar to the Drop Data Items Here area on the worksheet

The report now includes the sum of the quantity of each item sold to each of the stores in the data list, as shown in Figure 9-13.

FIGURE 9-13
Unfiltered PivotTable Report

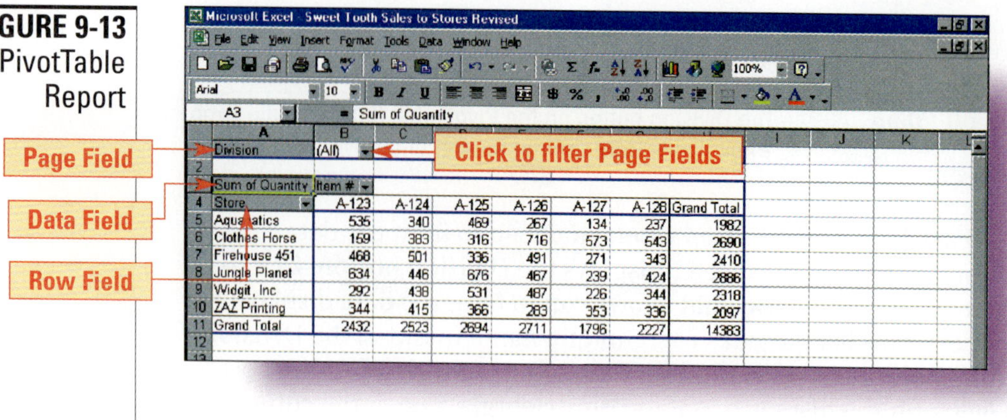

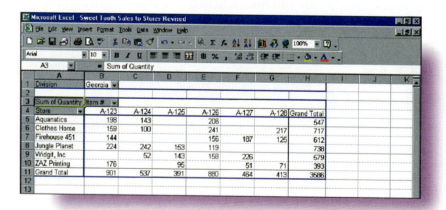

The final step in creating your report is to filter the list of divisions so that only data for Georgia is displayed.

Step 5	Click	the filter list arrow in the Page fields area (cell B1)
Step 6	Click	Georgia
Step 7	Click	OK

The filtered data is displayed as shown in Figure 9-14.

FIGURE 9-14
Filtered PivotTable Report

| Step 8 | Rename | the tab PivotTable |
| Step 9 | Save | the workbook |

An employee from Sweet Tooth's sales department just called and asked for the total sales to each client by division. You can quickly gather this information by modifying your PivotTable report.

9.d Modifying a PivotTable Report

The real power of a PivotTable report lies in the variety of ways in which you can quickly display data by rearranging fields included in the report. Instead of viewing the quantity of items sold to each store, you now want to see the total sales to each store. To rearrange the PivotTable report:

| Step 1 | **Drag** | the Sum of Quantity button off the chart |

This field is not necessary for the new report you want to create. As you drag button off the chart, a Remove Field pointer appears to indicate that you are removing the field out of your report.

| Step 2 | **Drag** | the Total Sales button to the Drop Data Items Here area |

Note that you cannot see the full field title on the button when it is on the PivotTable toolbar. As you move the pointer over the button, however, a ScreenTip displays the full name of the field; you can use this information to help find the desired field. The PivotTable now displays the total amount of sales by item for each store in Georgia. You want to display this information in the Accounting format.

| Step 3 | **Click** | the Field Settings button on the PivotTable toolbar |

The PivotTable Field dialog box displays, as shown in Figure 9-15.

FIGURE 9-15
PivotTable Field Dialog Box

> **MOUSE TIP**
>
> Access the PivotTable Field dialog box by right-clicking the cell or field name button and selecting Field Settings.

| Step 4 | **Click** | Number |

QUICK TIP

You can change the type of summary from Sum to Count, Min, Max, or Average or alter a number of other statistical summaries by selecting an item in the Summarize by list. The Options button allows you to change the way that data is displayed. For example, you might want to show the difference between sales amounts through a store-to-store comparison.

The Format Cells dialog box opens with only the Number tab visible.

| Step 5 | Click | Accounting in the Category: list |

Applying this number format affects only the data in the Total Sales field. If you change the data in the report, the numerical format changes back to the default setting.

| Step 6 | Click | OK |
| Step 7 | Click | OK |

Rather than displaying the sales by Item #, you want to show the sales by division for each store.

| Step 8 | Drag | the Item # field button off the PivotTable report |

When you remove the Item # field, the Total column displays only the sum of the sales made to each store in Georgia.

| Step 9 | Drag | the Division field from the Page fields area at the top of the worksheet to the Column fields area (cell B3), as shown in Figure 9-16 |

FIGURE 9-16
Adding an Additional Row Field

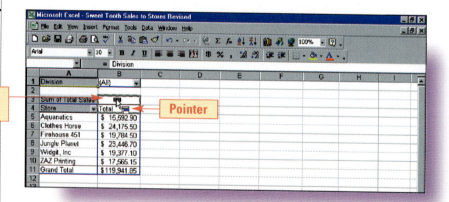

The new report shows the total sales to each store by division. For example, Aquanatics stores in Georgia purchased $4,015.65 worth of goods from Sweet Tooth. ZAZ Printing stores in New York purchased $5,607 worth of goods. Your screen should look similar to Figure 9-17.

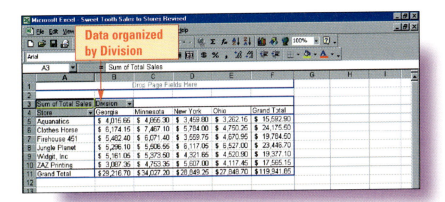

FIGURE 9-17
Organizing Row Fields by Division

| Step 10 | **Drag** | the Division field button to the left of the Store field |

You have successfully reorganized the report, providing a very different view of the same data. This view is organized more like an outline. Your screen should look similar to Figure 9-18.

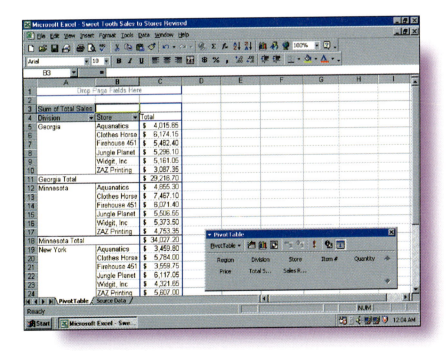

FIGURE 9-18
Organizing Row Fields by Division with Subtotals

Displaying and Hiding Detail in a Field

Excel provides many ways to display selected data in a PivotTable report. One feature allows you to extract selected data into a new table on a new worksheet. Georgia's division manager would like to see a detailed report for the Aquanatics stores in his division. Using your

PivotTable report, you can quickly extract the desired data. To show detailed data:

Step 1	Click	cell C5

This cell contains the sum of sales to the Aquanatics stores in the Georgia division.

Step 2	Click	the Show Detail button  on the PivotTable toolbar

The detail is extracted to a new worksheet.

Step 3	Click	cell A1
Step 4	Rename	the worksheet tab Georgia Aquanatics

The new worksheet contains a detailed summary of sales to the Aquanatics stores in Georgia. See Figure 9-19.

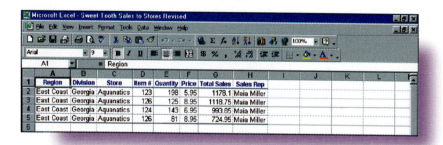

FIGURE 9-19
Detail Data Extracted from PivotTable

You can also alter the display of data so as to hide selected records. For example, suppose you want to see only a summary of the Minnesota and New York divisions, but detailed reports for all stores in the Georgia and Ohio divisions. The process used to modify the PivotTable is similar to collapsing levels in an outline.

To hide data:

Step 1	Click	the PivotTable worksheet tab
Step 2	Click	cell A12

You can actually click any cell in the range A12:B17. Because you organized the data with both the Division and Store fields in the Row fields area, the PivotTable has a format similar to that of an outline. Each of the cells in the range belongs to the Georgia division. Selecting Hide Detail while any of these cells is active will hide the details for the entire level.

Step 3	Click	the Hide Detail button on the PivotTable toolbar
Step 4	Click	cell A13
Step 5	Click	the Hide Detail button on the PivotTable toolbar

A summary of the Minnesota and New York divisions appears in your report, while the Georgia and Ohio divisions display detailed data. To show the details for the New York division:

Step 6	Click	the Show Detail button on the PivotTable toolbar
Step 7	Click	cell A12
Step 8	Click	the Show Detail button on the PivotTable toolbar

Show Detail acts differently when used to show the detail of a row or column field. Rather than extracting the data to a new worksheet, it includes additional data within the PivotTable report. Before moving on to the next section, save your workbook.

| Step 9 | Save | the workbook |

Your PivotTable report will be used in a presentation to the Sales department. As you can see, Excel offers an infinite variety of ways in which to organize data using PivotTables. Fortunately, rearranging reports is a simple drag-and-drop matter that has no effect on your source data. As a result, you can experiment, worry-free, with as many different combinations as you can dream up. In the next section, you apply AutoFormats to a PivotTable report. You learned about AutoFormats in Chapter 8, but formatting PivotTables presents a few new twists.

9.e Formatting a PivotTable Report

As you've already learned, AutoFormats enable you to quickly format tables. PivotTables can also be formatted similar to other tables. For PivotTables, AutoFormat provides 10 report styles and 10 table styles.

> **MOUSE TIP**
>
> You can hide data using a shortcut menu. Right-click any of the cells whose data you want to hide to access the PivotTable shortcut menu. Point to Group and Outline, then click Hide Detail.

> **MENU TIP**
>
> You can hide data from the Data menu. Point to Group and Outline on the Data menu, then click Hide Detail.

Applying AutoFormats rearranges the field layouts to a preset scheme. To format the PivotTable with an AutoFormat:

| Step 1 | **Click** | the Format Report button 📋 on the PivotTable toolbar |

The AutoFormat dialog box opens.

| Step 2 | **Click** | Table 8 (you need to scroll down) |
| Step 3 | **Click** | OK |

The report is reorganized and formatted using different font, border, and text orientation settings to emphasize the division names and grand totals in row 11. Notice that the detail data for Minnesota—which were hidden previously—appear when the PivotTable report is reorganized. Table AutoFormat styles arrange the data horizontally in the worksheet.

| Step 4 | **Click** | cell A1 |

Your screen should look similar to Figure 9-20.

> **MOUSE TIP**
>
> You can turn the Fields display (the blue borders around the PivotTable field areas) on and off by clicking the Hide/Display Fields button 📋 on the PivotTable toolbar.

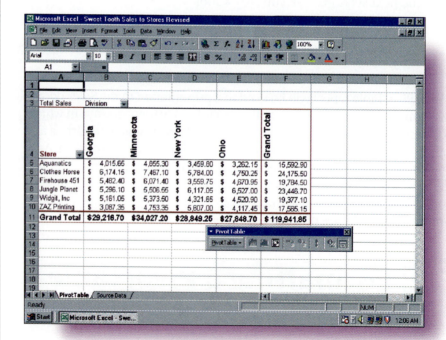

FIGURE 9-20
Applying an AutoFormat Report Style

The PivotTable is deselected, and the Page Fields area disappears because it is not used in the current report. The field buttons are not displayed on the PivotTable toolbar while the active cell remains outside the PivotTable report.

Rather than view your data in a simple table layout, you would rather examine the data in a report format.

Step 5	*Activate*	cell A4 in the PivotTable report
Step 6	*Click*	the Format Report button on the PivotTable toolbar
Step 7	*Click*	Report 4
Step 8	*Click*	OK
Step 9	*Click*	cell A1 to deselect the PivotTable report

The PivotTable is rearranged in a report style with a new color format. Report AutoFormat styles arrange the data vertically in the worksheet. Your screen should look similar to Figure 9-21.

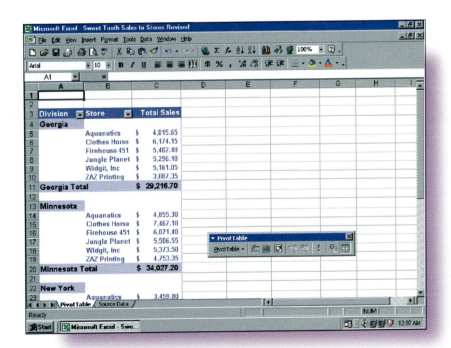

FIGURE 9-21
Applying an AutoFormat Table Style

Step 10	*Preview*	the worksheet
Step 11	*Print*	the worksheet
Step 12	*Save*	the workbook

This report will be very useful to Sweet Tooth's Sales department. You can also organize the data in a PivotChart, based on the PivotTable report.

9.f Creating PivotChart Reports

PivotCharts present another option for summarizing data. **PivotCharts** combine the features of both charts and PivotTable reports. Field buttons appear on the PivotChart. You can arrange to modify how data is grouped and displayed. When you reorganize PivotChart fields, you also alter the underlying PivotTable structure. In constructing a PivotChart, you can either use an existing PivotTable report or create a new PivotTable report when you create a PivotChart.

To create a PivotChart from an existing PivotTable:

| Step 1 | *Activate* | any cell within the PivotTable |
| Step 2 | *Click* | the Chart Wizard button on the Standard or PivotTable toolbar |

A PivotChart is created on a new worksheet named Chart1. When you use the Chart Wizard to create a chart from a PivotTable, the Chart Wizard makes all decisions for you.

| Step 3 | *Rename* | the chart tab PivotChart |
| Step 4 | *Close* | the PivotTable toolbar by clicking the Close button in the title bar |

> **MOUSE TIP**
>
> You can change the chart type by clicking the Chart Type button on the Chart toolbar.

The Chart Wizard creates the new chart as shown in Figure 9-22. The field buttons employed in the PivotTable are automatically placed on the chart. You can rearrange the field buttons on the chart to modify the data display.

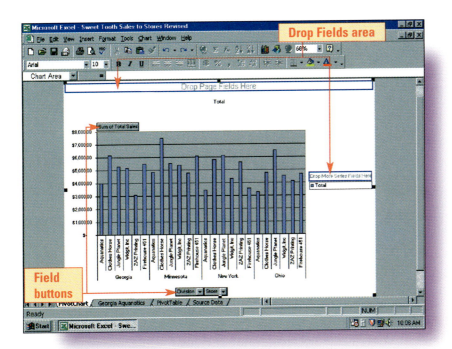

FIGURE 9-22
PivotChart

You decide to change the chart to show total sales for stores located in New York.

| Step 5 | Drag | the Division field button to the Page Fields area at the top of the chart |

You might have to drag the Chart toolbar to another location in the window to see the Division field button.

Step 6	Click	the list arrow next to the Division field button
Step 7	Click	New York
Step 8	Click	OK

MENU TIP

To change the chart type, click Type on the Chart menu.

The chart is updated, as shown in Figure 9-23.

FIGURE 9-23
Modifying a PivotChart

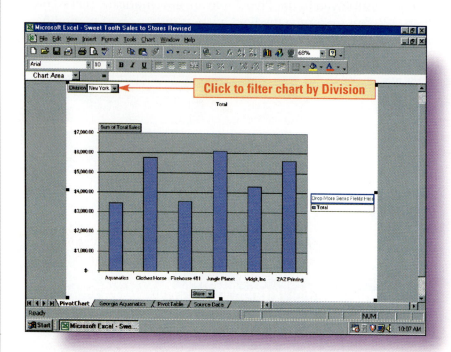

Step 9	*Print*	the PivotChart
Step 10	*Click*	the PivotTable worksheet tab

When you modify a PivotChart, you also change the PivotTable on which the chart is based. Thus the PivotTable now shows the total sales for stores in New York.

Step 11	*Save*	the workbook
Step 12	*Close*	the workbook

PivotTables and PivotCharts are very powerful tools for quickly summarizing data.

Summary

- Use data maps to display data by geographic region.
- Modify data map objects to display information according to specific needs.
- Use data analysis tools to examine data from a variety of angles using statistical calculations.
- Create PivotTable reports with the PivotTable and PivotChart Wizard to quickly display data in a variety of report layouts.
- Modify PivotTables by dragging and dropping fields to different locations on the PivotTable report.
- Extract data from a PivotTable by using Show Detail on a Data Field item.
- Hide and display data in row and column field items organized into an outline.
- Use AutoFormats to format a PivotTable report with preset report and table styles.
- Create a PivotChart based on a PivotTable report. Drag and drop fields on the PivotChart to modify the chart's data display.

Commands Review

Action	Menu Bar	Shortcut Menu	Toolbar	Keyboard
Create a data map			![icon]	
Use data analysis tools	Tools, Data Analysis			ALT + T, D
Create a PivotTable or PivotChart report	Data, PivotTable and PivotChart Report	Right-click a PivotTable, then PivotChart	Select a PivotTable, then ![icon]	ALT + D, P
Show detail	Data, Group and Outline, Show Detail	Group and Outline, Show Detail	![icon]	ALT + D, G, S
Hide detail	Data, Group and Outline, Hide Detail	Group and Outline, Hide Detail	![icon]	ALT + D, G, H
Format a PivotTable		Format Report	![icon]	
Change field settings of a PivotTable		Field Settings	![icon]	
Refresh data in a PivotTable or PivotChart	Data, Refresh	Refresh Data	![icon]	ALT + D, R

chapter nine

Concepts Review

Circle the correct answer.

1. To move a data map inside the Map window, use the:
   - [a] Select Objects tool.
   - [b] Grabber tool.
   - [c] Center Map tool.
   - [d] Map Labels tool.

2. Which of the following is *not* calculated using the Descriptive Statistics analysis tool?
   - [a] Mean
   - [b] Median
   - [c] Sum
   - [d] Average

3. Fields that you specify in a PivotTable or PivotChart report are represented by:
   - [a] Field buttons
   - [b] Field icons
   - [c] Data labels
   - [d] Field menus

4. PivotTables can be created from:
   - [a] the current workbook.
   - [b] an external file, such as a workbook or database.
   - [c] another PivotTable or PivotChart report.
   - [d] all of the above.

5. To restore a map to its original location in the Map window, use the:
   - [a] Grabber tool.
   - [b] Center Map tool.
   - [c] Display Entire tool.
   - [d] Redraw Map tool.

6. Field buttons can be removed from a PivotTable or PivotChart by:
   - [a] double-clicking the field button.
   - [b] right-clicking the field button and selecting Delete.
   - [c] dragging the field button off the report or chart.
   - [d] clicking Delete Field Button on the Edit menu.

7. To summarize data for one item at a time, drag the field button to the:
   - [a] Column Fields area.
   - [b] Row Fields area.
   - [c] Data Items area.
   - [d] Page Fields area.

8. When you want to show a field as a column header of a PivotTable, drag the field button to the:
   - [a] Column Fields area.
   - [b] Row Fields area.
   - [c] Data Items area.
   - [d] Page Fields area.

9. To finish editing a data map and return to editing the worksheet:
   - [a] click Close from the File menu.
   - [b] right-click the map object and click Close.
   - [c] double-click the map object.
   - [d] click anywhere on the worksheet outside the map object.

10. To change the number format in a PivotTable report, use the:
    - [a] Format Report button.
    - [b] PivotTable Wizard button.
    - [c] Field Settings button.
    - [d] Format Cells dialog box.

Circle **T** if the statement is true or **F** if the statement is false.

(T) F 1. Rearranging PivotTable fields has no effect on the data used to create the PivotTable report.

T **(F)** 2. Rearranging PivotChart fields has no effect on the PivotTable used to create the PivotChart.

(T)(F) 3. Using an AutoFormat Report style has no effect on the PivotTable layout, other than changing
p 124   attributes like colors, borders, and number formatting.

T **(F)** 4. Using an AutoFormat Table style has no effect on the PivotTable layout, other than changing
p 111   attributes like colors, borders, and number formatting.

T **(F)** 5. Data analysis reports contain formulas that are automatically updated when the data is changed.

T **(F)** 6. The PivotTable and PivotChart Wizard has a total of four steps.

T **(F)** 7. PivotTables and PivotCharts are created on new sheets by default.

T **(F)** 8. When you place multiple field buttons in a row or column, the arrangement of the field buttons
           does not affect the display of the data.

T F 9. Double-clicking a map object opens Microsoft Map.

T **(F)** 10. To remove a field button from a PivotTable or PivotChart, double-click it. drag

Skills Review

Exercise 1

1. Open the *Sweet Tooth Sales to Stores Q2* workbook on your Data Disk.

2. Sweet Tooth's warehouse division needs to know the quantity of each item being sold, so that it can keep adequate supplies in the warehouse. Create a new PivotTable report based on the data in cells A1:H97 using the PivotTable Wizard.

   a. Use default settings for all three steps of the wizard.

   b. Drag the Item # field button to the Row fields area.

   c. Drag the Quantity field button to the Data Items area.

3. Format the report using the Table 5 AutoFormat style.

4. Rename the worksheet tab as PivotTable Report.

5. Print the PivotTable report.

6. Save the workbook as *Sweet Tooth Sales to Stores Warehouse*.

chapter nine

Exercise 2

1. Open the *Sweet Tooth Sales to Stores Warehouse* workbook that you created in Exercise 1.

2. Shipping needs to know the quantity of each item being shipped to stores in the Minnesota division. Using the PivotTable Report tab, do the following:

  a. Remove all field buttons from the PivotTable report.

  b. Drag the Division field button to the Page Fields area.

  c. Select Minnesota from the filter list.

  d. Drag the Item # field button to the Row Fields area.

  e. Drag the Store field button to the Row Fields area and drop it to the left of the Item # field button.

  f. Drag the Quantity field button to the Data area.

3. Format your report using Report 4 style.

4. Print the report.

5. Save the workbook as *Sweet Tooth Sales to Stores Shipping*.

Exercise 3

1. Open the *Sweet Tooth Sales to Stores Shipping* workbook that you created in Exercise 2.

2. Marketing has asked you to create a data map illustrating which regions are generating the most sales.

  a. Remove all field buttons from the PivotTable.

  b. Drag the Division field button to the Row Fields area.

  c. Drag the Total Sales field button to the Data area.

3. Select cells A4:B7.

4. Create a data map using the United States in North America map.

5. Add labels to the four states in the PivotTable, using the Total Sales in column B as the values for the labels.

6. Change the data label font to red and bold by right-clicking each data label, then click Format Font. (*Hint:* After you've formatted one label, move the pointer over another label and click.)

7. Change the Title to Sales by Division.

8. Print your report.

9. Save the workbook as *Sweet Tooth Sales to Stores Marketing*.

Exercise 4

1. Open the *Sweet Tooth Sales to Stores Marketing* workbook that you created in Exercise 3.

2. Create a PivotChart based on the PivotTable report.

3. Change the chart type to Clustered Column with a 3-D visual effect; be sure that Default formatting is checked. (*Hint:* Use the Chart menu.)

4. Drag the Division field button to the Drop Page Fields Here area at the top of the chart.

5. Drag the Sales Rep field button from the PivotTable toolbar to the Drop More Category Fields Here area at the bottom of the chart.

6. Change the chart title to "Sales by Rep."

7. Change the chart title's font size to 20 and the style to Bold.

8. Print your chart.

9. Save the workbook as *Sweet Tooth Sales to Stores Marketing 2*.

Exercise 5

1. Open the *Sweet Tooth Sales to Stores Marketing 2* workbook that you created in Exercise 4. Management would like to see a breakdown of sales by sales representative within each division.

2. Click the PivotTable Report tab.

3. Delete the data map.

4. Format the data in column B using the Accounting number format.

5. Drag the Division Field button to the left of the Sales Rep field in the Row Fields area.

6. Print the report.

7. Save the workbook as *Sweet Tooth Sales to Stores Management*.

Exercise 6

1. Open the *Sweet Tooth Sales to Stores Management* that you created in Exercise 5.

2. Drag the Sales Rep field button off the PivotTable.

3. Drag the Store field button to the right of the Division button in the Row Fields area. (*Hint:* Position the pointer below the Division button.)

4. Format the report using the Table 2 style.

5. Print the report.

6. Save the workbook as *Sweet Tooth Sales to Stores Management 2*.

Exercise 7

1. Open the *Sweet Tooth Sales to Stores Management 2* workbook that you created in Exercise 6.

2. Click the Source Data tab.

3. Generate a Descriptive Statistics report using cells G2:G97 as your source.

4. Place the report on a new worksheet called Stats, using Summary Statistics.

5. Resize columns as necessary.

6. Print the report.

7. Save the workbook as *Sweet Tooth Sales to Stores Accounting*.

chapter nine

Exercise 8

1. Open the *Sweet Tooth Sales to Stores Accounting* workbook that you created in Exercise 7.
2. Click the PivotTable Report worksheet tab.
3. Display the PivotTable toolbar, if necessary.
4. Drag the Sales Rep field button to the Page Fields area.
5. Filter the Sales Rep to show data for Allen Winters only.
6. Print the worksheet.
7. Save the workbook as *Sweet Tooth Sales to Stores Personnel*.

Case Projects

Project 1

You own a computer retail store. Use the Web toolbar to search the Internet for computer component prices. Find at least three items in the following categories: hard drive, RAM, monitors, printers. Using the prices and product descriptions that your search turns up, create a table of information using the following column headings: Category, Item Description, Price, Q1 Quantity, Q2 Quantity, Q3 Quantity, Q4 Quantity, and Total Sales (use a formula to multiply Price by the sum of the quantity columns). Use fictitious sales data for the each quarter's quantities. Create a PivotTable that shows total sales for each item by category. Save the workbook as *Computer Sales* and print it.

Project 2

You own a successful catering business. Create a table to keep track of your clients. Include column headings for party name, menu item, quantity, price, and total sale. Create a menu of four items with prices for each item. Create fictitious data for three separate parties and indicate how many of each menu item were ordered for each of the parties. Use a lookup table to look up the price for each item, then use a formula to calculate the total sales for each item. Create a PivotChart showing which items are best-sellers. Save the workbook as *Catering* and print it.

Project 3

You are in charge of recordkeeping at a local veterinarian's office. You must keep track of owner names, pet names, pet visit dates, treatment, and treatment cost. Create a lookup table for five treatment types and prices into which you can enter a treatment and have the price looked up automatically. Create another lookup table for owner and pet names into which you can enter a pet name and have the owner's name looked up automatically. Create five pet/owner combinations. Use fictitious data to show each pet visiting the veterinarian's office at least twice for different treatments. Create a PivotTable showing each pet, the treatments the animal received, and the amount due for treatments provided. Save the workbook as *Veterinarian* and print it.

Project 4

Use the Web toolbar to search the Internet for PivotTable tutorials. Print at least one tutorial you find on the Web.

Project 5

You work at a busy convenience store. Create a workbook to keep track of sales for 20 items grouped in four different categories. Use fictitious sales data for seven days. Create a PivotChart showing the total items sold each day by category. Save the workbook as *Convenience Store* and print it.

Project 6

Use the Web toolbar to search the Internet for information about the latest trends in spreadsheet applications and/or office suites. Print Web pages containing reviews of at least two competing products.

Project 7

You work for a multinational oil company. Create a worksheet showing the company's sales totals for each continent. Use a data map to show the distribution of total sales by continent. Save the workbook as *Global Oil Sales* and print it.

Project 8

You work as a travelling sales representative. You have a trip scheduled to the southwestern United States with stops in Colorado, Utah, Arizona, and California. Use Map to create a map of this region of the country. Add highways and major cities to your map, and add labels identifying major highways and cities. Print your map and save the workbook as *Western US Map*.

Excel 2000

Linking Multiple Worksheets and Workbooks

Learning Objectives

- Group worksheets to share data, formatting, and formulas
- Link worksheets and use 3-D references
- Print multiple worksheets
- Work with multiple workbooks
- Link workbooks
- Insert hyperlinks

Chapter Overview

By grouping worksheets you can enter data simultaneously on all of the worksheets at once. In this chapter, you learn how to reference cells located on other worksheets or in other workbooks. By adding hyperlinks to your workbooks, you can easily open other workbooks, documents, or Web pages associated with your workbook. You can also add a hyperlink to automatically address an e-mail to someone.

Case profile

With four regional offices and a central office all collecting and combining data, Sweet Tooth employs numerous workbooks to keep track of this stream of information. You can combine the information from those various sources to ensure that your data stay up-to-date, even though the data may be revised daily. You use linked formulas to gather data from other worksheets and other workbooks, and you use hyperlinks to make short work of opening related documents.

chapter ten

10.a Grouping Worksheets to Share Data, Formatting, and Formulas

As you know, Sweet Tooth spreads its sales force across four regions, each of which is split into four divisions. Four sales representatives cover each division. Keeping track of the data generated by all of these sales personnel can be quite a chore. Fortunately, Excel provides some ways to not only help you save time when working with multiple worksheets, but also give your workbooks a more consistent and professional appearance.

When you select several worksheets at once, you create a **group**. When you group worksheets, you can enter data and formulas on one worksheet and have that information appear simultaneously on all of the other grouped worksheets. In Chapter 8, you created a group to apply formats to several worksheets at once. You can also perform operations such as spell checking and printing across grouped worksheets.

Sweet Tooth's *Central Region* workbook contains most of the data needed for the sales summary. None of the formulas or titles that you need for your report has been added to the workbook. You decide to group the worksheets so that you can enter information simultaneously on multiple pages. To group worksheets:

Step 1	Open	the *Central Region* workbook on your Data Disk
Step 2	Save	the workbook as *Central Region Revised*
Step 3	Click	the East Division worksheet tab
Step 4	Press & Hold	the SHIFT key
Step 5	Click	the South Division worksheet tab

See Figure 10-1. Each of the Division tabs is now selected or grouped, as indicated by the white tabs. The title bar also indicates that a group has been formed. When you group worksheets, any information that you enter and all formatting that you apply appear on all sheets in the group.

chapter ten

FIGURE 10-1
Grouping Worksheets

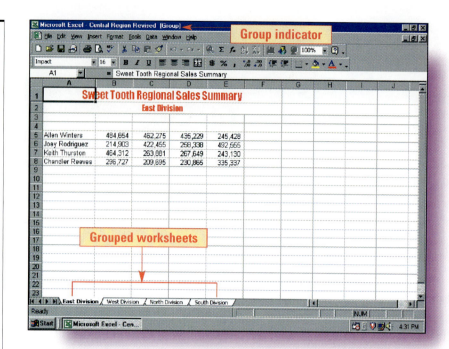

> **QUICK TIP**
>
> Select nonadjacent worksheets by holding the CTRL key down while clicking worksheet tabs. You can also use this method to remove worksheets from a group.

Table 10-1 contains the data you need to add to the worksheet group. As you enter the data on the East Division tab, the same information will automatically be added to the other worksheets in the group.

Step 6	*Enter*	the data shown in Table 10-1

TABLE 10-1
Data to Enter on Grouped Worksheets

Cell Address	Enter
A4	Rep Name
B4	Q1
C4	Q2
D4	Q3
E4	Q4
F4	Total
A9	Total

Step 7	*Select*	cells F5:F8
Step 8	*Click*	the AutoSum button ∑ on the Standard toolbar
Step 9	*Select*	cells B9:F9
Step 10	*Click*	the AutoSum button ∑ on the Standard toolbar

AutoSum automatically sums the cells to the left of or above the range. Now apply an AutoFormat to the table.

Step 11	*Click*	cell A4
Step 12	*Click*	Format
Step 13	*Click*	Autoformat
Step 14	*Click*	Simple
Step 15	*Click*	OK

See Figure 10-2. You can examine the changes to the other workbooks by clicking any of the tabs in the group. The group remains selected as long as you select a tab in the group.

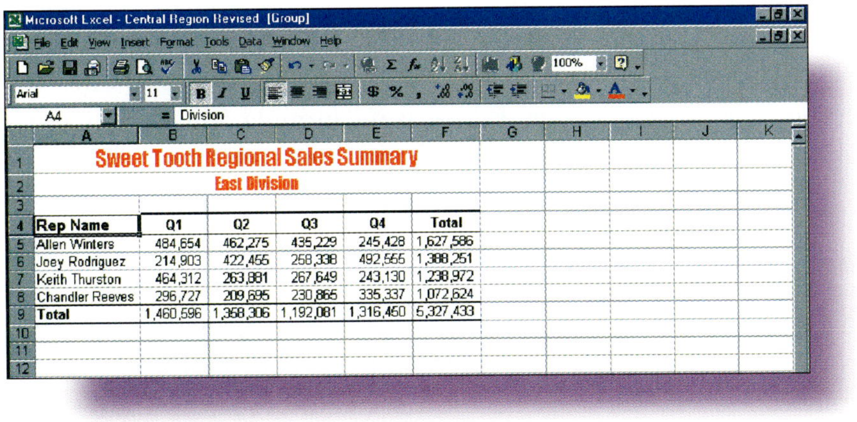

Rep Name	Q1	Q2	Q3	Q4	Total
Allen Winters	484,654	462,275	435,229	245,428	1,627,586
Joey Rodriguez	214,903	422,455	258,338	492,555	1,388,251
Keith Thurston	464,312	263,881	267,649	243,130	1,238,972
Chandler Reeves	296,727	209,695	230,865	335,337	1,072,624
Total	1,460,596	1,358,306	1,192,081	1,316,450	5,327,433

FIGURE 10-2
Adding Data and Formatting to Grouped Worksheets

Step 16	*Click*	the South Division worksheet tab

As you can see, the formatting and data have been applied to this worksheet as well as the original worksheet. Now that you have finished setting up the table, you need to ungroup the worksheets to avoid overwriting important data.

To ungroup the worksheets:

Step 1	*Right-click*	the South Division worksheet tab
Step 2	*Click*	Ungroup sheets

MOUSE TIP

You can click a worksheet tab outside the group to ungroup worksheets.

chapter ten

The sales representatives' names are missing from the South Division worksheet. To enter data:

| Step 1 | Enter | the data shown in Table 10-2 |

TABLE 10-2
South Division Sales Representatives' Names

Cell Address	Enter
A5	Raquel Olson
A6	Baka Hakamin
A7	Homer Hansen
A8	Ross Phillips

| Step 2 | Resize | column A to fit the names |
| Step 3 | Save | the workbook |

The sum formulas you entered in this section use references to cells located on the same worksheet as the formula. You can also use references to cells on other worksheets by linking formulas. You learn to link formulas in the next section.

10.b Linking Worksheets and Using 3-D References

As you have learned in previous chapters, you use cell references in formulas so that when a data value changes, the formula will recalculate and display the new result automatically. The simple formula =A1+B1, for example, links to cells A1 and B1 to calculate the sum of the values contained in those cells. You can also reference cells on other worksheets in formulas. In these **linking** formulas, the formulas are linked, or connected, to the cells on another worksheet. The linked formulas maintain a connection to the worksheet that holds the original formula. You can also create **3-D references**, which are ranges of cells that span multiple worksheets.

To create the Central Region Summary worksheet, you need to link the totals from each of the division worksheets. To add links to other worksheets:

| Step 1 | Click | the left end tab scrolling button |
| Step 2 | Click | the Central Region Summary worksheet tab |

| Step 3 | Activate | cell B5 |
| Step 4 | Key | = (equal sign) |

With the formula entry still active, you can click another cell (or cells) to create a link to the value in that cell.

Step 5	Click	the East Division worksheet tab
Step 6	Click	cell F9
Step 7	Click	the Enter button ✓ on the Formula Bar

See Figure 10-3. Excel returns to the Central Region Summary tab and displays the total sales for the East Division, calculated in cell F9 on the East Division tab.

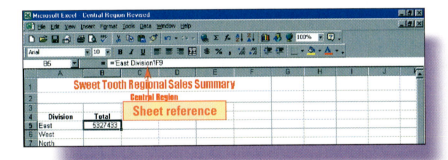

FIGURE 10-3
Linking Formula Between Worksheets

Notice the formula in the Formula Bar. It adds the worksheet name surrounded by apostrophes. An exclamation mark separates the worksheet name from the cell reference. Next, add links to the other worksheets.

Step 8	Repeat	steps 4–7 to link cell B6 to cell F9 on the West Division tab
Step 9	Repeat	steps 4–7 to link cell B7 to cell F9 on the North Division tab
Step 10	Repeat	steps 4–7 to link cell B8 to cell F9 on the South Division tab
Step 11	Enter	a formula to sum cells B5:B8 in cell B9

To find the Central Region's total sales for each quarter, you must reference the calculated totals for each division. Because these totals

QUICK TIP

You can link titles on charts to cells on other worksheets. Select a chart title, then enter = in the Formula Bar. Next, click the tab and cell you wish to link and press the ENTER key. The chart title displays the value of the referenced cell.

MENU TIP

You can create links to cells on other worksheets or workbooks by using Copy and Paste Special. Copy the cell(s) to which you want to link, then change to the workbook, worksheet, and cell(s) where the new link should appear. Click Edit, Paste Special, then click the Paste Link button to create an absolute reference to the cells you copied.

appear on different worksheets, you use a 3-D reference in your formula. To create a 3-D reference formula:

Step 1	Activate	cell B13
Step 2	Key	=sum(
Step 3	Click	the East Division worksheet tab

Notice that a reference to the East Division sheet appears in the Formula Bar.

Step 4	Click	cell B9
Step 5	Press & Hold	the SHIFT key
Step 6	Click	the South Division worksheet tab
Step 7	Click	the Enter button on the Formula Bar

The Formula Bar now shows the formula **=sum('East Division:South Division'!B9)**. This formula will sum the values in cell B9 in all of the worksheets, from the East Division to the South Division.

Step 8	Repeat	steps 2–7 to add a sum formula in cell B14 referencing cell C9 on each of the Division worksheets
Step 9	Repeat	steps 2–7 to add a sum formula in cell B15 referencing cell D9 on each of the Division worksheets
Step 10	Repeat	steps 2–7 to add a sum formula in cell B16 referencing cell E9 on each of the Division worksheets
Step 11	Enter	a formula in cell B17 to sum cells B13:B16

Cells B9 and B17 should be identical. Change the number format in your summary report.

Step 12	Select	cells B5:B17
Step 13	Click	the Currency Style button on the Formatting toolbar
Step 14	Resize	column B to show the calculated values
Step 15	Deselect	the range

Your worksheet should look similar to Figure 10-4.

> **QUICK TIP**
>
> It's easy to create 3-D references when the values to be referenced appear in the same cell on each worksheet. When the values are located in different cells on each worksheet, however, creating 3-D references is not quite as simple. In this case, you start the formula as you normally would. Click the first tab and select the cell(s) you want to add. Next, click the Formula Bar, key a comma (,), then click the next tab and select another cell. Continue building the formula, separating each cell reference with a comma. Press the ENTER key when the formula is complete.

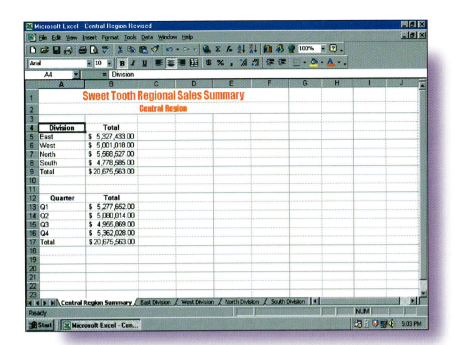

FIGURE 10-4
3-D Cell References Added

> **QUICK TIP**
>
> Another easy way to reference a cell or range from another worksheet is to use range names.

With the links in place on the Central Region Summary worksheet, you are ready to print your results. You can use worksheet grouping to print multiple worksheets.

10.c Printing Multiple Worksheets

You may want to print multiple worksheets at the same time. You can use the same grouping technique you employed to enter and format the Division worksheets earlier in this chapter. To print the *Central Region Revised* workbook:

Step 1	Group	the Central Region Summary tab and all of the Division summary tabs
Step 2	Click	the Print Preview button on the Standard toolbar
Step 3	Click	the Next and Previous buttons on the Print Preview toolbar to view each page of the print report

Each page corresponds to a worksheet.

Step 4	Click	the Print button on the Print Preview toolbar to print the worksheets

chapter ten

Step 5	Click	OK in the Print dialog box
Step 6	Ungroup	the worksheets
Step 7	Save	the workbook

Using linking techniques similar to those you've learned so far, you can also create links to other workbooks.

10.d Working with Multiple Workbooks

When working with multiple workbooks, you can arrange them to view several workbooks at once. If you must manipulate the same workbooks simultaneously, you can save a workspace, which speeds the editing process when you need to work with the same set of workbooks again. **Workspaces** remember which files are open and how the workbooks are arranged. First, you need to open the desired workbooks.

To open workbooks to save as a workspace:

| Step 1 | Open | the *Regional Sales Summary* workbook on your Data Disk |
| Step 2 | Save | the workbook as *Regional Sales Summary Revised* |

Now open the other workbooks that will act as sources.

| Step 3 | Open | the *East Coast Region, Mountain Region,* and *West Coast Region* workbooks |
| Step 4 | Save | each of these workbooks to your Data Files folder by placing "Revised" after the current filename |

The *Central Region Revised* workbook should still be open.

| Step 5 | Click | Window |
| Step 6 | Click | Regional Sales Summary Revised |

> **QUICK TIP**
>
> You can select multiple files to be opened by pressing the CTRL key as you click each file in the Open dialog box.

Arranging Workbooks

When working with multiple workbooks, you may want to display more than one workbook window at a time. Using the Arrange Windows dialog box, you can create several different arrangements. To arrange the workbook windows:

Step 1	Click	Window
Step 2	Click	Arrange
Step 3	Click	the Tiled option button
Step 4	Click	OK

Your screen should look similar to Figure 10-5. The exact arrangement of your windows will vary.

QUICK TIP

You can view multiple worksheets in a workbook at the same time. To do this, you need to create a new window of the current workbook. Click Window, then click New Window. A new window with the current workbook is displayed. You can arrange the windows using the Arrange Windows dialog box.

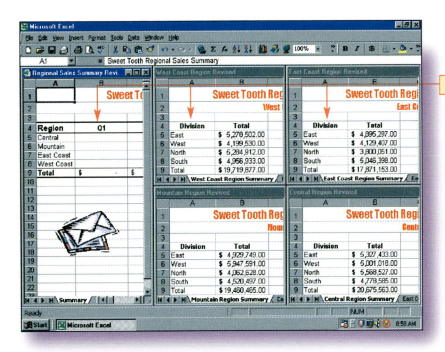

FIGURE 10-5
Tiled Windows

Using a Workspace

Workspaces are great time savers when you frequently use the same files simultaneously. Instead of opening several files and then using the Arrange Windows dialog box every time you need to work with that particular set of files, you can open a workspace, which automatically opens and arranges the desired files. Because you use this

chapter ten

set of Sweet Tooth's workbooks frequently, you decide to create a workspace. To create a workspace:

| Step 1 | **Click** | File |
| Step 2 | **Click** | Save Workspace |

The Save Workspace dialog box, which is very similar to the Save As dialog box, opens. In the Save as type: box, the option Workspaces is selected. When you save a workspace, this is the only option available.

Step 3	**Save**	the workspace as *Regional Sales Summary*
Step 4	**Press & Hold**	the SHIFT key
Step 5	**Click**	File
Step 6	**Click**	Close All

When you press the SHIFT key before clicking File, the Close command changes to Close All. Now open your workspace. Opening a workspace is very similar to opening any other Excel workbook. To open a workspace:

| Step 1 | **Click** | the Open button on the Standard toolbar |

It may be difficult to locate the workspace icon. It may be helpful to filter the list of files displayed in the Open file dialog box by changing the Files of type: selection.

| Step 2 | **Click** | the Files of type: list arrow |
| Step 3 | **Click** | Workspaces in the list (you need to scroll) |

Only workspace files are displayed, as shown in Figure 10-6.

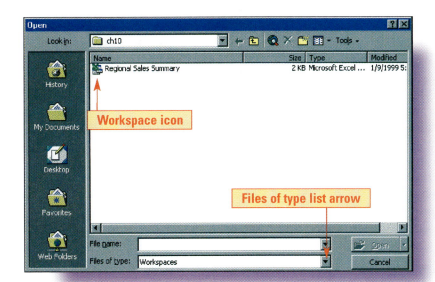

FIGURE 10-6
Opening a Workspace

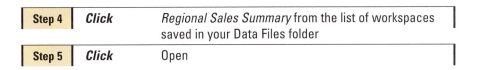

The workbooks open in the same arrangement in which you saved them. Now you're ready to finish the Regional Sales summary report by linking values from each of the Region workbooks to the *Regional Sales Summary Revised* workbook.

10.e Linking Workbooks

You need to prepare a final results workbook, linking the totals from each workbook's Region Summary tab. The Region workbooks are the **source** workbooks, and the *Regional Sales Summary Revised* workbook is the **target** workbook. Like linked worksheets, a workbook containing links maintains a connection with the source workbooks. The target workbook checks the values of the links in the source workbook every time that the file is opened or recalculated.

Creating Links

You need to create linking formulas in the *Regional Sales Summary Revised* to each of the Region workbooks. To add links to the other workbooks:

| Step 1 | Activate | cell B5 in the *Regional Sales Summary Revised* workbook |

Step 2	Key	= (equal sign)
Step 3	Click	the *Central Region Revised* workbook to activate this workbook
Step 4	Click	cell B13
Step 5	Click	the Enter button ✓ on the Formula Bar

Figure 10-7 shows the formula that appears in the Formula Bar. Single quotes surround the workbook name and the worksheet name. The workbook name appears in brackets. An exclamation point separates the workbook and worksheet name from the cell reference.

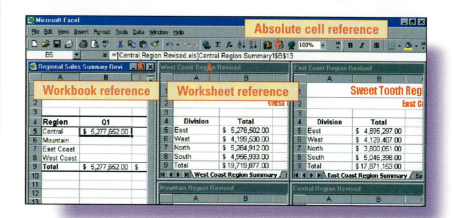

FIGURE 10-7
Linking Workbooks

Step 6	Repeat	steps 2–5 to link cell B6 of the *Regional Sales Summary Revised* workbook to cell B13 of the *Mountain Region Revised* workbook
Step 7	Repeat	steps 2–5 to link cell B7 of the *Regional Sales Summary Revised* workbook to cell B13 of the *East Coast Region Revised* workbook
Step 8	Repeat	steps 2–5 to link cell B8 of the *Regional Sales Summary Revised* workbook to cell B13 of the *West Coast Region Revised* workbook

Next, you need to link the cells for the second-, third-, and fourth-quarter data.

Step 9	Link	cells C5:E8 in the *Region Sales Summary Revised* workbook to the corresponding cells in the Region workbooks

QUICK TIP

🄲 If you need to copy the contents of a cell containing links, you can use the Paste Special command on the Edit menu. You have the option of pasting the calculated value, the formula, or all information. You can also click Paste Link to paste an absolute reference to the cell containing the formula.

Close the Region workbooks and continue working on the *Region Sales Summary Revised* workbook.

Step 10	Activate	cell B5 in the *Regional Sales Summary Revised* workbook
Step 11	Maximize	the *Regional Sales Summary Revised* workbook window by clicking the Maximize button
Step 12	Click	the Save button on the Standard toolbar

Your screen should look similar to Figure 10-8.

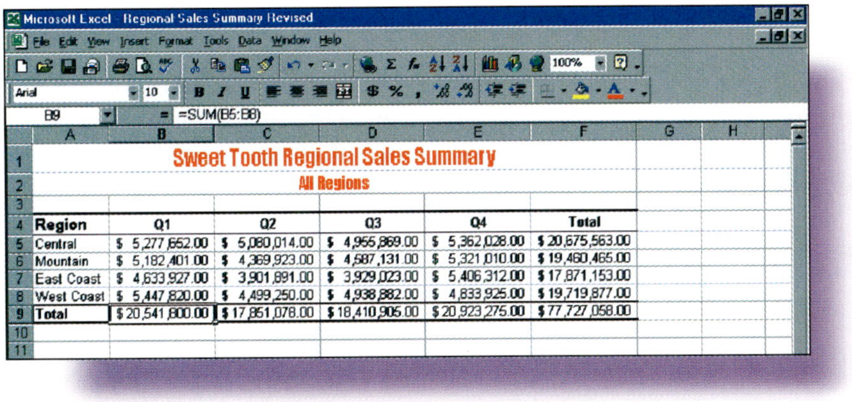

FIGURE 10-8
Links Completed

Step 13	Close	all open workbooks

Updating Links

When you open a workbook that contains links to other workbooks, that workbook attempts to reestablish the links. As long as the linked workbooks are still in the same directory they were in when you created the links, the links will be reestablished. You want to continue working on the *Regional Sales Summary Revised* workbook. To open a workbook and reestablish links:

Step 1	Change	the Files of type: list box to Microsoft Excel Files
Step 2	Open	the *Regional Sales Summary Revised* workbook

An alert box opens, asking if you want to update the links. If you click No, the workbook displays the calculated values that were in the workbook when you closed it. Clicking Yes means that the workbook should reestablish the links and recalculate the workbook. Unless you have a specific reason for not updating the links, it's a good idea to click Yes.

QUICK TIP

You can request link updates any time by clicking Links from the Edit menu. Select the source filename of the link to be updated, then click Update Now.

chapter ten

| Step 3 | **Click** | Yes |

In the next section, you add hyperlinks to the workbook to make it easy to look up information in other workbooks, send e-mail to someone, or open a Web page.

10.f Inserting Hyperlinks

You can add hyperlinks to your workbooks to make it easier to find information. In fact, not only can you create hyperlinks to Web pages on the Internet, but you can also construct hyperlinks to different locations in the workbook, to locations in other workbooks, or even to other types of Microsoft Office documents, such as a Word document or a PowerPoint presentation. You can even include a hyperlink to your own e-mail address, so that subsequent users can contact you for information about the workbook.

Adding an E-mail Hyperlink

You would like to create an e-mail hyperlink in the *Regional Sales Summary Revised* workbook. To add a hyperlink:

| Step 1 | **Click** | the envelopes clip art object to select it |

You can create a hyperlink attached to any object or to any value in a cell.

| Step 2 | **Click** | the Insert Hyperlink button 📎 on the Standard toolbar |

The Insert Hyperlink dialog box opens. You can add links to an existing file or Web page, a place in the current document (the workbook), create a new document (or workbook), or insert a link to send e-mail to someone.

| Step 3 | **Click** | E-mail Address in the Link to: section on the left |

The dialog box changes, allowing you to insert an e-mail address. See Figure 10-9.

MOUSE TIP

To remove a hyperlink, right-click any hyperlinked object or cell. Select Hyperlink, then Remove hyperlink.

QUICK TIP

Press the CTRL + K keys to insert a new hyperlink or to edit an existing hyperlink. This shortcut key combination works in all Office 2000 applications.

Linking Multiple Worksheets and Workbooks **EI 151**

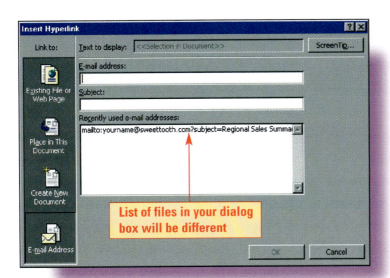

FIGURE 10-9
Insert Hyperlink Dialog Box

| Step 4 | Key | your e-mail address in the E-mail address: box |

As you begin to enter your e-mail address, notice that "mailto:" is inserted in front of the address. When a user clicks this hyperlink, the user's e-mail program will launch and start a new message. The e-mail address you specify here will automatically be entered as the "To" address of the new e-mail message.

| Step 5 | Key | Regional Sales Summary.xls in the Subject: box |

This information will be entered automatically as the subject line of the new message whenever a user clicks this link.

| Step 6 | Click | ScreenTip |

Here you key the text that users will see in the ScreenTip that displays when they point to your hyperlink.

Step 7	Key	Need help? E-mail me!
Step 8	Click	OK
Step 9	Click	OK in the Insert Hyperlink dialog box
Step 10	Deselect	the clip art object

MOUSE TIP

When you add a hyperlink to an object, you can't click the object to select it, because clicking the object activates the hyperlink. To select an object with a hyperlink attached, right-click the object. You can then use the shortcut menu to modify the object, or press ESC to close the shortcut menu and move or resize the object.

chapter ten

> **QUICK TIP**
>
> When creating hyperlinks, you don't have to type in the address. Open the Insert Hyperlink dialog box, then click Web Page on the right to open your browser. Use your browser to find the Web page, click in the address box in the browser, then switch to Excel. The address currently in your browser appears in the Type the file or Web page name: box.

Now test your new hyperlink. To use the newly constructed hyperlink:

| Step 1 | Move | the pointer over the envelope |

Your custom ScreenTip appears, displaying the tip, "Need help? E-mail me!"

| Step 2 | Click | the envelope |

Your e-mail program starts automatically and creates a new mail message with the address and subject lines already filled in.

| Step 3 | Close | the e-mail message without saving changes |

Adding a Hyperlink to Another Workbook

To make it easier to look up information, you can add hyperlinks to other workbooks. To add a hyperlink to another workbook:

| Step 1 | Right-click | cell A5 |
| Step 2 | Click | Hyperlink |

The Insert Hyperlink dialog box opens.

| Step 3 | Click | Existing File or Web Page in the Link to: area |

The dialog box changes, allowing you to insert a file or Web page name. The list in the middle of the dialog box displays filenames, network drives, and Internet addresses that you've visited recently, depending on which button is selected to the left of the list.

| Step 4 | Click | File under Browse for: on the right side of the dialog box |

The Link to File dialog box opens. This dialog box looks very similar to the Open dialog box.

> **MENU TIP**
>
> On the Insert menu, click Hyperlink to open the Insert Hyperlink dialog box.

Step 5	*Delete*	any text in the File name: box at the bottom of the dialog box
Step 6	*Locate*	the *Central Region Revised* workbook in your Data Files folder
Step 7	*Click*	OK
Step 8	*Click*	ScreenTip
Step 9	*Key*	Go to Central Region Revised.xls
Step 10	*Click*	OK

The dialog box on your screen should look similar to Figure 10-10.

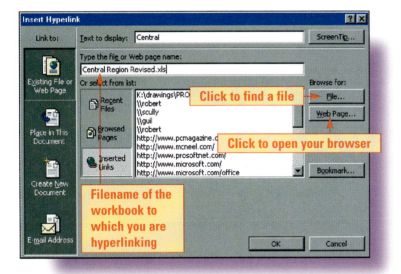

FIGURE 10-10
Adding a Hyperlink to a File

> **QUICK TIP**
>
> You can modify the formatting of a cell containing a hyperlink by using the normal formatting commands. Altering the formatting does not affect the hyperlink.

| Step 11 | *Click* | OK |

The value in cell A5 changes to blue and is underlined. This format is the default for hyperlinks.

| Step 12 | *Repeat* | steps 1–11 to add hyperlinks in cells A6:A8 to each of your revised Region workbooks |

Now check your new hyperlinks.

| Step 13 | *Move* | the pointer over cell A8 |

Your screen should look similar to Figure 10-11.

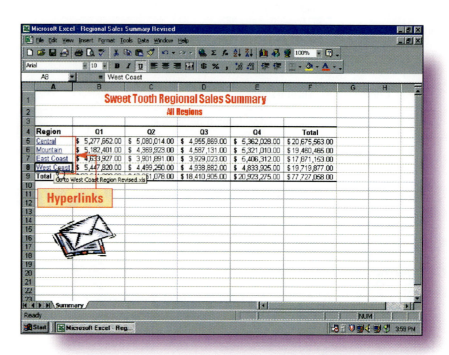

FIGURE 10-11
Adding Hyperlinks to Other Workbooks

CAUTION TIP

If you move a file to which you have created hyperlinks, you must edit the hyperlink to point to the new location. Right-click the hyperlink or object and select Hyperlink, then Edit Hyperlink.

QUICK TIP

Activate a cell containing a hyperlink by moving to it using the ARROW keys, then jump to the hyperlink location by pressing the ENTER key.

| Step 14 | Click | the West Coast hyperlink |

The *West Coast Region Revised* workbook opens.

| Step 15 | Close | the *West Coast Region Revised* workbook |

Notice that the hyperlink in cell A8 changes to purple. This color indicates a hyperlink that you have already followed.

Step 16	Print	the *Regional Sales Summary Revised* workbook
Step 17	Save	the workbook
Step 18	Close	the workbook

Hyperlinks make it easy to connect to a variety of information sources. You can add hyperlinks to Web pages on the Internet or to other Office documents. This approach can speed up your work by reducing the amount of time needed to locate information associated with the workbook(s) with which you are working.

Summary

- ▶ Group worksheets using SHIFT + Click or CTRL + Click. Grouping worksheets makes it easy to add the same data, titles, headings, and formatting to several worksheets at a time. You can also group worksheets for printing.

- ▶ Use references to cells or ranges on other worksheets. References to cells on other worksheets have the following syntax: 'SheetName'!A1.

- ▶ Create 3-D references when ranges span across multiple worksheets.

- ▶ Use the Arrange Windows dialog box to view several worksheets simultaneously.

- ▶ Save workspaces to open and rearrange several workbooks simultaneously.

- ▶ Use references to cells or ranges in other workbooks. References to cells in other workbooks have the following syntax: 'c:\pathname\[workbook name.xls]SheetName'!A1.

- ▶ Add an e-mail or hyperlinks to cell values or drawing objects. Click an e-mail link to automatically address a new message with the address and subject lines already filled in. Click hyperlinks to open other files, jump to other cells or ranges in the current workbook, or access an Internet Web site.

chapter ten

Commands Review

Action	Menu Bar	Shortcut Menu	Toolbar	Keyboard
Ungroup worksheets		Ungroup Sheets		
Arrange windows	Window, Arrange			ALT + W, A
Save a workspace	File, Save Workspace	Save Workspace		ALT + F, W
Add a hyperlink to an object or cell	Insert, Hyperlink	Hyperlink		CTRL + K ALT + I, I
Edit a hyperlink	Insert, Hyperlink	Hyperlink, Edit Hyperlink		CTRL + K ALT + I, I
Remove a hyperlink		Hyperlink, Remove Hyperlink		

Concepts Review

Circle the correct answer.

1. Hyperlinks can jump to:
   - [a] other cells.
   - [b] other workbooks.
   - [c] Web pages.
   - [d] all of the above.

2. Which of the following formulas contains a valid reference to a range on another worksheet?
   - [a] =sum(Totals!A1:B5)
   - [b] =sum('Totals'!A1:B5)
   - [c] =sum("Totals"!A1:B5)
   - [d] =sum(Totals:A1:B5)

3. Which of the following formulas contains a valid reference to a range in another workbook?
   - [a] =sum(RegionSales['Sheet1'!A1:B5])
   - [b] =sum('[RegionSales]Sheet1'!A1:B5)
   - [c] =sum('[RegionSales]Sheet1!A1:B5')
   - [d] =sum("[RegionSales]Sheet1"!A1:B5)

4. 3-D references in formulas:
   - [a] cannot be modified.
   - [b] allow formatting to be applied across multiple worksheets.
   - [c] span across worksheets.
   - [d] none of the above.

5. An e-mail link:
   - [a] jumps to a Web site.
   - [b] automatically addresses a new e-mail message.
   - [c] jumps to another workbook.
   - [d] jumps to another worksheet.

6. A referenced workbook name is surrounded by:
   - [a] [ ]
   - [b] { }
   - [c] ( )
   - [d] < >

7. A referenced worksheet, workbook, and worksheet name is surrounded by:
   - [a] ' '
   - [b] " "
   - [c] ~ ~
   - [d] (: :)

8. Hyperlinks can be attached to:
   - [a] lines.
   - [b] clip art.
   - [c] cells.
   - [d] all of the above.

Circle **T** if the statement is true or **F** if the statement is false.

T **F** 1. You can select groups of worksheets only in one continuous group.

T F 2. You can use the SHIFT or CTRL key to create a worksheet group.

T **F** 3. You can group worksheets for printing, but not for formatting.

T **F** 4. You can view only one workbook at a time.

T **F** 5. You can view only one worksheet of a workbook at a time. p.145 quick tip

T **F** 6. You cannot link worksheet text to charts.

T F 7. If linked workbooks are open simultaneously, changes are immediately reflected in either workbook.

p149 QT **T** F 8. Once a workbook is open, you cannot update its links to other workbooks without closing the original workbook and reopening it.

p148 **T** F 9. Use Paste Link from the Paste Special dialog box to create a quick reference to another cell or cells.

T F 10. ScreenTips added to a hyperlink appear only when the pointer is positioned over the hyperlink.

Skills Review

Exercise 1

1. Open the *Sweet Tooth Summary* workbook on your Data Disk.

2. In cells B5:B10 on the Summary worksheet, use a linking formula to link to the total items sold, which is calculated in cell D24 of each item's tab.

3. In cells C5:C10 on the Summary worksheet, use a linking formula to link to the total gross sales, which is calculated in cell F24 of each item's tab.

4. In cell B14, enter a formula to sum the total number of items sold to Aquanatics stores. (*Hint:* Switch to each item tab, select the appropriate cells, then enter a comma in the Formula Bar before selecting the next range.)

5. Repeat step 4 to sum the total number of items sold to each of the stores in cells B15:B19.

6. Repeat step 4 to sum the total sales to each of the stores in cells C14:C19.

7. Print the Summary worksheet.

8. Save the workbook as *Sweet Tooth Summary Revised*.

Exercise 2

1. Create a new workbook.

2. Use the Drawing toolbar to insert five AutoShape or clip art objects of your choice.

3. Add a hyperlink linking each of the objects to a different search engine, such as Yahoo!, Excite, Lycos, AltaVista, or Ask Jeeves. (*Hint:* Use the Existing File or Web Page button in the Insert Hyperlink dialog box, then click Web Page in the Browse for section to open your browser and locate a Web address.)

4. Add a ScreenTip and text to the objects to identify the hyperlinks.

5. Save the workbook as *Search Links* and print it.

chapter ten

Exercise 3

1. Open the *Mountain Region*, *West Coast Region*, and *East Coast Region* workbooks on your Data Disk. Also open the *Central Region Updated* workbook on your Data Disk.
2. Save the workbooks as *Mountain 1*, *West Coast 1*, *East Coast 1*, and *Central 1*.
3. Arrange the windows using the Tile layout.
4. Save the workspace as *Region Workbooks* in your Data Files folder.
5. In cell D4 of the *Central 1* workbook, enter "Go to Mountain." Add a hyperlink to jump to the *Mountain 1* workbook.
6. In cell D4 of the *Mountain 1* workbook, enter "Go to West Coast." Add a hyperlink to jump to the *West Coast 1* workbook. (*Hint:* Use the Recent Files button in the Insert Hyperlinks dialog box.)
7. In cell D4 of the *West Coast 1* workbook, enter "Go to East Coast." Add a hyperlink to jump to the *East Coast 1* workbook.
8. In cell D4 of the *East Coast 1* workbook, enter "Go to Central." Add a hyperlink to jump to the *Central 1* workbook.
9. Save and close all of the workbooks, leaving only the *Central 1* workbook open.
10. Test the hyperlinks, printing the Summary worksheet of each workbook as it opens.
11. Close all open workbooks.

Exercise 4

1. Create a new workbook.
2. In cell A1, enter "Jump to Cell."
3. In cell A2, enter "Jump to Worksheet."
4. In cell A3, enter "Jump to Workbook."
5. In cell A4, enter "Jump to Web."
6. Create a hyperlink in cell A1 to another cell on the same worksheet.
7. Create a hyperlink in cell A2 to another worksheet in the same workbook.
8. Create a hyperlink in cell A3 to any of the workbooks you've created in the Skills Review exercises.
9. Create a hyperlink in cell A4 to one of your favorite Web site address.
10. Include ScreenTips to indicate where the hyperlink points.
11. Save the workbook as *Jump Around*.

Exercise 5

1. ZXY Accounting is a large accounting firm with offices in Orlando, San Diego, Phoenix, and Washington, D.C. Open the *ZXY Accounting* workbook on your Data Disk.
2. Group the worksheets.
3. Insert a column in front of column A.
4. Insert a row above row 1.
5. Add the information indicated in the table below:

Cell	Enter
A2	Auditing
A3	Tax Preparation
A4	Consulting
A5	Total
B1	January
C1	February
D1	March
E1	Total

6. Bold and center the titles in row 1.
7. Bold cell A5.
8. Use the SUM formula in row 5 and column E to sum the data.
9. Ungroup the worksheets and enter the city name (shown on each tab) in cell A1 of each worksheet.
10. Save the workbook as *ZXY Accounting Revised* and print all four worksheets.

Exercise 6

1. Open the *ZXY Accounting Revised* workbook that you created in Exercise 5.
2. Insert a new worksheet to the left of the Washington, D.C., tab named "Summary."
3. Create a summary table to add the totals for each month across all cities. Use linking formulas to link the data from each of the worksheets.
4. Format the data using the Currency format.
5. Find the average income for each month by adding a formula below the Total row in each column.
6. Create a chart showing the income by month for each city on a new sheet called "Summary Chart."
7. Title the chart "1st Quarter Income."
8. Print the chart.
9. Save the workbook as *ZXY Accounting Summary*.

chapter ten

Exercise 7

1. Open the *ZXY Accounting Summary* workbook that you created in Exercise 6.

2. Group all the worksheets except the Summary Chart worksheet.

3. Use Page Setup from the File menu to set print options to center the data vertically and horizontally.

4. Add a centered header "ZXY Accounting" using 20 point, bold type.

5. Preview and print all five worksheets.

6. Ungroup the worksheets.

7. Save the workbook as *ZXY Accounting Summary Print*.

Exercise 8

1. Open the *ZXY Accounting Summary Print* workbook that you created in Exercise 7.

2. Group all the worksheets except the Summary Chart and Summary worksheets.

3. Apply the AutoFormat style List 2 to cells A1:E5.

4. Set print options to landscape orientation and 150% scale.

5. Print the worksheets.

6. Ungroup the worksheets.

7. Save the workbook as *ZXY Accounting Summary Print 2*.

Case Projects

Project 1

You work for the local newspaper. You're currently researching historical weather trends in the United States. Use the Web toolbar to search the Internet for average monthly temperatures for New York City and Los Angeles in the last year. Create a workbook that includes the temperatures for each city on two separate worksheets. Create a 3-D reference formula on a third worksheet to display the average temperature of the two cities for each month of the previous year. Create a chart comparing the average temperatures for each city. Use axis and chart titles to clarify the purpose of the chart. Save the workbook as *Temperature Averages* and print it.

Project 2

The Paste Special command provides many ways to copy data from one cell to another. Use the Office Assistant to learn about each option. Write a four-paragraph document explaining each of the options. Save the document as *Paste Special Options.doc* and print it.

Project 3

You work for a small architectural firm that tracks income in one of two categories: contract and consulting work. Create a *Business Income* workbook showing receipts in both categories for four quarters. Name the tab 1999 Income, then remove any unused worksheets. Sum the totals and save the workbook.

The firm lumps expenses into four categories: advertising, office, auto, and rent. Create a *Business Expenses* workbook showing expenses in each category for four quarters. Name the tab 1999 Expenses, then remove any unused worksheets. Sum the totals and save the workbook.

Create a *Business Projection* workbook. Set up separate tables to show both income categories and the four expense categories. Use columns for each quarter. Using a 5% projected growth rate for consulting work, create a formula to link the *Business Income* cells to the *Business Projection* cells and then add 5% to last year's totals to project this year's consulting income totals. Do the same for contract work, using a projected growth percentage of 7.5%. For expense categories, link the *Business Expense* figures to the *Business Projection* workbook and then calculate an inflation adjustment of 4% over last year's totals. Name the worksheet 2000 Projection and remove any unused worksheets. Print the worksheets in each of the workbooks. Save each workbook when you are finished.

Project 4

As a worker in the financial sector, you need to understand the concept of inflation. Use the Web toolbar to search the Internet for information about inflation. Write a two-paragraph summary explaining what inflation is and how it affects the economy. Save the document as *Inflation.doc* and print it.

Project 5

As a small business owner who uses Excel for a variety of functions, you need to use your time effectively. When you need help with Excel, you immediately look for information on the Internet. It takes time to locate helpful sites, however. Create a new workbook called *Excel Internet Resources*. Using your Web browser and a search engine, locate five useful sites containing tips and other information about Excel. Add hyperlinks to each site to your workbook. When you have finished adding the hyperlinks, print the worksheet and save the workbook.

Project 6

You have sent several linked workbooks to a colleague. When she opened those workbooks, the links were broken because the source files were stored in a different folder system than you use on your computer. Using online Help, find out how to reconnect linked objects if the source file is moved. In your own words, write a Word document explaining how to reconnect the links. Save the file as *Reconnect Links.doc* and print it.

Project 7

You work in the budgeting department of a large publishing company. Create two workbooks, one called *Budget Data* and one called *Budget Summary*. In the *Budget Data* workbook, create column and row labels to identify sales numbers, production costs, and marketing costs by quarter. Create labels for the totals. In the *Budget Summary* workbook, link the cells from the *Budget Data* workbook that will hold the totals. Arrange the two workbooks vertically. Save the workspace as *Budget*. Print both workbooks.

Project 8

You would like to setup an Internet e-mail account. Many companies offer free e-mail services. Use the Internet to locate at least two companies offering free e-mail. Print the page on each site which explains the policies or "terms of service" for the e-mail account.

chapter ten

Excel 2000

Customizing Excel Templates, Toolbars, and Menus

Chapter Overview

Templates are special Excel files that you can use to create new workbooks with formulas, data, and special formatting already applied. You can modify existing templates, create your own templates, or use existing workbooks as templates. You can customize the Excel window to accommodate the way you work by repositioning toolbars. Toolbars can be docked, or they may float in the application window to provide maximum accessibility. Using the Customize dialog box, you can create your own toolbars and menus by dragging commands to the custom toolbar or menu.

Learning Objectives

- Use and edit templates to create a new workbook
- Create custom templates
- View, hide, and dock toolbars
- Customize toolbars
- Create a custom menu

Case profile

Your work at Sweet Tooth routinely involves creating the same type of workbook for invoices, expense statements, and reports. Using templates, you can create new workbooks that already contain all of the necessary formulas and formatting. You also can customize toolbars and templates to access additional commands, and to help you work more efficiently in Excel.

chapter eleven

11.a Using and Editing Templates to Create a New Workbook

When you create a new workbook by clicking the New button on the Standard toolbar, you are actually creating a new workbook based on Excel's default workbook template, which contains three blank worksheets. A **template** is a special type of workbook into which formatting, settings, and formulas are already inserted. You can create and use your own templates that contain a set number of worksheet pages, customized formatting, formulas, macros, menus, toolbars, print options, and layout settings specifically designed for a single use.

Using a Built-in Template

Many templates are designed for very specific applications. For example, an invoice template holds the formulas needed to multiply an item's quantity by the price, subtotal the item costs, then add shipping and sales tax. The user needs to fill in only the purchaser's information, shipping address, and items ordered. Likewise, purchase orders and expense statements are often created as templates. Excel supplies templates—named Expense Statement, Invoice, and Purchase Order templates—for these three common forms as examples to help you see the many possibilities offered by templates.

You modify the Invoice template for use at Sweet Tooth. First, you need to know how to use the template. To create a new workbook based on the Invoice template:

Step 1	Click	File
Step 2	Click	New

The New dialog box opens.

Step 3	Click	the Spreadsheet Solutions tab
Step 4	Click	the Invoice icon

CAUTION TIP

You must use the New command on the File menu to access the New dialog box. Clicking the New button on the Standard toolbar opens a new, blank workbook.

chapter eleven

You should see a preview of the template in the Preview window, as shown in Figure 11-1.

FIGURE 11-1
Creating a New Workbook Using a Template

CAUTION TIP

Some workbooks contain macros that were written by other users to automate certain routine tasks in the workbook. You create your own macros in Chapter 15. Unfortunately, some macros are programmed to do malicious things. These are called macro viruses. Whenever you open a workbook containing macros, you receive a warning about the possibility of macro viruses. Excel simply alerts you to the fact that the workbook contains macros. It cannot tell you whether the macros will do anything harmful. If you have downloaded a workbook off the Internet and are not sure of its origin, you should take a cautious approach and disable the workbook macros. The data remains intact, even though macros are disabled.

Step 5	*Click*	OK

 notes If you do not see a preview in the Preview box but instead see instructions on how to install additional templates, then insert the Office 2000 CD in your CD-ROM drive, click OK, and continue with step 6.

An alert box warns you that the file you are opening contains macros.

Step 6	*Click*	<u>E</u>nable Macros

A new workbook, based on the Invoice template, opens. The title bar identifies this workbook as "invoice1," and the Invoice toolbar appears somewhere in the window. Changes you make to this workbook do not affect the template itself. Your screen should look similar to Figure 11-2.

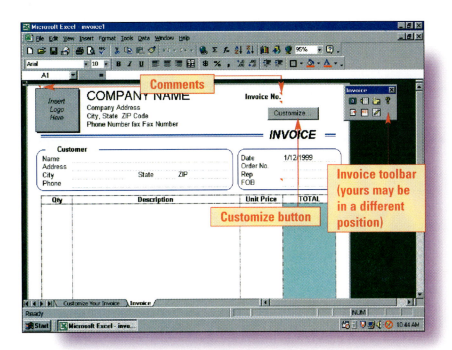

FIGURE 11-2
New Invoice Workbook

> **QUICK TIP**
>
> If the Invoice toolbar covers part of the invoice, drag it by its title bar to another location in the window.

As you can see, the new workbook looks nothing like the workbooks you're used to seeing. Gridlines and column and row headings are turned off to reduce the amount of distracting elements in the template. This workbook includes a special Help file to explain how to use the template. To get help with the Invoice template:

Step 1 | *Click* | the Template Help button on the Invoice toolbar

Read the Help file to familiarize yourself with the template's features.

Step 2 | *Click* | the Close button in the Help window title bar

Another source for help is built directly into the workbook. You may have noticed several cells containing little red triangles. These cells hold comments, or notes from the creator of the workbook. You learn to create your own comments in Chapter 12.

Step 3 | *Move* | the pointer over a cell with a red triangle in the corner

chapter
eleven

The comment in that cell appears after a moment, similar to Figure 11-3.

FIGURE 11-3
Viewing Comments

| Step 4 | *Scroll* | the worksheet to view the rest of the Invoice worksheet |

Once you've familiarized yourself with the template, you're ready to add Sweet Tooth's company information.

Editing a Built-in Template

You can customize built-in templates to display your company's information. Your workbook contains a tab called Customize Your Invoice. You can click this tab or the Customize button to customize the invoice. Once you make changes, this tab disappears, but you can return to it at any time by clicking the Customize button. Changes made on the Customize tab are saved as part of the template. Once you customize the template, new workbooks based on this template contain the customized information. To customize the Invoice template:

| Step 1 | *Click* | the Customize button in the upper-right corner of the Invoice worksheet |

The Customize Your Invoice worksheet becomes active. This worksheet also has several comments. See Figure 11-4.

| Step 2 | *Scroll* | the worksheet and read the comments to familiarize yourself with this worksheet |

Because column and row headings are turned off, navigating this worksheet may seem a little bit more difficult than usual. Nevertheless, the Name Box still indicates the current active cell. You can use the Name Box to enter a cell reference. Many of the cells have already been named, and you may decide to select these names from the Name Box instead.

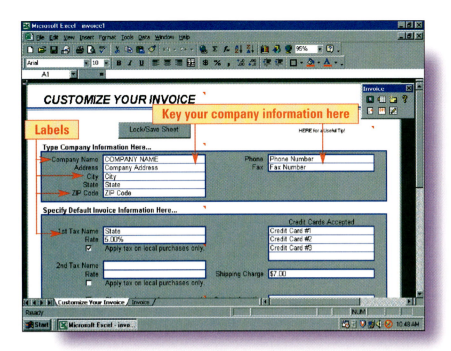

FIGURE 11-4
Customize Your Invoice Worksheet Tab

CAUTION TIP

Editing any of the labels in the gray area of an information group on the Customize Your Invoice tab changes the label permanently in the workbook, and the Undo command is disabled on this tab. To correct a mistake, you must reenter the data.

This worksheet includes several information "groups" consisting of gray boxes surrounded by a blue border. Within each group, you enter the data that should appear on your template in the white cells. Labels next to each white cell guide you as you fill in the information.

To add Sweet Tooth's company information to the template:

| Step 1 | *Click* | the white cell next to the label Company Name |

A yellow outline surrounds the cell. This cell is named vital1 in the Name Box.

| Step 2 | *Key* | SWEET TOOTH (see Figure 11-5) |

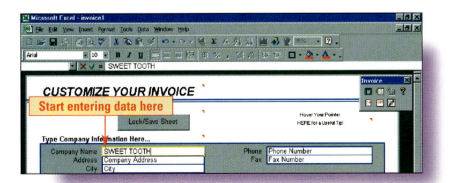

FIGURE 11-5
Customizing the Invoice Data

chapter eleven

| Step 3 | Press | the ENTER key |

The active cell moves down to the cell with Company Address in it (cell "vital2").

| Step 4 | Key | 1234 Candy Cane Lane |
| Step 5 | Press | the ENTER key |

Continue entering Sweet Tooth's company data in the white areas.

Step 6	Enter	Phoenix in the City cell (cell "vital4")
Step 7	Enter	AZ in the State cell (cell "vital5")
Step 8	Enter	85001 in the ZIP Code cell (cell "vital6")
Step 9	Enter	(555) 555-1234 in the Phone cell (cell "vital8")
Step 10	Enter	(555) 555-1235 in the Fax cell (cell "vital9")

This entry completes the company information that will appear at the top of the invoice. Next, fill in the Default Invoice Information.

Step 11	Enter	AZ in the 1st Tax Name cell (cell "dflt1")
Step 12	Enter	6.8% in the Rate cell (cell "dflt2")
Step 13	Enter	Visa in the Credit Card #1 cell
Step 14	Enter	MasterCard in the Credit Card #2 cell
Step 15	Enter	Discover in the Credit Card #3 cell

The suggested shipping charge of $7.00 is what Sweet Tooth charges.

| Step 16 | Scroll | the worksheet to the bottom |

The Formatted Information area shows you how the company address (which appears at the top of the invoice) will look.

| Step 17 | **Click** | Change Plate Font |

The Format Cells dialog box opens.

| Step 18 | **Select** | Impact from the Font: list, Red from the Color: palette, and 10 from the Size: list |
| Step 19 | **Click** | OK |

To view the customized Invoice worksheet:

| Step 1 | **Click** | the Invoice worksheet tab |

Your worksheet should look similar to Figure 11-6.

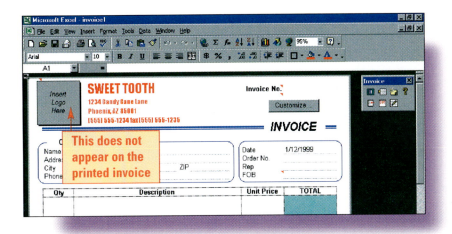

FIGURE 11-6
Adding Company Information to a Template

Using the Invoice toolbar, you can view the invoice with sample data. To view sample data:

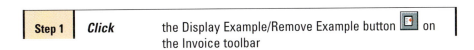

| Step 1 | **Click** | the Display Example/Remove Example button on the Invoice toolbar |

After a few seconds, sample data appears on the Invoice. Take a moment to review the formulas in the workbook.

| Step 2 | **Activate** | cell L18 (the first cell under TOTAL in the blue column) |

Don't forget to look at the Name Box to see which cell is the active cell. Look at the Formula Bar. This logical IF formula assesses the value in cell D18 (the first cell under Qty) to see whether a quantity has been entered (<> means not equal to and "" means no data). If a quantity has been entered, the formula multiplies the quantity (cell D18) by the price (cell K18); otherwise it displays nothing.

Step 3	*Scroll*	to the bottom of the worksheet
Step 4	*Activate*	cell L35 (next to SubTotal)

This formula sums the TOTAL column. When you are finished reviewing the formulas, remove the sample data.

Step 5	*Click*	the Display Example/Remove Example button 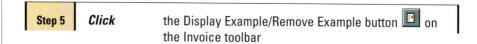 on the Invoice toolbar

After a few seconds, the data is removed.

Step 6	*Click*	the Save button on the Standard toolbar

The Template File – Save to Database dialog box appears. This template has a special add-on feature enabled, called Template Wizard with Data Tracking. It allows you to save the information you entered using this template in a special database. By default, the database is an Excel workbook but you can also use the Template Wizard to create an Access database to store the data, however. By storing the data in a database, you can create reports and gather information from all other workbooks you create based on this same template.

Step 7	*Click*	the Continue without updating option button
Step 8	*Click*	OK

The Save As dialog box opens. Remember that you created a new workbook based on the Invoice template, so you are saving a new workbook, not a modified template.

Step 9	*Key*	Sweet Tooth Invoice 1 in the File name: box
Step 10	*Click*	Save

In the next section, you create your own custom template by modifying an existing template.

11.b Creating Custom Templates

You can create your own custom templates, similar to the Invoice template. For example, you can develop a workbook that contains all the formatting, borders, text, data, formulas, and macros you want, then save the new workbook as a template. You can also create a template from an existing workbook or template.

Create a Template Based on an Existing Workbook

The workbook you saved in the previous exercise is not a template. If you reuse the Invoice template, it does not include the company information that you entered. For Sweet Tooth, users shouldn't have to re-enter this information every time they use the template. You therefore save the workbook as a template with all the company information already in place. To save a workbook as a template:

Step 1	Click	File
Step 2	Click	Save As
Step 3	Click	the Save as type: list arrow at the bottom of the dialog box
Step 4	Click	Template

Notice that the Save in box changes to the default Templates directory. When you save a template in this directory, it appears on the General tab of the New dialog box.

Step 5	Change	the Save in: list box to the folder where you are storing your Data Files
Step 6	Key	Sweet Tooth Invoice in the File name: box
Step 7	Click	Save
Step 8	Close	the template file

You can also create templates based on other workbooks you've created. Sweet Tooth's Central region office, for example, has created a nicely formatted report that would make a good template for other

Regional Sales Summary workbooks. All you need to do is erase the data and save the workbook as a template.

To prepare a workbook for use as a template:

Step 1	Open	the *Region Sales* file on your Data Disk
Step 2	Group	all the tabs in the workbook
Step 3	Select	the range B5:E8
Step 4	Press	the DELETE key
Step 5	Activate	cell A1

An employee in the Central region office mistakenly used "Area" in place of "Division" throughout the workbook. Excel's Find and Replace feature can help you quickly correct this mistake.

Using Find and Replace

Find and Replace are two related tools that help you locate and replace values in a workbook. Find can help you locate data in a cell value, formula, or comment. Replace can quickly find and replace individual instances or all instances of a given value. Replace cannot search comments or formulas, however.

You need to search the entire workbook for the text value "Area" and replace it with the value "Division." By default, Find and Replace search the current active worksheet only. When you group worksheets, these tools searches all worksheets in the group. To use Find:

| Step 1 | Click | Edit |
| Step 2 | Click | Find |

The Find dialog box opens, similar to Figure 11-7.

> **QUICK TIP**
>
> You can access the Find dialog box by pressing the CTRL + F keys.

FIGURE 11-7
Find Dialog Box

| Step 3 | *Key* | Area in the Find what: box |

If matching the case is important, click the Match case check box. This option is useful when you want to find instances of "Area" but not "area." You can search by rows or by columns.

| Step 4 | *Click* | the list arrow in the Search: box |
| Step 5 | *Click* | By Columns |

You can search formulas, values, or comments.

Step 6	*Click*	the list arrow in the Look in: box
Step 7	*Click*	Values
Step 8	*Click*	Find Next

Cell A4 is selected on the Central Region Summary tab. Because the Replace command is closely related to the Find command, you can click the Replace button in the Find dialog box and begin replacing values.

| Step 9 | *Click* | Replace |

The Replace dialog box, which is very similar to the Find dialog box, appears. See Figure 11-8.

CAUTION TIP
Find and Replace does not search chart objects or worksheet tabs.

MENU TIP
If you know you will be replacing values, click Replace from the Edit menu.

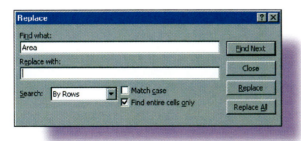

FIGURE 11-8
Replace Dialog Box

| Step 10 | *Key* | Division in the Replace with: box |
| Step 11 | *Click* | Replace |

QUICK TIP

You can access the Replace dialog box by pressing the CTRL + H keys.

The value in cell A4 is replaced with the new value. Excel then automatically searches for the next instance of "Area," which happens to be located in cell A2 on the South Division tab. You can continue replacing each instance one by one, which is a good approach when you don't need to replace all instances. In this case, however, you want all instances to be replaced.

Step 12	Click	Replace All

All instances are replaced throughout the workbook.

Step 13	Ungroup	the grouped worksheets
Step 14	Double-click	the Central Region Summary worksheet tab
Step 15	Key	Region Summary
Step 16	Press	the ENTER key
Step 17	Enter	<Add Region or Division Title> in cell A2

When you finish, your workbook should look similar to Figure 11-9.

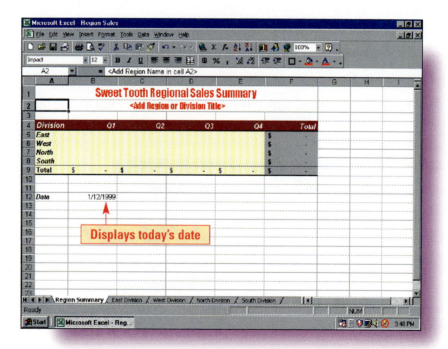

FIGURE 11-9
Preparing a Template from an Existing Workbook

Save a New Template

Now that you have finished creating your template, you need to save it. To save the template:

Step 1	Click	File
Step 2	Click	Save As
Step 3	Click	the Save as type: list arrow
Step 4	Click	Template
Step 5	Key	Region Sales Summary Template in the File name: box

Notice that the current folder is Templates. If you save a template to this folder, it appears on the General tab of the New dialog box.

Step 6	Click	the Save in: list arrow
Step 7	Switch	to the drive and directory where you are storing your Data Files
Step 8	Click	Save

If you are interested in creating professional-looking templates, study the three sample templates provided by Excel. Pay special attention to how the templates use column widths, row heights, cell borders, and cell fills.

11.c Viewing, Hiding, and Docking Toolbars

You can turn toolbars on and off to keep your screen uncluttered. As you've seen, some toolbars, like the Chart and WordArt toolbars, appear automatically when you're editing a chart or a WordArt object.

Toolbars can also "float" in the application window or "dock" on the left, right, top, or bottom of the application window. A **floating** toolbar can be repositioned within Excel's working area. A **docked** toolbar stays anchored in the same position at one edge of the application window.

> **MENU TIP**
>
> You can turn toolbars on and off from the View menu. Point to Toolbars on the View menu, then click the desired toolbar. A check mark appears next to toolbars that are turned on.

Displaying and Hiding Toolbars

You decide to practice displaying and moving toolbars using the Forms toolbar. To display a toolbar:

Step 1	**Right-click**	anywhere in the toolbar area of the Excel window
Step 2	**Click**	Forms

The Forms toolbar appears as a floating toolbar, as shown in Figure 11-10.

FIGURE 11-10
Floating and Docked Toolbars

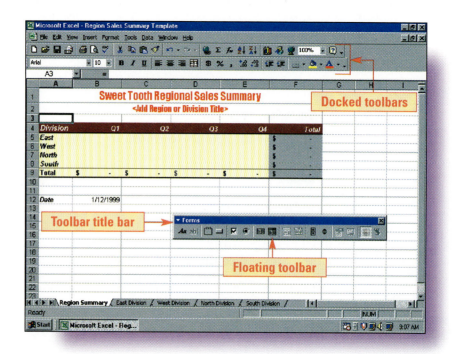

QUICK TIP

You can use the Forms toolbar to add special controls to a template, such as option buttons, check boxes, and spinner controls. The Invoice template, for example, contained option buttons in the Payment Details section near the bottom of the Invoice form.

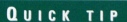

MOUSE TIP

To hide a floating toolbar, click the Close button on the toolbar.

To hide a toolbar:

Step 1	**Right-click**	anywhere in the toolbar area of the Excel window
Step 2	**Click**	Forms

The Forms toolbar closes.

Docking and Undocking Toolbars

By default, the Standard and Formatting toolbars are docked at the top of the application window, underneath the menu bar. You can, however, dock toolbars in other locations. Alternatively, you can keep toolbars floating in the application window to make them easier to access. To practice docking and undocking toolbars:

| Step 1 | **Right-click** | anywhere in the toolbar area of the Excel window |
| Step 2 | **Click** | Forms |

To move a floating toolbar, click the toolbar's title bar and drag the toolbar to a new location. To dock a floating toolbar, drag it to an edge of the window. To move and dock a floating toolbar:

| Step 1 | **Drag** | the title bar of the Forms toolbar anywhere else in the window |
| Step 2 | **Drag** | the title bar of the Forms toolbar to the left side of the application window |

When the pointer is close to the left edge of the application window, the toolbar automatically docks on the left side, as shown in Figure 11-11.

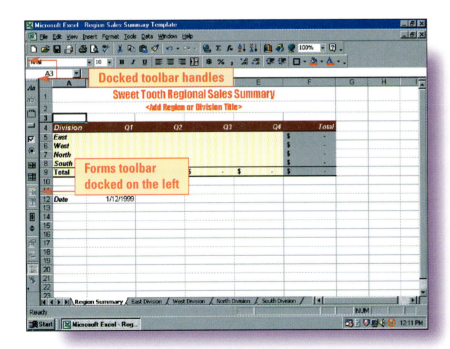

FIGURE 11-11
Docking a Toolbar

To move a docked toolbar and undock it:

| Step 1 | **Move** | the pointer to the Forms toolbar handle at the top of the toolbar |

The pointer changes to the four-headed arrow pointer ✥.

| Step 2 | Drag | the toolbar up |

The toolbar automatically docks at the top of the window. If you drag the toolbar past the Formula Bar, the toolbars change positions, with the Forms toolbar becoming docked at the top of the application window.

| Step 3 | Drag | the Forms toolbar handle to the middle of the application window |

The toolbar undocks.

| Step 4 | Click | the Close button on the Forms toolbar |

You may wish to display all of the Excel toolbars and dock them in various positions around the application window. Many of the toolbars, like the Forms toolbar, are useful only at certain times and for specific tasks. To keep the application window uncluttered, you should leave most toolbars off until you need them; when you're finished with a toolbar, turn it off.

11.d Customizing Toolbars

As you become more familiar with Excel, you may find certain commands that you use more frequently than other commands. Excel is extremely flexible in allowing you to create your own toolbars and customize existing toolbars to enhance your productivity.

You would like to create a special toolbar to attach to the Region Sales Summary Template. When you attach a toolbar to a template, it is available to anyone who uses that template to create new workbooks. To open the Customize dialog box:

| Step 1 | Right-click | anywhere in the toolbar area of the Excel window |
| Step 2 | Click | <u>C</u>ustomize |

Customizing Excel Templates, Toolbars, and Menus

The Customize dialog box opens.

| Step 3 | Click | the Tool<u>b</u>ars tab |

Figure 11-12 shows the Tool<u>b</u>ars tab.

FIGURE 11-12
Toolbars Tab of the Customize Dialog Box

You use the Tool<u>b</u>ars tab to create new toolbars and edit or delete existing toolbars. You cannot delete or rename Excel toolbars, however.

To create a new toolbar:

| Step 1 | Click | <u>N</u>ew |

The New Toolbar dialog box opens, allowing you to name the new toolbar.

| Step 2 | Key | Region Sales in the <u>T</u>oolbar name: box |
| Step 3 | Click | OK |

An empty toolbar appears in the application window and My Toolbar appears in the Toolbars list in the dialog box. Your screen should look similar to Figure 11-13.

QUICK TIP

If you modify any of Excel's toolbars, you can later reset them to the default settings by clicking <u>R</u>eset in the Customize dialog box.

MOUSE TIP

You can remove items from a toolbar or menu while the Customize dialog box remains open. Drag the item from the toolbar or menu and drop it anywhere on the worksheet. This operation is similar to removing items from a PivotTable report.

chapter
eleven

FIGURE 11-13
New Toolbar

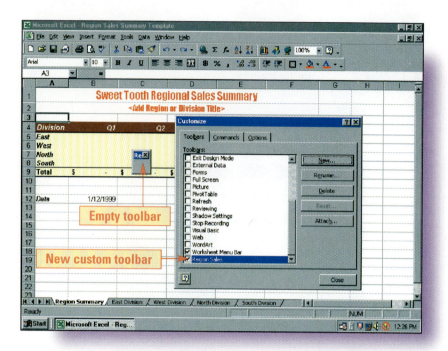

To add commands to your toolbar, use the Commands tab. To add buttons to a custom toolbar:

| Step 1 | Click | the Commands tab in the Customize dialog box |

Figure 11-14 shows the Commands tab.

FIGURE 11-14
Commands Tab of the Customize Dialog Box

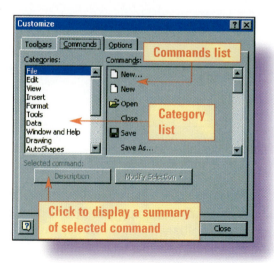

| Step 2 | Click | Format in the Categories: list |

| Step 3 | Click | AutoFormat in the Comma<u>n</u>ds: list |

As you browse through the Comma<u>n</u>ds: list, you see the same commands that appear on the F<u>o</u>rmat menu, as well as many other commands that you can access only by adding them to a toolbar.

| Step 4 | Click | Descrip<u>t</u>ion at the bottom of the dialog box |

A ScreenTip appears describing the function of the selected command.

| Step 5 | Click | anywhere in the dialog box to close the ScreenTip |
| Step 6 | Drag | the AutoFormat button to the Region Sales toolbar, as shown in Figure 11-15 |

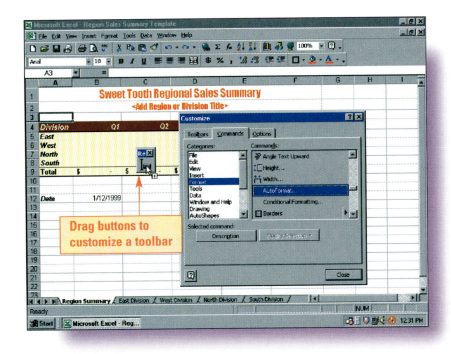

FIGURE 11-15
Adding Buttons to a Custom Toolbar

The AutoFormat button does not have an icon associated with it, so it appears as text on the toolbar. When you have finished adding buttons, attach the toolbar to the template. To attach a toolbar to a workbook or template:

| Step 1 | Click | the Tool<u>b</u>ars tab |

QUICK TIP

To delete, or unattach, a custom toolbar from a workbook, open the Attach Toolbars dialog box, select the toolbar name in the Toolbars in workbook: list, then click Delete.

Step 2	Click	Attach

The Attach Toolbars dialog box opens, displaying a list of custom toolbars and a list of toolbars that have been attached to the workbook.

Step 3	Click	Region Sales in the Custom toolbars: list
Step 4	Click	Copy>>

The Region Sales toolbar now appears in the Toolbars in workbook: list.

Step 5	Click	OK
Step 6	Click	Close to close the Customize dialog box
Step 7	Save	the template

Creating custom menus is basically the same as creating custom toolbars. In the next section, you add a custom menu to the Region Sales toolbar.

11.e Creating a Custom Menu

Excel allows you to modify its menus by adding or removing existing commands, or you can create your own menus. Menus can be added to the menu bar or to toolbars. You would like to add a custom menu to the Region Sales toolbar. To create a custom menu:

Step 1	Right-click	anywhere in the toolbar area of the Excel window
Step 2	Click	Customize
Step 3	Click	the Commands tab
Step 4	Click	New Menu in the Categories: list
Step 5	Drag	New Menu from the Commands: list to the Region Sales toolbar

Your screen should look similar to Figure 11-16.

MOUSE TIP

You can drag New Menu to the menu bar to create a new menu on the menu bar.

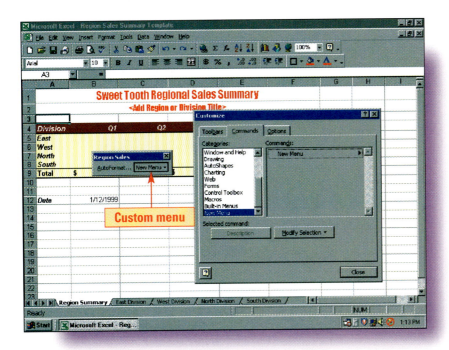

FIGURE 11-16
Creating a Custom Menu

| Step 6 | Right-click | the New Menu that you added to the toolbar |

The New Menu shortcut menu appears. This shortcut menu appears only when the Customize dialog box is open.

Step 7	Drag	to select the entry in the Name: box
Step 8	Key	Special Format in the Name: box
Step 9	Press	the ENTER key

The menu name is renamed. Next, you need to add commands to your menu. To add a command to the menu:

| Step 1 | Click | Format in the Categories list in the Customize dialog box |
| Step 2 | Drag | Cycle Font Color from the Commands: list to the Special Format menu name on the menu bar, as shown in Figure 11-17 |

QUICK TIP

When you press the ALT + F keys, the File menu opens. The F key is a **mnemonic** character that provides access to the menu using the keyboard. You can define mnemonic characters on custom menus and menu items by inserting the ampersand (&) character in front of the letter that should be used as a shortcut in the Name: box. For example, when you name the Special Format menu, you could use *p* as the mnemonic by entering S&pecial Format as the menu name.

chapter eleven

FIGURE 11-17
Adding Commands to a Custom Menu

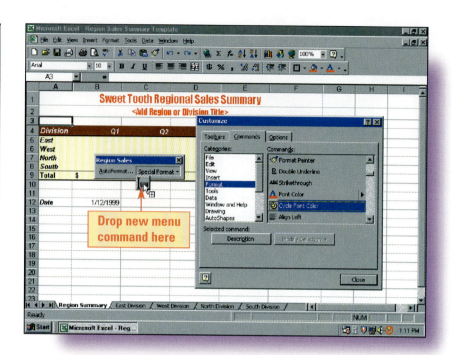

CAUTION TIP

Make sure that you drop the Cycle Font Color on the blank box that appears below the Special Format menu name and not on the toolbar; otherwise, a new item appears next to Special Format. If that happens, just drag the new command off the toolbar to remove it.

You can add or change a button image on items you've added to a toolbar or menu. For your custom menu, you want to add a button image to the AutoFormat command. To add a button image to a command:

Step 1	*Right-click*	the AutoFormat button on the Region Sales toolbar
Step 2	*Point to*	Change Button Image
Step 3	*Select*	the yellow happy face button from the Button Image palette
Step 4	*Click*	Close in the Customize dialog box
Step 5	*Click*	Special Format on the Region Sales toolbar

QUICK TIP

If you want to display only the button image, open the Customize dialog box, right-click the button, then click Default Style on the shortcut menu.

Your toolbar should look similar to Figure 11-18.

FIGURE 11-18
Custom Menu Added to a Toolbar

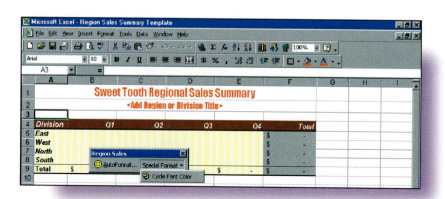

Now attach the modified toolbar. To reattach a toolbar:

Step 1	**Right-click**	any toolbar
Step 2	**Click**	Customize
Step 3	**Click**	the Toolbars tab
Step 4	**Click**	Attach
Step 5	**Click**	Region Sales in the Toolbars in workbook: list
Step 6	**Click**	Delete
Step 7	**Click**	Region Sales in the Custom toolbars: list on the left
Step 8	**Click**	Copy>>
Step 9	**Click**	OK
Step 10	**Click**	Close
Step 11	**Save & Close**	the template

> **QUICK TIP**
>
> You can move a menu from a toolbar to the menu bar, or vice versa, while the Customize dialog box remains open. Just drag the menu item from the toolbar to the menu bar, or from the menu bar to the toolbar.

The template is now ready for distribution and use by Sweet Tooth's division managers. If you no longer need your custom toolbar, you may want to delete it. To delete a toolbar:

Step 1	**Right-click**	any toolbar
Step 2	**Click**	Customize
Step 3	**Click**	the Toolbars tab
Step 4	**Click**	Region Sales in the Toolbars: list
Step 5	**Click**	Delete

Excel asks if you are sure you want to delete the selected toolbar.

Step 6	**Click**	OK
Step 7	**Click**	Close

The custom toolbar is still attached to the *Region Sales Summary Template*. Using this template will save the managers a lot of time when preparing data, and will save you a lot of time in reformatting the data to have a consistent appearance when you need to create reports.

chapter eleven

Summary

- Templates are used to start a new workbook with preset formatting, data, and formulas. Use templates whenever you need to reuse a workbook.
- Customize Excel's built-in templates by adding your own information to the template.
- Create a custom template by changing the Save as type setting in the Save As dialog box. Save customized templates or other existing workbooks as templates.
- Find can be used to locate values within cell values, formulas, or comments. Replace can find and replace values throughout a workbook.
- View toolbars when you need to use them. Hide toolbars when you no longer need them.
- Dock a floating toolbar by dragging the toolbar's title bar to an edge of the application window. Move a docked toolbar by dragging the toolbar's handle located at the left or top of the docked toolbar.
- Create custom toolbars by dragging command buttons onto the toolbar.
- Create custom menus by dragging command items onto the toolbar. Right-click menu items while in Customize mode to edit menu items. Remove items from a toolbar or menu by dragging them off the toolbar or menu.

Commands Review

Action	Menu Bar	Shortcut Menu	Toolbar	Keyboard
Create a new workbook based on a template	File, New			ALT + F, N
Open the Find dialog box	Edit, Find			ALT + E, F CTRL + F
Open the Replace dialog box	Edit, Replace			ALT + E, E CTRL + H
View or hide toolbars	View, Toolbars, (toolbar name)	Right-click a toolbar, (toolbar name)		ALT + V, T
Customize toolbars or menus	View, Toolbars, Customize	Right-click a toolbar, Customize		ALT + V, T, C

Concepts Review

Circle the correct answer.

1. Toolbars can be docked:
   - [a] only at the top and bottom edges of the application window.
   - [b] only at the left or right edges of the application window.
   - **[c]** on any edge of the application window.
   - [d] none of the above; toolbars must always float in the application window.

2. Find cannot be used on which of the following?
   - [a] formulas
   - [b] comments
   - [c] cell values
   - **[d]** worksheet tabs

3. Templates:
   - **[a]** save time by eliminating repetitious formatting and setup tasks.
   - [b] are difficult to create.
   - [c] cannot be modified.
   - [d] can be used by clicking the New button on the Standard toolbar.

4. To move a docked toolbar:
   - [a] click and drag the toolbar's title bar.
   - [b] click and drag the toolbar's fill handle.
   - **[c]** click and drag the toolbar's handle.
   - [d] turn it off, then turn it on again to make it float.

5. Customizing toolbars:
   - [a] is easy to do.
   - [b] can help you work more efficiently.
   - [c] gives you access to commands not available on the toolbars or menus by default.
   - **[d]** all of the above.

6. Custom menus:
   - [a] are difficult to modify.
   - **[b]** can be placed on the menu bar or a toolbar.
   - [c] cannot be created in Excel.
   - [d] can contain only items found on other menus.

7. Excel's built-in templates:
   - [a] are located on the General tab of the New dialog box.
   - **[b]** are located on the Spreadsheet Solutions tab of the New dialog box.
   - [c] are available when you click the New button on the Standard toolbar.
   - [d] can be viewed using the Templates item on the View menu.

8. To create a custom toolbar:
   - [a] drag buttons off the Standard toolbar.
   - [b] drag the name of the toolbar from the Toolbars list in the Customize dialog box.
   - [c] right-click an open toolbar, then click New Toolbar.
   - **[d]** click the New button on the Toolbars tab of the Customize dialog box.

9. Once you've created a template, you can use it to create a new workbook:
   - [a] only after you open the Customize dialog box.
   - [b] only by clicking New from the File menu.
   - **[c]** after you click the Save As Workbook command on the File menu.
   - [d] after clicking the New button on the Standard toolbar.

10. To rename a menu, open the Customize dialog box, then:
    - **[a]** right-click the menu item and use the Name box to enter a new name.
    - [b] key the new name.
    - [c] double-click the menu name and key a new name.
    - [d] drag the menu off the menu bar and change its name.

chapter eleven

Circle **T** if the statement is true or **F** if the statement is false.

T F 1. You can remove items from a custom menu by dragging them off the menu while in Customize mode.

T **F** 2. Custom menus can be added to the menu bar, but not to custom toolbars.

T F 3. The Reset button in the Customize dialog box is used to return Excel toolbars to their default settings.

T **F** 4. The Attach button in the Customize dialog box is used to attach, or dock, a toolbar to an edge of the application window.

T F 5. You can change or add button images to any item you have added to a toolbar or menu.

T F 6. You can set up a template to use only customized menus and toolbars.

T **F** 7. Once you've placed a menu item or toolbar button, you cannot reposition it.

T F 8. You can save any workbook as a template using the File menu, then clicking Save As and setting the Save as type: to Template.

T **F** 9. When you edit a workbook created using a template and then save the changes, the changes are updated in the template as well.

T **F** 10. You cannot add other menu items to Excel's default menus.

Skills Review

Exercise 1

1. Start a new workbook.

2. Create a new toolbar named Special Edit.

3. Add the following Edit category commands:

   a. Paste Formatting

   b. Paste Values

   c. Clear Contents

   d. Clear Formatting

   e. Select Current Region

4. Attach the toolbar to the workbook.

5. Save the workbook as *Special Edit*.

6. Close the workbook.

7. Delete the Special Edit toolbar (the toolbar will still be available when you open the *Special Edit* workbook because you attached it).

Exercise 2

1. Start a new workbook.

2. Create a Custom Formatting toolbar.

3. Add a new menu to the toolbar.

4. Name the menu Borders, using B as the mnemonic. (*Hint:* Use the & character in front of the B.)

5. Add the following Format category commands to the <u>B</u>orders menu:

   a. Apply Inside Borders

   b. Inside Vertical Border

   c. Inside Horizontal Border

   d. Diagonal Down Border

   e. Diagonal Up Border

6. Attach the toolbar to the workbook.

7. Save the workbook as *Custom Formatting*.

8. Close the workbook.

9. Delete the Custom Formatting toolbar.

Exercise 3

1. Open the *Custom Formatting* workbook that you created in Exercise 2.

2. Add a second menu to the Custom Formatting toolbar.

3. Name the menu Rotation, with a mnemonic R.

4. Add the following Format category commands to the <u>R</u>otation menu:

   a. Vertical Text

   b. Rotate Text Up

   c. Rotate Text Down

   d. Angle Text Downward

   e. Angle Text Upward

5. Rename the toolbar Custom Formatting 2. (*Hint:* Select the toolbar name in the Toolba<u>r</u>s: list on the Tool<u>b</u>ars tab, then click <u>R</u>ename.)

6. Attach the Custom Formatting 2 toolbar to the workbook and unattach the Custom Formatting toolbar.

7. Save the workbook as *Custom Formatting 2*.

8. Close the workbook.

9. Delete the Custom Formatting 2 toolbar.

Exercise 4

1. Create a new expense statement using the Expense Statement template in the Spreadsheet Solutions tab. (*Hint:* If you need to install the template, insert the CD into the drive, then click OK in the alert box.) Enable macros.

2. Click Customize.

3. Enter the Sweet Tooth company information listed below:

   a. SWEET TOOTH in the Company Name cell

   b. 1234 Candy Cane Lane in the Address cell

   c. Phoenix in the City cell

    d. AZ in the State cell

    e. 85001 in the ZIP Code cell

    f. (555) 555-1234 in the Phone cell

    g. (555) 555-1235 in the Fax cell

4. Click the Change Plate Font button.

5. Change the font style to Impact, the size to 10, and the color to red.

6. Click the Expense Statement tab.

7. Save the workbook as a new template called *Sweet Tooth Expense Statement Template* and print it.

Exercise 5

1. Open the *Region Sales with Chart* workbook on your Data Disk.

2. Save the workbook as a template named *Region Sales with Chart Template*.

3. Close the template file.

4. Create a new workbook using the *Region Sales with Chart Template* template.

5. Enter West Coast Region in cell A2.

6. Enter fictitious sales data in cells B5:E8.

7. Display the data table on the Region Summary Chart sheet.

8. Print the Region Summary Chart.

9. Save the workbook as *West Coast Region Sales with Chart*.

Exercise 6

1. Open the *Locate* workbook on your Data Disk.

2. A named range, Qtr4, has been deleted from the workbook, causing an error in one of the formulas. Use the Find dialog box to search for Qtr4, by searching formulas.

3. Fix the formula so that it correctly sums the values in cells E4:E7.

4. Use Find and Replace to replace all instances of "Q" with "Quarter " (include a space after Quarter).

5. Print the worksheet.

6. Save the workbook as *Locate Revised*.

Exercise 7

1. Open the *Video Rental* workbook on your Data Disk.

2. Bold and center the column headings in row 2.

3. Use a red cell fill with white text in row 2.

4. Select cells B3:G7 and add All Borders to the selection.

5. Select cells G3:G10 and add a Thick Box Border to the selection.

6. Select cells B1:G10 and add a Thick Box Border to the selection.

7. Set the print area to this selection and print it.

8. Save the workbook as a template named *Video Rental Template*.

Exercise 8

1. Create a new workbook using the *Video Rental Template* template.
2. Fill in fictitious data on the form for two video rentals.
    a. Fill in today's date in the Check Out date column for each video.
    b. Fill in a video title for each video.
3. Print the Video Rental form.
4. Save the workbook as *Video Rental 1*.

Case Projects

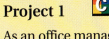

Project 1

As an office manager, you receive a large volume of phone calls each day. Create a custom phone message template. Include cells to record the time and date of the call, the name of the person whom the message is for, the message text, the caller's phone number, and the requested response. Be creative in your use of borders, shading, drawing objects, font styles, and so on. Apply number formats as appropriate. Set print settings to print messages correctly. Save the template as *Phone Message Template* and print it.

Project 2

Use the Web toolbar to go to *www.microsoft.com*. Search the site for "free stuff" and look for other Excel templates that you can download and use. With your instructor's permission, download two templates and save them to the drive and directory where you are storing your Data Files and print them.

Project 3

As a traveling sales representative, you know that keeping track of your schedule is very important. Use Excel to create a calendar template for one month. Format the calendar, and set print areas. Save the template as *Calendar Template*. Create two new calendars using this template for the next two months. Save each workbook as the month name covered by the calendar. Print the two calendars and the *Calendar Template*.

Project 4

You have just launched your own sales business. As a new business owner, you don't have templates for any of the routine tasks you need to accomplish in the course of a day. Use the Web toolbar to search the Internet for companies selling Excel template productivity packs geared toward business. Print the home pages of at least two companies that market templates for use in Excel.

Project 5

You own a retail computer store. In addition to selling custom computers, you service computers that aren't working. You need a template to enter service order information. In the client information section, you need to enter the client's name, address, city, state, and ZIP code. In the computer information section, you need to enter the CPU speed, amount of RAM, hard drive space, and operating system. In the problem description section, you need to enter a description of the problem as explained by the client. In the estimate section, you need to enter an estimate of the number of hours it will take a technician to repair the problem, plus the estimated cost of any parts that may need to be replaced. Create formulas to (1) multiply the number of estimated hours by the current rate of $45/hour; (2) add the estimated

technician cost to the estimated parts cost;
(3) calculate the sales tax on the estimate; and
(4) add the subtotal and the calculated sales tax to provide a total. Create a new template including all these sections named *Service Order Template* and print it.

Project 6

As the owner of a small book store, you would like to create a receipt template to record sales. Your template should include the current date and time of the transaction, a place to enter the title of the books purchased, and the price of each book. It should also include formulas to calculate the subtotal of items sold, sales tax, and the total sale amount. Save the template as *Book Sales Receipt Template* and print it.

Project 7

You are the project manager at an architectural firm. One of your duties is to generate a "To Do" list for the office staff. Create a template for the To Do list. This template should automatically display the current date and contain columns for the due date, project name, task to complete, and the employee who is assigned to each task. The template should contain enough entry blanks to record 15–20 tasks. Save the template as *To Do List Template* and print it.

Project 8

You're looking for other ways to make it easier to find text values in a worksheet. In Chapter 7, you learned about several Text functions. However, there are other text functions that weren't covered in that chapter. Use online Help to lookup information on the following functions: FIND, FINDB, SEARCH and SEARCHB. Write a half-page summary of your findings in Word. Save the document as *Find and Search Functions.doc* and print it.

Sharing Workbooks with Others

Chapter Overview

Changes in today's software reflect the way the business world works. Documents are shared between departments and among coworkers. Excel workbooks can be edited simultaneously by many different people connected to a network. During the editing process, Excel keeps track of all changes made to a workbook. Workbooks can be distributed electronically, then merged into a single workbook after several people make modifications. You can add comments to cells to clarify results or add an informative note.

Case profile
Each department of Sweet Tooth is responsible for tracking data pertinent to the department. Sales maintains information on how many units are sold and works with production and management to set pricing for each item. At the beginning of each year, you set up a Projected Profit workbook, with estimated income and expense figures. By sharing your workbook, the other departments can update your workbook with real figures as they become available. You can see who made what changes and when, and choose whether to accept those changes.

Learning Objectives
- Protect worksheets and workbooks and use passwords
- Share a workbook
- Track changes
- Change workbook properties
- Merge workbooks
- Create, edit, and remove comments

chapter twelve

12.a Protecting Worksheets and Workbooks and Using Passwords

When sharing a workbook, you may want to prevent other users from changing the data or formatting in that workbook. You do this by enabling workbook protection. If security is a concern, you can add a password to your workbooks as well. You need to distribute the *Sweet Tooth Projected Profit 2000* workbook to several managers in the company. You would like to protect the workbook from unnecessary changes by retaining the work you've done.

To open the workbook:

Step 1	Open	the *Sweet Tooth Projected Profit 2000* workbook on your Data Disk
Step 2	Save	the workbook as *Sweet Tooth Projected Profit 2000 Revised* in your Data Files folder

Excel provides two ways to protect individual cells from being altered. **Hiding** cells prevents the formula from appearing in the Formula Bar when a user clicks the cell, but still calculates the result as usual. **Locking** cells prevents other users from changing them. To set these options, you use the Format Cells Dialog box, then enable worksheet protection.

To set cell protection options:

Step 1	Select	cells B6:F10 and cell F5
Step 2	Press	the CTRL + 1 keys to open the Format Cells dialog box
Step 3	Click	the Protection tab
Step 4	Click	the check box next to Hidden
Step 5	Click	OK

The Locked check box is selected by default. Neither option affects the selected cells until you protect the worksheet.

To apply worksheet protection:

Step 1	Click	Tools
Step 2	Point to	Protection
Step 3	Click	Protect Sheet

The Protect Sheet options allow you to protect cell contents, drawing objects, and scenarios. If security is an issue, you can apply a password to prevent anyone who does not have that password from changing the settings.

To apply a password:

| Step 1 | Key | your first name in the Password box (use lowercase letters) |

As you enter your password, an asterisk (*) replaces each letter you type, as a security measure.

| Step 2 | Click | OK |

Excel prompts you to reenter your password to ensure that you entered it correctly. Passwords are case-sensitive, so *Your Name* is not the same password as *your name*.

Step 3	Key	your first name again, exactly as you keyed it before
Step 4	Click	OK
Step 5	Click	cell F5

Notice you can no longer see the formula in the Formula Bar.

> **QUICK TIP**
>
> You can protect either individual worksheets or the entire workbook. In protecting a workbook, you prevent users from inserting, moving, or deleting worksheets, or even opening the workbook. On the Tools menu, point to Protection, then click Protect Workbook. You can add an optional password, if necessary.

> **CAUTION TIP**
>
> Be sure to remember your password. If you forget it, you may not be able to access your workbook.

chapter twelve

QUICK TIP

You can change your user name with the Options dialog box. Click Options on the Tools menu. On the General tab, key your name in the User name box, then click OK.

| Step 6 | Press | any letter key to change the contents of the cell |

Excel notifies you that the cell is protected.

| Step 7 | Click | OK |

To remove worksheet protection:

Step 1	Click	Tools
Step 2	Point to	Protection
Step 3	Click	Unprotect sheet
Step 4	Key	your password (your first name) exactly as you entered it previously
Step 5	Click	OK
Step 6	Save	the workbook

12.b Sharing a Workbook

To work more efficiently, you can share workbooks with other people. When **sharing** a workbook, you can track modifications to the workbook. You can share a workbook by routing it to other users via e-mail or by working simultaneously with other users on a network. When you collaborate with others via a network, each user is notified when another user has saved changes. You want to share the *Sweet Tooth Projected Profit 2000 Revised* workbook with other departments to collect final data. To share a workbook:

Step 1	Click	Tools
Step 2	Click	Share Workbook to open the Share Workbook dialog box
Step 3	Click	the check box next to Allow changes by more than one user at the same a time

The Share Workbook dialog box on your screen should look similar to Figure 12-1.

MOUSE TIP

The Advanced tab of the Share Workbook dialog box includes advanced tracking options. For more information about these settings, click the Help button, then click the setting about which you want to learn.

FIGURE 12-1
Share Workbook Dialog Box

QUICK TIP

Limitations exist regarding what changes can and cannot be made to a shared workbook. To obtain a complete list of these limitations, use the Office Assistant.

| Step 4 | **Click** | OK |

An alert box warns you that the workbook will be saved.

| Step 5 | **Click** | OK |

The workbook is saved automatically and the title bar reflects the fact that the workbook is [Shared].

12.c Tracking Changes

Tracking changes allows you to see what changes have been made to a workbook. When you track changes, highlighted borders quickly identify cells whose contents have been edited. When several people work together on the same workbook, each user's changes are assigned a different color, making it easy to see who made changes to different cells. Note that the color assigned to each user's changes may differ each time you open the workbook. To highlight changes:

Step 1	**Click**	Tools
Step 2	**Point to**	Track Changes
Step 3	**Click**	Highlight Changes

The Highlight Changes dialog box, shown in Figure 12-2, allows you to select which changes to show.

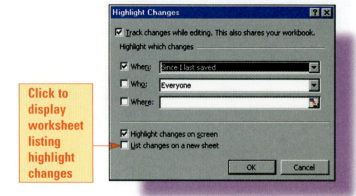

FIGURE 12-2
Track Changes Dialog Box

Step 4	*Click*	the Whe<u>n</u>: list arrow
Step 5	*Click*	All
Step 6	*Click*	OK

Excel notifies you that it did not find any changes.

Step 7	*Click*	OK
Step 8	*Enter*	10250 in cell B5
Step 9	*Move*	your pointer over cell B5

See Figure 12-3. A ScreenTip indicates the user name of the person who made the change, the date and time when the change was made, and the modification that was made to the cell. The border of the cell changes to a colored border and a small triangle is added in the upper-left corner, indicating that the cell's contents have changed.

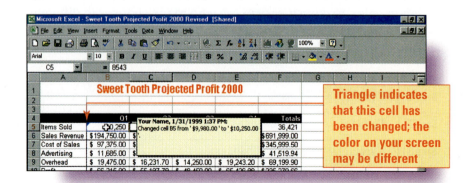

FIGURE 12-3
Viewing Changes to a Shared Workbook

QUICK TIP

When working simultaneously with multiple users, conflicting changes may occur. Excel can either save the latest changes—known as the "whoever saves last, wins" rule—or it can display the Resolve Conflicts dialog box to allow you to select which change to accept. This option appears on the Advanced tab of the Share Workbook dialog box.

QUICK TIP

A quick way to enable workbook sharing and track changes simultaneously is to open the Track Changes dialog box, then click the check box next to <u>T</u>rack changes while editing.

| Step 10 | Enter | 10000 in cell C5 |

You can accept or reject any change to the workbook. To accept or reject changes:

Step 1	Click	Tools
Step 2	Point to	Track Changes
Step 3	Click	Accept or Reject Changes
Step 4	Click	OK to save the changes to your workbook

The Select Changes to Accept or Reject dialog box opens. This dialog box allows you to filter the changes made since a certain date, changes made by a certain user, or changes affecting certain cells. The default is to select changes that you haven't reviewed yet.

| Step 5 | Click | OK |

When you click OK, the Accept or Reject Changes dialog box opens, allowing you to accept or reject individual or group changes. Your dialog box should look similar to Figure 12-4.

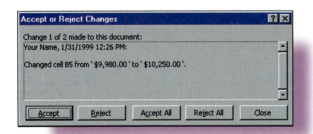

| Step 6 | Click | Accept to accept the first change |
| Step 7 | Click | Reject to reject the second change |

The value in cell C5 returns to its original value, and the colored triangle and border that indicated a change disappear from the cell.

| Step 8 | Save | the workbook |

QUICK TIP

Excel keeps track of changes on a separate worksheet. Normally, this worksheet remains hidden from view, but you can display it by clicking the check box next to List changes on a new sheet in the Highlight Changes dialog box. This history list displays detailed information about all changes made to the workbook because the "track changes" feature was enabled.

FIGURE 12-4
Accept or Reject Changes Dialog Box

QUICK TIP

Click Accept All or Reject All to quickly accept or reject all cells currently being reviewed.

chapter twelve

When you disable workbook sharing, you also turn off the track changes feature and erase the History list.

12.d Changing Workbook Properties

Workbook **properties** comprise information about the workbook that can be stored with the workbook. This information includes file size, creation date, company and author name, and date that the workbook was last modified or accessed. You can change some of this information through the workbook Properties dialog box. Before you can change workbook properties, you need to turn off workbook sharing.

To disable workbook sharing:

Step 1	Click	Tools
Step 2	Click	Share Workbook
Step 3	Click	the check box next to Allow changes to remove the check mark
Step 4	Click	OK
Step 5	Click	Yes after reading the warning about turning off the sharing feature

Now you can change the workbook's properties. To change a workbook's properties:

Step 1	Click	File
Step 2	Click	Properties
Step 3	Key	your name in the Author: box (if it's not already there)
Step 4	Key	Sweet Tooth in the Company: box

The dialog box on your screen should look similar to Figure 12-5.

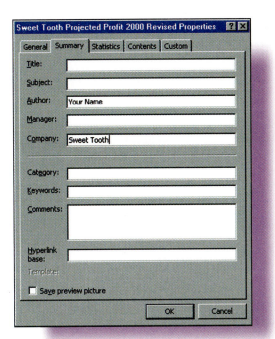

FIGURE 12-5
Workbook Properties Dialog Box

QUICK TIP

You can view a workbook's properties without opening the workbook. In Windows Explorer or in the Open dialog box, right-click any workbook, then click Properties.

Step 5	*Click*	OK
Step 6	*Save & Close*	the workbook

12.e Merging Workbooks

Occasionally, you may need to distribute copies of a shared workbook to users who do not have access to your network. Although you can route the workbook via e-mail, if you must continue editing the workbook simultaneously, this option may not work. In this case, you can save copies of the workbook and distribute them. When other users return these copies to you with their changes, you can incorporate the additional changes into the original workbook by using the Merge workbooks command.

To merge workbooks, you must follow several rules. First, you must create copies of a workbook for which the sharing and track changes features are enabled. Second, each copy must have a unique filename. Third, each workbook must have a common password or no password. Fourth, when you enable workbook sharing, you can specify the length of time for which you want to track changes on the Advanced tab of the Share Workbook dialog box (the default is 30 days). You must merge the copies within this period. For example, if you set the "keep change" history to 30 days, and the workbook copies were made 45 days ago, you can no longer merge the workbooks. If necessary, you can set the "keep change" history to 32,767 days.

chapter twelve

When you perform the merge, only the target (workbook receiving the changes) can be open. To create a copy and merge changes:

| Step 1 | Open | the *Sweet Tooth Projected Profit 2001* workbook on your Data Disk |

Note that this workbook is designated as being shared.

Step 2	Save	the workbook as *Sweet Tooth Projected Profit 2001 Final* in your Data Files folder
Step 3	Save	the workbook again as *Sweet Tooth Projected Profit 2001 Revised* in your Data Files folder
Step 4	Enter	11000 in cell B5
Step 5	Enter	12000 in cell E5
Step 6	Save & Close	the workbook
Step 7	Open	the *Sweet Tooth Projected Profit 2001 Final* workbook in your Data Files folder
Step 8	Click	Tools
Step 9	Click	Merge Workbooks
Step 10	Click	OK to save the workbook
Step 11	Select	the *Sweet Tooth Projected Profit 2001 Revised* workbook in your Data Files Folder
Step 12	Click	OK

The changes in the revised (source) workbook become merged into the target workbook. The colored border indicates the changed cells. Your screen should look similar to Figure 12-6.

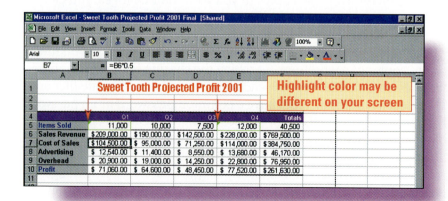

FIGURE 12-6
Merged Workbooks

Sharing Workbooks with Others   EA 11

| Step 13 | Save | the workbook |

12.f Creating, Editing, and Removing Comments

To clarify information in your workbooks, you can add comments to individual cells. Comments might explain how a formula was set up, why you made a certain assumption, or question a colleague about the value of a particular cell. Comments are identified by a small, red triangle in the upper-right corner of a cell.

To add a comment:

| Step 1 | Right-click | cell F10 |
| Step 2 | Click | Insert Comment |

A comment note appears, similar to Figure 12-7.

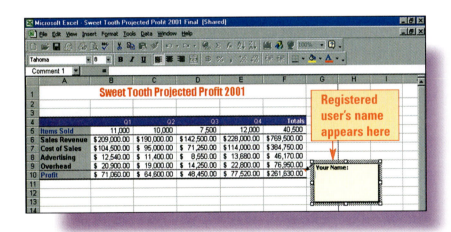

MENU TIP

To insert a comment, click Comment from the Insert menu.

To view all comments on a worksheet, click Comments on the View menu. The Reviewing toolbar opens, and you can then use this toolbar to add, edit, delete, and display comments.

FIGURE 12-7
Adding a Comment

MOUSE TIP

To delete a comment from a worksheet, right-click the cell with the comment, then click Delete comment.

| Step 3 | Key | Merged Sweet Tooth Projected Profit 2001 Revised workbook on DATE |
| Step 4 | Click | cell F10 to close the comment |

Comment boxes appear when you hover the pointer over the cell.

To read a comment:

| Step 1 | **_Move_** | your pointer over cell F10 |

The comment appears as a ScreenTip. You can also modify comments in a worksheet. To modify a comment:

Step 1	**_Right-click_**	cell F10
Step 2	**_Click_**	Edit comment
Step 3	**_Replace_**	DATE with the current date
Step 4	**_Click_**	cell F10
Step 5	**_Save & Close_**	the workbook

Sharing workbooks can be a good way to boost productivity by allowing multiple users to work on and modify the same workbook simultaneously. Tracking changes is an easy way to monitor changes to your workbooks.

> **QUICK TIP**
>
> You can print worksheet comments by printing them at the end of the print report or as they are displayed on the page. On the Sheet tab of the Page Setup dialog box, click the Comments list arrow, then select an option.

Summary

▶ Protect a workbook from changes by enabling protection. You can also add a level of security by providing password protection to a worksheet or workbook.

▶ Multiple users can edit a workbook simultaneously on a network. While a workbook is shared, certain features remain unavailable, such as chart and drawing tools.

▶ Track changes to see which modifications have been made and who made them.

▶ Merge workbooks to combine information from multiple copies of a shared workbook.

▶ Add comments to clarify information or to act as a reminder.

Commands Review

Action	Menu Bar	Shortcut Menu	Toolbar	Keyboard
Protect a worksheet	Tools, Protection, Protect Sheet			ALT + T, P, P
Unprotect a worksheet	Tools, Protection, Unprotect Sheet			ALT + T, P, P
Protect a workbook	Tools, Protection, Protect Workbook			ALT + T, P, W
Unprotect a workbook	Tools, Protection, Unprotect Workbook			ALT + T, P, W
Share a workbook	Tools, Share workbook			ALT + T, H
Highlight changes	Tools, Track changes, Highlight changes			ALT + T, T, H
Accept or reject changes	Tools, Track changes, Accept or Reject changes			ALT + T, A
Merge workbooks	Tools, Merge Workbooks			ALT + T, W
Add a comment	Insert, Comment	Insert Comment	☐	ALT + I, M
Edit a comment	Insert, Edit Comment	Edit Comment	☐	ALT + I, E
Delete a comment		Delete Comment	☐	
Hide a comment		Hide Comment	☐	
Show a comment	View, Comments	Show Comment	☐	ALT + V, C

chapter twelve

Concepts Review

Circle the correct answer.

1. **When you hide formulas using worksheet protection:**
   - [a] formulas do not calculate.
   - [b] the formula is displayed but not the calculated value.
   - **[c] formulas calculate but are not displayed in the Formula Bar.**
   - [d] formulas display and calculate as usual.

2. **You can identify modified cells using Track Changes by a colored:**
   - [a] border and triangle in the upper-right corner.
   - **[b] border and triangle in the upper-left corner.**
   - [c] triangle in the upper-right corner.
   - [d] triangle in the upper-left corner.

3. **You can identify comments by a colored:**
   - [a] border and triangle in the upper-right corner.
   - [b] border and triangle in the upper-left corner.
   - **[c] triangle in the upper-right corner.**
   - [d] triangle in the upper-left corner.

4. **To select view options for changes, click Tools, then:**
   - [a] Merge Workbook.
   - [b] Share Workbook.
   - [c] Track Changes, Highlight changes.
   - [d] Track Changes, Accept or Reject changes,

5. **The History list shows:**
   - [a] the results of a Solver operation.
   - [b] the results of a Goal Seek operation.
   - **[c] all changes that have been made to a shared workbook.**
   - [d] a list of recently accessed files.

6. **When merging workbooks:**
   - **[a] both workbooks can be open.**
   - [b] only the target workbook can be open.
   - [c] only the source workbook can be open.
   - [d] neither of the workbooks has to be open.

7. **You can use comments to:**
   - [a] point out important information.
   - [b] remind yourself or someone else to do something.
   - [c] explain a cell's function or value.
   - **[d] all of the above.**

8. **Workbook properties:**
   - [a] cannot be modified.
   - **[b] contain fields of additional data that are stored with the workbook.**
   - [c] cannot be displayed unless the workbook is open.
   - [d] can be displayed only outside of Excel.

9. When should you use Merge workbooks instead of another method of viewing changes to a workbook?
   [a] When several users are sharing the file on the network.
   [b] When another user does not have access to the network, but you must continue working on the workbook at the same time.
   [c] When you need to route a workbook to several users in a certain order.
   [d] Merging workbooks is just as easy as sharing a single workbook.

10. In Excel, you can protect:
    [a] worksheets, but not workbooks.
    [b] only selected cells.
    [c] selected cells, entire worksheets, or entire workbooks.
    [d] only worksheets in which changes are highlighted.

Circle **T** if the statement is true or **F** if the statement is false.

T F 1. "Whoever saves last, wins" is one way to deal with conflicting changes in a shared workbook.

T F 2. You must enable sharing before multiple users can access a workbook simultaneously.

T **F** 3. You can track changes without enabling workbook sharing.

T **F** 4. To view information about a change made to a shared workbook, you must display the History list worksheet.

T **F** 5. You can view charts in a shared workbook.

T **F** 6. Excel automatically saves the workbook before (after) enabling the sharing feature.

T **F** 7. Merged workbooks can be merged anytime regardless of how many days are specified to track changes.

T **F** 8. You can change workbook properties while sharing is enabled.

T F 9. You can protect a worksheet or workbook without applying a password.

T F 10. To merge workbooks, you must merge copies of a shared workbook.

Skills Review

Exercise 1

1. Create a new workbook.
2. Enter the information shown in the table below. (Enter Division in cell A1.)

Division	Sales Rep	Total Sales
East		
East		
East		
East		
West		
West		
West		
West		
North		
North		
North		
North		
South		
South		
South		
South		

3. Save the workbook as *Division Sales*.
4. Share the workbook.
5. Save the workbook and print it.

Exercise 2

1. Open the *Division Sales* workbook that you created in Exercise 1.
2. Enable track changes and set the When option to All.
3. In column B, add fictitious sales representative names for each division.
4. In column C, create fictitious sales data between $1,000 and $5,000.
5. Save the workbook as *Division Sales 1* and print it.

Exercise 3

1. Open the *Division Sales 1* workbook that you created in Exercise 2.

2. Display the change History list. (*Hint:* Use the Track Changes dialog box, and make sure the When: list is set to All.)

3. Print the History worksheet.

4. Save the workbook. Note that when you save the workbook, the History list becomes hidden again.

Exercise 4

1. Open the *Division Sales 1* workbook that you created in Exercise 2.

2. Save the workbook as *Division Sales 2*.

3. Disable workbook sharing.

4. Add a title to the workbook properties, change the Author name to your name, and change the company name to Sweet Tooth.

5. Save the workbook and print it.

Exercise 5

1. Open the *Division Sales 2* workbook that you created in Exercise 4.

2. Protect the worksheet, and add your last name in small caps as the password.

3. Try to change the value in cell C2 to $3,000.00.

4. Disable worksheet protection, and change the value of cell C2 to $3,000.00.

5. Save the workbook as *Division Sales 3*.

Exercise 6

1. Open the *Division Sales 3* workbook that you created in Exercise 5.

2. Add a comment to the name of any sales representative who made less than $2,000. Ask for information from the division managers regarding how the sales representative has performed historically. Ask for recommendations on the sales representative's future with the company.

3. Save the workbook as *Division Sales 4*.

4. Enable workbook sharing.

5. E-mail the workbook to yourself as an attachment.

chapter twelve

Exercise 7

1. You should receive an e-mail containing an attached workbook from Exercise 6. (*Hint:* Use your e-mail program to send/receive messages.)

2. Read the comments in the workbook.

3. In column D, write a response comment suggesting future action for each sales representative.

4. Save the workbook with the new name *Division Sales 4a,* and e-mail the modified workbook back to yourself. (Be sure to close this workbook in Excel.)

Exercise 8

1. If the *Division Sales 4a* workbook is still open, close it.

2. Open the *Division Sales 4* workbook that you created in Exercise 6.

3. After you receive the workbook *Division Sales 4a* that you sent to yourself as an e-mail attachment, merge the *Division Sales 4a* workbook into the *Division Sales 4* workbook.

4. Print the workbook with the comments at the end of the report.

5. Save the workbook as *Division Sales Recommendations*.

Case Projects

Project 1

You are the personnel manager for a small company. You maintain information about the company's employees using a worksheet. Create a workbook with fictitious names, home phone numbers, and Social Security numbers for 10 employees. You want to prevent unauthorized users from viewing the contents of this workbook. In addition to protecting worksheets and workbooks, you can add a password to keep users from opening a workbook when you save the file. Use Save <u>A</u>s from the <u>F</u>ile menu to save your workbook as *Employee Info*. Before clicking save, click the <u>T</u>ools menu, then General <u>O</u>ptions. Add a password consisting of your first name in uppercase letters in the Password to open box.

Project 2

Your boss is concerned about securing information contained in some workbooks that you are sharing with other staff members. Use the Office Assistant to research how to limit what others can see and change in a shared workbook. Write a half-page summary of your findings, including any steps necessary to hide or protect portions of a workbook from other users. Name your document *Securing Workbook Information.doc*.

Project 3

As a small business owner just learning Excel, you would like to take a class to help you become familiar with this program more rapidly. Use the Internet to search for businesses offering Excel training in your area. Print a Web page containing contact information for a company near you.

Project 4

You are looking for a new job where you can apply your Excel skills. Use the Internet to search for jobs (*Hint:* Search for Job Sites first) where Excel is a required skill. Print at least two job descriptions that sound intriguing.

Project 5

Play a game of Othello using a shared Excel workbook. Open the *Othello* workbook on your Data Disk. Share the workbook, then start a game of Othello. View comments for instructions or ask someone who knows how to play Othello for help. Make sure that both players save their workbooks after each player's turn ends.

Project 6

You are in charge of documenting and managing workbook files created in your company. You use file properties to make it easy for others to find out information without opening the workbook. Using at least two of the workbooks you created in this chapter or in one of the Skills Review Exercises, edit the file properties by adding a Title, Subject, and Keywords to the workbook file. Save and close the workbooks with new filenames. Open the Open dialog box, click Tools, then click Find to use the Find dialog box to search for one of the keywords you entered in one of the Properties dialog boxes. Be sure to select Keywords in the Property: box in the Find dialog box, and be sure the Look in: box lists the folder where you are storing your Data Files.

Project 7

You work for a large publishing company tracking sales data for the Computer Books division. Create a worksheet with four fictitious book titles and columns to keep track of the sales data for each quarter of the current year. Add fictitious sales data to your workbook for each book in all quarters. Save the workbook as *Book Sales 1*. Enable Highlight Changes. Save the workbook as *Book Sales 2*. Change the sales data in several cells, then save and close the workbook. Open *Book Sales 1* and merge the changes from *Book Sales 2*. Print a history list of the changes you made.

Project 8

You are a clerk working in the warehouse of a large shipping company. You have created a custom number format for keeping track of items in your warehouse. Create a workbook with a custom number format that automatically inserts several non-numeric characters. Format the column using your number format. Next, add 5–10 items, then add a comment to one of the entries explaining how to enter data using your custom number format. Finally, enable workbook sharing so others can edit the workbook. Save the workbook as *Warehouse Entries*.

chapter twelve

Excel 2000

Using Lists in Excel

Chapter Overview

Some workbooks in Excel store lists of data, much as a database does. In this chapter, you learn about the components of a list. To ensure proper data entry in a list, you can specify validation criteria for each column. You can use data forms to enter, edit, find, and delete records from a list. Use AutoFilters or advanced filters to view subsets of a list.

Learning Objectives

- Identify components of a list
- Use data validation
- Use the data form
- Apply data filters

Case profile

You have been asked to create a personnel data list to keep track of information about each of Sweet Tooth's employees. By using data validation, you can ensure that other users will enter the appropriate data in each field. Using data forms and filters, you can then locate specific records.

chapter thirteen

13.a Identifying Components of a List

In earlier chapters, you saw examples of lists in Excel. Sometimes these **lists** are referred to as **databases**. A database stores data in a structure called a **table**, similar to a list in Excel. Each row in a data table contains a unique record, and each column contains entries in a particular field. A **field** contains a collection of characters or numbers, such as a person's name or a phone number. The **field name** identifies the contents of that particular field. A group of field entries is known as a **record**. At the top of the list, or data table, is a **header row**, which identifies the field names used in the table.

The *Sweet Tooth Personnel Data* workbook contains several records that you have already entered. This list contains fields for each employee's last name, first-name initial, division, salary, and "Rec. No.," a field that stores a unique record number for each record in the list. To open the workbook:

| Step 1 | **Open** | the *Sweet Tooth Personnel Data* workbook on your Data Disk |
| Step 2 | **Save** | the workbook as *Sweet Tooth Personnel Data Revised* to your Data Files folder |

Figure 13-1 shows the Sweet Tooth Personnel database.

QUICK TIP

Record numbers are often used in large database tables to speed up indexing and data retrieval. They also provide an easy way to sort the list by the order in which the records were entered into the list.

FIGURE 13-1
Typical List in Excel

You must remember some important guidelines when creating lists. First, you should format the header row differently from the rest of the data, using bold, italics, or a different font, so that Excel recognizes that it is the header row and not just another record. Second, the header row should appear as the first row of your list. Don't separate the header row from the first row of data by inserting a blank row. If necessary, use borders or cell fill to distinguish the header row from the data in the list. Third, each field entry in a field must contain the

same type of data. For example, don't place a phone number in the Last Name field of a phone directory list. Take note of the following guidelines as well:

- Create only one list per worksheet. If you need more than one list, use a separate worksheet for each new list. This strategy helps you avoid the potential problem of mixing lists when you perform a sort.
- Always leave one column and one row blank on both sides and above and below a list. Excel can then automatically detect the list boundaries, saving you the hassle of selecting the list, or else make sure it starts in row 1 and column A for sorting, outlining, and AutoFormat operations.
- Avoid using spaces at the beginning of a field entry. Spaces affect the sort order of a list, because the space character comes before alphabetic characters. Entries that have spaces as their first character are placed at the top of a sorted list.
- Format data in a column in a consistent manner. Don't make some names bold and others italic.
- Never place critical data to the left or right of a list. When filters are later applied to the list, you may not be able to see important data.
- Always include a record number field so as to give each record a unique record number. This strategy enables you to return the list to its original entry order after you've performed other sort operations.

13.b Using Data Validation

You want to ensure that anyone who uses the *Sweet Tooth Personnel Data Revised* workbook enters the correct data in each field. For example, the Salary field should contain only numerical data. To help the user meet these expectations, you will set up data validation for each column. **Data validation** restricts the entry in a field to parameters that you set. You can, for example, apply data validation to each field in a list to restrict the entry to specific types of data.

You want to limit the entry in the record number field to whole numbers between 1 and 999. To use data validation:

Step 1	*Select*	cells A7:A10
Step 2	*Click*	Data
Step 3	*Click*	Validation
Step 4	*Click*	the Allow: list arrow on the Settings tab

Figure 13-2 shows the Allow: list.

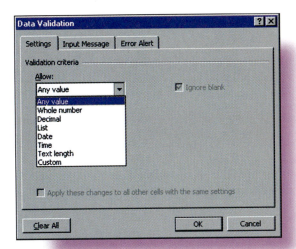

FIGURE 13-2
Allow List on the Settings Tab of the Data Validation Dialog Box

Each choice in the list restricts the data in the selected cells to different types. For example, the Whole number validation option restricts entry to whole numbers, and the Decimal validation option allows entry of any numerical value. The List validation option permits you to supply a list of valid entries from which the user can select one choice from a drop-down list. The Text length validation option allows you to limit the number of characters that can be entered in a field.

| Step 5 | Click | Whole number from the Allow: list |

The options on the Settings tab change for each validation option in the Allow list. For whole numbers, you specify an operator (less than, greater than, between, and so on) and minimum and maximum values to restrict which numerical values are permitted.

Step 6	Select	between from the Data: list
Step 7	Key	1 in the Minimum: box
Step 8	Key	999 in the Maximum: box

You want to ensure that every new record receives a record number. By default, Excel does not count blank entries as invalid.

| Step 9 | Click | the check box next to Ignore blank to deselect it |

Input messages display entry instructions, to make it easier for the user to understand what should be entered into a field.

To add an input message to the selected cells:

Step 1	Click	the Input Message tab
Step 2	Key	Record Number in the Title: box
Step 3	Press	the TAB key to move to the Input message: box
Step 4	Key	Enter a whole number between 1 and 999.

Your dialog box should look similar to Figure 13-3.

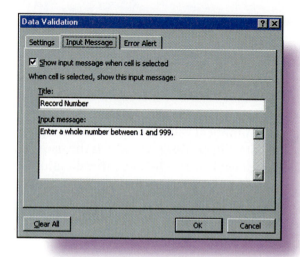

FIGURE 13-3
Input Message Tab

When the user enters invalid data, you can have the worksheet display one of three types of error messages. To set the error messages:

Step 1	Click	the Error Alert tab
Step 2	Verify	that the Show error alert after invalid data is entered check box is checked
Step 3	Click	the Style: list arrow

Each option produces a different type of error message alert box. The Stop style generates an alert box that contains Retry and Cancel buttons. The Warning style alert box contains Yes and No buttons. The Information style alert box contains OK and Cancel buttons. As you will not allow the entry of invalid data into the worksheet, you will prompt the user to enter the correct entry or cancel the operation.

Step 4	Click	Stop
Step 5	Key	Record Number in the Title: box

Step 6	Press	the TAB key to move to the Error message: box
Step 7	Enter	You must enter a whole number between 1 and 999.

Your dialog box should look similar to Figure 13-4.

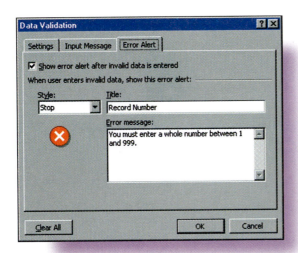

FIGURE 13-4
Error Alert Tab

Step 8	Click	OK

The dialog box closes, and the input message that you just created appears near the selected cells. Next, test the new data validation rules. To test data validation:

Step 1	Activate	cell A7

QUICK TIP

If you have the Office Assistant open, the Input Message appears in an Office Assistant dialog balloon instead of next to the cell.

The Input Message appears, similar to Figure 13-5.

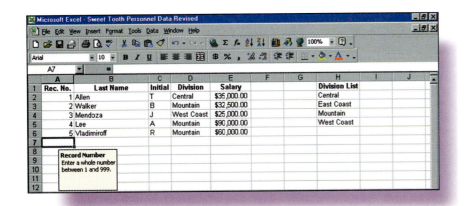

FIGURE 13-5
Input Message

chapter
thirteen

| Step 2 | **Key** | 1000 |
| Step 3 | **Press** | the ENTER key |

The error message box you created appears, similar to Figure 13-6.

FIGURE 13-6
Invalid Entry Dialog Box

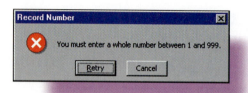

Step 4	**Click**	Retry
Step 5	**Key**	6
Step 6	**Press**	the TAB key

This entry is valid and accepted. Next, you enter validation criteria for each of the other fields. Table 13-1 briefly describes the type of validation criteria you will use.

TABLE 13-1
Setting Validation Criteria

Field Name	Validation Characteristic Settings	Input Message	Error Alert
Last Name	Text length maximum of 20 characters	Yes	Stop
Initial	Text length maximum of 1 character	Yes	Stop
Division	Select from a list	Yes	Stop
Salary	Decimal number should not exceed $75,000 without special authorization	Yes	Information

For the Last Name and Initial fields, you want users to enter only text, and you want to limit the number of characters permitted in each field. To set data validation for the Last Name column:

| Step 1 | **Select** | cells B7:B10 |
| Step 2 | **Click** | Data |

Step 3	Click	Validation
Step 4	Click	the Settings tab
Step 5	Select	Text length from the Allow: list
Step 6	Key	1 in the Minimum: box
Step 7	Key	20 in the Maximum: box
Step 8	Click	the Ignore blank check box to clear the check mark
Step 9	Click	the Input Message tab
Step 10	Key	Last Name in the Title: box
Step 11	Key	"Limit last name to 20 characters. Abbreviate if necessary." in the Input message: box (do not key the quotation marks)
Step 12	Click	the Error Alert tab
Step 13	Select	Stop from the Style: list
Step 14	Key	Last Name in the Title: box
Step 15	Key	"Please limit last name to 20 characters. Abbreviate if necessary." in the Error message: box
Step 16	Click	OK
Step 17	Enter	Rawlins in cell B7

Next, you add the validation criteria for the Initial column. To add the validation criteria for the Initial column:

Step 1	Select	cells C7:C10
Step 2	Open	the Data Validation dialog box
Step 3	Select	Text length from the Allow: list on the Settings tab
Step 4	Key	1 in the Minimum: box
Step 5	Key	1 in the Maximum: box
Step 6	Click	the Ignore blank check box to clear it
Step 7	Click	the Input Message tab
Step 8	Key	Initial in the Title: box
Step 9	Key	"Enter first initial of employee's first name." in the Input message: box

> **QUICK TIP**
>
> If you set data validation for a range of cells but later need to update the validation settings, you can have the update apply to all cells with similar data validation settings. Select any cell that contains the data validation setting you wish to change, then open the Data Validation dialog box to modify the setting. On the Settings tab, check the box next to Apply these changes to all other cells with the same settings.

Step 10	Click	the Error Alert tab
Step 11	Key	Initial in the Title: box
Step 12	Key	"You must enter a one-character initial." in the Error message: box
Step 13	Click	OK
Step 14	Enter	J in cell C7

The next field, Division, contains only four valid entries. You can create a list of these valid entries from which the user can select. To set list validation criteria:

Step 1	Select	cells D7:D10
Step 2	Open	the Data Validation dialog box
Step 3	Select	List from the Allow: list on the Settings tab
Step 4	Click	the Collapse Dialog button in the Source: box
Step 5	Select	cells H2:H5
Step 6	Click	the Expand Dialog button
Step 7	Verify	the In-cell dropdown check box is checked
Step 8	Click	the Ignore blank check box to remove the check

Your dialog box should look similar to Figure 13-7.

> **QUICK TIP**
>
> To prevent changes to data validation, choose Protection on the Tools menu, then click Protect Sheet. Verify that the Contents box is checked before you click OK.

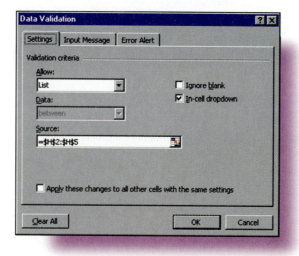

FIGURE 13-7
List Validation Options

Step 9	Click	the Input Message tab
Step 10	Key	Division in the Title: box
Step 11	Key	"Select a Division from the list." in the Input message: box
Step 12	Click	the Error Alert tab
Step 13	Key	Division in the Title: box
Step 14	Key	"You must select an entry from the list." in the Error message: box
Step 15	Click	OK
Step 16	Click	cell D7
Step 17	Click	the list arrow next to cell D7

Your screen should look similar to Figure 13-8.

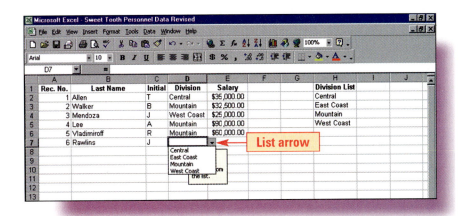

FIGURE 13-8
Using a List to Enter Valid Data in a Field

| Step 18 | Click | East Coast |

Using Paste Special to Copy Data Validation Criteria

You do not have to select all cells to which you want to add validation criteria when you set up the data validation. Instead, you can copy the validation criteria using the Paste Special command. Employee salaries are entered as decimal numbers not greater than $75,000; salaries higher than this figure cannot be entered without permission from Amy Lee, Sweet Tooth's president. To enter the validation criteria for the Salary field:

| Step 1 | Select | cell E7 |

Step 2	*Open*	the Data Validation dialog box
Step 3	*Select*	Decimal from the Allow: list on the Settings tab
Step 4	*Select*	less than or equal to from the Data: list
Step 5	*Key*	75000 in the Maximum: box
Step 6	*Click*	the Ignore blank check box to remove the check
Step 7	*Click*	the Input Message tab
Step 8	*Key*	Salary in the Title: box
Step 9	*Key*	"Enter a salary under $75,000. For salaries over $75,000, get permission from A. Lee." in the Input message: box
Step 10	*Click*	the Error Alert tab

QUICK TIP

To find out more about data validation options, use the Office Assistant.

Because you sometimes need to enter values greater than $75,000, you will use the Information style error alert, which gives you the option of ignoring the validation criteria.

Step 11	*Select*	Information from the Style: list
Step 12	*Key*	Salary in the Title: box
Step 13	*Key*	"Salary must be under $75,000 unless authorized by A. Lee." in the Error message: box
Step 14	*Click*	OK
Step 15	*Click*	cell E7, if necessary
Step 16	*Key*	80000
Step 17	*Click*	the Enter button ✓ on the Formula Bar

The Information dialog box displays the error alert message. In this case, you have been authorized to add this salary to the list. Clicking OK accepts the entry; clicking Cancel clears the entry so that you can key another value.

| Step 18 | *Click* | OK |

Next, copy the validation criteria to cells E8:E10. To copy the data validation criteria:

| Step 1 | *Click* | the Copy button 📋 on the Standard toolbar |

Step 2	**Select**	cells E8:E10
Step 3	**Right-click**	the selected cells
Step 4	**Click**	Paste Special
Step 5	**Click**	the Validation option button
Step 6	**Click**	OK
Step 7	**Save**	the workbook

Entering Data in a List

You do not have to add data validation to enter data in a list. Nevertheless, data validation is important to ensure that the user enters the appropriate type of data in each field. To enter the rest of the data in the list:

| Step 1 | **Enter** | the records, as shown in Table 13-2 |

Rec. No.	Last Name	Initial	Division	Salary
7	Munns	R	East Coast	$45,000
8	Greenwood	J	West Coast	$30,000
9	Chin	M	Central	$25,000

TABLE 13-2
Additional Records for Sweet Tooth Personnel List

When you finish, your screen should look similar to Figure 13-9.

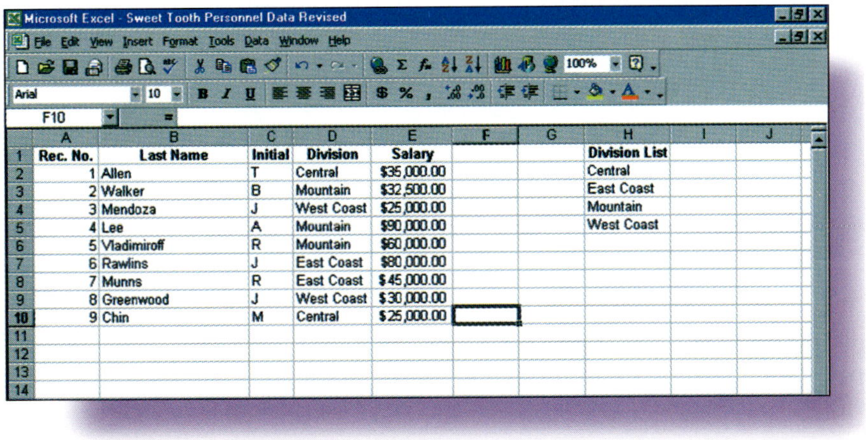

FIGURE 13-9
Completed Data List

chapter
thirteen

13.c Using the Data Form

An alternative method of entering data in a list is to use a data form. A data form simplifies data entry by allowing the user to enter each field of a record using a simple dialog box, rather than the worksheet itself. You can also use the data form to edit and locate specific records in a list.

Entering Data in a List with a Data Form

You need to add another record to the list. To use a data form to enter a new record:

Step 1	Activate	any cell that is part of the list, including the header row
Step 2	Click	Data
Step 3	Click	Form

The Form dialog box opens, with the worksheet tab name as the title of the dialog box, as shown in Figure 13-10. You can use the scroll bar or the Find Prev and Find Next buttons to scroll through the records.

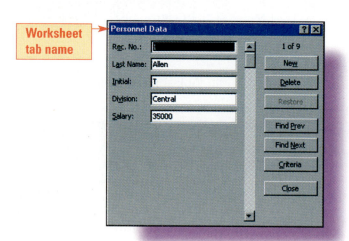

FIGURE 13-10
Form Dialog Box

Step 4	Click	New
Step 5	Key	10 in the Rec. No.: box
Step 6	Press	the TAB key
Step 7	Key	Tate in the Last Name: box
Step 8	Press	the TAB key

Step 9	Key	J in the Initial: box
Step 10	Press	the TAB key
Step 11	Key	Central in the Division: box
Step 12	Press	the TAB key
Step 13	Enter	65000 in the Salary: box
Step 14	Press	the ENTER key

The record is added to the bottom of your list, and a new record is started in the Form dialog box. You can enter a new record at this point or close the Form dialog box.

| Step 15 | Click | Close |

Finding Specific Records Using the Data Form

The data form allows you to readily locate specific records in a list; however, scrolling through a list of hundreds or thousands to find a certain record would be very time-consuming. You want to review records of Sweet Tooth employees whose annual salaries are $40,000 or more. Using the data form, you can set criteria for the records you want to see. To search for specific records:

Step 1	Open	the Form dialog box
Step 2	Click	Criteria
Step 3	Click	the Salary: box
Step 4	Key	>40000
Step 5	Click	Find Next

The first record meeting the criteria appears in the Form dialog box.

| Step 6 | Click | Find Next |

The next record meeting the criteria appears in the Form dialog box.

| Step 7 | Click | Find Next four more times |

CAUTION TIP

One drawback to using the Form dialog box is that data validation criteria are not active with this method of data entry. In other words, you will not see input messages or error alert messages, and the list option is not available.

QUICK TIP

You can use the Find Prev button to step back through the records meeting the specified criteria.

chapter thirteen

The computer indicates that no more records meet your criteria by making a sound. To clear the criteria and view all records again:

Step 1	Click	Criteria
Step 2	Click	Clear
Step 3	Click	Form to return to the Form dialog box

Deleting a Record from a List Using the Data Form

Occasionally, you will need to remove records from a list. To delete a record using the data form:

| Step 1 | Drag | the scroll box in the Form dialog box up until 6 of 10 appears in the upper-right corner |
| Step 2 | Click | Delete to delete the record for J. Rawlins |

A confirmation dialog box opens, indicating that the record will be permanently deleted.

| Step 3 | Click | OK |

The record is removed from the list.

| Step 4 | Click | Close |
| Step 5 | Save | the workbook |

MOUSE TIP

You can delete a record by deleting the row in the worksheet or the cells containing the data. Right-click the row number, then click Delete; alternatively, select all cells in the record, right-click the selection, click Delete, then choose the appropriate option.

13.d Applying Data Filters

Filtering a list allows you to work with a subset of a list. You can use the Find command in the data form to filter the records displayed in the Form dialog box, or you can filter records in the worksheet. When you apply a filter, only those records meeting the specified criteria are displayed. You can format, edit, chart, and print the filtered list. When you have finished, turn the filter off and the rest of the records in the list reappear.

Using AutoFilter

The AutoFilter feature offers a fast, easy way to apply multiple filters to a list. When you apply AutoFilter to a list, a filter list arrow appears next to each of the column labels. Clicking the filter list arrow displays the filter list, which includes the following information:

- Each unique entry in the list
- A Top 10 option that you can customize
- A custom option to apply conditional operators (AND and OR) and logical operators (greater than, equal to, and less than)
- Options to filter for blank or nonblank fields
- An option to show all records

You need to compile a list of the employees in Sweet Tooth's Central division who make less than $40,000 per year.

To apply an AutoFilter:

Step 1	*Activate*	any cell in the list
Step 2	*Click*	<u>D</u>ata
Step 3	*Point to*	<u>F</u>ilter
Step 4	*Click*	Auto<u>F</u>ilter

The AutoFilter list arrows appear next to each column label, as shown in Figure 13-11.

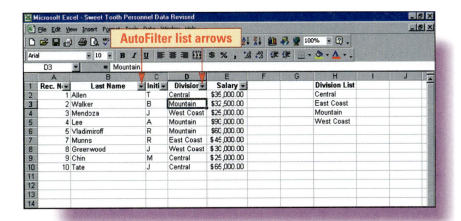

FIGURE 13-11
AutoFilter Applied

Step 5	*Click*	the Filter list arrow in the Division field
Step 6	*Click*	Central
Step 7	*Click*	the Filter list arrow in the Salary field
Step 8	*Click*	(Custom…)

The Custom AutoFilter dialog box opens, as shown in Figure 13-12.

FIGURE 13-12
Custom AutoFilter Dialog Box

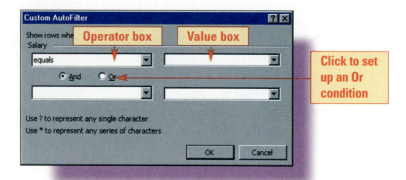

The default in the Custom AutoFilter dialog box is for the And option button to be selected.

Step 9	*Click*	the operator list arrow on the left side of the dialog box
Step 10	*Click*	is greater than or equal to
Step 11	*Click*	the value list arrow on the right side of the dialog box
Step 12	*Click*	$35,000.00
Step 13	*Click*	OK

The list is filtered, as shown in Figure 13-13. Notice that the filter list arrows of the filtered columns and the row headings appear in blue. Filtered rows remain hidden.

FIGURE 13-13
A Filtered List

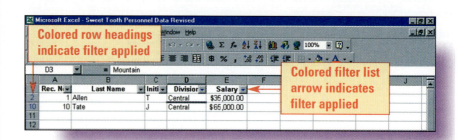

When you want to display all of the records again, use the Show All command.

To clear the filters:

Step 1	Click	Data
Step 2	Point to	Filter
Step 3	Click	Show All

You can also use wildcards in your custom filters. A **wildcard** is used in place of other characters. Suppose you want to filter a list for all last names starting with R. You could enter R* in the Custom AutoFilter dialog box, where the asterisk (*) represents any characters after the R. The question mark (?) can be used in place of a single character. If you used the filter r?n on a list of words, for example, you would see ran and run.

To apply a wildcard filter:

Step 1	Click	the Last Name filter arrow
Step 2	Click	(Custom...)
Step 3	Click	the operator list arrow
Step 4	Click	begins with
Step 5	Key	m* in the value box
Step 6	Click	OK

The list is filtered to show all last names beginning with M. When you have finished filtering a list, you can turn off AutoFilter. To turn off AutoFilter:

Step 1	Click	Data
Step 2	Point to	Filter
Step 3	Click	AutoFilter
Step 4	Save	the workbook

You can also use filters that are more advanced.

> **MOUSE TIP**
>
> You can remove the filter from one column by clicking the filter list arrow and selecting (All).

Using Advanced Filters

Another way to filter records is to use advanced filters. Advanced filters allow you to work with multiple AND and OR operators in each field so as to filter a list. These types of filters are more difficult to set up than AutoFilters, however. To take advantage of advanced filters, you must establish a criteria range in the worksheet. The column labels in the criteria range must match the column labels of your list. Rows beneath the column labels in the criteria range indicate the filter criteria. You should also follow these guidelines when using advanced filtering:

- Place the criteria range above or below the rows containing your list data. Do not set up the range in the same rows as the list, because filtered rows remain hidden from view.
- The first row of the criteria range identifies the columns to be filtered. Although its formatting does not have to match that of the column labels in the list you are filtering, the spelling must match exactly.
- Adding multiple criteria in the same row creates an AND condition. For example, to list employees who have an annual salary greater than $40,000 AND who work in the Central division, you would enter >40000 under the column heading Salary and Central under the column label Division; both of these entries would appear in the same row.
- Entering criteria in subsequent rows specifies an OR condition. For example, if you wanted to find all employees who made more than $40,000 OR less than $30,000 per year, you would enter >40000 in one row under the Salary column label and <30000 in the next row under the column label. Each time you add another row to the criteria, you specify another OR condition.

To create a criteria range:

Step 1	Insert	six blank rows above row 1
Step 2	Enter	Last Name in cell D1
Step 3	Enter	Salary in cell E1

Your criteria range now appears above your list. Next, enter the criteria you want to use in your filter. To add criteria to a criteria range:

Step 1	Enter	a* in cell D2

This filter will display records that start with the letter "A" in the Last Name field.

| Step 2 | **Enter** | m* in cell D3 |
| Step 3 | **Enter** | >40000 in cell E3 |

This multiple-column condition will display records that start with the letter "M" in the Last Name field AND have a salary greater than $40,000.

| Step 4 | **Enter** | g* in cell D4 |

This complex filter will display records for all employees whose last name starts with A or G, as well as records for any employee whose salary is more than $40,000 and whose last name starts with M.

To apply the advanced filter:

| Step 1 | **Click** | cell A8 |

You must select a cell within the list that you want to filter. Excel automatically searches for the header row.

Step 2	**Click**	Data
Step 3	**Point to**	Filter
Step 4	**Click**	Advanced Filter

The Advanced Filter dialog box opens, as shown in Figure 13-14. In this dialog box, you can select the list range and criteria range and specify whether you want to create a copy of the filtered records or filter the list in place. The default is to filter the list in place. The list range is automatically selected.

chapter thirteen

FIGURE 13-14
Advanced Filter Dialog Box

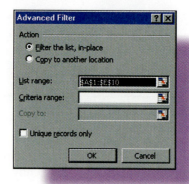

QUICK TIP

You can use named ranges as references in the Advanced Filter dialog box.

Step 5	*Click*	in the Criteria range: box
Step 6	*Key*	D1:E4
Step 7	*Click*	OK

The list is filtered to produce only records meeting the criteria specified in the criteria range D1:E4, as shown in Figure 13-15.

FIGURE 13-15
Filtered List

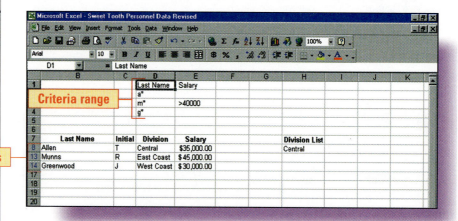

QUICK TIP

To find out about other advanced filtering techniques, use the Office Assistant to search for information about advanced filters and examples of advanced filter criteria.

You can clear the filter to show all records in the list. To show all records:

Step 1	*Click*	Data
Step 2	*Point to*	Filter
Step 3	*Click*	Show All

The complete list is displayed.

Extracting Data

When you use the advanced filter copy option, you leave the original list of data unfiltered and **extract** the records meeting your filter criteria to a new location. You want to extract a list of all employees who make more than $35,000 per year.

To extract data:

Step 1	Delete	the contents of cells D2:E4
Step 2	Enter	>35000 in cell E2
Step 3	Click	cell A8
Step 4	Click	Data
Step 5	Point to	Filter
Step 6	Click	Advanced Filter
Step 7	Drag	to select the contents of the Criteria range: box
Step 8	Key	D1:E2
Step 9	Click	the Copy to another location option button
Step 10	Click	the Copy to: box
Step 11	Click	cell I1 in the worksheet

Note that you can copy filtered data only to the active worksheet. Once you have extracted the records, you can move or copy them wherever you like.

Step 12	Click	OK
Step 13	Scroll	the worksheet to view the extracted data
Step 14	Increase	the width of column M to show the data

The filtered records are copied to the new location, starting in cell I1. Notice that the column headings are included with the extracted records, as shown in Figure 13-16.

FIGURE 13-16
Extracted Records

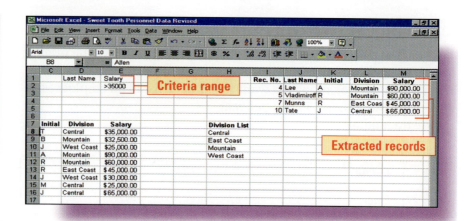

Step 15 ***Save & Close*** the workbook

It may take you some time to become comfortable when working with data lists and filters, but these features provide powerful tools for storing and retrieving data.

Summary

- Identify the main components of a list. Know the guidelines for creating lists.
- Enter data in a list. Preselect a list to permit quicker data entry.
- Create data validation criteria to ensure that the user enters proper data in each field of a record.
- Use the data form to add, modify, locate, and delete records.
- Use AutoFilter to add simple filters to a list.
- Use advanced filters to build complex filters using AND and OR operators.
- Extract records from a list for use elsewhere.

Commands Review

Action	Menu Bar	Shortcut Menu	Toolbar	Keyboard
Open the Data Validation dialog box	Data, Validation			ALT + D, L
Use a data form to enter records	Data, Form			ALT + D, O
Apply AutoFilter	Data, Filter, AutoFilter			ALT + D, F, F
Apply an advanced filter	Data, Filter, Advanced Filter			ALT + D, F, A
Show all records	Data, Filter, Show All			ALT + D, F, S

chapter thirteen

Concepts Review

Circle the correct answer.

1. **The field name:**
   - [a] is a collection of characters or numbers that make up one part of a record.
   - [b] is the collection of fields that make a complete entry.
   - [c] identifies the contents of each column.
   - [d] can appear anywhere on the worksheet.

2. **A record:**
   - [a] is a collection of characters or numbers that make up one part of a record.
   - [b] is the collection of fields that make a complete entry.
   - [c] identifies the contents of each column.
   - [d] can appear anywhere on the worksheet.

3. **Why should you leave one column and one row blank between the list and any other data on the worksheet?**
   - [a] This approach makes it easier to return the list to its original sort order.
   - [b] Excel can autodetect list boundaries more easily.
   - [c] You should not leave blank rows or columns, because spaces affect the sort order of a list.
   - [d] It does not matter, as long as you format each field in the same way.

4. **Data validation is used to:**
   - [a] sort fields using criteria you define.
   - [b] restrict the data that can be entered in each field.
   - [c] search for records containing certain characters.
   - [d] make a copy of filtered records in another location.

5. **How would you remove the filter from one field in a list that has AutoFilter applied?**
   - [a] (All)
   - [b] (Top 10)
   - [c] (Custom...)
   - [d] Mountain

6. **Multiple criteria in the same row in an advanced filter criteria range indicate:**
   - [a] an AND condition.
   - [b] an OR condition.
   - [c] a wildcard character.
   - [d] the inclusion of additional fields in the result.

7. **Criteria in additional rows beneath a criteria column heading indicate:**
   - [a] an AND condition.
   - [b] an OR condition.
   - [c] a wildcard character.
   - [d] the inclusion of additional records in the result.

8. **Extracted data refers to records:**
   - [a] meeting filter criteria that are moved from the list.
   - [b] meeting filter criteria that are copied from the list.
   - [c] not meeting filter criteria.
   - [d] that are randomly removed from the database.

9. **A data form can be used to:** — dialog box
   - [a] add records to a list.
   - [b] locate records meeting specific criteria in a list.
   - [c] delete records from a list.
   - [d] all of the above.

10. **One drawback of a data form is that:**
    - [a] you cannot delete records from a list.
    - [b] the data validation criteria are not active.
    - [c] you cannot move from record to record.
    - [d] you cannot edit records once they are entered.

Using Lists in Excel EA 45

Circle **T** if the statement is true or **F** if the statement is false.

- **T** F 1. Column headings for advanced filter criteria must be spelled exactly like the column headings in the list you are filtering.
- **T** F 2. "Part No." would be a likely field name in a warehouse database.
- T **F** 3. The terms "record" and "field" refer to the same thing.
- **T** F 4. The term "list" in Excel can often be used interchangeably with "database."
- **T** F 5. Spaces at the beginning of a field entry affect the sort order of a list.
- T **F** 6. You cannot specify AND or OR conditions using AutoFilters.
- T **F** 7. The header row can be placed anywhere in a list, as long as it is formatted differently than the rest of the list.
- **T** F 8. Filters allow you to work with a subset of records in a list.
- **T** F 9. When you apply a filter to a list, you hide all other records that don't meet the criteria.
- **T** F 10. When using advanced filters, the top row of the criteria area must contain column headings spelled exactly the same way as the field names in the list you are filtering.

Skills Review

Exercise 1

1. Create a new workbook.
2. Use the following field names to create a product list for use in the warehouse: Part No.; Description; Manufacturer; Cost; Quantity; and Value. Start your entries in cell A8.
3. Select 15 rows per column. Use data validation to set the rules in the table below, using the following instructions:
   a. Do not allow blank entries for any fields.
   b. The valid manufacturer names are Price Mfg., Sunrise Products Inc., Watershed Mfg., and Irontown Mfg.
   c. Use a formula in the Value column to calculate the value of stock on hand by multiplying the quantity of each item times the cost.

Field Name	Validation Characteristic	Input Message	Error Alert Type
Part No.	Whole number between 1,000 and 4,999	Yes	Stop
Description	Text limited to 20 characters	Yes	Information
Manufacturer	Use the list of four valid manufacturer names	Yes	Stop
Cost	Decimal number limited to less than $100.00	Yes	Information
Quantity	Whole number limited to less than 1,000	Yes	Stop

4. Review your list setup to make sure that it fits the list guidelines discussed in at the beginning of this chapter.
5. Save the workbook as *Warehouse Parts* and print it.

chapter thirteen

Exercise 2

1. Using the *Warehouse Parts* workbook that you created in Exercise 1, enter the data shown in the table below. Calculate the Value column using a formula.

Part No.	Description	Manufacturer	Cost	Quantity	Value
1010	Sugar, 50 lb	Price Mfg.	19.95	333	(use a formula)
1020	Sugar, 125 lb	Price Mfg.	39.95	693	(use a formula)
1030	Molasses	Watershed Mfg.	45.95	282	(use a formula)
2100	Sprinkles, 1,000 gross	Sunrise Products Inc.	70.95	314	(use a formula)
2200	Rainbow Sprinkles, 10 gross	Watershed Mfg.	6.95	838	(use a formula)
2300	Chocolate Sprinkles, 50 gross	Irontown Mfg.	34.95	279	(use a formula)
3001	Flour, 25 lb	Irontown Mfg.	12.95	940	(use a formula)
3002	Flour, 5 lb	Irontown Mfg.	5.95	412	(use a formula)
3003	Wheat flour, 150 lb	Price Mfg.	99.95	758	(use a formula)
4020	Honey, 30 gallons	Sunrise Products Inc.	89.95	687	(use a formula)
4030	Honey, 2 gallons	Sunrise Products Inc.	6.95	769	(use a formula)
4040	Honey, 1 quart	Watershed Mfg.	1.95	930	(use a formula)

2. Resize columns to fit, as necessary.
3. Format columns D and F using the Accounting format, two decimal places.
4. Sort the list by Manufacturer and Cost.
5. Save the workbook as *Warehouse Parts Inventory* and print it.

Exercise 3

1. Open the *Warehouse Parts Inventory* that you developed in Exercise 2.
2. Use a data form to edit part number 3003. Change the description to Wheat Flour, 175 lb.
3. Use a data form to eliminate part number 4040.
4. Use a data form to add a new record using the information in the table below.

Part No.	Description	Manufacturer	Cost	Quantity
4041	Honey, 25 gallons	Price Mfg.	35.95	750

5. Apply AutoFilters to the list.
6. Using the AutoFilter list arrows, filter the list to find only items manufactured by Price Mfg.
7. Sort the list in order of cost, from lowest to highest.
8. Print the filtered list.
9. Save the workbook as *Warehouse Parts Inventory Filter 1*.

Exercise 4

1. Open the *Warehouse Parts Inventory Modified* workbook that you created in Exercise 3.
2. Create an advanced filter criteria that will find any records with a quantity of more than 500 items, or any item that costs less than $30.00 (be sure you don't create an "AND" condition).
3. Filter the list with the criteria set up in step 2.
4. Sort the list by quantity.
5. Print the filtered list.
6. Save the workbook as *Warehouse Parts Inventory Filter 2*.

Exercise 5

1. Open the *Sweet Tooth Sales Data* workbook on your Data Disk.
2. Apply AutoFilters to the list.
3. Filter the list for all names starting with D or M.
4. Sort the filtered list alphabetically by first name.
5. Use an advanced filter to extract records for sales representatives whose first names begin with D and who work in the Mountain Region. Copy the records starting in cell J1.
6. Resize columns to display all data, if necessary.
7. Set the print area to print only the extracted records.
8. Print the extracted records.
9. Save the workbook as *Sweet Tooth Sales Data Extracted Records*.

Exercise 6

1. Open the *Sweet Tooth Sales Data Extracted Records* workbook that you created in Exercise 5.
2. Create a new advanced filter to find records of employees whose Gross Sales were less than $3,000 or more than $4,500.
3. Filter the list in place.
4. Sort the filtered list by Gross Sales from highest to lowest.
5. Print the filtered list.
6. Save the workbook as *Sweet Tooth Sales Data Extracted Records 1*.

Exercise 7

1. Open the *Sweet Tooth Sales Data Extracted Records 1* workbook that you created in Exercise 6.
2. Display all records.
3. Click any cell in the data list, then use a data form to add the following record to the list:

    Mountain   South   Sun Li $4,500

4. Save the workbook as *Sweet Tooth Sales Data 1*.

chapter thirteen

Exercise 8

1. Open the *Sweet Tooth Sales Data 1* workbook that you created in Exercise 7.

2. Use a data form to locate the record for all employees whose name starts with W.

3. Use the Find Next button to locate the record for Walter Jacobs.

4. Delete the record.

5. Close the Form dialog box.

6. Print the data list.

7. Save the workbook as *Sweet Tooth Sales Data 2*.

Case Projects

Project 1

You are reviewing workbooks in use at your company. The personnel data workbook is a mess because no one used data validation when creating the workbook. Use the Office Assistant and what you learned in this chapter to create a document explaining what data validation is and how to set it up for use in a workbook. Include instructions for dealing with text, number, and date entries. Be sure to describe how to set up an input message and an error alert. Save the document as *Data Validation.doc*.

Project 2

As the personnel director for a small retail sales company, you are in charge of tracking personnel information. Create a list of 15 employees. Include a unique record number for each employee, starting at 1. Each record should include a record number, last name, first initial, hire date (within the last five years), date of last pay increase, current salary, and department (use at least three departments). Use appropriate data validation for each field. Prepare and print a series of sorted reports showing employees sorted by record number, alphabetically by last name, by hire date, by department (alphabetically by last name within each department), and by current salary. Use subtotals to prepare a pie chart showing salary percentages by department. Print the chart. Save the workbook as *Personnel Information*.

Project 3

Use the Office Assistant to find out how to locate cells that have data validation rules applied. Write a step-by-step summary of this process. Save the document as *Find Data Validation Cells.doc*.

Project 4

As a financial advisor for personnel in a large corporation, you are constantly asked for investment resources. Use the Internet to locate 6 to 10 sites that provide investment information. Find sites that offer more than just stock quotes, such as investment advice, market trend analysis, financial reports for different companies, and investment research tools. Create a workbook with at least six hyperlinks to these Web sites. Print five Web pages providing investment advice.

Project 5

Programmers sometimes add "Easter Eggs" to a program. If a user follows a certain sequence of commands, they might see a special message containing the names of the programmers or something else fun. Use the Internet to search for Excel Easter Eggs and see if any of them work with Excel 2000. You could also try searching for Easter Eggs in other programs you use. Print at least one page explaining how to display an Easter Egg.

Project 6

You are the data manager at a shipping company. Create a workbook to track shipping dates, company names, addresses, and four-digit item numbers. Use a data form to add five records to the list. Print the list and save the workbook as *Shipping*.

Project 7

Your marketing firm is preparing a commercial that it would like to release in the 10 largest cities in the United States. Use the Internet to find a list of populations of cities in the United States. In a new workbook, set up field names for each city, its state, and its population. Apply data validation to each column. Limit the data in the city field to a text length of 15 characters, the state field to a text length of 2 characters, and the population field to a whole number greater than 1,000,000. Enter the data for the 10 largest cities you can find. Save the workbook as *Population*.

Project 8

You work at a telemarketing company. Create a list to log the date, time, and duration of each call. Use data validation to restrict the data entry for each cell to the appropriate type of data (limit call length to less than 60 minutes). Enter fictitious data for five calls. Save the workbook as *Phone Log*.

Excel 2000

Auditing a Worksheet

Chapter Overview

Auditing tools help you identify relationships between cells. The Auditing toolbar provides tools to identify precedents and dependents, trace errors to their source, and locate invalid data.

Learning Objectives

- Use Range Finder to check and review data
- Identify relationships between precedent and dependent cells
- Trace errors
- Identify invalid data

Case profile

Many of Sweet Tooth's employees use the Excel workbooks you've created, and they also create their own workbooks. As you share workbooks with other workers, you occasionally find errors (not to mention your own *rare* errors) or need to review the sources of values referenced by a certain formula. Using Excel's auditing tools, you can make quick work of tracking down the source of errors or identifying locations where values are used throughout even the most complex worksheets.

chapter fourteen

14.a Using Range Finder to Check and Review Data

Whenever you open a workbook created by someone else, it is a good idea to review the worksheet's assumptions and calculations before you begin editing data. **Range Finder** can help you track down references used in formulas. The *Sweet Tooth Projected Profit* workbook contains several errors that should be corrected. To open the file and save it with a new name:

Step 1	**Open**	the *Sweet Tooth Projected Profit with Errors* workbook on your Data Disk
Step 2	**Save**	the workbook as *Sweet Tooth Projected Profit Revised* to your Data Files folder

The Projected Profit worksheet contains projections for income and expenses for the coming year. Rows 17–22 contain multipliers used in some of the formulas on the worksheet to calculate expense amounts. Because the information for the third and fourth quarters consists of projected data, it is italicized. To use Range Finder to revise a formula:

Step 1	**Click**	cell E13 on the Projected Profit worksheet

The formula in cell E13 is supposed to calculate the projected profit for the third quarter, but it currently shows a value of zero (shown as a dash in the Accounting format). The formula refers to empty cells G6 and G8:G12. You could key in the correction so that the formula refers to the correct cells in the column E, but Range Finder can make this type of correction even more easily.

Step 2	**Double-click**	cell E13

Your screen should look similar to Figure 14-1. The formula highlights each cell or range reference, using a different color for each reference to make it easier to identify the reference.

chapter fourteen

FIGURE 14-1
Use Range Finder to Locate References

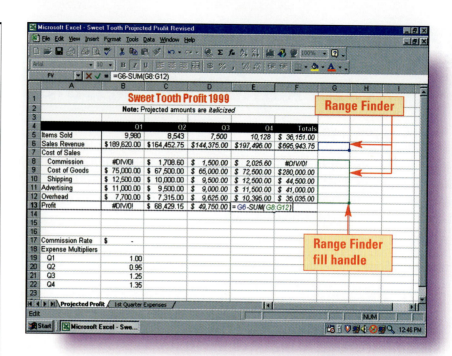

You can see that the references point to the wrong column. To adjust the reference, drag the border to the correct location in column E. If necessary, you can drag the Range Finder fill handle to increase or decrease the size of the range.

| Step 3 | Drag | the blue Range Finder border to cell E6 |

As you drag the border, the formula in the Formula Bar adjusts itself automatically.

| Step 4 | Drag | the green Range Finder border to cells E8:E12 |

The total $88,575.40 should appear in cell E13.

| Step 6 | Save | the workbook |

14.b Identifying Relationships Between Precedent and Dependent Cells

As workbooks grow larger and more complicated, it becomes increasingly difficult to locate and review relationships between cells. Excel provides auditing features to simplify this job.

Tracing Precedents

Precedents are the cells referred to by a formula. You can locate precedents by using the Auditing commands on the Tools menu and on the Auditing toolbar. To show the Auditing toolbar:

Step 1	Click	Tools
Step 2	Point to	Auditing
Step 3	Click	Show Auditing Toolbar

The formula in cell F6 adds the total Sales Revenue figures for each quarter. To trace the precedents for this formula:

Step 1	Click	cell F6
Step 2	Click	the Trace Precedents button on the Auditing toolbar

A heavy blue tracer arrow identifies the precedent(s) for this formula. When the precedent consists of a range of cells, the tracer arrow is indicated with a heavy line and the range is highlighted with a blue border. When the precedent consists of a single cell, the tracer arrow is indicated with a thin line. Your screen should look similar to Figure 14-2.

> **MENU TIP**
>
> To trace precedents, point to Auditing on the Tools menu, then click Trace Precedents.

FIGURE 14-2
Tracing Precedents

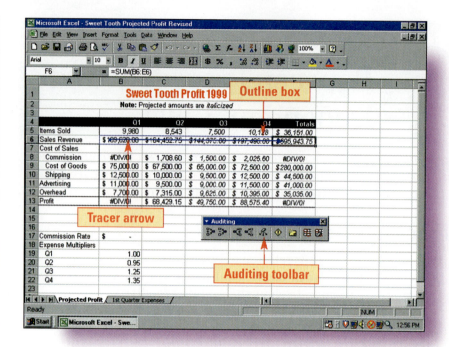

> **MOUSE TIP**
>
> You can jump to a referenced cell using the tracer arrow lines. Double-click an arrow line and the active cell moves back and forth between the referenced cells and the formula.

Many times, the results of a formula are not based on a single level of precedents. For example, the formula in cell F6 refers to the range B6:E6, but the values in this range are derived from still other formulas. To view a second level of precedents:

| Step 1 | **Click** | the Trace Precedents button  on the Auditing toolbar |

Your screen should look similar to Figure 14-3.

FIGURE 14-3
Tracing Multiple Levels of Precedents

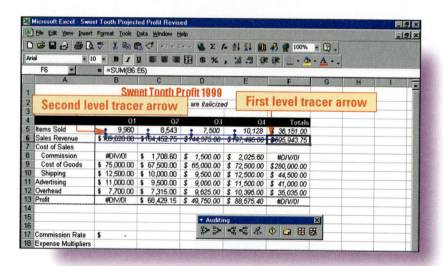

You can continue to click the Trace Precedents button until you have revealed all of the precedent levels. If your computer has a sound card and speakers attached, an alert sound indicates when Excel has reached the last level of precedents. Once you have finished viewing the precedents for a cell, you may want to clear the precedent arrows to view your worksheet more easily. To clear all precedent arrows:

| Step 1 | Click | the Remove All Arrows button on the Auditing toolbar |

The arrows are removed from the display.

Tracing Dependents

Dependents are all cells containing formulas that rely on the value of another cell. A cell may be referenced by one or several formulas throughout a workbook. You can locate dependents in the same manner that you located precedents. To trace dependents:

| Step 1 | Click | cell B5 |
| Step 2 | Click | the Trace Dependents button  on the Auditing toolbar |

Thin blue tracer arrows point to cells B6, B8, and F5. Each of these cells contains a formula that references cell B5. Your screen should look similar to Figure 14-4.

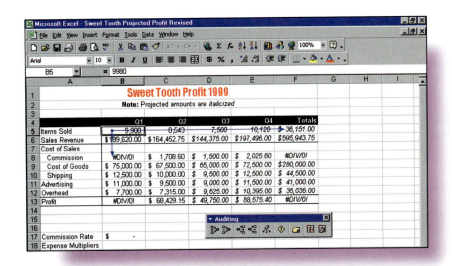

FIGURE 14-4
Tracing Dependents

You can identify multiple levels of dependents by continuing to click the Trace Dependents button on the Auditing toolbar. The number of items sold, which appears in cell B5, is referenced by the formula in cell B8, which calculates the commission expense. This amount is then referenced by still other formulas. Cell B5 is also referenced by the formula in cell B6, which is then referenced by cell F6.

| Step 3 | Click | the Trace Dependents button  on the Auditing toolbar |

A second level of tracer arrows is added to the display. A thin blue tracer arrow now points to cell F6. Because the formula in cell B8 contains an error, red tracer arrows point to the two cells that use cell B8 in their formulas. You take care of this error in the next section.

You can remove a single level of arrows rather than removing all arrows at once. To remove a single level of arrows:

| Step 1 | Click | the Remove Dependent Arrows button on the Auditing toolbar |

The second level of tracer arrows disappears.

| Step 2 | Click | the Remove Dependent Arrows button on the Auditing toolbar |

The first level of tracer arrows disappears.

Tracing Cell Relationships Between Worksheets

As you learned in previous chapters, you can reference cells located on other worksheets as well as those on the current worksheet. Excel's auditing tools help you trace references to these cells. To trace precedents between worksheets:

| Step 1 | Click | cell B12 |
| Step 2 | Click | the Trace Precedents button on the Auditing toolbar |

A worksheet icon and a black tracer arrow appear, indicating that a reference in cell B12 is located on another worksheet. Check the

> **MENU TIP**
>
> To remove all precedent and dependent tracer arrows, click Tools, point to Auditing, then click Remove All Arrows.

formula in the Formula Bar to verify this relationship. Your screen should look similar to Figure 14-5. You can quickly jump to the referenced cell.

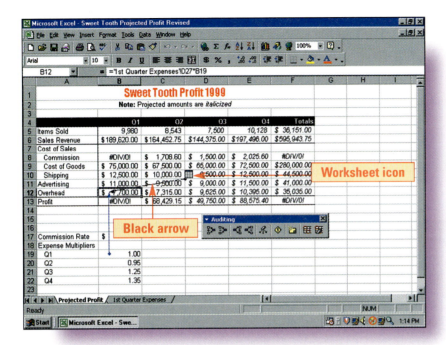

FIGURE 14-5
Tracing Relationships Between Worksheets

| Step 3 | **Double-click** | the black tracer arrow |

The Go To dialog box opens.

| Step 4 | **Click** | the reference listed at the top of the Go to: list box |
| Step 5 | **Click** | OK |

The 1st Quarter Expenses worksheet is activated, and the active cell moves to cell D27. The total in cell D27 is used in cell B12 on the Projected Profit worksheet.

Step 6	**Click**	the Projected Profit worksheet tab
Step 7	**Click**	the Remove All Arrows button on the Auditing toolbar
Step 8	**Save**	the workbook

chapter fourteen

14.c Tracing Errors

The formulas in cells B8, F8, B13, and F13 display the #DIV/0! error. This error indicates that at least one of these cells contains a formula that attempts to divide a value by zero. To trace and correct the source of this error:

Step 1	Click	cell F13
Step 2	Click	the Trace Error button on the Auditing toolbar

Your screen should look similar to Figure 14-6.

Menu Tip

You can trace errors by clicking Tools, then pointing to Auditing and clicking Trace Error.

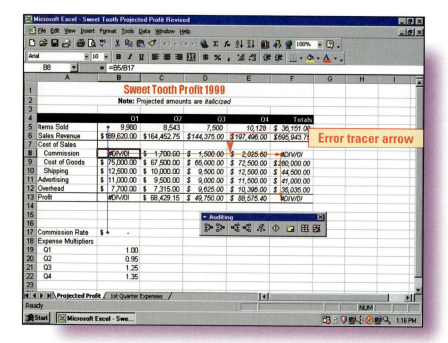

FIGURE 14-6 Tracing Errors

The formula in cell F13 refers to the range F8:F12. Because an error occurs in cell F8, you see a red error arrow. Cell F8 adds the range B8:F8 and therefore a second error arrow stretches back to cell B8. Cell B8 contains a formula that divides the value of cell B5 by the value of cell B17. The blue arrows, as you know, indicate precedents of cell B8. By examining the value of B17, you find the source of the problem—cell B17 contains a value of 0.

Step 3	Enter	5 in cell B17

This correction solves the "divide by 0" error in cell B8, and consequently eliminates the problems in cells B13, F8, and F13. Now blue tracer arrows, indicating the formulas are working correctly, replace the red error arrows.

| Step 4 | Click | the Remove All Arrows button  on the Auditing toolbar |

14.d Identifying Invalid Data

In Chapter 13, you learned how to use data validation when creating lists of data. You also learned about the three different types of error alert messages. Two of the error alert messages—Information and Warning—allow a user to input invalid data, even though the user is informed that the information is invalid. To help you identify cells in a list that contain data violating data validation rules, you can use an auditing command. To find invalid data:

Step 1	Click	the 1st Quarter Expenses worksheet tab
Step 2	Click	the Circle Invalid Data button on the Auditing toolbar
Step 3	Scroll	the worksheet up until you can see row 1

All cells containing invalid data are circled in red. Your screen should look similar to Figure 14-7.

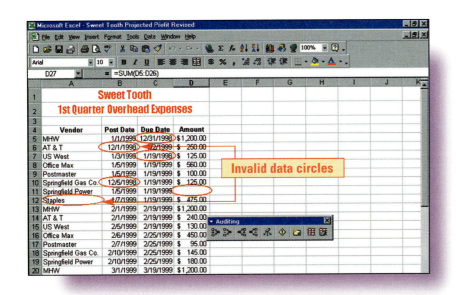

FIGURE 14-7
Identifying Invalid Data

MOUSE TIP

You can turn the circles off by clicking the Clear Validation Circles button  on the Auditing toolbar.

CAUTION TIP

The invalid data circle should disappear when you select Office Max from the list. But sometimes it doesn't "take," so be sure to key the entry if necessary as we did here.

Step 4	Click	cell A12
Step 5	Click	the list arrow in cell A12
Step 6	Select	Office Max from the list
Step 7	Key	Of
Step 8	Press	the ENTER key to accept the AutoComplete entry

Office Max is a valid entry. As you correct the errors, the validation circles disappear.

Step 9	Enter	1/1/99 in cell B6
Step 10	Enter	1/5/99 in cell B10
Step 11	Enter	1/31/99 in cell C5
Step 12	Enter	1/19/99 in cell C7
Step 13	Enter	185 in cell D11
Step 14	Click	the Circle Invalid Data button on the Auditing toolbar to double-check for additional errors
Step 15	Close	the Auditing toolbar
Step 16	Save & Close	the workbook

The Auditing toolbar can be helpful when your worksheets include complicated formulas that use many precedents.

Summary

▶ Use Range Finder to quickly edit cell references in a formula. Click and drag Range Finder borders to move a reference. Use the Range Finder fill handle to "resize" a range reference.

▶ Precedents are cells or ranges referenced by a specific formula. Select a cell containing a formula, then use the Trace Precedents tool to identify cells and ranges referenced in that particular formula.

▶ Dependents are cells containing formulas that depend on the value of a certain cell. Select a cell containing a value or formula, then use the Trace Dependents tool to identify other cells containing formulas that reference that particular cell.

▶ Use the Trace Error tool to quickly locate the source of a formula error.

▶ Locate data that violates data validation rules by using the Circle Invalid Data auditing tool.

Commands Review

Action	Menu Bar	Shortcut Menu	Toolbar	Keyboard
Trace precedents	Tools, Auditing, Trace Precedents			ALT + T, U, T
Trace dependents	Tools, Auditing, Trace Dependents			ALT + T, U, D
Trace errors	Tools, Auditing, Trace Error			ALT + T, U, E
Remove all arrows	Tools, Auditing, Remove All Arrows			ALT + T, U, A
Circle invalid data				
Clear validation circles				

chapter fourteen

Concepts Review

Circle the correct answer.

1. **Precedents are cells that:**
   [a] are referred to by a formula.
   [b] depend on the value of another cell.
   [c] have blue arrow lines showing the relationship between two cells.
   [d] have red arrow lines showing the source of an error.

2. **Dependents are cells that:**
   [a] are referred to by a formula.
   [b] depend on the value of another cell.
   [c] have blue arrow lines showing the relationship between two cells.
   [d] have red arrow lines showing the source of an error.

3. **Traced errors are indicated by a:**
   [a] blue arrow. — *correct — another wk sheet in the wk bk*
   [b] black arrow.
   [c] red arrow.
   [d] blinking cell border.

4. **A heavy tracer arrow indicates a:**
   [a] serious error.
   [b] multiple-cell reference.
   [c] single-cell reference.
   [d] reference on another worksheet.

5. **A black arrow indicates a:**
   [a] traced error.
   [b] traced precedent.
   [c] traced dependent.
   [d] precedent or dependent cell located on another worksheet.

6. **To locate data that violates data validation, use the:**
   [a] Trace Precedents button.
   [b] Trace Error button.
   [c] Trace Dependents button.
   [d] Circle Invalid Data button.

7. **To quickly jump to a precedent or dependent in another worksheet that has been traced:**
   [a] click the worksheet icon that appears in the worksheet.
   [b] double-click the black tracer arrow.
   [c] drag the black tracer arrow to the worksheet tab.
   [d] double-click the cell to which the black tracer arrow points.

8. **You can trace errors in worksheet formulas by:**
   [a] clicking the Trace Errors button on the Auditing toolbar.
   [b] double-clicking the tracer arrows until they point to the errors.
   [c] clicking the Find Errors button on the Auditing toolbar.
   [d] dragging the red tracer arrows to the precedent cell.

9. **If data in a worksheet has a red circle around it, you should:**
   [a] fix the precedent cells.
   [b] reenter the value currently in the cell.
   [c] enter a valid entry in the cell.
   [d] erase the red circles using the Eraser button on the Drawing toolbar.

Circle **T** if the statement is true or **F** if the statement is false.

T F 1. You can view multiple levels of precedents and dependents.

T F 2. It is a good idea to review the relationships between cells when using a workbook prepared by someone else or when using a workbook with which you haven't worked for a long time.

T **F** 3. You can jump between ends of a tracer arrow by double-clicking the arrow line.

T **F** 4. You can open the Auditing toolbar by right-clicking a toolbar and clicking Auditing. *Tools ↓ Auditing → Show Auditing Toolbar*

T F 5. The #DIV/0! error indicates a number that Excel cannot display.

T (F) 6. Red arrows indicate precedents and dependents.

(T) F 7. If a cell containing a formula that results in an error is a precedent of a formula in another cell, both cells will display the error.

T (F) 8. To move a range with Range Finder, click and drag the Range Finder fill handle. — click & drag the RF border
— the fill handle expands or contracts the range

T F 9. You can use Trace Errors tool to find invalid data entered in a list.

(T) F 10. As you correct invalid entries in a list, the validation circles disappear.

Skills Review

Exercise 1

1. Open the *Warehouse Inventory Errors* file on your Data Disk.

2. Use the Auditing toolbar to locate cells containing invalid data.

3. Select rows 17–24.

4. Use the Clear All command to clear data validation settings from rows 17–24.

5. Click the Circle Invalid Data button on the Auditing toolbar again.

6. Print the worksheet with the circles displayed.

7. Save the workbook as *Warehouse Inventory Errors 1*.

Exercise 2

1. Open the *Warehouse Inventory Errors 1* file that you created in Exercise 1.

2. Use the Auditing toolbar to circle invalid entries.

3. Correct the errors using data that is compatible with the validation rules.

4. Save the workbook as *Warehouse Inventory Fixed* and print it.

Exercise 3

1. Open the *Fee Calculator Errors* file on your Data Disk.

2. Click cell H7.

3. Use auditing tools to trace the #NAME? error to its source.

4. The formula in cell C3 refers to a named range, percentage, that does not exist in the worksheet. Edit the formula to properly refer to cell C2. If necessary, check the formula in the cell to the right of cell 3.

5. Save the workbook as *Fee Calculator Errors Fixed 1* and print it.

Exercise 4

1. Open the *Fee Calculator Errors Fixed 1* file that you created in Exercise 3.

2. Click cell H7.

3. Use Range Finder to correct the formula so that it adds cells H3:H6.

4. Save the workbook as *Fee Calculator Errors Fixed 2* and print it.

chapter fourteen

Exercise 5

1. Open the *Fee Calculator Errors Fixed 2* file that you created in Exercise 4.
2. Trace the source of the #DIV/0! error in cell B10.
3. Change the value of the erroneous cell to 5.
4. Remove the arrows.
5. Print the worksheet.
6. Save the workbook as *Fee Calculator Fixed 3*.

Exercise 6

1. Open the *XYZ Accounting* file on your Data Disk.
2. Click cell B2 and trace its precedents.
3. Print the worksheet with the arrows displayed.
4. Double-click the black arrow line.
5. Select the reference to the San Diego tab and click OK.
6. Print the worksheet.
7. Save the workbook as *XYZ Accounting 1*.

Exercise 7

1. Open the *XYZ Accounting 1* file that you created in Exercise 6.
2. Click cell E5 on the San Diego worksheet.
3. Display the first-level precedents for cell E5.
4. Display the second-level precedents for cell E5.
5. Print the worksheet.
6. Save the workbook as *XYZ Accounting 2*.

Exercise 8

1. Open the *XYZ Accounting 2* file that you created in Exercise 7.
2. Activate cell B2 on the Summary tab.
3. Trace all dependents of cell B2.
4. Print the worksheet.
5. Save the workbook as *XYZ Accounting 3*.

Case Projects

Project 1

Use the Web toolbar to connect to your favorite search engine. Most search engines have a News section. Locate and read two articles one specifically about business or technology, and a subject of some interest to you (non-sports-related!). Print both articles.

Project 2

Some of your clients work with other spreadsheet applications that use the R1C1 cell reference style. Use the Office Assistant to research the R1C1 reference style. Write a description of the differences between the two styles, and how to use absolute and relative cell references in R1C1 style. Include instructions on how to change Excel to use the R1C1 reference style. Save the document as *R1C1 Instructions.doc*.

Project 3

Use the Office Assistant to look up "circular references." Write an explanation of circular reference, explaining how to turn on the Circular Reference toolbar and how to resolve the problem. Save the document as *Circular References.doc*.

Project 4

You are in charge of hiring new employees for the accounting division. Part of your hiring procedure is to test applicants using a workbook containing several errors, to see how they resolve the problems. Create a workbook similar to the one used in this chapter, using your own row and column headings, and data. Create erroneous formulas using incorrect references, named ranges that don't exist, circular references, and a divide by 0 error. Trace the source of each of your errors, and document them in another section of the worksheet. Save your workbook as *Error Test*.

Project 5

A popular method of transferring files on the Internet is FTP. Use an Internet search engine to find out what FTP stands for. Print a Web page containing a simple explanation of FTP. The article may suggest several FTP programs you can download, or you may need to use the search engine again to locate FTP programs. Find at least one FTP program you can download and print the page you find it on.

Project 6

Use the Internet to see if you can find out who invented the first spreadsheet application. Print a page explaining who invented it, why it was invented and what it was called.

chapter fourteen

Excel 2000

Automating Excel with Macros

Chapter Overview

Many tasks you perform in Excel can be very repetitive. Macros can record these steps, then play them back automatically and much more rapidly than you could do normally. In this chapter, you record and edit macros. You even learn how to program a dialog box that gets text from a user to use in your macro.

Learning Objectives

- Record a macro
- Run a macro
- Edit a macro
- Use workbooks containing macros
- Add Visual Basic functions to a macro

Case profile

Every time you create a new worksheet for Sweet Tooth, you spend precious time keying a worksheet title and formatting it the same way you do all other worksheet titles. You can streamline this tedious process to a couple of mouse clicks by recording a macro to do the work for you.

chapter fifteen

15.a Recording a Macro

A **macro** is a set of instructions that automatically executes a set of commands. Using macros, you can automate repetitive tasks. For example, you format Sweet Tooth's worksheet titles with the Impact font, 16 point size, red color, and centered across several cells. This formatting is a perfect candidate for a simple macro: repetitive, specific commands that you use over and over again. Other good candidates for macros include tasks such as adding headers and footers to a print report, creating charts, sorting lists, and setting up worksheets.

Macros are written or recorded in a programming language called Visual Basic. Visual Basic is used in all of the Office 2000 applications. It is fairly easy to learn, and if you take the time to learn its basics, you can create macros that work in Word, Access, PowerPoint, or Excel.

Now, take a deep breath. Yes, we said "programming." And yes, you're going to do it. Keep a few things in mind: (1) Programming is not just for geeks anymore; and (2) by learning how to do a little bit of programming (deep breath), you can actually lighten your workload and free yourself to do other things.

The simplest way to create a macro is to record it. When you record a macro, Excel takes note of every command you use and every keystroke you press. The first macro you record adds Sweet Tooth's company title to a worksheet using the company's preferred font style, size, color, and alignment. To start recording a macro:

Step 1	**Create**	a new, blank workbook
Step 2	**Click**	Tools
Step 3	**Point to**	Macro
Step 4	**Click**	Record New Macro

The Record Macro dialog box opens. Macros can be stored as part of the current workbook or in a hidden workbook called the Personal Macro Workbook.

| Step 5 | **Key** | Sweet_Tooth_Title in the Macro name: box |

Macro names cannot contain spaces, so use the underscore (_) character instead.

| Step 6 | **Select** | This Workbook from the Store Macro in: list box |

> **QUICK TIP**
>
> When creating macros, a very helpful technique is to write down or practice each step in the task you want to automate. When you are sure that you have written down all of the steps involved, begin recording your macro.
>
> If you want your recorded macros to be available whenever you use Excel, store them in the Personal Macro Workbook.

Step 7	Drag	to select all of the text in the Description: box
Step 8	Key	Create and format a worksheet title

The Shortcut key: box allows you to assign a shortcut key to the macro. For now, leave this box blank. Your dialog box should look similar to Figure 15-1.

FIGURE 15-1
Record Macro Dialog Box

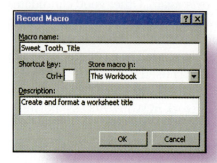

Step 9	Click	OK

The Stop Recording toolbar appears, and Recording appears in the status bar, as shown in Figure 15-2.

FIGURE 15-2
Stop Recording Toolbar

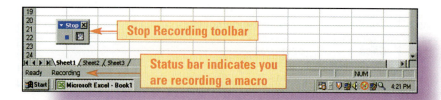

Now enter and format the titles you want on your worksheet. To enter the titles:

Step 1	Enter	Sweet Tooth in cell A1
Step 2	Enter	<Add a subtitle in cell A2> in cell A2 (include the brackets)
Step 3	Select	cells A1:F1
Step 4	Click	the Merge and Center button on the Formatting toolbar

Step 5	Repeat	steps 3 and 4 with cells A2:F2
Step 6	Select	cells A1:A2
Step 7	Open	the Format Cells dialog box by pressing the CTRL + 1 keys
Step 8	Click	the Font tab
Step 9	Select	Impact from the Font: list
Step 10	Select	16 from the Size: list
Step 11	Select	Red from the Color: palette
Step 12	Click	OK
Step 13	Activate	cell A1
Step 14	Click	the Stop Recording button on the Stop Recording toolbar

Your macro is saved as part of the workbook, and the Stop Recording toolbar closes.

15.b Running a Macro

To test the macro, you must run it. You can use the Macro dialog box to run macros stored in any currently open workbook or macros stored in your Personal Macro Workbook. To run the macro:

Step 1	Click	the Sheet2 worksheet tab
Step 2	Click	Tools
Step 3	Point to	Macro
Step 4	Click	Macros

The Macro dialog box opens.

| Step 5 | Click | Sweet_Tooth_Title from the list of available macros |

QUICK TIP

If you want to see additional information about recording macros, use Microsoft Visual Basic Help from the Visual Basic Editor.

MENU TIP

The Personal Macro workbook is hidden by default. You can hide other open workbooks or view hidden workbooks. To hide a workbook, click Window, then Hide. To view a hidden workbook, click Window, then Unhide.

chapter fifteen

The description that you keyed when you recorded the macro appears at the bottom of the dialog box. Your dialog box should look similar to Figure 15-3.

FIGURE 15-3
Macro Dialog Box

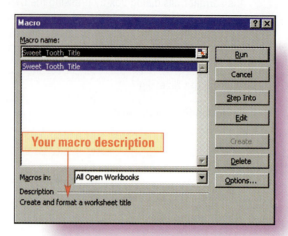

> **QUICK TIP**
>
> You can access the Macro dialog box by pressing the ALT + F8 keys.

Step 6	Click	Run

The macro performs the steps that you recorded earlier. Your screen should look similar to Figure 15-4.

FIGURE 15-4
Running the Sweet_Tooth_Title Macro

15.c Editing a Macro

Using the Visual Basic Editor, you can edit macros that you've previously recorded or written. The Visual Basic Editor is a separate program that runs in its own window, outside of Excel, and provides toolbars and menus specifically intended for working with Visual Basic programming code. To edit the Sweet_Tooth_Title macro:

> **QUICK TIP**
>
> You can access the Visual Basic Editor by pressing the ALT + F11 keys.

Step 1	Click	Tools
Step 2	Point to	Macro
Step 3	Click	Macros

| Step 4 | **Select** | the Sweet_Tooth_Title macro |
| Step 5 | **Click** | <u>E</u>dit |

The Visual Basic Editor opens, with the selected macro open on the right side, as shown in Figure 15-5. Notice that the Visual Basic Editor program button appears in the taskbar.

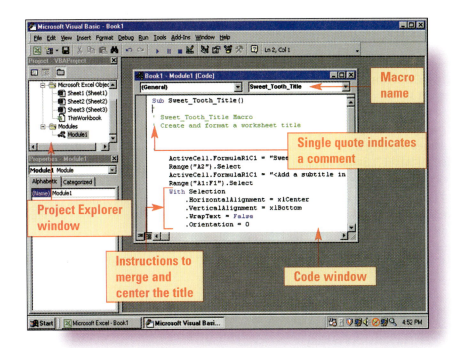

FIGURE 15-5
Visual Basic Editor

> **QUICK TIP**
>
> You can also write new macros, test, debug, and delete macros from the Visual Basic Editor.

On the left side of the Visual Basic Editor window, you see the Project Explorer window. Project Explorer displays a hierarchical list of all open projects and each of the items associated with each particular project. A **project** includes objects in the workbook, including the worksheets, **modules** (where macro code is stored), and **forms** (custom dialog boxes). In addition to these items, projects can contain other items, such as ActiveX controls, class modules, and references to other projects. Visual Basic Help provides information about other items that can be included in a project.

The Code window to the right contains the macro code for the Sweet_Tooth_Title macro.

| Step 6 | **Scroll** | the Code window to review the code |

chapter
fifteen

Table 15-1 explains different sections of the code.

TABLE 15-1
Macro Code Description

Macro Line	Description
Sub Sweet_Tooth_Title()	Sub appears in blue text and defines the beginning of a procedure. The title of the macro appears on the Sub line and appears in black text.
Green text lines	Green text lines are remark, or comment, lines. Everything you enter after an apostrophe or REM (short for REMARK) is considered a remark. You use remarks to explain certain steps in your program. Notice that the description you entered in the Record Macro dialog box appears at the top of your code.
ActiveCell.FormulaR1C1 = "Sweet Tooth"	Enters the text "Sweet Tooth" in the current cell. (Uses R1C1 style cell references; use Office Assistant to learn more about this topic).
Range("A2").Select	Activates cell A2.
All lines starting with Range("A1:F1").Select to Selection.Merge	Merges and centers cells A1:F1.
All lines beginning with Range("A1:F2").Select to End With	Selects cells A1:F2 and sets the font options.
End Sub	Indicates the end of the macro

> **MOUSE TIP**
>
> Click the Maximize button in the Code window to make the Code window fill the space on the right.

Whenever a Sweet Tooth employee uses this macro, the current date should be added in a blue font to cell A3. To modify the code:

Step 1	Locate	the line that reads Range ("A1:F1").Select near the end of the macro
Step 2	Drag	the I-beam pointer over A1:F1 to select it
Step 3	Key	A3
Step 4	Press	the END key to move to the end of the line
Step 5	Press	the ENTER key
Step 6	Key	ActiveCell.FormulaR1C1 = "=TODAY()"

This line enters the TODAY date formula in the current cell, A3.

Step 7	Press	the ENTER key
Step 8	Key	Selection.Font.ColorIndex = 5

This line sets the font color to 5, which is the color index code for the color blue.

Step 9	Press	the ENTER key
Step 10	Key	Range("A1").

After you type the period, a list appears displaying a list of valid actions belonging to the Range group of functions.

Step 11	Scroll	down the list until you see Select
Step 12	Double-click	Select

Your screen should look similar to Figure 15-6.

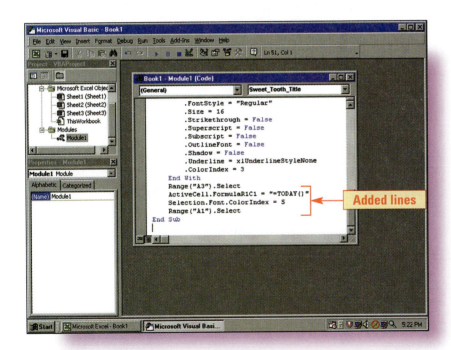

FIGURE 15-6
Editing a Macro

Now you can run your revised macro. To run your revised macro:

Step 1	Click	the Excel taskbar button
Step 2	Click	the Sheet3 worksheet tab
Step 3	Click	Tools
Step 4	Point to	Macro

Step 5	Click	Macros
Step 6	Select	Sweet_Tooth_Title from the list of available macros
Step 7	Click	Run

Your screen should look similar to Figure 15-7.

FIGURE 15-7
Results of the Revised Macro

To print the macro code and close the Visual Basic Editor:

Step 1	Click	the Visual Basic Editor taskbar button
Step 2	Click	File
Step 3	Click	Print
Step 4	Click	OK to print the current module
Step 5	Click	File
Step 6	Click	Close and Return to Microsoft Excel

The Visual Basic Editor closes, and the Excel window becomes the active window.

| Step 7 | Save | the workbook as *Sweet Tooth Title Macro* |

CAUTION TIP

If cell A3 displays TODAY(), click the Visual Basic taskbar button, click before the T in TODAY, and key an equal sign. Switch back to Excel and run the macro again.

15.d Using Workbooks Containing Macros

When you share workbooks with other users or download files from the Internet, your file(s)—or the downloaded files—could be infected with viruses. Viruses are malicious programs that can destroy files and data. **Macro viruses** are a special class of viruses that embed themselves in macros. When you open a workbook containing a macro virus, the virus can replicate itself to other workbooks, destroy files on your hard drive, and do other types of damage. Because of this threat, Excel prompts you before opening any file containing macros.

Opening a Workbook with Macros

The *Sweet Tooth Header Macro* workbook on your Data Disk contains a macro to automatically set up a header, and you want to edit it. To open a workbook containing a macro:

| Step 1 | Open | the *Sweet Tooth Header Macro* workbook on your Data Disk |

Excel displays a warning dialog box, as shown in Figure 15-8.

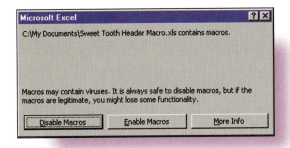

FIGURE 15-8
Macro Virus Warning Dialog Box

Excel cannot determine whether a macro is actually a macro virus. If you are not sure about the origins of the workbook, you would select Disable Macros. The contents of the workbook can still be edited, but any special macros stored in the notebook cannot be executed. If possible, contact the person who created the workbook to find out which macros should appear in the workbook. Because you know that the source of this workbook is safe, you can open the file with macros enabled.

| Step 2 | Click | Enable Macros |

Copying Macro Code to Another Workbook

You would like to copy the macro in this workbook to the *Sweet Tooth Title Macro* you created earlier. To copy macro code:

| Step 1 | Click | Tools |
| Step 2 | Point to | Macro |

> **QUICK TIP**
>
> To scan your files for viruses, you must purchase special antivirus software capable of scanning your files, hard drive(s), and floppy drive(s). Most newer antivirus programs can scan files containing macros for macro viruses. For more information about macro viruses, use the Office Assistant.

chapter fifteen

| Step 3 | Click | Visual Basic Editor |

Visual Basic Editor opens to the Sweet_Tooth_Header macro module.

| Step 4 | Press | the CTRL + A keys to select all of the code |
| Step 5 | Click | the Copy button on the Visual Basic Editor Standard toolbar |

In the Project Explorer window, you can expand the view for the Sweet Tooth Title project.

| Step 6 | Click | the + icon next to VBAProject (Sweet Tooth Title Macro.xls) |

If a – (minus sign) appears next to VBAProject (Sweet Tooth Title Macro.xls), do not click it.

Step 7	Scroll	down the Project Explorer window, if necessary
Step 8	Right-click	the Modules folder indented under VBAProject (Sweet Tooth Title Macro.xls)
Step 9	Point to	Insert
Step 10	Click	Module

A blank macro module opens.

| Step 11 | Click | the Paste button on the Visual Basic Editor Standard toolbar |

The macro from *Sweet Tooth Header Macro* is pasted into the *Sweet Tooth Title Macro* workbook.

> **CAUTION TIP**
>
> Make sure you are clicking the + icon next to the VBAProject for Sweet Tooth Title Macro.xls, not Sweet Tooth Header Macro.xls.

15.e Adding Visual Basic Functions to a Macro

Of course, macros can do more than modify font and alignment settings for a few cells. They can create charts, set header and footer options, and perform many other tasks. By adding a special Visual

Basic function called an InputBox, you can retrieve information from the user while the macro is running. You decide to add an InputBox to the Sweet_Tooth_Header macro that prompts Sweet Tooth employees to key in a header title. The macro automatically creates a custom header for printing reports from the header that the employee inputs. To add the InputBox function to the macro:

Step 1	Press	the CTRL + HOME keys to move to the top of the macro module
Step 2	Move	the insertion point in front of the W on the line With ActiveSheet.PageSetup (the first one)
Step 3	Press	the ENTER key to insert a new line
Step 4	Press	the UP ARROW key
Step 5	Key	HeaderText = InputBox("Enter a Header Title")

QUICK TIP

To find out more about Visual Basic functions, use Visual Basic Editor Help.

A **variable** is a placeholder for data; it is replaced by the actual data. By adding this line, you have assigned a variable called *HeaderText* to the result of a Visual Basic function called *InputBox*. This function displays a box with a space in which the user can enter new text. The text between quotes in the line you added appear as a prompt in the InputBox. Your screen should look similar to Figure 15-9.

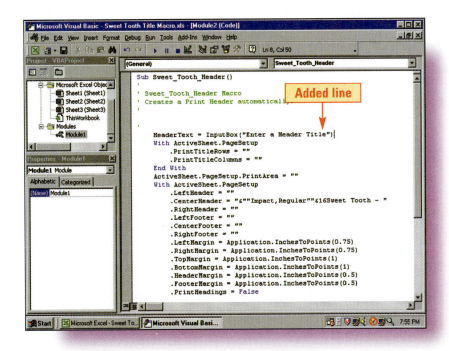

FIGURE 15-9
Adding an InputBox Function to a Macro

Now you need to tell the macro where to use the data held by the variable HeaderText.

Step 6	Move	the insertion point down eight lines to the line that reads .CenterHeader = "&""Impact,Regular""&16Sweet Tooth – "
Step 7	Press	the END key to move to the end of the line
Step 8	Press	the SPACEBAR
Step 9	Key	& HeaderText

This line adds the text "Sweet Tooth – " to the data held by the variable HeaderText. Your screen should look similar to Figure 15-10.

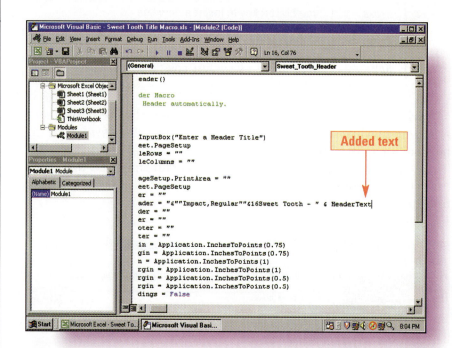

FIGURE 15-10
Using a Variable to Replace Values

QUICK TIP

You can assign a macro to a toolbar button. Open the Customize dialog box, and click the Commands tab. Right-click a custom button that you've added to a toolbar, then click Assign Macro. Select the desired macro, then click OK.

Now test your macro. To run the macro:

Step 1	Click	the Excel taskbar button
Step 2	Click	Window
Step 3	Select	Sweet Tooth Title Macro from the menu list
Step 4	Click	Tools
Step 5	Point to	Macro
Step 6	Click	Macros
Step 7	Select	This workbook from the Macros in: list

| Step 8 | Run | the Sweet_Tooth_Header macro |

The macro runs, and you see a dialog box similar to Figure 15-11.

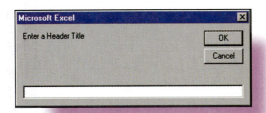

FIGURE 15-11
An InputBox

| Step 9 | Key | Central Region in the box |
| Step 10 | Click | OK |

After a moment (depending on the speed of your computer), you can edit your worksheet. To view your header:

Step 1	Click	the Print Preview button  on the Standard toolbar
Step 2	Print	the worksheet
Step 3	Save & Close	the *Sweet Tooth Title Macro* workbook
Step 4	Click	the Visual Basic Editor taskbar button
Step 5	Click	File
Step 6	Click	Print
Step 7	Click	OK
Step 8	Click	File
Step 9	Click	Close and Return to Microsoft Excel
Step 10	Close	the *Sweet Tooth Header Macro* workbook

The macro you created will make it a snap to create new workbooks.

chapter fifteen

Summary

- A macro is a set of instructions that executes several commands automatically. Macros can be simple recorded steps, or they can be complex programs capable of making decisions based on user input.

- Recording a macro is the simplest way to create a macro. During the recording process, Excel records exactly what you do.

- Once a macro is recorded, it must be run to perform the desired task.

- Edit macros using the Visual Basic Editor. Visual Basic is the programming language used by Excel and other Office 2000 applications. The Visual Basic Editor is a separate application used to create, edit, delete, and test Visual Basic modules or macros.

- Some macros can contain viruses, or programs that can damage file on your computer system. If you are unsure of a workbook's origin, disable macros when you open the workbook. You can still view and edit data in the workbook.

- Copy macro code between Visual Basic projects (other workbooks) using the Cut and Paste commands.

- Use Visual Basic functions, like InputBox, to retrieve information from the user, assign that information to a variable, and then use the variable in other locations throughout your program.

Commands Review

Action	Menu Bar	Shortcut Menu	Toolbar	Keyboard
Record a macro	Tools, Macro, Record New Macro			ALT + T, M, R
Run or edit a macro	Tools, Macro, Macros then Run or Edit button			ALT + T, M, M, then R or E ALT + F8
Open the Visual Basic Editor	Tools, Macro, Visual Basic Editor			ALT + T, M, V ALT + F11

Concepts Review

Circle the correct answer.

1. Macros:
   [a] are much too difficult for the average user to program.
   [b] waste time because they run every time you open a workbook.
   [c] consist of a set of instructions that automatically executes a set of commands.
   [d] can never be modified.

2. Which of the following tasks can be performed by macros?
   [a] printing worksheets
   [b] creating and modifying charts
   [c] sorting lists
   [d] all of the above

3. To make a macro available in all workbooks, you should save it:
   [a] in every workbook you use.
   [b] in the Personal Macro Workbook.
   [c] on a floppy disk.
   [d] to the All Macros folder on your hard drive.

4. You edit macros in the:
   [a] Excel application window.
   [b] Macro dialog box.
   [c] Visual Basic Editor program window.
   [d] Record Macro dialog box.

5. Visual Basic is the programming language used by:
   [a] only Microsoft Excel.
   [b] only Microsoft Word.
   [c] only Microsoft Access.
   [d] all Office 2000 applications.

6. If you see REM, or an apostrophe (') in Visual Basic, what does it signify?
   [a] a shortened version of the REMOVE command
   [b] a blank line follows
   [c] a shortened version of REMARK, preceding a comment section
   [d] a shortened version of REMEMBER, preceding a programmer's reminder section

7. When you record a macro, you:
   [a] must write all the actions you want to perform, then key them in the Visual Basic Editor program window.
   [b] start recording, then Excel automatically records every keystroke.
   [c] must open the Visual Basic Editor first before Excel will record your keystrokes.
   [d] click the Record button after each keystroke so that mistakes are not recorded.

chapter fifteen

8. If you see a message telling you that a workbook contains macros, you should:
   [a] always click Disable Macros because the workbook contains a virus.
   [b] always click Enable Macros because the workbook will not display all the data unless you do.
   [c] cancel the operation quickly because the macro may contain a virus.
   [d] decide whether the workbook comes from a reliable source, then click either Disable or Enable Macros.

Circle **T** if the statement is true or **F** if the statement is false.

T F 1. Macros save a lot of time.

T F 2. It is nearly impossible to add user input to a macro.

T F 3. The Visual Basic Editor is part of the Excel application.

T F 4. You can write macros that work across several Office 2000 applications.

T F 5. Learning the basics of Visual Basic can help you write macros in all of the Office 2000 applications.

T F 6. The easiest way to create a macro is to open the Visual Basic Editor and key in the code by hand.

T F 7. If you make a mistake recording a macro, you have to record a new macro.

T F 8. When you see the macro virus warning when opening an Excel workbook, you should not open the workbook because it contains a macro virus.

T F 9. Macro viruses are usually harmful programs capable of copying themselves to other files and destroying data.

T F 10. A module is the basic storage unit for macros.

Skills Review

Exercise 1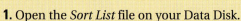

1. Open the *Sort List* file on your Data Disk.
2. Click any cell within the list of data on Sheet1.
3. Record a new macro called Sort1 and save it in the current workbook.
4. Sort the list by name in ascending order.
5. Stop recording the macro.
6. Record a second macro called Sort2 and save it in the current workbook.
7. Sort the list by region and then by name in ascending order.
8. Stop recording the macro.
9. Save the workbook as *Sort List with Macros*.

Exercise 2

1. Open the *Sort List with Macros* workbook that you created in Exercise 1.
2. Display the Drawing toolbar.
3. Insert two bevel shapes from the Basic Shapes palette of the AutoShapes button.
4. Add Text to the first bevel shape that reads "Sort by Name."
5. Add Text to the second bevel shape that reads "Sort by Region & Name."
6. Resize the buttons so as to make it possible to read all text, if necessary.
7. Right-click the "Sort by Name" bevel object and select Assi<u>g</u>n Macro.
8. Select Sort1 from the <u>M</u>acro name: list, and click OK.
9. Repeat steps 7 and 8 to assign the Sort2 macro to the "Sort by Region & Name" bevel object.
10. Make sure that the active cell is within the list, then move your pointer over either of the bevel objects.
11. Click the bevel object to sort the list. Try the other bevel object. (*Hint:* You get a run-time error if the active cell is not within the list when you click one of the bevel objects. Click the <u>E</u>nd button and return to Excel. Move the active cell within the list and try again.)
12. Save the workbook as *Sort List with Macros 2*.

Exercise 3

1. Open the *Sort List with Macros 2* workbook that you created in Exercise 2.
2. Record a new macro called Filter_Region, and save it in the current workbook.
3. Activate a cell within the list.
4. Apply AutoFilters.
5. Click the AutoFilter arrow for the Region column and select Central.
6. Open the Page Setup Dialog box (from the <u>F</u>ile menu), and select Landscape layout on the Page tab.
7. Click the Print button, then click OK to print the report.
8. Click the AutoFilter arrow for the Region column and select (All).
9. Stop recording the macro.
10. Save the workbook as *Sort List with Macros 3*.

Exercise 4

1. Open the *Sort List with Macros 3* workbook that you created in Exercise 3.

2. Select the Filter_Region macro from beginning to end. (*Hint:* Press the CTRL + A keys in the code window to select all.)

3. Copy the code using the Copy button on the Visual Basic Editor Standard toolbar.

4. Move the insertion point to a new line below End Sub.

5. Paste the code using the Paste button on the Visual Basic Editor Standard toolbar.

6. Change the name of the second macro to Filter_Region2 by modifying the second Sub Filter_Region() line.

7. Edit the Filter_Region2 macro as follows (**bold** identifies added or modified sections):

…Leave the remarks section of the macro as is.
CriteriaName = InputBox("Enter Region Name (Central, Mountain, East Coast, West Coast)")
Selection.AutoFilter Field:=1, Criteria1:=**CriteriaName**
With ActiveSheet.PageSetup
…Leave the rest of the macro as is.
This change adds an InputBox that prompts the user for a region to filter and print. The response is assigned to the variable, CriteriaName, which is then used as the filter criteria.

8. Save the changes to your macro, print your macro, and return to Excel.

9. Run the new Filter_Region2 macro from the Macro dialog box.

10. Save the workbook as *Sort List with Macros 4*, then print the worksheet.

Exercise 5

1. Open the *Central Region Sales 2* workbook on your Data Disk.

2. Record a macro called Chart. Store the macro in This Workbook.

3. Select cells A4:E8, and click the Chart Wizard button on the Standard toolbar.

4. Create a chart with the following characteristics:

a. Select the Clustered Column with a 3-D visual effect chart subtype.

b. Enter "Central Region Summary" for the Chart title.

c. Create the chart as a new sheet.

d. Name the new sheet "Central Region Summary Chart."

5. When the chart appears, click the Stop Recording button to stop recording the macro.

6. Delete the new chart sheet tab.

7. Run the macro to verify that it works correctly.

8. Save the workbook as *Central Region Sales 2 Chart*.

Exercise 6

1. Open the *Central Region Sales 2 Chart* workbook that you created in Exercise 5.

2. Open the Macro dialog box, and select the Chart macro for editing.

3. In the Visual Basic Editor, edit the macro code as follows (insert the text in **bold**):

   a. Insert **NM = ActiveSheet.Name** before the line Range("A4:E8").Select

   b. Use Replace (press the CTRL + H keys) to replace "Central Region Summary" (including the quotation marks) with **NM**

   c. Use Replace to replace all occurrences of "Central Region Summary Chart" (including the quotation marks) with **NM & " Summary Chart"** (include a space between the first quotation mark and the letter S).

   d. In the line .ChartTitle.Characters.Text = "Central Region Summary Chart" replace "Central Region Summary Chart" with **NM & " Summary Chart"**

These changes find the current worksheet tab name and assign it to the variable NM. The macro then uses this variable to create and automatically give a title to a new chart, on a new chart sheet that it also names automatically.

4. Click the Excel taskbar button.

5. Click the South Division worksheet tab.

6. Run the Chart macro.

7. Create charts for each of the Division pages of your workbook using the Chart macro.

8. Print the charts.

9. Save the workbook as *Central Region Sales 2 Chart Revised*.

Exercise 7

1. Open the *Central Region Sales 2 Chart Revised* workbook that you created in Exercise 6.

2. Record a new macro called "Set_Footer."

3. Use the Page Setup dialog box to set the following Footing options:

   a. In the left section, print the Date.

   b. In the center section, print the Tab name.

   c. In the right section, print the Time.

4. Click OK to close the Footer and Page Setup dialog boxes.

5. Stop recording the macro.

6. Click the Central Region Summary Chart worksheet tab, and test your macro.

7. Print the macro.

8. Preview and print the chart.

9. Save the workbook as *Central Region Sales 2 Chart Revised 2*.

Exercise 8

1. Open the *Central Region Sales 2 Chart Revised 2* workbook that you created in Exercise 7.

2. Save the workbook as *Central Region Sales 2 Chart Revised 3*.

3. Open the Macro dialog box, and click the Set_Footer macro.

4. Click Options.

5. Hold down the SHIFT key and press the F key to assign the hotkey CTRL + SHIFT + F to your macro.

6. Close the Macro dialog box.

7. Click the West Division Summary Chart tab.

8. Use the new hotkey to run the macro.

9. Print the worksheet.

10. Create a new toolbar called "Chart Tools."

11. Add two new Custom buttons to the toolbar from the Macro category on the Commands tab of the Customize dialog box.

12. Right-click the first button, and name it &Chart.

13. Click Assign Macro and assign the Chart macro to the button.

14. Right-click the second button and name it &Set Footer.

15. Click Assign Macro and assign the Set_Footer macro to the button.

16. Click the Toolbars tab in the Customize dialog box, then click Assign Macro.

17. Attach the toolbar to the workbook.

18. Save and close the workbook.

19. Open the Customize dialog box and delete the Chart Tools toolbar on the Toolbars tab.

Case Projects

Project 1

As a busy student who uses Excel for many homework assignments, you find it tedious to constantly add your name, class, and date to your workbooks before you turn them in. In a new workbook, record a macro to insert three rows at the top of your workbook, and insert your name in cell A1, the class name in cell A2, and today's date in cell A3. Name the macro Name_Stamp. Test your macro on Sheet2 of your workbook. Save the workbook as *Name Stamp Macro*. Print your macro code and the worksheet.

Project 2

Use the Web toolbar to locate your favorite search engine. Search the Internet for information about Visual Basic and Visual Basic for Applications. Focus your search on tutorials, especially those intended for beginners. Print at least two beginner tutorials, and save five links in your browser's Favorites or Bookmarks.

Project 3

As the manager of a retail music store, you create a chart every week listing the best-selling CDs. Use the Internet to search for the Top 15 Best-Selling CDs for the current week. Create a new workbook containing the album title, artist name, and number of CDs sold. Generate fictitious sales data (for your store) for each CD.

Record a macro to do the following:

1. Sort the list by number of CDs sold, then by album title.
2. Create a chart selecting the top 10 best-selling albums.
3. Create a centered header with your store's name.
4. Create a footer with the date on the left and the time on the right.
5. Change the page layout to landscape orientation.
6. Print the chart.

Randomly change the number of albums sold, then run the macro again. Save the workbook as *Record Sales*. Print your macro code and the worksheet.

Project 4

As an accountant who deals with a high volume of clients every day, you would like to be able to see the current date and time when you switch between clients. Start a new blank workbook, and save it as *Time Clock*. Using the Drawing tools, draw something resembling a clock face and group the objects. Open the Visual Basic Editor and double-click Module 1 of the Time Clock.xls project in the Project Explorer window. Use Visual Basic Help to create a message box that displays the current date and time. (*Hint:* Search for the MsgBox, Date, and Time functions.) Assign the macro to your clock object. Save the workbook as *Time Clock*. Print your macro code and the worksheet.

Project 5

As a busy account manager, you are constantly adding new worksheets to existing workbooks. Create a macro to automatically insert a new sheet and prompt the user for a sheet name using an InputBox. Assign the shortcut keys CTRL + SHIFT + N to your macro. (*Hint:* Record the steps to insert and name a worksheet first, then add the InputBox function using the Visual Basic Editor. Just after the Sheets.Add line, insert a new line: NM = ActiveSheet.Name to assign the new sheet name to the variable NM. Next, replace sheet name references with the variable. Your macro will then insert new sheets as often as you want.) Save the workbook as *Insert New Sheet*. Print your macro code and the worksheet.

chapter fifteen

Project 6

As the newly hired personnel manager, you have located several workbooks on your computer that list employees' first names, but not their last names. Create a new workbook with five first names. Copy this list to Sheet2 in your workbook. Record a macro called Replace_Names to find and replace one of the names on the worksheet with the first and last name of the employee. In the Visual Basic Editor, copy the two lines recorded by the macro four additional times (above the End Sub line). Modify the copied code to search and replace each of the names you listed on Sheet1 with the first and last names of each employee. Go back to Excel, and run your macro on Sheet2. Save the workbook as *Replace Names*. Print your macro code and the worksheets.

Project 7

You are worried about the security of workbooks that you share with other people over the Internet. Search the Internet for information about Excel macro viruses. Print at least one page identifying one existing Excel macro virus, explaining what it does, and describing how you can eliminate it.

Project 8

You would like to find out more about writing macros to automate Excel. Search the Internet for pages that contain macro tutorials or explain how to create macros in Excel. Print at least one page.

Excel 2000

Using What-If Analysis

Chapter Overview

Finding solutions to complex business problems is one of the things that Excel does best. Data tables allow you to quickly recalculate a formula by replacing one argument with several values. Goal Seek and Solver help you reach a desired outcome. Scenarios let you save and restore several variables in your worksheets.

Learning Objectives

- Create data tables
- Use Goal Seek and Solver
- Create scenarios

Case profile

To be successful in business, you must know how to analyze information and how to make decisions based on the analysis of that information. This month, Sweet Tooth is looking to expand its fleet of cars and needs to know how much the company can afford to borrow. The warehouse division is also seeking a solution to some scheduling problems. Using a variety of what-if analysis tools, you can resolve all of these problems.

chapter

16.a Creating Data Tables

One of Excel's key strengths is its ability to help you perform what-if analyses. In a **what-if analysis,** you change data values and then observe the effect on calculations—for example, "What if I change the value in cell A2?" To make this kind of trial-and-error process easier, you can use **data tables** to show the results of a formula by replacing one or two of the variables with several different values. **One-variable data tables** can be created to show the results of changing one variable in several formulas at once. **Two-variable data tables** can show the results of changing two variables in a single formula.

Creating a One-Variable Data Table

You learned about using variables when creating macros. A variable is a placeholder for a value. You can assign different values to a **variable**, then use that variable in a formula or calculation. A **one-variable data table** uses a variable to replace one of the arguments in a given formula and then calculates results using several different values for that one argument.

Sweet Tooth is considering purchasing a fleet of automobiles for some of its sales representatives. The purchase amount of each car is $25,000, with a loan interest rate of 10%. The company wants to find out what the monthly payment will be per car, and how much interest will be paid depending on the term of the loan. In this case, the term argument is the variable.

To set up a one-variable data table:

Step 1	**Open**	the *Interest Calculator* workbook on your Data Disk
Step 2	**Save**	the workbook as *Interest Calculator Revised* in your Data Files folder

Recall from Chapter 7, the CUMIPMT function calculates the cumulative interest paid, given a start and end period. The PMT function calculates the monthly payment on a loan. Both of these financial functions share common arguments, including the rate (percentage), nper (number of periods in the life of the loan), and pv (present value of the loan).

In this workbook, the loan information has already been entered. Cell B5 holds the value representing the nper argument used in both the CUMIPMT and the PMT functions. This value will be replaced by the values in cells C5:C8, which are shaded in green. (In this case, the

---

QUICK TIP

For more information about these functions, use the Office Assistant.

period of time for the nper argument is months.) The payment (PMT) calculation takes place in column D. The cumulative interest (CUMIPMT) is calculated in column E.

| Step 3 | Enter | =PMT(B4/12,B5,B6) in cell D4 |
| Step 4 | Enter | =CUMIPMT(B4/12,B5,B6,1,B5,1) in cell E4 |

Your screen should look similar to Figure 16-1.

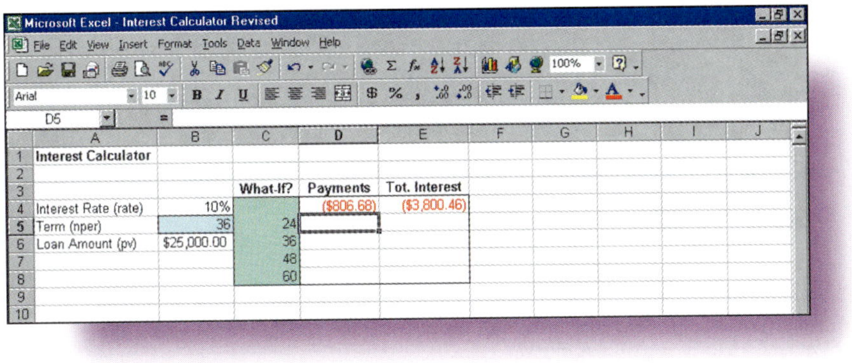

FIGURE 16-1
Setting Up a One-Variable Data Table

Now that the formulas and information are set up, you can see what happens if you change the term of the loan.

To perform a what-if analysis using a one-variable data table:

Step 1	Select	cells C4:E8
Step 2	Click	Data
Step 3	Click	Table

The Table dialog box opens. Because the replacement values you will use are arranged in a column, you use a Column input cell.

| Step 4 | Click | in the Column input cell: box |
| Step 5 | Click | cell B5 |

The data table automatically replaces the value in cell B5 with each of the values in the leftmost column of the data table you've selected.

chapter sixteen

First, Excel calculates the PMT function using the value 24 (the first value in column C) instead of the current value of cell B5. Then, Excel calculates the PMT function again, using the next value in column C, 36, in place of the current value of cell B5. Excel continues this process until it reaches the end of the table you selected. See Figure 16-2.

FIGURE 16-2
Choosing the Variable in a One-Variable Data Table

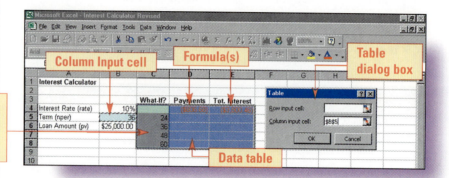

Step 6	**Click**	OK
Step 7	**Click**	cell A1

The monthly payment and cumulative interest for each term length are calculated, as shown in Figure 16-3.

FIGURE 16-3
One-Variable Data Table Calculated

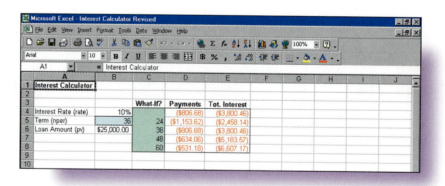

Step 8	**Save**	the workbook

Creating a Two-Variable Data Table

Two-variable data tables allow you to see the results of a formula that uses two variables. You want to calculate the monthly payments on the auto loan for various terms at different interest rates.

To set up a two-variable data table:

Step 1	Click	the Two Variable worksheet tab
Step 2	Enter	=PMT(B4/12,B5,B6) in cell C4

Two-variable data tables can use only one formula at a time, and this formula must be located in the cell directly above the column of the first replacement values and to the right of the second replacement values. The result of the formula, ($806.68), appears in cell C4, as shown in Figure 16-4.

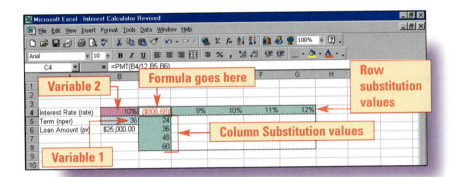

FIGURE 16-4
Preparing a Two-Variable Data Table

Now you can perform the what-if calculations. To perform a what-if analysis using a two-way data table:

Step 1	Select	cells C4:G8
Step 2	Click	Data
Step 3	Click	Table
Step 4	Click	cell B4 so that it appears as an absolute reference in the Row input cell: box
Step 5	Click	in the Column input cell: box
Step 6	Click	cell B5
Step 7	Click	OK
Step 8	Click	cell A1

Your final data table should look similar to Figure 16-5.

FIGURE 16-5
Two-Variable Data Table

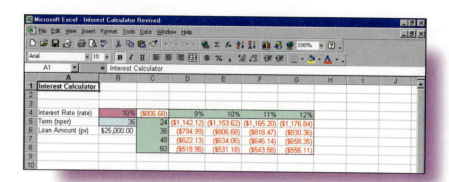

| Step 9 | **Save & Close** the workbook |

16.b Using Goal Seek and Solver

Excel includes several tools to help you solve complex problems. When you know the desired result of a formula but the values currently used in the formula don't produce the correct result, you can use the **Goal Seek** tool to change a variable in the formula and obtain the correct result. Goal Seek can modify only one variable. **Solver** works in much the same way, but it allows you to change the values of several variables; at the same time, it sets constraints on how much you can alter those variables.

Using Goal Seek

Sweet Tooth has decided to purchase 40 new cars for the company, at a total cost of $1,000,000. The company would like to pay off the loan in 36 months, but it has a budget of only $30,000 per month available to make payments. The Board of Directors needs to know how much money Sweet Tooth can borrow at 10%, and how much cash it needs to meet this budget limitation.

To set up the workbook:

Step 1	**Open**	the *Car Purchase* workbook on your Data Disk
Step 2	**Save**	the workbook as *Car Purchase Revised* in your Data Files folder
Step 3	**Enter**	=PMT(B8/12,B9,B10) in cell B13

The monthly payment is calculated at $32,267.19. You need to adjust the loan amount so that the monthly payment fits the budget of $30,000. To use Goal Seek:

Step 1	**Activate**	cell B13
Step 2	**Click**	**T**ools
Step 3	**Click**	**G**oal Seek
Step 4	**Click**	in the To **v**alue: box
Step 5	**Key**	-30000

The company will be paying this amount out, so you use a negative number to indicate it is an expense.

| Step 6 | **Press** | the TAB key to move to the By **c**hanging cell: box |
| Step 7 | **Click** | cell B10 |

The completed Goal Seek dialog box is shown in Figure 16-6.

FIGURE 16-6
Goal Seek Dialog Box

Goal Seek finds the solution and displays the Goal Seek Status dialog box. When you click the OK button, Excel changes the value of the variable cell—B10 in this case—so that the formula in cell B13 meets your goal.

| Step 8 | **Click** | OK |

Figure 16-7 shows the results of the Goal Seek operation. To meet the budgeted payment amount of $30,000 per month, Sweet Tooth can borrow a maximum of $929,737.

FIGURE 16-7
Goal Seek Status Dialog Box

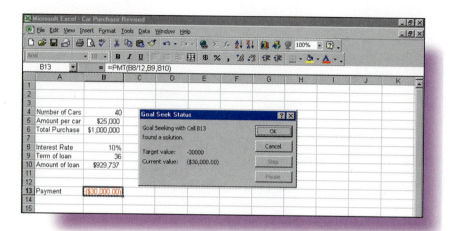

| Step 9 | **Click** | OK to accept the Goal Seek solution |
| Step 10 | **Save & Close** the workbook | |

Solver is an Excel Add-In that must be installed before you can use it. If you do not have a Sol<u>v</u>er option on the <u>T</u>ools menu, click <u>T</u>ools, then click Add-<u>I</u>ns. Click Solver Add-In, and then click OK to install Solver.

Using Solver

Amy Lee, Sweet Tooth's president, has requested that all divisions of the company study ways to save the company money. Many departments are overstaffed, but some departments are understaffed or are not scheduling employees efficiently. The warehouse has especially serious scheduling problems.

The warehouse division currently employs 64 employees and runs seven days a week. Each employee works a schedule of five days on, two days off. Under the current schedule, approximately 45 employees are scheduled each day, but this system creates problems. More employees are needed during the week, when the warehouse is at its busiest. The goal is to minimize the amount of payroll paid out each week, by reducing the staff required to meet the demand for each day. Sound like a complicated problem? It is, and that's why Solver is so useful.

To open the workbook and save it with a new name:

Step 1	Open	the *Warehouse Personnel Scheduling* workbook on your Data Disk
Step 2	Save	the workbook as *Warehouse Personnel Scheduling Solution* in your Data Files folder

This worksheet shows the scheduling for employees in the warehouse. The number of employees currently assigned to each shift appears in cells C5:C11, with the total number of employees being displayed in cell C13. Cells D13:J13 calculate the number of employees working each day by multiplying the number of employees on each shift by the on value of 1 or the off value of 2 for each day on the schedule. Cells D15:J15 indicate the actual numbers of employees that the warehouse needs on staff each day. Cells C18 and C19 calculate the payroll total for each week. Each warehouse employee is paid $70 per day.

To use Solver to create the most efficient schedule:

Step 1	Click	Tools
Step 2	Click	Solver

The Solver Parameters dialog box appears, as shown in Figure 16-8.

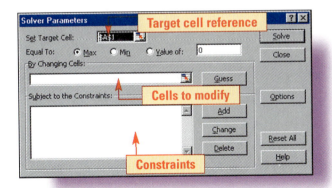

FIGURE 16-8
Solver Parameters Dialog Box

The goal of this activity is to reduce the total payroll, so cell C19 is the target. To set the Solver target:

Step 1	Click	cell C19
Step 2	Click	the Min option button next to Equal To:

Solver looks for the solution that results in the lowest possible value for the target cell C19. Next, you need to specify which cells can be changed to reach the goal.

To identify which cells can be changed:

Step 1	Click	the Collapse Dialog button 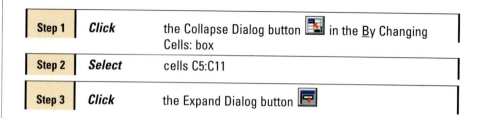 in the By Changing Cells: box
Step 2	Select	cells C5:C11
Step 3	Click	the Expand Dialog button

Solver now changes the number of employees on each shift to best reduce the amount of payroll paid each week. Before Solver eliminates the entire warehouse staff, you should apply some constraints. The first constraint is to make sure that at least one employee serves on each shift. Second, the number of employees on each shift must be greater than or equal to the total demand for each day. Finally, you need to force Excel to use whole numbers—after all, it's difficult to get 0.58 of a worker to appear at work on any given day.

To add constraints:

Step 1	Click	Add

The Add Constraint dialog box appears with the insertion point blinking in the Cell Reference box.

Step 2	Select	cells D13:J13
Step 3	Select	>= in the constraint type list (in the middle of the dialog box)
Step 4	Key	1 in the Constraint: box

Your screen should look similar to Figure 16-9.

FIGURE 16-9
Add Constraint Dialog Box

| Step 5 | Click | OK |

The constraint is displayed in the Subject to the Constraints list. Next, you add a constraint to ensure that the total demand for employees for each day is met.

To add this constraint:

Step 1	Click	Add
Step 2	Select	cells D13:J13 in the Cell Reference: box
Step 3	Select	>= in the constraint type list
Step 4	Select	cells D15:J15 in the Constraint: box

This constraint requires the values in cells D13:J13 to be greater than or equal to the values in cells D15:J15. You need the number of employees on each schedule to be a whole number, so you also apply an integer constraint.

| Step 5 | Click | Add |

This adds the constraint, and clears the Add Constraint dialog box for a new entry.

Step 6	Select	cells C5:C11
Step 7	Select	int in the constraint type list
Step 8	Click	OK
Step 9	Click	Solve

Depending on the worksheet and the speed of your computer, Solver may take a few seconds to perform its calculations. Solver figures out the solution, displays the results on your worksheet, and opens the Solver Results dialog box.

> **QUICK TIP**
>
> The Options button provides settings to optimize Solver's calculation methods; it also allows you to save and load Solver models for use in other worksheets. If you want to change the way that Solver calculates solutions, open the Solver dialog box, then click Options. Use the What's This? command or the Office Assistant to learn more about the Solver Options dialog box.

chapter sixteen

Your screen should look similar to Figure 16-10.

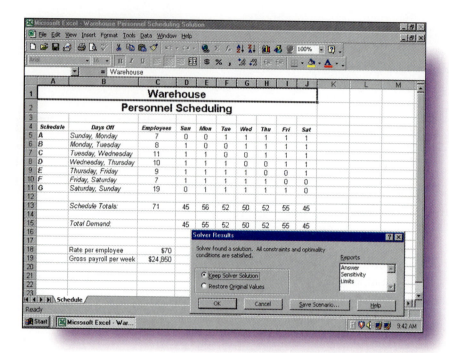

FIGURE 16-10
Solver Results Dialog Box

CAUTION TIP

Once you complete the Solver operation, you cannot undo it. Before closing the Solver Results dialog box, you have the option of restoring the original values. Click the Restore Original Values option button, then click OK.

Interestingly, the best solution for the warehouse is to add more employees. By doing so, Solver came up with a scheduling solution that provides the correct number of employees for each day of the week. Only once does the number of employees exceed the required number of employees.

Step 10	Click	Answer in the Reports list box
Step 11	Click	OK

The Answer Report 1 worksheet tab is added to your workbook.

Step 12	Click	the newly created Answer Report 1 worksheet tab

The Answer Report provides information about the calculations and constraints used by Solver to generate the solution. It displays information about the date on which this solution was created, and provides all data used in the solution, including the target cell, adjustable cells, and constraints. Original cell values are shown adjacent to the final cell values after Solver is run. Your screen should look similar to Figure 16-11.

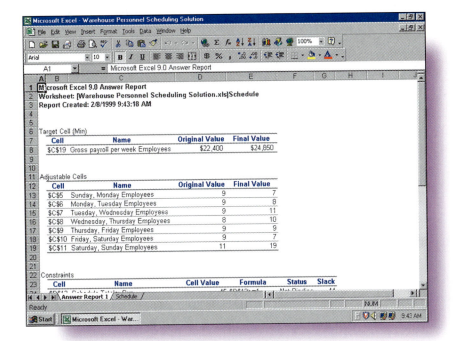

FIGURE 16-11
Solver Answer Report

> **QUICK TIP**
>
> To find out more information about the Limits and Sensitivity reports, use the Office Assistant.

| Step 13 | **Save** | the workbook |

16.c Creating Scenarios

The tools introduced in this chapter—data tables, Goal Seek, and Solver—are designed to allow you maximum flexibility in asking the question, "What if?" Many times, you need to quickly see the results of several "What if?" situations. For example, what if the current level of activity in the warehouse drops off? What if the current level of activity in the warehouse increases, as it always does during the holiday season?

The demand values in cells D15:J15 indicate how many employees are needed on a given day. By using scenarios, you can change the values contained in these cells and run Solver using the new set of values to find a solution that satisfies the constraints of the given scenario.

chapter sixteen

Creating Scenarios

Scenarios allow you to quickly replace the values in several cells with another set of values, which you can then use in formulas throughout the worksheet. To create scenarios:

Step 1	*Click*	the Schedule worksheet tab
Step 2	*Select*	cells D15:J15
Step 3	*Click*	Tools
Step 4	*Click*	Scenarios

The Scenario Manager dialog box appears, as shown in Figure 16-12.

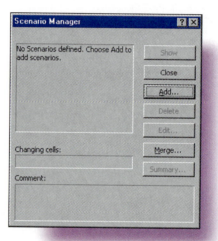

FIGURE 16-12
Scenario Manager Dialog Box

| Step 5 | *Click* | Add |

The Add Scenario dialog box opens. In this dialog box, you can name your scenario, select the cells to be changed under the new scenario, and add descriptive comments about your scenario.

Step 6	*Enter*	Normal Demand in the Scenario name: box
Step 7	*Verify*	that the Changing cells: box references D15:J15
Step 8	*Click*	at the end of the Created by…on MM/DD/YY comment in the Comment: box
Step 9	*Press*	the ENTER key

> **QUICK TIP**
>
> Drag the scroll box down to see the rest of the cells you selected.

| Step 10 | Key | This is normal demand for April-September. |
| Step 11 | Click | OK |

The Scenario Values dialog box appears, allowing you to enter different values for each of the changing cells. See Figure 16-13. Because the values currently in those cells are the Normal Demand values, you can leave them alone.

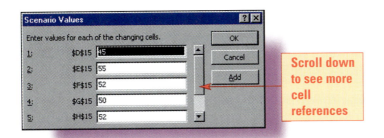

FIGURE 16-13
Scenario Values Dialog Box

QUICK TIP

Press the TAB key to move from box to box in the Scenarios Values dialog box.

Step 12	Click	OK to return to the Scenario Manager dialog box
Step 13	Click	Add and create another scenario named Low Demand that covers January-March
Step 14	Click	OK in the Add Scenario dialog box
Step 15	Key	20 in the 1: box next to D15
Step 16	Press	the TAB key
Step 17	Continue	replacing the current values in Table 16-1

Changing Cell	New Value
D15	20
E15	45
F15	45
G15	40
H15	45
I15	50
J15	20

TABLE 16-1
Low Demand

| Step 18 | Click | OK |
| Step 19 | Create | a scenario named High Demand that covers October-December and uses the values in Table 16-2 |

TABLE 16-2
High Demand

Changing Cell	New Value
D15	40
E15	60
F15	60
G15	60
H15	60
I15	65
J15	40

Displaying Scenarios

Once you've created different scenarios, you can display each one and replace the values in row 15, then run Solver to calculate the number of employees needed for each period.

To display different scenarios:

Step 1	Select	Low Demand in the Scenarios: list in the Scenario Manager dialog box
Step 2	Click	Show
Step 3	Click	Close

The values in cells D15:J15 have changed to display the scenario values you created.

Step 4	Click	Tools
Step 5	Click	Scenario
Step 6	Show	the High Demand scenario
Step 7	Click	Close

You can create a scenario report to display the values contained in each scenario. To create a scenario report:

Step 1	Open	the Scenario Manager dialog box
Step 2	Click	Summary
Step 3	Verify	that the Scenario summary option button is selected
Step 4	Click	OK

> **QUICK TIP**
>
> To show your scenario as a PivotTable, select the Scenario PivotTable option button. You must also select Result cells that perform calculations on the cells saved in your scenario(s).

A scenario summary is created and inserted on a new worksheet named Scenario Summary, which automatically becomes the active worksheet. Your summary should look similar to Figure 16-14.

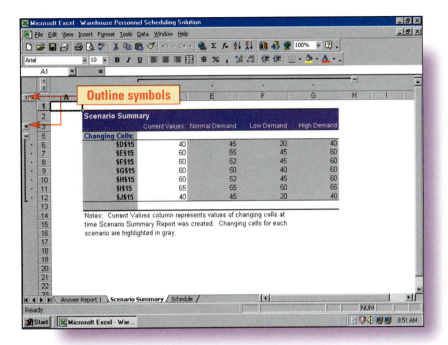

FIGURE 16-14
Scenario Summary

MOUSE TIP

Click the Outline symbols on the left to expand the outline and view the comments for each scenario.

This scenario summary lists the current values of the changing cells as well as the values for each of the defined scenarios.

Step 5	**Print**	the workbook
Step 6	**Save**	the workbook
Step 7	**Close**	the workbook

Using these different scenarios, you can run Solver to find the best solution for each period of the year.

QUICK TIP

Report Manager is a useful add-in that helps you create and organize a **report**, a combination of a worksheet, a custom view, and a scenario. Using Report Manager you can create multiple reports for each workbook, making it easy to print several different areas of your workbook at once. Once installed and activated in the Add-Ins dialog box, you can find the Report Manager command on the View menu. For more information about creating reports with Report Manager, use the Office Assistant.

chapter
sixteen

Summary

- Use a one-variable data table to replace one variable of a formula(s) with multiple values.
- Use a two-variable data table to replace two variables of a single formula with multiple values.
- Use Goal Seek to change the values of variables used in a formula to obtain a certain result.
- Use Solver to change the values of multiple cells and apply constraints to limit the changes of those cells so as to obtain a certain result.
- Create a solution report to summarize the changes made by Solver.
- Use scenarios to store cell values for different situations.
- Create a scenario report to see the information saved in Scenario Manager.

Commands Review

Action	Menu Bar	Shortcut Menu	Toolbar	Keyboard
Create a data table	Data, Table			ALT + D, T
Use Goal Seek	Tools, Goal Seek			ALT + T, G
Use Solver	Tools, Solver			ALT + T, V
Create scenarios	Tools, Scenarios			ALT + T, E

Concepts Review

Circle the correct answer.

1. If you want to see how different interest rates and different terms affect the payment of a loan, which of the following tools would you use?
   - [a] one-variable data table
   - [b] two-variable data table
   - [c] Solver
   - [d] Goal Seek

2. Solving complex business problems often requires you to:
   - [a] look at a problem several ways.
   - [b] know the expected outcome of a formula.
   - [c] perform a what-if analysis.
   - [d] all of the above.

3. Which of the following is not a Solver report?
   - [a] Answer
   - [b] Sensitivity
   - [c] Limits
   - [d] Scenario

4. Which of the following is not a setting used by Solver?
   - [a] Target
   - [b] Changing cells
   - [c] Constraints
   - [d] Summary

5. Goal Seek is useful when you:
   - [a] know the outcome and have to change only one variable.
   - [b] know the outcome and have to change multiple variables.
   - [c] don't know the outcome, but know one of the variables.
   - [d] don't know the outcome, but know two of the variables.

6. Constraints:
   - [a] cannot be modified.
   - [b] set limits regarding how much a cell's value can be changed.
   - [c] help Solver run faster.
   - [d] set limits regarding the speed at which Solver runs.

7. A what-if analysis can show you:
   - [a] how changing data affects various calculations.
   - [b] how to set up one-variable data tables if you don't know the value of any of the variables.
   - [c] which feature is the better choice to solve your problem—Goal Seek or Solver.
   - [d] which calculations change if you change a variable.

chapter sixteen

8. In a two-variable data table you can replace:
   [a] two variables in more than one formula.
   [b] two variables in a single formula.
   [c] one variable in two formulas.
   [d] one variable in one formula.

9. The Scenario Manager allows you to:
   [a] add a new scenario.
   [b] delete a scenario.
   [c] generate a Scenario Summary Report.
   [d] all of the above.

10. If you know the outcome you want for a given formula and can change multiple values, which tool should you use?
    [a] scenarios
    [b] Solver
    [c] one-variable data table
    [d] Goal Seek

Circle **T** if the statement is true or **F** if the statement is false.

T F 1. You can use more than one formula in a one-variable data table.

T F 2. You can use more than one formula in a two-variable data table.

T F 3. You can create a what-if analysis by manually changing the values of cells referenced in a formula.

T F 4. Goal Seek can create a report when it finds a solution.

T F 5. Solver is the best tool to use whenever you're trying to do a what-if analysis.

T F 6. Solver can create three different reports when it has found a solution.

T F 7. You can save a scenario from Solver.

T F 8. The formula for a two-variable data table must appear immediately above the column variables and immediately to the right of row variables.

T F 9. Once you run Solver, you cannot get back your original data.

T F 10. A Scenario Summary Report and the Solver Answer Report are the same thing.

Skills Review

Exercise 1

1. Open the *Warehouse Personnel Scheduling 2* file on your Data Disk.

2. Set up constraints in the Solver Parameters dialog box to accomplish the following:

   a. The goal is to reduce the value of cell C19 to a minimum.

   b. The values in cells C5:C11 can change, but must be integers and must be greater than or equal to 1.

   c. The values in cells D13:J13 must meet the total demand in cells D15:J15.

3. Solve the workbook and create an Answer Report.
4. Print the schedule and the Answer Report.
5. Save the workbook as *Warehouse Personnel Scheduling Solution 1*.

Exercise 2

1. Open the *Warehouse Personnel Scheduling Solution 1* workbook that you created in Exercise 1.
2. Create four scenarios called 1st Quarter, 2nd Quarter, 3rd Quarter, and 4th Quarter by changing cells D15:J15 on the Schedule tab. Values for each scenario are listed below:
    a. 1st Quarter—use values as currently set
    b. 2nd Quarter—D15=37, E15=54, F15=56, G15=56, H15=60, I15=52, J15=40
    c. 3rd Quarter—D15=35, E15=52, F15=52, G15=50, H15=55, I15=48, J15=37
    d. 4th Quarter—D15 = 45, E15 = 55, F15 = 55, G15 = 55, H15 = 60, I15 = 55, J15 = 45
3. Create and print the Answer Report.
4. Save the workbook as *Warehouse Personnel Scheduling Scenarios*.

Exercise 3

1. Open the *Warehouse Personnel Scheduling Scenarios* workbook that you created in Exercise 2.
2. Rename the Answer Report 1 tab to 1st Quarter Answer.
3. Show the 2nd Quarter scenario.
4. Run Solver and create an Answer Report.
5. Rename the tab 2nd Quarter Answer.
6. Repeat steps 3–5 to show the 3rd and 4th Quarter scenarios, run Solver and generate an Answer Report, and rename the Answer Report tab.
7. Print the Answer Report tabs.
8. Save the workbook as *Warehouse Personnel Scheduling Scenarios 2*.

Exercise 4

1. Open the *Warehouse Personnel Scheduling Scenarios 2* workbook that you created in Exercise 3.
2. Click the Schedule tab.
3. Generate a Scenario summary.
4. Print the Scenario summary.
5. Save the workbook as *Warehouse Personnel Scheduling Scenarios 3*.

Exercise 5

1. Open the *Home Purchase* workbook on your Data Disk.

2. Use Goal Seek to find the maximum amount of loan given the following:

   a. Use B8 as the goal, with a value of 650.

   b. Change the value in cell B5.

3. Save the workbook as *Home Purchase Loan* and print the workbook.

Exercise 6

1. Open the *System Purchase* file on your Data Disk.

2. Use Solver to find the optimum purchasing solution given the following parameters:

   a. Seek the minimum total purchase price in cell D7.

   b. Change cells C4:C7.

   c. Use the following constraints:
   C4:C7 must be integers.
   You need to buy at least 65 new computers.
   At least 15 computers need to be PII-450s.
   At least 20 computers need to be PII-333s.
   The total number of K6-2 333s cannot exceed 20.

3. Generate an Answer Report.

4. Print your solution and the Answer Report.

5. Save the workbook as *System Purchase Solution*.

Exercise 7

1. Open the *Manufacturing Production* workbook on your Data Disk.

2. Use Solver to find a solution to maximize total profit (cell G8). Use the following constraints.

   a. The number of cases to be produced can be changed with the constraints.

   b. Number of cases must be an integer.

   c. Number of cases of each product must be at least 1.

   d. Minimum number of A-123 to produce is 100.

   e. Maximum number of A-128 to produce is 25.

f. Minimum number of A-128 to produce is 10.

g. The total storage space must not exceed 25,000.

h. The maximum production hours is 80.

3. Create an Answer Report.
4. Print the Answer Report and the solution.
5. Create a scenario using the constraint values in cells B11:B15. Name it "Normal Production Schedule."
6. Save the workbook as *Manufacturing Production Solution*.

Exercise 8

1. Open the *Manufacturing Production Solution* workbook that you created in Exercise 7.
2. Create a new scenario, called Low Production Schedule, using the following constraint values:

    a. Warehouse storage available=15000

    b. Minimum A-123=75

    c. Maximum A-128=20

    d. Minimum A-128=10

    e. Total Production Hours=60

3. Create and print a solution for maximum profit.
4. Create another scenario called High Production Schedule using the following constraint values:

    a. Warehouse storage available=40000

    b. Minimum A-123=200

    c. Maximum A-128=50

    d. Minimum A-128=40

    e. Total production hours = 120

5. Create a solution for each of the above scenarios.
6. Create and print a solution for maximum profit.
7. Save the workbook as *Manufacturing Production Solution 2*, and close the workbook.

chapter sixteen

Case Projects

Project 1

You want to buy a new house. To buy the house you want, you need a loan of $100,000. You've been shopping for loans and found one offering an interest rate of 9.5% with a 15-year term, 8.5% with a 20-year term, 7.5% with a 25-year term, and 7% with a 20-year term. Use a data table(s) to calculate your monthly payments for each interest rate, and what your total interest would be for each loan. Save the workbook as *Home Loan Calculator*.

Project 2

Use the Web toolbar to search the Internet for Excel Solver tutorials. Locate at least one tutorial and print the Web page(s) containing the tutorial.

Project 3

You want to buy a car for $18,500. The car dealer has offered to finance your purchase at 8.5% for 48 months. You can afford to make payments of $250.00 per month. Use Goal Seek to find the maximum amount you can borrow at this interest rate. Save the workbook as *Car Loan* and print the solution.

Project 4

Use the Office Assistant to look up guidelines for designing a model to use with Solver. Write a two-paragraph summary describing what you learned. Save this document as *Creating Workbooks for Solver.doc*.

Project 5

Set up a budget for a sales company with an estimated gross sales income of $25,000 per month. Figure an amount for rent of $5,000, utilities and overhead of $5,000, payroll of $8,500, and advertising costs of $2,500. Set up a workbook to calculate the net profit or loss using these figures. Save the gross sales income, payroll, and advertising costs as a scenario called Best Case. Create a second scenario called Worst Case, with the following amounts: income = $17,500, payroll = $5,000, advertising = $1,000. Save the workbook as *Best and Worst Case Sales*.

Project 6

You are deciding between two jobs located in two different cities. Job offer #1 provides a salary of $35,000 per year. Job offer #2 includes a salary of $40,000 per year. Create a workbook to calculate a budget based on each scenario. In your budget, you estimate that 30% of your salary can be spent on house payments, 10% can be spent on car payments, 30% on living expenses, and 10% for savings. Also include a formula to sum the total budgeted expenses, then subtract this amount from the salary. Save the workbook as *Job Offers*.

Project 7

You would like to reduce the length of time needed to pay off your car loan. Instead of paying off the $10,000 loan (at 8%) in 48 months, you would like to see what your monthly payments would be if you paid off the loan in 42, 36, and 30 months. Create a one-variable table to calculate these payments, and save the workbook as *Quick Payoff*.

Project 8

You are applying for a student loan for college. You want to find out how much you can borrow at 5% interest, paid back over 120 payments (10 years) with a maximum payment of $150.00. Use Goal Seek to help you find the solution. Save the workbook as *Student Loan*.

Working with Windows 98

Appendix Overview

The Windows 98 operating system creates a workspace on your computer screen, called the desktop. The desktop is a graphical environment that contains icons you click with the mouse pointer to access your computer system resources or to perform a task such as opening a software application. This appendix introduces you to the Windows 98 desktop by describing the default desktop icons and showing how to access your computer resources, use menu commands and toolbar buttons to perform a task, and select dialog box options.

Learning Objectives

- Review the Windows 98 desktop
- Access your computer system resources
- Use menu commands and toolbar buttons
- Use the Start menu
- Review dialog box options
- Use Windows 98 shortcuts
- Understand the Recycle Bin
- Shut down Windows 98

appendix A

A.a Reviewing the Windows 98 Desktop

Whenever you start your computer, the Windows 98 operating system automatically starts and the Windows 98 desktop appears on your screen. To view the Windows 98 desktop:

Step 1	**Turn on**	your computer and monitor
Step 2	**Observe**	the Windows 98 desktop, as shown in Figure A-1

FIGURE A-1
Windows 98 Desktop

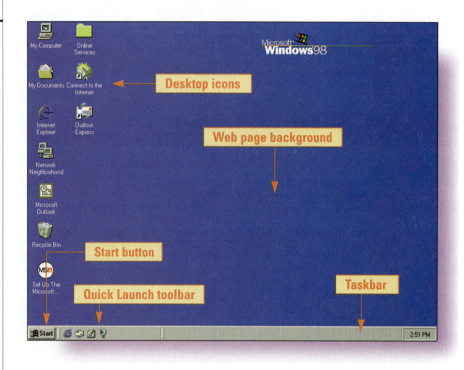

> ### QUICK TIP
>
> Internet **channels** are Web pages you subscribe to that automatically send updated information to your computer. An **active desktop** contains live Web content. You can create an active desktop by adding windows to the desktop that contain automatically updated Web pages. To add Web pages to your desktop, right-click the desktop, point to Active Desktop, click Customize my Desktop, and click the Web tab in the Display Properties dialog box. For more information on Active Desktop features, see online Help.

The Windows 98 desktop contains three elements: icons, background, and taskbar. The icons represent Windows objects and shortcuts to opening software applications or performing tasks. Table A-1 describes some of the default icons. By default, the background is Web-page style. The taskbar, at the bottom of the window, contains the Start button and the Quick Launch toolbar. The icon types and arrangement, desktop background, or Quick Launch toolbar on your screen might be different.

The Start button displays the Start menu, which you can use to perform tasks. By default, the taskbar also contains the **Quick Launch toolbar**, which has shortcuts to open Internet Explorer Web browser, Outlook Express e-mail software, and Internet channels, as well as to switch between the desktop and open application windows. You can customize the Quick Launch toolbar to include other toolbars.

TABLE A-1
Common Desktop Icons

Icon	Name	Description
	My Computer	Provides access to computer system resources
	My Documents	Stores Office 2000 documents (by default)
	Internet Explorer	Opens Internet Explorer Web browser
	Microsoft Outlook	Opens Outlook 2000 information manager software
	Recycle Bin	Temporarily stores folders and files deleted from the hard drive
	Network Neighborhood	Provides access to computers and printers networked in your workgroup

A.b Accessing Your Computer System Resources

The My Computer window provides access to your computer system resources. To open the My Computer window:

Step 1	*Point to*	the My Computer icon on the desktop
Step 2	*Observe*	a brief description of the icon in the ScreenTip
Step 3	*Double-click*	the My Computer icon to open the My Computer window shown in Figure A-2

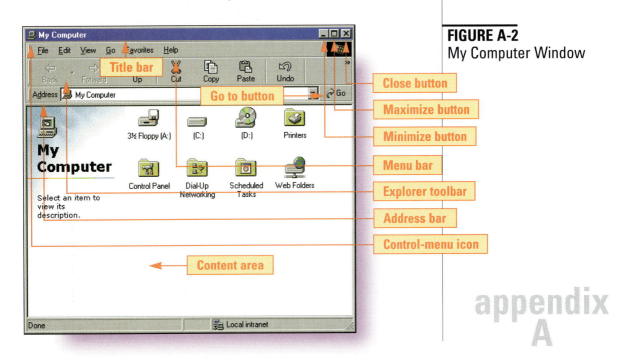

FIGURE A-2
My Computer Window

appendix A

MOUSE TIP

Point means to place the mouse pointer on the command or item. **Click** means to press the left mouse button and release it. **Right-click** means to press the right mouse button and release it. **Double-click** means to press the left mouse button twice very rapidly. **Drag** means to hold down the left mouse button as you move the mouse pointer. **Right-drag** means to hold down the right mouse button as you move the mouse pointer. **Scroll** means to use the application scroll bar features or the IntelliMouse scrolling wheel.

A window is a rectangular area on your screen in which you view operating system options or a software application, such as Internet Explorer. Windows 98 has some common window elements. The **title bar**, at the top of the window, includes the window's Control-menu icon, the window name, and the Minimize, Restore (or Maximize), and Close buttons. The **Control-menu icon**, in the upper-left corner of the window, accesses the Control menu that contains commands for moving, restoring, sizing, minimizing, maximizing, and closing the window. The **Minimize** button, near the upper-right corner of the window, reduces the window to a taskbar button. The **Maximize** button, to the right of the Minimize button, enlarges the window to fill the entire screen viewing area above the taskbar. If the window is already maximized, the Restore button appears in its place. The **Restore** button reduces the window size. The **Close** button, in the upper-right corner, closes the window. To maximize the My Computer window:

Step 1	Click	the Maximize button on the My Computer window title bar
Step 2	Observe	that the My Computer window completely covers the desktop

When you want to leave a window open, but do not want to see it on the desktop, you can minimize it. To minimize the My Computer window:

Step 1	Click	the Minimize button on the My Computer window title bar
Step 2	Observe	the My Computer button added to the taskbar

The minimized window is still open but not occupying space on the desktop. To view the My Computer window and then restore it to a smaller size:

Step 1	Click	the My Computer button on the taskbar to view the window
Step 2	Click	the Restore button on the My Computer title bar
Step 3	Observe	that the My Computer window is reduced to a smaller window on the desktop

You can move and size a window with the mouse pointer. To move the My Computer window:

Step 1	Position	the mouse pointer on the My Computer title bar

| Step 2 | **Drag** | the window down and to the right approximately ½ inch |
| Step 3 | **Drag** | the window back to the center of the screen |

Several Windows 98 windows—My Computer, My Documents, and Windows Explorer—have the same menu bar and toolbar features. These windows are sometimes called **Explorer-style windows**. When you size an Explorer-style window too small to view all its icons, a vertical or horizontal scroll bar may appear. A scroll bar includes scroll arrows and a scroll box for viewing different parts of the window contents.

To size the My Computer window:

Step 1	**Position**	the mouse pointer on the lower-right corner of the window
Step 2	**Observe**	that the mouse pointer becomes a black, double-headed sizing pointer
Step 3	**Drag**	the lower-right corner boundary diagonally up approximately ½ inch and release the mouse button
Step 4	**Click**	the right scroll arrow on the horizontal scroll bar to view hidden icons
Step 5	**Size**	the window twice as large to remove the horizontal scroll bar

> **QUICK TIP**
>
> The Explorer-style windows and the Internet Explorer Web browser are really one Explorer feature integrated into Windows 98 that you can use to find information on your hard drive, network, company intranet, or the Web. Explorer-style windows have a Web-browser look and features. You can use Internet Explorer to access local information by keying the path in the Address bar or clicking an item on the F̲avorites list.

You can open the window associated with any icon in the My Computer window by double-clicking it. Explorer-style windows open in the same window, not separate windows. To open the Control Panel Explorer-style window:

| Step 1 | **Double-click** | the Control Panel icon |
| Step 2 | **Observe** | that the Address bar displays the Control Panel icon and name, and the content area displays the Control Panel icons for accessing computer system resources |

A.c Using Menu Commands and Toolbar Buttons

> **MOUSE TIP**
>
> You can display four taskbar toolbars: Quick Launch, Address, Links, and Desktop. The Quick Launch toolbar appears on the taskbar by default. You can also create additional toolbars from other folders or subfolders and you can add folder or file shortcuts to an existing taskbar toolbar. To view other taskbar toolbars, right-click the taskbar, point to T̲oolbars, and then click the desired toolbar name.

You can click a menu command or toolbar button to perform specific tasks in a window. The **menu bar** is a special toolbar located below the window title bar that contains the F̲ile, E̲dit, V̲iew, G̲o, F̲avorites, and H̲elp menus. The **toolbar**, located below the menu bar, contains shortcut "buttons" you click with the mouse pointer to execute a variety of commands. You can use the Back and Forward

QUICK TIP

You can use Start menu commands to create or open Office 2000 documents, connect to the Microsoft Web site to download operating system updates, open software applications, open a favorite folder or file, or open one of the last fifteen documents you worked on. You can also change the Windows 98 settings, search for files, folders, and resources on the Internet, get online Help, run software applications, log off a network, and shut down Windows 98.

buttons on the Explorer toolbar or the Back or Forward commands on the Go menu to switch between My Computer and the Control Panel. To view My Computer:

Step 1	Click	the Back button ⬅ on the Explorer toolbar to view My Computer
Step 2	Click	the Forward button ➡ on the Explorer toolbar to view the Control Panel
Step 3	Click	Go on the menu bar
Step 4	Click	the My Computer command to view My Computer
Step 5	Click	the Close button ❌ on the My Computer window title bar

A.d Using the Start Menu

The **Start button** on the taskbar opens the Start menu. You use this menu to access several Windows 98 features and to open software applications, such as Word or Excel. To open the Start menu:

| Step 1 | Click | the Start button 🏁Start on the taskbar to open the Start menu (see Figure A-3) |

FIGURE A-3
Start Menu

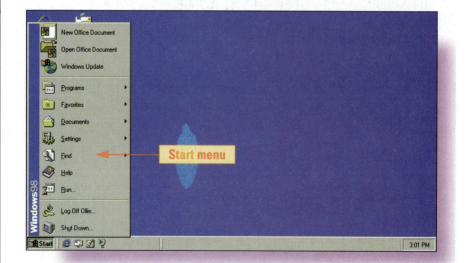

| Step 2 | Point to | Programs to view the software applications installed on your computer |
| Step 3 | Click | the desktop outside the Start menu and Programs menu to close them |

A.e Reviewing Dialog Box Options

A **dialog box** is a window that contains options you can select, turn on, or turn off to perform a task. To view a dialog box:

Step 1	Click	the Start button [Start] on the taskbar
Step 2	Point to	Settings
Step 3	Point to	Active Desktop
Step 4	Click	Customize my Desktop to open the Display Properties dialog box
Step 5	Click	the Effects tab (see Figure A-4)

> **QUICK TIP**
>
> Many dialog boxes contain sets of options on different pages organized on **tabs** you click. Options include drop-down lists you view by clicking an arrow, text boxes in which you key information, check boxes and option buttons you click to turn on or off an option, and buttons that access additional options.

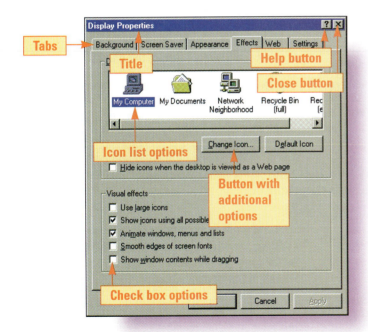

FIGURE A-4
Effects Tab in the Display Properties Dialog Box

Step 6	Click	each tab and observe the different options available (do not change any options unless directed by your instructor)
Step 7	Right-click	each option on each tab and then click What's This? to view its ScreenTip
Step 8	Click	Cancel to close the dialog box without changing any options

A.f Using Windows 98 Shortcuts

> **QUICK TIP**
>
> Many of the Windows 98 shortcuts are also available in Windows 95 and NT 4.0 if you have Internet Explorer 4.0 or later and Windows Desktop Update installed.

You can use the drag-and-drop method to reposition or remove Start menu commands. You can also right-drag a Start menu command to the desktop to create a desktop shortcut. To reposition the Windows Update item on the Start menu:

Step 1	Click	the Start button [Start] on the taskbar
Step 2	Point to	the Windows Update item
Step 3	Drag	the Windows Update item to the top of the Start menu

To remove the Windows Update shortcut from the Start menu and create a desktop shortcut:

Step 1	Drag	the Windows Update item to the desktop
Step 2	Observe	that the desktop shortcut appears after a few seconds
Step 3	Verify	that the Windows Update item no longer appears on the Start menu

To add a Windows Update shortcut back to the Start menu and delete the desktop shortcut:

Step 1	Drag	the Windows Update shortcut to the Start button [Start] on the taskbar and then back to its original position when the Start menu appears
Step 2	Close	the Start menu
Step 3	Drag	the Windows Update shortcut on the desktop to the Recycle Bin
Step 4	Click	Yes

> **MOUSE TIP**
>
> One way to speed up tasks is to single-click (rather than double-click) a desktop icon just like you single-click a Web page hyperlink. You can create a Web-style, single-click environment by opening the Folder Options dialog box from the View menu in any Windows 98 Explorer-style window or from the Settings command on the Start menu. The Web Style option adds an underline to icon titles, similar to a hyperlink.

You can close multiple application windows at one time from the taskbar using the CTRL key and a shortcut menu. To open two applications and then use the taskbar to close them:

Step 1	Open	the Word and Excel applications (in this order) from the Programs menu on the Start menu

Step 2	Observe	the Word and Excel buttons on the taskbar (Excel is the selected, active button)
Step 3	Press & Hold	the CTRL key
Step 4	Click	the Word application taskbar button (the Excel application taskbar button is already selected)
Step 5	Release	the CTRL key
Step 6	Right-click	the Word or Excel taskbar button
Step 7	Click	Close to close both applications

You can use the drag-and-drop method to add a shortcut to the Quick Launch toolbar for folders and documents you have created. To create a new subfolder in the My Documents folder.

Step 1	Click	the My Documents icon on the desktop to open the window
Step 2	Right-click	the contents area (but not a file or folder)
Step 3	Point to	New
Step 4	Click	Folder
Step 5	Key	Example
Step 6	Press	the ENTER key to name the folder
Step 7	Drag	the Example folder to the end of the Quick Launch toolbar (a black vertical line indicates the drop position)
Step 8	Observe	the new icon on the toolbar
Step 9	Close	the My Documents window
Step 10	Position	the mouse pointer on the Example folder shortcut on the Quick Launch toolbar and observe the ScreenTip

You remove a shortcut from the Quick Launch toolbar by dragging it to the desktop and deleting it, or dragging it directly to the Recycle Bin. To remove the Example folder shortcut and delete the folder:

Step 1	Drag	the Example folder icon to the Recycle Bin
Step 2	Click	Yes
Step 3	Open	the My Documents window
Step 4	Delete	the Example folder icon using the shortcut menu
Step 5	Close	the My Documents window

CAUTION TIP

Selecting items in a single-click environment requires some practice. To **select** (or highlight) one item, simply point to the item. *Be careful not to click the item; clicking the item opens it.*

You can use the SHIFT + Click and CTRL + Click commands in the single-click environment. Simply *point to* the first item. Then press and hold the SHIFT or CTRL key and *point to* the last item or the next item to be selected.

MENU TIP

In the Windows environment, clicking the right mouse button displays a **shortcut menu** of the most commonly used commands for the item you right-clicked. For example, you can use a shortcut menu to open applications from the Programs submenu. You can right-drag to move, copy, or create desktop shortcuts from Start menu commands.

appendix A

MENU TIP

You can open the Recycle Bin by right-clicking the Recycle Bin icon on the desktop and clicking Open. To restore an item to your hard drive after opening the Recycle Bin, click the item to select it and then click the Restore command on the File menu. You can also restore an item by opening the Recycle Bin, right-clicking an item, and clicking Restore.

To empty the Recycle Bin, right-click the Recycle Bin icon and click Empty Recycle Bin.

A.g Understanding the Recycle Bin

The **Recycle Bin** is an object that temporarily stores folders, files, and shortcuts you delete from your hard drive. If you accidentally delete an item, you can restore it to its original location on your hard drive if it is still in the Recycle Bin. Because the Recycle Bin takes up disk space you should review and empty it regularly. When you empty the Recycle Bin, its contents are removed from your hard drive and can no longer be restored.

A.h Shutting Down Windows 98

It is very important that you follow the proper procedures for shutting down the Windows 98 operating system when you are finished, to allow the operating system to complete its internal "housekeeping" properly. To shut down Windows 98 correctly:

| Step 1 | Click | the Start button [Start] on the taskbar |
| Step 2 | Click | Shut Down to open the Shut Down Windows dialog box shown in Figure A-5 |

FIGURE A-5
Shut Down Windows Dialog Box

You can shut down completely, restart, and restart in MS-DOS mode from this dialog box. You want to shut down completely.

| Step 3 | Click | the Shut down option button to select it, if necessary |
| Step 4 | Click | OK |

Managing Your Folders and Files Using Windows Explorer

Appendix Overview

Windows Explorer provides tools for managing your folders and files. This appendix introduces the Windows Explorer options of expanding and collapsing the folder view, creating new folders, renaming folders and files, deleting folders and files, and creating desktop shortcuts.

LEARNING OBJECTIVES

- ▶ Open Windows Explorer
- ▶ Review Windows Explorer options
- ▶ Create a new folder
- ▶ Move and copy folders and files
- ▶ Rename folders and files
- ▶ Create desktop shortcuts
- ▶ Delete folders and files

appendix

> **notes** The default Windows 98 Custom folder options are used in the hands-on activities and figures. If you are using the Windows 95 operating system, your instructor will modify the hands-on activities and your screen will look different.

B.a Opening Windows Explorer

You can open Windows Explorer from the Programs command on the Start menu or from a shortcut menu. To open Windows Explorer using a shortcut menu:

Step 1	*Right-Click*	the Start button on the taskbar
Step 2	*Click*	Explore
Step 3	*Maximize*	the Windows Explorer window, if necessary (see Figure B-1)

FIGURE B-1
Windows Explorer Window

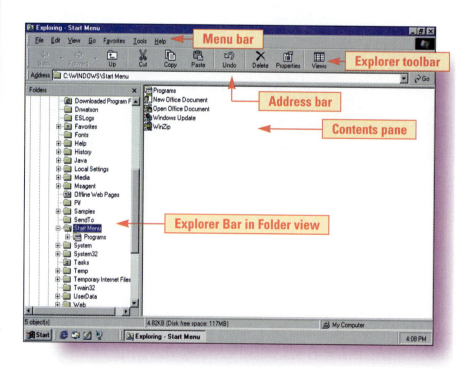

QUICK TIP

You can also use the My Computer Explorer-style window to manage your files and folders. If you are using Windows 95, the list of disk drives and folders is called the **Tree pane**.

The window below the menu bar, toolbar, and Address bar is divided into two panes: The **Explorer Bar** on the left shows the computer's organizational structure, including all desktop objects, My Computer objects, and the disk drive folders. The **Contents pane** on the right shows all subfolders and files for the folder selected in the Explorer Bar. The panes are divided by a **separator bar** that you drag left or right to resize the panes.

B.b Reviewing Windows Explorer Options

You can view disk drive icons, folders, and files (called **objects**) for your computer by selecting an item from the Address bar list or by clicking an object in the Explorer Bar. To view all your computer's disk drives and system folders:

Step 1	Click	the Address bar list arrow
Step 2	Click	My Computer to view a list of disk drives and system folders in the Contents pane
Step 3	Click	the (C:) disk drive object in the Explorer Bar to view a list of folders (stored on the C:\ drive) in the Contents pane

You can expand or collapse the view of folders and other objects in the Explorer Bar. To collapse the view of the C:\ drive in the Explorer Bar:

Step 1	Click	the minus sign (–) to the left of the (C:) disk drive object in the Explorer Bar
Step 2	Observe	that the C:\ drive folders list is hidden and the minus sign becomes a plus sign (+)
Step 3	Click	the plus sign (+) to the left of the (C:) disk drive object in the Explorer Bar
Step 4	Observe	that the list of folders stored on the C:\ drive is again visible

You can view a folder's contents by clicking the folder in the Explorer Bar or double-clicking the folder in the Contents pane. To view the contents of the folder that contains the Data Files:

Step 1	Click	the disk drive in the Explorer Bar where the Data Files are stored

MOUSE TIP

Point means to place the mouse pointer on the command or item. **Click** means to press the left mouse button and release it. **Right-click** means to press the right mouse button and release it. **Double-click** means to press the left mouse button twice very rapidly. **Drag** means to hold down the left mouse button and then move the mouse pointer. **Right-drag** means to hold down the right mouse button and then move the mouse pointer. **Scroll** means to use the application scroll bar features or the IntelliMouse scrolling wheel.

MENU TIP

By default, the Explorer Bar shows your local and network folders. This is the Explorer Bar Folder view option. You can view Internet resources and a list of favorites by clicking View, pointing to Explorer Bar, and clicking Search, Favorites, or History.

> **QUICK TIP**
>
> The minus sign (–) indicates all the items stored in that object are displayed, or expanded, below the icon. The plus sign (+) indicates these items are hidden, or collapsed.
>
> You can sort the list of files and folders by name, size, type, and date modified in ascending or descending order by clicking the Name, Size, Type, or Modified buttons above the list in the Contents pane.

| Step 2 | *Double-click* | the Data Files folder in the Contents pane (scroll, if necessary) to view a list of Data Files and folders |

You can resize and reposition folders and files in the Contents pane and add more details about the file size, type, and date modified. To change the size and position of the Data Files and folders:

Step 1	*Click*	the Views button list arrow on the Explorer toolbar
Step 2	*Click*	Large Icons to view horizontal rows of larger folder and file icons in the Contents pane
Step 3	*Click*	Small Icons on the Views button list to view horizontal rows of smaller folder and file icons in the Contents pane
Step 4	*Click*	Details on the Views button list to view a vertical list of folders and files names, sizes, types, and dates modified
Step 5	*Click*	List on the Views button list to view a simple list of the files and folders

B.c Creating a New Folder

You can create a new folder for an object in the Explorer Bar or the Contents pane. To add a folder to the My Documents folder in the C:\ drive folder list:

Step 1	*Click*	the My Documents folder in the Explorer Bar to select it (scroll, if necessary)
Step 2	*Click*	File
Step 3	*Point to*	New
Step 4	*Click*	Folder
Step 5	*Observe*	the newly created folder object in the Contents pane with the selected temporary name New Folder

> **CAUTION TIP**
>
> After you move or copy files or folders or add or remove files or folders, you may need to refresh the view of the folder list in the Explorer Bar and the Contents pane to see the changes. Click the Refresh command on the View menu.

To name the folder and refresh the Explorer Bar view:

Step 1	*Key*	Practice Folder
Step 2	*Press*	the ENTER key
Step 3	*Observe*	the new folder name in the Contents pane
Step 4	*Click*	View

Step 5	Click	Refresh
Step 6	Observe	that the My Documents folder has a plus sign, indicating that the folder list can be expanded

B.d Moving and Copying Folders and Files

You select folders and files by clicking them. You can then copy or move them with the Cut, Copy and Paste commands on the Edit menu or shortcut menu, the Copy and Paste buttons on the Explorer toolbar, or with the drag-and-drop or right-drag mouse methods. To copy a file from the Data Files folder to the Practice Folder using the right-drag method:

Step 1	View	the list of Data Files in the Contents pane
Step 2	Right-drag	any file to the My Documents folder in the Explorer Bar and pause until the My Documents folder expands to show the subfolders
Step 3	Continue	to right-drag the file to the Practice Folder subfolder under the My Documents folder in the Explorer Bar
Step 4	Click	Copy Here on the shortcut menu
Step 5	Click	the Practice Folder in the Explorer Bar to view the copied file's icon and filename in the Contents pane

B.e Renaming Folders and Files

Sometimes you want to change an existing file or folder name to a more descriptive name. To rename the copied file in the Practice Folder:

Step 1	Verify	the icon and filename for the copied file appears in the Contents pane
Step 2	Right-click	the copied file in the Contents pane
Step 3	Click	Rename
Step 4	Key	Renamed File
Step 5	Click	the Contents area (not the filename) to accept the new filename

MOUSE TIP

You can use the SHIFT + Click method to select adjacent multiple folders and files in the Contents pane by clicking the first item to select it, holding down the SHIFT key, and then clicking the last item. You can use the CTRL + Click method to select nonadjacent files and folders in the Contents pane by clicking the first item, holding down the CTRL key, and then clicking each additional item.

MENU TIP

You can quickly copy a file to a disk from a hard disk or network drive, create a desktop shortcut, or send the file as an attachment to an e-mail message by right-clicking the file, pointing to Send To, and clicking the appropriate command.

> **QUICK TIP**
>
> To erase all the files stored on a disk, you can reformat it. Insert a used disk in drive A, right-click the drive A icon in the Explorer Bar, and click For_m_at. Specify the disk's capacity. Select the _F_ull option to erase all files and check the disk for bad sectors. Click the _S_tart button.

B.f Creating Desktop Shortcuts

You can add a shortcut for folders and files to the Windows desktop by restoring the Windows Explorer window to a smaller window and right-dragging a folder or file icon to the desktop. You can also right-drag a folder or file icon to the Desktop icon in the Explorer Bar inside the Windows Explorer window. To create a desktop shortcut to the Practice Folder using the Desktop icon:

Step 1	Expand	the My Documents folder in the Explorer Bar, if necessary, to view the Practice Folder subfolder
Step 2	Right-drag	the Practice Folder to the Desktop icon at the top of the Explorer Bar
Step 3	Click	Create _S_hortcut(s) Here
Step 4	Minimize	the Windows Explorer window to view the new shortcut on the desktop
Step 5	Drag	the Shortcut to Practice Folder desktop shortcut to the Recycle Bin to delete it
Step 6	Click	_Y_es
Step 7	Click	the Exploring-Practice Folder taskbar button to maximize the Windows Explorer window

B.g Deleting Folders and Files

When necessary, you can delete a folder and its contents or a file by selecting it and then clicking the _D_elete command on the _F_ile menu or shortcut menu, or pressing the DELETE key. You can also delete multiple selected folders and files at one time. To delete the Practice Folder and its contents:

Step 1	Click	the Practice Folder in the Explorer Bar to select it, if necessary
Step 2	Press	the DELETE key
Step 3	Click	_Y_es to send the folder and its contents to the Recycle Bin

> **MOUSE TIP**
>
> You can delete a file or folder by dragging or right-dragging it to the Recycle Bin object on the desktop or the Recycle Bin object in the Explorer Bar. If you hold down the SHIFT key while dragging the file or folder to the Recycle Bin, Windows deletes the file or folder without placing it in the Recycle Bin.

Formatting Tips for Business Documents

Appendix Overview

Most organizations follow specific formatting guidelines when preparing letters, envelopes, memorandums, and other documents to ensure the documents present a professional appearance. In this appendix you learn how to format different size letters, interoffice memos, envelopes, and formal outlines. You also review a list of style guides and learn how to use proofreader's marks.

Learning Objectives

- ▶ Format letters
- ▶ Insert mailing notations
- ▶ Format envelopes
- ▶ Format interoffice memorandums
- ▶ Format formal outlines
- ▶ Use proofreader's marks
- ▶ Use style guides

appendix C

C.a Formatting Letters

The quality and professionalism of a company's business correspondence can affect how customers, clients, and others view a company. That correspondence represents the company to those outside it. To ensure a positive and appropriate image, many companies set special standards for margins, typeface, and font size for their business correspondence. These special standards are based on the common letter styles illustrated in this section.

Most companies use special letter paper with the company name and address (and sometimes a company logo or picture) preprinted on the paper. The preprinted portion is called a **letterhead** and the paper is called **letterhead paper**. When you create a letter, the margins vary depending on the style of your letterhead and the length of your letter. Most letterheads use between 1 inch and 2 inches of the page from the top of the sheet. There are two basic business correspondence formats: block format and modified block format. When you create a letter in **block format**, all the text is placed flush against the left margin. This includes the date, the letter address information, the salutation, the body, the complimentary closing, and the signature information. The body of the letter is single spaced with a blank line between paragraphs.[1] Figure C-1 shows a short letter in the block format with standard punctuation.

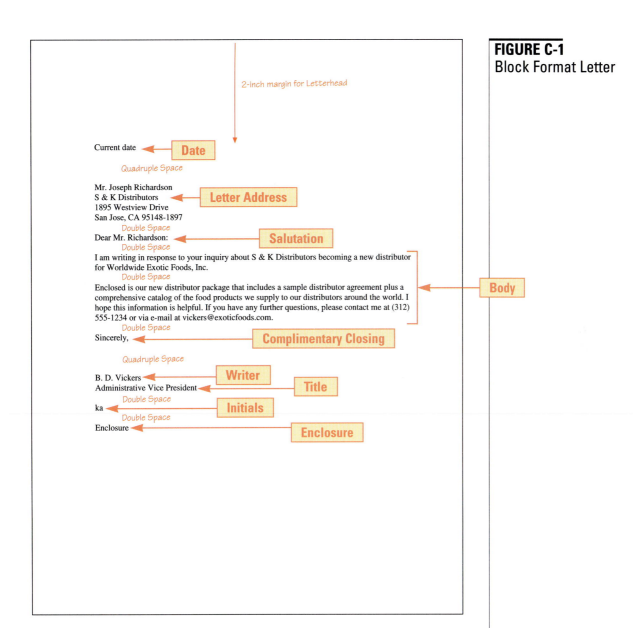

FIGURE C-1
Block Format Letter

appendix C

Quick Tip

When you key a letter on plain paper in the modified block format, the return address usually appears near the right margin and above the date, with one blank line between the return address and the date.

In the **modified block format**, the date begins near the center of the page or near the right margin. The closing starts near the center or right margin. Paragraphs can be either flush against the left margin or indented. Figure C-2 shows a short letter in the modified block format with standard punctuation.

Both the block and modified block styles use the same spacing for the non-body portions. Three blank lines separate the date from the addressee information, one blank line separates the addressee information from the salutation, one blank line separates the salutation from the body of the letter, and one blank line separates the body of the letter from the complimentary closing. There are three blank lines between the complimentary closing and the writer's name. If a typist's initials appear below the name, a blank line separates the writer's name from the initials. If an enclosure is noted, the word "Enclosure" appears below the typist's initials with a blank line separating them. Finally, when typing the return address or addressee information, one space separates the state and the postal code (ZIP+4).

Formatting Tips for Business Documents — AP 21

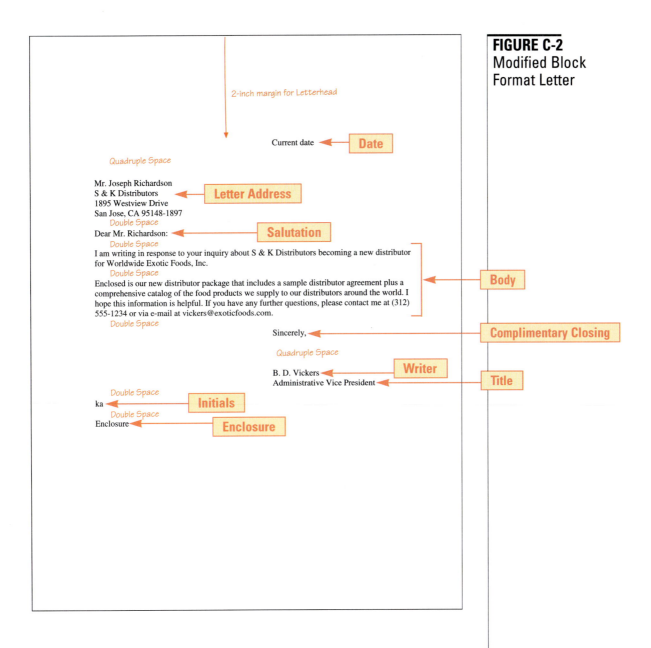

FIGURE C-2
Modified Block Format Letter

C.b Inserting Mailing Notations

Mailing notations add information to a business letter. For example, the mailing notations CERTIFIED MAIL or SPECIAL DELIVERY indicate how a business letter was sent. The mailing notations CONFIDENTIAL or PERSONAL indicate how the person receiving the letter should handle the letter contents. Mailing notations should be keyed in uppercase characters at the left margin two lines below the date.[2] Figure C-3 shows a mailing notation added to a block format business letter.

Formatting Tips for Business Documents AP 23

FIGURE C-3
Mailing Notation on Letter

Current date
Double Space
CERTIFIED MAIL ← **Mailing Notation**
Double Space
Mr. Joseph Richardson
S & K Distributors
1895 Westview Drive
San Jose, CA 95148-1897

Dear Mr. Richardson:

I am writing in response to your inquiry about S & K Distributors becoming a new distributor for Worldwide Exotic Foods, Inc.

Enclosed is our new distributor package that includes a sample distributor agreement plus a comprehensive catalog of the food products we supply to our distributors around the world. I hope this information is helpful. If you have any further questions, please contact me at (312) 555-1234 or via e-mail at vickers@exoticfoods.com.

Sincerely,

B. D. Vickers
Administrative Vice President

ka

Enclosure

appendix C

C.c Formatting Envelopes

Two U. S. Postal Service publications, *The Right Way* (Publication 221), and *Postal Addressing Standards* (Publication 28) available from the U. S. Post Office, provide standards for addressing letter envelopes. The U. S. Postal Service uses optical character readers (OCRs) and barcode sorters (BCSs) to increase the speed, efficiency, and accuracy in processing mail. To get a letter delivered more quickly, envelopes should be addressed to take advantage of this automation process.

Table C-1 lists the minimum and maximum size for letters. The post office cannot process letters smaller than the minimum size. Letters larger than the maximum size cannot take advantage of automated processing and must be processed manually.

TABLE C-1
Minimum and Maximum Letter Dimensions

Dimension	Minimum	Maximum
Height	3½ inches	6⅛ inches
Length	5 inches	11½ inches
Thickness	.007 inch	¼ inch

The delivery address should be placed inside a rectangular area on the envelope that is approximately ⅝ inch from the top and bottom edge of the envelope and ½ inch from the left and right edge of the envelope. This is called the **OCR read area**. All the lines of the delivery address must fit within this area and no lines of the return address should extend into this area. To assure the delivery address is placed in the OCR read area, begin the address approximately ½ inch left of center and on approximately line 14.[3]

Formatting Tips for Business Documents

The lines of the delivery address should be in this order:

1. any optional nonaddress data, such as advertising or company logos, must be placed above the delivery address
2. any information or attention line
3. the name of the recipient
4. the street address
5. the city, state, and postal code (ZIP+4)

The delivery address should be complete, including apartment or suite numbers and delivery designations, such as RD (road), ST (street), or NW (northwest). Leave the area below and on both sides of the delivery address blank. Use uppercase characters and a sans serif font (such as Arial) for the delivery address. Omit all punctuation except the hyphen in the ZIP+4 code.

Figure C-4 shows a properly formatted business letter envelope.

> **QUICK TIP**
>
> Foreign addresses should include the country name in uppercase characters as the last line of the delivery address. The postal code, if any, should appear on the same line as the city.

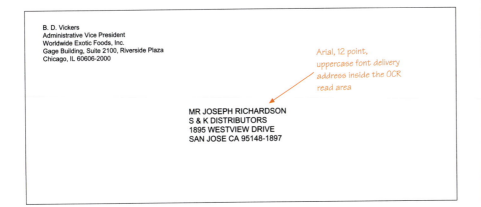

FIGURE C-4
Business Letter Envelope

appendix C

C.d Formatting Interoffice Memorandums

Business correspondence that is sent within a company is usually prepared as an **interoffice memorandum**, also called a **memo**, rather than a letter. There are many different interoffice memo styles used in offices today, and word processing applications usually provide several memo templates based on different memo styles. Also, just as with business letters that are sent outside the company, many companies set special standards for margins, typeface, and font size for their interoffice memos.

A basic interoffice memo should include lines for "TO:", "FROM:", "DATE:", and "SUBJECT:" followed by the body text. Memos can be prepared on blank paper or on paper that includes a company name and even a logo. The word MEMORANDUM is often included. Figure C-5 shows a basic interoffice memorandum.

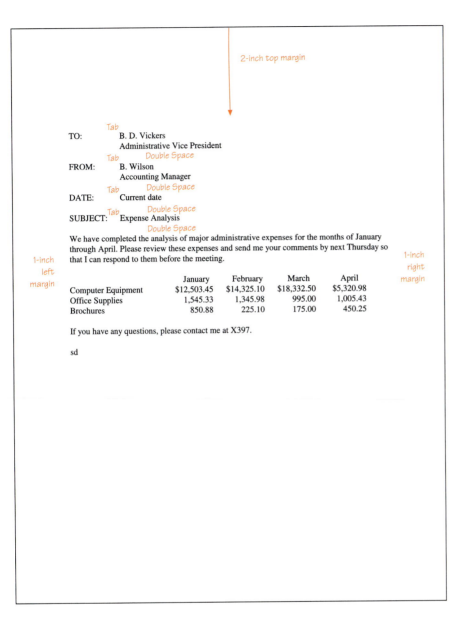

FIGURE C-5
Interoffice Memorandum

C.e Formatting Formal Outlines

Companies use outlines to organize data for a variety of purposes, such as reports, meeting agenda, and presentations. Word processing applications usually offer special features to help you create an outline. If you want to follow a formal outline format, you may need to add formatting to outlines created with these special features.

Margins for a short outline of two or three topics should be set at 1½ inches for the top margin and 2 inches for the left and right margins. For a longer outline, use a 2-inch top margin and 1-inch left and right margins.

The outline level-one text should be in uppercase characters. Second-level text should be treated like a title, with the first letter of the main words capitalized. Capitalize only the first letter of the first word at the third level. Double space before and after level one and single space the remaining levels.

Include at least two parts at each level. For example, you must have two level-one entries in an outline (at least I. and II.). If there is a second level following a level-one entry, it must contain at least two entries (at least A. and B.). All numbers must be aligned at the period and all subsequent levels must begin under the text of the preceding level, not under the number.[4]

Figure C-6 shows a formal outline prepared using the Word Outline Numbered list feature with additional formatting to follow a formal outline.

Formatting Tips for Business Documents AP 29

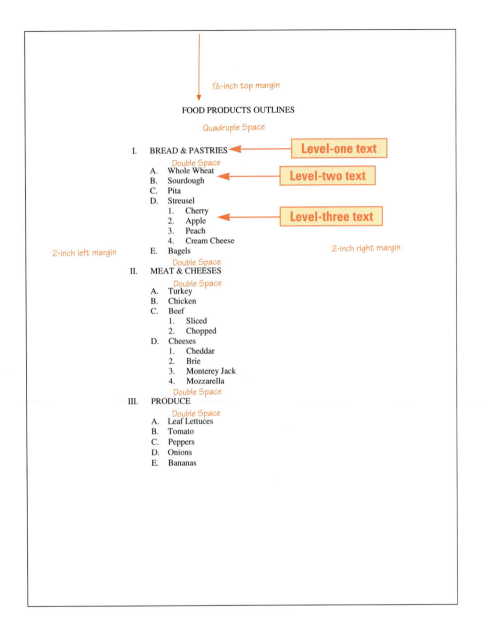

FIGURE C-6
Formal Outline

C.f Using Proofreader's Marks

Standard proofreader's marks enable an editor or proofreader to make corrections or change notations in a document that can be recognized by anyone familiar with the marks. The following list illustrates standard proofreader's marks.

Defined	Mark	Examples
Paragraph	¶	¶ Begin a new paragraph at this
Insert a character	∧	point. Ins∧rt a letter here.
Delete	ℓ	Delete these words. Disregard
Do not change	stet or ...	the previous correction. To
Transpose	tr	transpose is to around turn.
Move to the left	⌐	⌐Move this copy to the left.
Move to the right	⌐	⌐Move this copy to the right.
No paragraph	No ¶	No ¶ Do not begin a new paragraph
Delete and close up	ℓ̃	here. Delete the hyphen from pre-empt and close up the space.
Set in caps	Caps or ≡	a sentence begins with a capital
Set in lower case	lc or /	letter. This Word should not
Insert a period	⊙	be capitalized. Insert a period⊙
Quotation marks	∨∨	∨∨Quotation marks and a comma
Comma	∧	should be placed here∧ he said.
Insert space	#	Space between these#words. An
Apostrophe	∨	apostrophe is what∨s needed here.
Hyphen	=	Add a hyphen to Kilowatt=hour. Close
Close up	⌒	up the extra spa⌒ce.
Use superior figure	∨	Footnote this sentence.∨ Set
Set in italic	ital. or ___	the words, sine qua non, in italics.
Move up	⊔	This word is too ⊔low.⊔ That word is
Move down	⊓	too ⊓high.⊓

C.g Using Style Guides

A **style guide** provides a set of rules for punctuating and formatting text. There are a number of style guides used by writers, editors, business document proofreaders, and publishers. You can purchase style guides at a commercial bookstore, an online bookstore, or a college bookstore. Your local library likely has copies of different style guides and your instructor may have copies of several style guides for reference. Some popular style guides are *The Chicago Manual of Style* (The University of Chicago Press), *The Professional Secretary's Handbook* (Barron's), *The Holt Handbook* (Harcourt Brace College Publishers), and the *MLA Style Manual and Guide to Scholarly Publishing* (The Modern Language Association of America).

Endnotes

[1] Jerry W. Robinson et al., *Keyboarding and Information Processing* (Cincinnati: South-Western Educational Publishing, 1997).
[2] Ibid.
[3] Ibid.
[4] Ibid.

Index

Special Characters

& ampersand, EI 183

* asterisk, EA 3, EA 37

= equal sign, EB 14

− (minus sign), AP 14

+ (plus sign), AP 14

? question mark, EA 37

(_) underscore, EA 67

A

absolute cell references, in formulas, EB 63, EB 64

Accept or Reject Changes dialog box, EA 7

Access 2000, OF 3, OF 10, OF 17, OF 21, OF 31

Access, integrating Excel with
   exporting Excel data to, EX 9–11
   querying Excel data from, EX 11–14

active cell, EB 4
   editing in, EB 11–12

active desktop, AP 2

Add Constraint dialog box, EA 98

adding
   borders, EB 40–42, EB 45
   cell references to formulas, EB 15–16
   commands to toolbar, EI 180–181
   data tables to charts, EB 104–105
   e-mail hyperlinks, EI 150–152
   hyperlinks to other workbooks, EI 152–154
   labels to columns, EB 30–32
   labels to data maps, EI 104–105
   labels to rows, EB 32
   named ranges, EB 65–66
   shading, EB 40, EB 42–43
   shadow and 3-D effects to objects, EI 12–15
   text to AutoShape objects, EI 9–10

Address bar, AP 5, OF 57

Address Book, EX 16, EX 18, EX 19

Advanced Filter dialog box, EA 39–40

advanced filters, EA 38–40

alignment of cell content, changing, EB 35–36, EB 45

All Borders command, EB 41

ALT key, EB 4, EB 55, EX 3

AltaVista, OF 60, OF 61

America OnLine, OF 55, OF 62

Analysis ToolPak, EI 27

AND function, EI 44, EI 45–49

AND operator, EA 38

application Control-menu icon, OF 4

applications. *See also specific applications*
   closing, OF 16, OF 17
   starting, OF 7, OF 17

arguments, EB 16, EI 27
   for financial functions, EI 39

ARPAnet, OF 51, OF 62

Arrange Windows dialog box, EI 145

Arrow button, EI 11

arrow keys, EB 9, EB 104

Arrow Style button, EI 11

arrowheads, changing, EI 11

Attach Toolbars dialog box, EI 182

Attendee Availability tab, OF 41. *See also* Outlook Meeting Window

auditing worksheets
   commands, review of, EA 61
   identifying invalid data, EA 59–60

identifying relationships between precedent and dependent cells, EA 53–57

Range Finder, EA 51–52

tracing errors, EA 58–59

AutoComplete, EB 61

AutoFill, EB 30

AutoFilter, EA 35–37, EA 43

AutoFit, EB 32–33, EB 45

AutoFormat button, EI 181

AutoFormat dialog box, EI 84–85, EI 124

AutoFormats, EI 84–86, EI 93

AutoHide, OF 29

AutoShapes
 adding text to, EI 9–10
 button, EI 7, EI 9
 changing from one shape to another, EI 9
 defined, EI 2
 deleting, EI 2
 inserting, EI 7–9
 resizing text objects, EI 10–11
 toolbar, EI 7

AutoSum button, EB 17

AVERAGE function, EI 28, EI 31

axes, formatting, EB 103–104

B

Back button, OF 59

block format, AP 18–19

boldface, EB 33, EB 35, EB 45

Boolean operators, OF 61

Border tab, EB 41, EB 42

borders
 adding, EB 40–42, EB 45
 dotted, EB 59

browser. *See* Web browser

button(s), OF 21
 adding to toolbar, OF 23, OF 27
 default, OF 23

button functions, list of, EB 87

C

category axis, EB 103

cell content, modifying alignment of, EB 35–36

cell references, EB 4
 absolute, EB 63, EB 64
 adding to formulas, EB 15–16
 commands, review of, EB 74
 mixed, EB 63, EB 64
 relative, EB 63–64

cells, EB 4
 clearing contents and formatting, EB 13
 commands, review of, EB 22
 deleting, EB 61–62
 editing, EB 11–12
 inserting, EB 61–62
 merging, to create worksheet title, EB 29

range of, EB 9–10

selecting, EB 9–11

tracing relationships, EA 56–57

Center button, EB 29, EB 35

change(s)
 commands, review of, EA 13
 e-mail notice of, OF 46
 limitations with shared workbooks, EA 5
 multiple users and making, EA 6
 properties, EA 8–9
 tracking, EA 5–8

channel. *See* Internet channel

chart(s), OF 3
 Chart Wizard for creating, EB 88–102
 commands, review of, EB 108
 components of, EB 102
 creating PivotChart reports, EI 126–128
 embedded, EB 99, EB 106–107
 linking to PowerPoint presentation, EX 5–8
 objects, EB 101, EB 102
 previewing, EB 105–106
 printing, EB 105–106, EB 107
 resizing, EB 106–107, EX 6
 sheets, EB 99
 titles, changing, EB 103

charts, formatting and modifying, EB 102
 adding data tables, EB 104–105

axes, EB 103–104
   fonts, changing, EB 103

Chart Wizard, EB 88–102, EI 126–127

Chart Wizard button, EB 99

chat, OF 39, OF 47, OF 53

Clear All command, EB 13

Clear Contents command, EB 13

Clear Formats command, EB 13

clearing contents and formatting of cells, EB 13

click, AP 4, AP 13, OF 8

clip art
   defined, EI 2
   deleting, EI 2
   inserting, EI 2–4
   resizing, EI 4–6

Clipboard. *See* Office Clipboard toolbar

Clip Gallery/clip art, using, EI 2–7

Clips Online button, EI 3

Close button, AP 4, AP 7, EB 20, EB 61, OF 4

Close Window button, EB 20, OF 6

closing workbooks, EB 20, EB 22

collaboration, OF 37, OF 38, OF 39, OF 47
   tools, OF 47

collapsing outlines, EB 70

collating, EB 91

color
   of fonts, changing, EB 34, EB 45
   shading, adding, EB 40, EB 42–43

column chart, EB 99

column headings, EB 3

columns, EB 3
   adding labels to, EB 30–32
   capitalization in, EB 16
   deleting, EB 62
   freezing and unfreezing, EB 67–68
   hiding and unhiding, EB 67–68
   inserting, EB 62
   modifying size of, EB 32–33, EB 45
   selecting, EB 10

Column Width dialog box, EB 32

commands. *See also specific command*
   adding to toolbar, EI 180–181
   review of, EA 13, EA 43, EA 61, EA 81, EA 107, EB 22, EB 45, EB 74, EB 92, EB 108, EI, 20, EI 65, EI 93, EI 129, EI 156, EI 186, EX 26

Commands tab, EI 180

comma-separated text files, EX 15

comments
   commands, review of, EA 13
   creating, editing, and removing, EA 11–12
   printing, EA 12
   viewing, EI 165–166

commercial network, OF 55. *See also* America Online, Microsoft Network

CONCATENATE function, EI 59, EI 114

conditional formatting, EI 79–84, EI 93

Conditional Formatting dialog box, EI 80–81

conditional number formats, creating, EI 77–79

conferencing, OF 36

connection points, EI 7

connector line, EI 2, EI 7

Contents pane, AP 13

Control-menu icon, AP 4, OF 6

CONVERT function, EI 53–55

copy and paste, to copy data, EB 59–61, EB 74

Copy button, EB 59

Copy command, EB 59, EB 60

copying
   macro code to another workbook, EA 75–76
   styles, EI 92
   worksheets, EB 57–58, EB 74

copying data
  copy and paste, EB 59–61
  drag and drop, EB 54–55
  fill handle, EB 30
  Paste Special command for, EA 29–31

COUNT function, EI 28, EI 30

CTRL key, EB 57, EX 5

CTRL + ALT keys, EB 55

CUMIPMT function, EA 90–91, EI 38, EI 39–41

Custom AutoFilter dialog box, EA 36

Customize button, EI 166

Customize dialog box, EI 101–102, EI 178–179

customizing. *See also* editing toolbars, EI 178–182

cut and paste, to move data, EB 58–59, EB 74

Cut command, EB 58, EB 59

D

data
  analysis, EI 109–113, EI 129
  copying and moving, EB 54–55, EB 58–61
  detail, EB 68
  embedding, in a Word document, EX 2–5
  entering, EB 7–9
  entering, in a list, EA 31, EA 32–33
  exporting, to Access database, EX 9–11
  extracting, EA 41–42
  filters, EA 34–42
  importing, from other applications, EX 15–16
  labels, EB 102, EB 104
  points, EB 102, EB 105
  querying, from Access database, EX 11–14
  series, EB 102

Data Analysis dialog box, EI 109

database(s), EA 21, OF 3

data form
  deleting records from a list using, EA 34
  entering data in a list with, EA 32–33
  finding specific records using, EA 33–34

data maps
  commands, review of, EI 129
  creating, EI 102–104
  formatting, EI 104–109

data tables
  adding to charts, EB 104–105
  commands, review of, EA 107
  creating, EA 90–94
  one-variable, EA 90–92
  two-variable, EA 92–94

data validation, EA 22–31, EA 43
  characteristic settings, EA 26
  error messages, EA 24
  identifying invalid data, EA 59–60
  Paste Special command to copy data validation criteria, EA 29–31
  preventing changes, EA 28
  updating, EA 27

Data Validation dialog box, EA 23

dates
  entering, EB 7–9
  functions, EI 33–38
  values of, EB 40

decimals, EB 37–39

default settings, OF 25

Define Name dialog box, EB 65–66

Delete command, EB 13, EB 56

Delete dialog box, EB 61

DELETE key, EB 13, EB 59, EB 107, EI 2

deleting
  cells, EB 61–62
  clip art or AutoShape, EI 2
  columns, EB 62
  commands, review of, EB 74
  formats, EI 75
  named ranges, EB 65–66
  records from a list using data form, EA 34
  rows, EB 62
  style, EI 88
  worksheets, EB 56, EB 59

delimiters, EX 15

dependents, tracing, EA 55–56

Descriptive Statistics dialog box, EI 110

desktop, AP 1
  default, OF 8
desktop shortcuts
  creating, AP 16
Desktop toolbar, AP 5
detail data, EB 68
dialog box, OF 9, AP 7
  Accept or Reject Changes, EA 7
  Add Constraint, EA 98
  Advanced Filter, EA 39–40
  Arrange Windows, EI 145
  Attach Toolbars, EI 182
  AutoFormat, EI 84–85, EI 124
  Column Width, EB 32
  Conditional Formatting, EI 80–81
  Custom AutoFilter, EA 36
  Customize, EI 101–102, EI 178–179
  Data Analysis, EI 109
  Data Validation, EA 23
  Define Name, EB 65–66
  Delete, EB 61
  Descriptive Statistics, EI 110
  Edit Text Object, EI 104
  Find, EI 172–173
  Form, EA 32–33
  Format, EB 102, EB 103
  Format AutoShape, EI 5, EI 10
  Format Cells, EB 29, EB 35, EB 36, EB 39, EB 41–42, EI 80, EI 87–88, EI 120, EI 169
  Format Properties, EI 106
  Goal Seek, EA 95

Goal Seek Status, EA 95–96
Go To, EA 57, EI 81–82
Go To Special, EI 82–84
Header/Footer, EB 86–87
Highlight Changes, EA 6, EA 7
Import Text File, EX 15
Insert, EB 61
Insert ClipArt, EI 3
Insert Hyperlink, EI 150–151, EI 152–153
Link to File, EI 152
Macro, EA 69–70
Map Labels, EI 105
Merge Styles, EI 91
New, EI 163–164
Open, EB 6, EI 144
Options, EA 4, EB 8
Page Setup, EB 82–83
Paste Function, EI 28–29
Paste Name, EB 67
Paste Special, EX 3
PivotTable Field, EI 119
Print, EB 88, EB 90–91
Properties, EA 8
Record Macro, EA 67–68
Replace, EI 173–174
Resolve Conflicts, EA 6
Routing Slip, EX 18–19
Row Height, EB 32, EB 33
Save As, EB 18, EB 19
Scenario Manager, EA 102
Scenario Values, EA 103
Series, EB 31
Share Workbook, EA 4–5, EA 6
Solver Parameters, EA 97

Solver Results, EA 99–100
Sort, EB 53–54
Spelling, EB 71–72
Style, EI 87
Subtotal, EB 69
Symbol, EI 107–108
tabs, AP 7
Track Changes, EA 6
View, EB 68
directory, OF 53, OF 60
discussion groups, OF 53
discussion items, OF 42, OF 47
disk
  reformatting, AP 16
disk drive icon, AP 13
displaying toolbars, EI 176
docked toolbar, EI 175
docking and undocking toolbars, EI 176–178
document(s)
  creating, OF 9
  e-mail notice of changes to, OF 46
  formatting, AP 17–29
documentation worksheet, EB 71
domains, OF 55
  .com, OF 55
  .edu, OF 55
  .gov, OF 55
  .mil, OF 55
  .net, OF 55
  .org, OF 55
double-clicking, EX 7, OF 8

download, OF 51

drag, AP 4, AP 13, OF 8,

drag and drop, AP 8, EB 54–55, EB 74

dragging clip art, EI 4

drawing
   AutoShapes, using, EI 78
   Clip Gallery/clip art, using, EI 2–7
   commands, review of, EI 20
   lines, EI 11
   shadow and 3-D effects to objects, EI 12–15
   WordArt, using, EI 17–18

Drawing button, EI 2

Drawing toolbar, EI 2

E

Edit Text Object dialog box, EI 104

editing
   active cell, EB 11–12
   cell content, EB 11–12
   comments, EA 11–12
   data maps, EI 104
   Formula Bar for, EB 12
   macros, EA 70–74
   templates, EI 163–170

electronic bulletin board, OF 53

electronic "mail box" OF 54

e-mail, sending workbooks via, EX 16–20

e-mail hyperlinks, adding, EI 150–152

e-mail message, OF 9, OF 40, OF 53
   attaching document to, OF 40

embedded charts, EB 99, EB 106–107

embedding Excel data in a Word document, EX 2–5

encryption/decryption, OF 56

endnotes, AP 32

engineering functions, EI 53–55

ENTER key, EB 8, EB 11, EB 59

entering
   data in a list, EA 31, EA 32–33
   formulas and functions, EB 14–18
   text, dates, and numbers, EB 7–9
   values, EB 31

envelopes
   formatting, AP 24–25

error(s)
   messages, EA 24
   tracing, EA 58–59

ESC key, EB 59

EVEN function, EI 37

Excel 2000, OF 3, OF 8, OF 17, OF 31
   components of, EB 3–5
   exiting, EB 20, EB 22
   opening/starting, EB 3, EB 22

Excel, integrating
   Access, with, EX 9–14
   commands, review of, EX 26
   embedding Excel data in a Word document, EX 2–5

exporting data to Access database, EX 9–11
importing data from other applications, EX 15–16
Internet, with the, EX 20–25
linking Excel chart to PowerPoint presentation, EX 5–8
querying data from Access database, EX 11–14
sending workbooks via e-mail, EX 16–20
with Word and PowerPoint, EX 2–8

exiting Excel, EB 20, EB 22

Explorer bar, AP 13, OF 59

Explorer-style windows, AP 5
   Contents pane, AP 13
   separator bar, AP 13
   Tree pane, AP 12

exporting data to Access database, EX 9–11

Extend List Format command, EB 37–38

External Data toolbar, EX 14

extracting data, EA 41–42

F

F2 key, EB 11

F3 key, EB 67

F4 key, EB 64

F11 key, EB 99

F12 key, EB 18

FALSE function, EI 44, EI 50

favorites, OF 58

Favorites folder, OF 59

field, EA 21

field name, EA 21

file(s)
    creating, AP 14
    deleting, AP 16
    e-mail notice of changes to, OF 46
    managing, AP 12–16
    moving and copying, AP 15
    renaming, AP 15

file access services, Internet, OF 53

file extensions, EB 6

file names, special characters in, EB 19

File Transfer Protocol (FTP), OF 53

Fill commands, EB 30–31, EB 45

fill handle, EB 30

filtering, EA 34–42

financial functions, EI 38–44

Find command, EA 34

Find dialog box, EI 172–173

FIND function, EI 59, EI 60–64

floating toolbar, EI 175

folder(s)
    creating, AP 14
    deleting, AP 16
    e-mail notice of changes to, OF 46
    managing, AP 12–16
    moving and copying, AP 15
    selecting multiple, AP 14

Folder button, EB 19

font style, changing, EB 35

Font tab, EB 33

fonts
    changing, EB 33–34, EI 10
    changing chart, EB 103
    color, EB 34, EB 45
    defined, EB 33

footers, setting up, EB 86–88

Format AutoShape dialog box, EI 5, EI 10

Format Cells dialog box, EB 29, EB 35, EB 36, EB 39, EB 41–42, EI 80, EI 87–88, EI 120, EI 169

Format dialog box, EB 102, EB 103

Format Painter, EB 34, EB 45, EI 17, EI 92

Format Properties dialog box, EI 106

formatting. *See also* charts, formatting; worksheets, formatting
    data maps, EI 104–109
    PivotTable reports, EI 123–126
    toolbar, EB 5, EX 4, OF 6, OF 22, OF 31

Form dialog box, EA 32–33

forms, EA 71

Forms toolbar, EI 176

Formula Bar, EB 5
    editing with, EB 12

Formula Palette, EI 29–31

formulas
    absolute cell references in, EB 63, EB 64
    adding cell references to, EB 15–16
    commands, review of, EB 22
    entering, EB 14–18
    mixed cell references in, EB 63, EB 64
    named ranges in, EB 66–67
    natural language, EI 32–33
    relative cell references in, EB 63–64
    syntax and rules of precedence, EB 15

Forward button, OF 59

Freeze Panes command, EB 67

FrontPage 2000, OF 3, OF 4, OF 21, OF 31

FTP. *See* File Transfer Protocol

FTP site, OF 56

function names, EI 27

functions
    commands, review of, EB 22, EI 65
    date and time, EI 33–38
    engineering, EI 53–55
    entering, EB 14–18, EI 29–31
    financial, EI 38–44
    logical, EI 44–50
    lookup and reference, EI 55–58

MAX, EB 17–18

MIN, EB 17–18

Paste Function, EI 27–29

role of, EI 27

statistical, EI 50–53

SUM, EB 16–17

text, EI 59–64

FV function, EI 38, EI 41–43

G

Galaxy, OF 61

general discussion item, OF 43, OF 47

Goal Seek, EA 94–96, EA 107

Goal Seek dialog box, EA 95

Goal Seek Status dialog box, EA 95–96

Go To dialog box, EA 57, EI 81–82

Go To Special dialog box, EI 82–84

gridlines, turning on or off, EI 9

grouping

commands, review of, EI 156

multiple worksheets and workbooks, EI 137–156

shapes, EI 16

H

hardware requirements, OF 4

header row, EA 21

headers, setting up, EB 86–88

HeaderText, EA 77–78

help, AP 6, EB 86, OF 7, OF 11, OF 12, OF 14, OF 17

button, AP 7

menu, OF 15

window, OF 14

hiding

cells, EA 2

rows and columns, EB 67–68

toolbars, EI 176

highlight, AP 9

Highlight Changes dialog box, EA 6, EA 7

History folder, OF 59, OF 60

hits, OF 61

HLOOKUP function, EI 56, EI 58

horizontal scroll bar, OF 7

host, OF 37, OF 38

host computer, OF 54, OF 62

HotBot, OF 60

HTML mail, sending worksheets as, EX 17–18

hyperlinks, EI 150–154, OF 28, OF 56, OF 60

I

icons, AP 1, OF 9

IF function, EI 44–45

Import Text File dialog box, EX 15

importing tables from Web pages, EX 24–25

indents, changing, EB 36–37, EB 45

INFO function, EI 43

inline discussion item, OF 43, OF 45, OF 47

InputBox, EA 77

Insert Clip Art button, EI 3

Insert ClipArt dialog box, EI 3

Insert dialog box, EB 61

Insert Hyperlink dialog box, EI 150–151, EI 152–153

inserting

AutoShapes, EI 7–9

cells, EB 61–62

clip art objects, EI 2–4

columns, EB 62

commands, review of, EB 74

Excel data into PowerPoint presentation, EX 2

hyperlinks, EI 150–154

page breaks, EB 88–90

rows, EB 62

worksheets, EB 56–57

insertion point, blinking, EB 8

installation, OF 4

integrating Excel. *See* Excel, integrating

IntelliMouse, EB 7

Internet

accessing art clips on, EI 3

address, OF 54, OF 62

channel, AP 2

connecting to, OF 52

history of, OF 51–52, OF 62

integrating Excel with, EX 20–25

security issues of, OF 56

using, OF 55–61

Internet Explorer folder, AP 3

Internet Explorer Web browser, AP 2, AP 5, OF 51, OF 62

changing start page of, OF 56

using, OF 56–59

Internet Service Provider (ISP), OF 53, OF 54, OF 55, OF 62

Internet services, OF 53

interoffice memorandum

formatting, AP 26–27

INT function, EI 37

invalid data, identifying, EA 59–60

IP address OF 54, OF 62

IPMT function, EI 40

ISP. *See* Internet Service Provider

italics, EB 33, EB 35, EB 45

K

keyboard shortcuts, EB 4, EB 7, EB 59, EB 99, EX 18, OF 22, OF 47

keys, to select cells, EB 10–11

L

labels

adding to columns, EB 30–32

adding to data maps, EI 104–105

landscape orientation, EB 83

LEFT function, EI 59, EI 60–64

legend, EB 102

letter(s), OF 12

formatting, AP 18–21

minimum/maximum dimensions, AP 24

letterhead, AP 18

lines, drawing, EI 11

Link to File dialog box, EI 152

linking

commands, review of, EI 156

defined, EX 2

Excel chart to PowerPoint presentation, EX 5–8

multiple worksheets and workbooks, EI 137–156

links

creating, EI 147–149

updating, EI 149–150

Links bar, OF 57, OF 60

Links toolbar, AP 5

lists

commands, review of, EA 43

data filters, EA 34–42

data form, EA 32–34

data validation, EA 22–31

entering data in, EA 31

error messages, EA 24

identifying components of, EA 21–22

locking cells, EA 2

logical functions, EI 44–50

lookup and reference functions, EI 55–58

M

Macro dialog box, EA 69–70

macros, EI 164

adding Visual Basic functions to, EA 76–79

code descriptions, EA 72

commands, review of, EA 81

editing, EA 70–74

recording, EA 67–69

running, EA 69–70

using workbooks containing, EA 74–76

viruses, EA 74–75

mailing list, OF 53

mailing notations, AP 22–23

Magellan Internet Guide, OF 60

Map button, EI 101

Map Labels dialog box, EI 105

margins, setting and centering, EB 84–86

MAX function, EB 17–18

Maximize button, AP 4, OF 4

Maximize Window, OF 6

meeting
  scheduling, OF 36–42, OF 47
memo(s)
  formatting, AP 26–27
menu, OF 5, OF 21
  closing, OF 15
  expanding, OF 22
  personalized, OF 21, OF 31
menu, creating a custom, EI 182–186
menu bar, AP 5, EB 4, OF 4, OF 5, OF 6,
  customizing, OF 27, OF 31
Merge button, EB 29
Merge Styles dialog box, EI 91
merging workbooks, EA 9–11
Microsoft
  Internet Explorer, EX 24
  Map, EI 101–102, EI 103
  Network, OF 55, OF 62
  Outlook, AP 3, EX 16
  Query, EX 12
MID function, EI 59, EI 60–64
MILnet, OF 52
MIN function, EB 17–18
Minimize button, AP 4, OF 4
Minimize Window, OF 6
mixed cell references, in formulas, EB 63, EB 64
mnemonic character, EI 183
modem, OF 52, OF 53, OF 54, OF 56, OF 62
modified block format, AP 20–21

modules, EA 71
More Buttons list, OF 23
More Buttons drop-down lists, EB 5
mouse, using the, EB 7
mouse operations, OF 8
mouse settings
  changing, OF 6
move handle, OF 23
move pointer, OF 23
moving clip art, EI 4–6
moving data
  cut and paste, EB 58–59
  drag and drop, EB 54–55
  fill handle, EB 30
moving worksheets, EB 57–58, EB 74
My Computer folder, AP 3
My Documents folder, AP 3

N

Name Box, EB 5, EB 10, EB 59
named ranges
  adding and deleting, EB 65–66
  in Advanced Filter dialog box, EA 40
  commands, review of, EB 74
  in formulas, EB 66–67
natural language formulas, EI 32–3
navigating worksheets, EB 6–7

NetMeeting, OF 36–42, OF 47
network, OF 51, OF 62
network cable, OF 52
Network Neighborhood, AP 3
network server, OF 51
NETWORKDAYS function, EI 35–36
New command, EI 163
New dialog box, EI 163–164
Northern Light, OF 60
NOT function, EI 44, EI 50
NOW function, EI 34–35
NSFnet, OF 52
number formats
  applying, EB 37–40, EB 45, EI 71–72
  codes for, EI 74
  creating conditional, EI 77–79
  creating custom, EI 72–75
  modifying, EI 75–77
numbers, entering, EB 7–9

O

objects, AP 13. *See also* disk drive icon, folder, file
  adding hyperlinks to, EI 151
  chart, EB 101, EB 102
  inserting clip art, EI 2–4
OCR. *See* optical character reader
OCR read area, AP 24

ODD function, EI 37

Office 97 compatibility, OF 6

Office 2000, EB 4

Office applications. *See individual applications*

Office Assistant, OF 7, OF 11, OF 12, OF 13
   displaying or hiding, EB 5, OF 13

Office Clipboard toolbar
   closing, EB 61
   copying with, EB 60

Office documents
   switching between, OF 11

Office Serve Extensions, OF 42

Office Shortcut Bar, OF 28, OF 29, OF 30, OF 31

online Help. *See* Help

online meeting
   control in, OF 37, OF 38
   disconnecting from, OF 40
   scheduling, OF 36, OF 40

Online Meeting toolbar, OF 38

one-variable data table, EA 90–92

Open dialog box, EB 6, EI 144

opening
   Excel, EB 3
   existing workbook, EB 5–6, EB 22
   workbook with macros, EA 75

operands, EB 14

operating system, AP 1

operators, EB 14

optical character reader, AP 24

Options dialog box, EA 4, EB 8

OR function, EI 44, EI 49

OR operator, EA 38

outlines, EB 68–71, EB 74
   formatting, AP 28–29

Outlook, OF 3, OF 17, OF 40
   global address book, OF 41

Outlook Meeting window, OF 41

P

Page Break Preview dialog box, EB 89

page breaks, inserting and removing, EB 88–90

page margins, setting and centering, EB 84–86

page orientation and scale, changing, EB 82–84

Page Setup
   commands, review of, EB 92
   dialog box, EB 82–83
   header and footer, setting up, EB 86–88
   page margins, setting and centering, EB 84–86
   page orientation and scale, changing, EB 82–84
   print area, clearing, EB 88

   print area, setting, EB 81
   print preview, using, EB 81–82
   Sheet tab, EB 87

parallel projection, EI 15

participant, OF 37, OF 38, OF 39

passwords, EA 3

paste
   copy and, EB 59–61
   cut and, EB 58–59

Paste button, EB 60

Paste command, EB 59

Paste Function, EI 27–29

Paste Function button, EI 28

Paste Function dialog box, EI 28–29

Paste Name dialog box, EB 67

Paste Special command, EA 29–31, EI 148

Paste Special dialog box, EX 3

PERCENTILE function, EI 50, EI 51–53

personal information manager, OF 4

perspective projection, EI 15

PhotoDraw 2000, OF 4

PIM. *See* personal information manager

PivotChart reports, creating, EI 126–128, EI 129

PivotChart Wizard, EI 114–115

PivotTable Field dialog box, EI 119

PivotTable reports, EX 11–12, EX 24
  commands, review of, EI 129
  creating, EI 113–118
  displaying and hiding detail in a field, EI 121–123
  formatting, EI 123–126
  modifying, EI 119–123
  scenarios as, EA 104

plot area, EB 102

Place a Call dialog box, OF 37

PMT function, EA 90–92

point, AP 4, AP 13, OF 8

point size, EB 33

portrait orientation, EB 83–84

PowerPoint 2000, OF 3, OF 10, OF 17, OF 31
  integrating Excel with, EX 2–8
  linking Excel chart to PowerPoint, EX 5–8

PPMT function, EI 40

precedents, tracing, EA 53–55

presentation, OF 3

previewing
  charts, EB 105–106
  worksheets, EB 80–92

print area
  clearing, EB 88
  setting, EB 81

Print button, EB 90

Print dialog box, EB 88, EB 90–91

printing
  charts, EB 105–106, EB 107
  commands, review of, EB 92
  comments, EA 12
  an entire workbook, EB 90–91
  multiple worksheets, EI 143–144
  options, EB 87

print preview, using, EB 81–82, EB 105–106

program window
  bottom of, EB 5
  top of, EB 4–5

project, EA 71

Project Explorer, EA 71

proofreader's marks, AP 30

PROPER function, EI 59, EI 60

properties, changing workbook, EA 8–9

Properties dialog box, EA 8

protecting worksheets and workbooks, EA 2–4, EA 13

proximal operators, OF 61

Publisher 2000, OF 3, OF 4, OF 17, OF 21

PV function, EI 41

Q

Query Wizard, EX 12–14

querying data from Access database, EX 11–14

Quick launch toolbar, AP 2, AP 5, OF 7, OF 8

R

RAND function, EI 37

RANDBETWEEN function, EI 37

range, cell, EB 9–10

Range Finder, EA 51–52, EA 61

rank and percentile reports, EI 111–113

RANK function, EI 50–51, EI 102

record, EA 21

recording macros, EA 67–69, EA 81

Record Macro dialog box, EA 67–68

Recycle Bin, AP 3, AP 10

Redo command, EB 13–14, EB 22

relative cell references, in formulas, EB 63–64

removing
  comments, EA 11–12
  page breaks, EB 88–90

renaming worksheets, EB 56, EB 74

Replace dialog box, EI 173–174

report, EA 105

Report Manager, EA 105

resizing
  charts, EB 106–107, EX 6
  clip art, EI 4–6
  text objects, EI 10–11

Resolve Conflicts dialog box, EA 6

Restore button, AP 4, OF 4

Restore Window, OF 6

restoring named views, EB 68

right-click, AP 4, AP 13, OF 8, OF 25

right-drag, AP 4, AP 13, OF 8

right-dragging, EX 6

robot , OF 60

ROMAN function, EI 37

rotating text and changing indents, EB 36–37, EI 13, EI 14

ROUND function, EI 37

Routing Recipient button, OF 28

Routing Slip dialog box, EX 18–19

routing workbooks, EX 18–20

row headings, EB 3

Row Height dialog box, EB 32, EB 33

rows, EB 3
   adding labels to, EB 32
   deleting, EB 62
   freezing and unfreezing, EB 67–68
   hiding and unhiding, EB 67–68
   inserting, EB 62
   modifying size of, EB 32–33, EB 45
   selecting, EB 10
   running macros, EA 69–70

S

Save As command, EB 18–19, EB 22

Save As dialog box, EB 18, EB 19

Save command, EB 19–20, EB 22

saving
   named views, EB 68
   new templates, EI 175
   workbooks, EB 18–20, EB 22
   workbooks as Web pages, EX 21–22

scaling, EB 82–83
   clip art, EI 4–6

Scenario Manager dialog box, EA 102

scenarios
   commands, review of, EA 107
   creating, EA 102–104
   displaying, EA 104–105

Scenario Values dialog box, EA 103

ScreenTip, OF 6
   help message, OF 15

scroll, AP 4, AP 13, OF 8
   index, OF 60
   search engine, OF 53, OF 60

scroll bars, OF 6, OF 7

searching tools, OF 53

select, AP 9

sending workbooks via e-mail, EX 16–20

separator bar, AP 13

serial values, EB 40

Series dialog box, EB 31

Set Print Area command, EB 81

shading, adding, EB 40, EB 42–43, EB 45

Shadow button, EI 12

shadows, adding, EI 12

shapes
   changing stack order, EI 15
   grouping, EI 16

Share Workbook dialog box, EA 4–5, EA 6

sharing workbooks, EA 4–5, EA 13

Sheet tabs, EB 57, EB 87

sheets. See worksheets

shortcut menu, AP 9, OF 25, OF 31

shortcuts, AP 8

Show All command, EA 36

shutdown options, AP 10

single-click option, AP 8

slide, OF 3

SLN function, EI 38, EI 43–44

Solver, EA 94, EA 96–101, EA 107

Solver Parameters dialog box, EA 97

Solver Results dialog box, EA 99–100

sort criteria, EB 53

Sort dialog box, EB 53–54

sorts, single and multi-level, EB 53–54, EB 74

source file, EI 91, EI 147, EX 2

spelling, checking, EB 71–72, EB 74

Spelling dialog box, EB 71–72

spider, OF 60

spreadsheets, EB 3. *See also* worksheet

SQRT function, EI 37

stack order, EI 15

Standard toolbar, EB 5, EX 4, OF 6, OF 22, OF 31

Start button, AP 6, OF 7

Start menu, AP 6

start page, OF 57

starting Excel, EB 3

statistical functions, EI 50–53

status bar, EB 5

Stop Recording toolbar, EA 68–69

style
    applying, EI 86–88
    creating from a previously formatted cell, EI 89
    defined, EI 86
    deleting, EI 88
    merging from other workbooks, EI 91–92
    modifying, EI 89–90

Style dialog box, EI 87

style guide, AP 31

Subtotal dialog box, EB 69

Subtotals command, EB 68, EB 70

SUM function, EB 16–17, EB 69

Symbol dialog box, EI 107–108

syntax and rules of precedence for formulas, EB 15

T

tab-delimited text files, EX 15

TAB key, EB 11, EX 3

tab scrolling buttons, EB 5, EB 57–58

tables, EA 21
    See also PivotTable reports
    data tables, adding to charts, EB 104–105
    importing from Web pages, EX 24–25

tabs, AP 7, EB 3. *See also* dialog box tabs

target file, EI 91, EI 147, EX 2

taskbar, AP 2, OF 7

taskbar button, OF 4

taskbar toolbars, AP 5

telephone line, high-speed, OF 56

templates
    commands, review of, EI 186
    creating custom, EI 171–175
    editing, EI 163–170

Temporary Internet Files folder, OF 59

text
    adding to AutoShape objects, EI 9–10
    boxes, EI 11
    entering, EB 7–9
    functions, EI 59–64
    resizing, in AutoShape, EI 10–11
    rotating, EB 36–37

Text Box button, EI 11

threading, OF 42

3-D references, linking worksheets using, EI 140–143

3-D shapes, creating and modifying, EI 12–15

tick marks, EB 102

time functions, EI 33–38

time values, EB 40

title bar, AP 4, EB 4, OF 4

titles
    chart, changing, EB 103
    merging cells to create worksheet, EB 29

TODAY function, EI 34

toolbar(s), AP 5, OF 6, OF 21. *See also individual toolbar names, type of*
    commands, review of, EI 186
    customizing, EI 178–182
    displaying and hiding, EI 176
    docking and undocking, EI 176–178, OF 25, OF 26, OF 31

floating, OF 25, OF 26
Formatting, EB 5, EX 4
hiding, OF 25
move handle of, OF 23
move pointer of, OF 23
personalized, OF 21, OF 24
resetting, OF 28
resizing, OF 22
Standard, EB 5, EX 4
updating, OF 23, OF 24
viewing, OF 25

tracing
   cell relationships, EA 56–57
   commands, review of, EA 61
   dependents, EA 55–56
   errors, EA 58–59
   precedents, EA 53–55

Track Changes dialog box, EA 6

Tree pane, AP 12

TRUE function, EI 44, EI 50

tutorials, OF 4

two-variable data table, EA 92–94

typeface, EB 33

U

U.S. Postal Service standards, AP 24

underlined, EB 33, EB 35, EB 45

Undo button, EB 62

Undo command, EB 13–14, EB 22

Unfreeze Panes command, EB 67

unhiding rows and columns, EB 67–68

Uniform Resource Locator (URL), OF 57

updating links, EI 149–150

upload, OF 51

UPPER function, EI 59, EI 60

URL. *See* Uniform Resource Locator

USENET, OF 54, OF 62

user name, OF 55

V

value axis, EB 103–104

values, EB 4

variable, EA 77, EA 90

vertical scroll bar, OF 7

View dialog box, EB 68

views, saving and restoring, EB 68

viruses, macro, EA 74–75

Visual Basic Editor, EA 70–74, EA 81

Visual Basic functions, adding to macros, EA 76–79

VLOOKUP function, EI 56–57, EI 113–114

W

Web browser, OF 51, OF 52, OF 56, OF 62

Web discussions, OF 42–46, OF 47

Web Discussions toolbar, OF 43, OF 44

Web pages, OF 56, OF 62
   creating interactive, EX 22–24
   importing tables from, EX 24–25
   loading, OF 57
   saving workbooks as, EX 21–22

Web sites, OF 53. *See also* Web pages

WEEKDAY function, EI 37–38

what-if analysis, EA 90
   data tables, EA 90–94
   Goal Seek, EA 94–96, EA 107
   scenarios, EA 101–105, 107
   Solver, EA 94, EA 96–101, EA 107

What's This? command, OF 15

Whiteboard, OF 39, OF 40

wildcard, EA 37

window, OF 4

window, active, OF 11

Windows 98, AP 1
   desktop, AP 1
   operating system, AP 1
   settings, AP 6
   shutting down AP 10

Windows Explorer
   opening, AP 12
   options, AP 13–14
wizard, OF 12
Word 2000, OF 3, OF 9, OF 17
   embedding Excel data in, EX 2–5
   integrating Excel with, EX 2–8
WordArt, using, EI 17–18
word processing, OF 3
workbooks, EB 3
   adding hyperlinks to other, EI 152–154
   arranging, EI 145
   changing properties, EA 8–9
   closing, EB 20, EB 22
   commands, review of, EB 22
   containing macros, EA 74–76
   grouping/linking multiple, EI 137–156
   merging, EA 9–11
   opening, EB 5–6, EB 22
   printing entire, EB 90–91
   protecting, EA 2–4
   publishing, EX 21
   routing, EX 18–20
   saving, EB 18–20, EB 22
   saving as Web pages, EX 21–22
   sending, via e-mail, EX 16–20
   sharing, EA 4–5

workgroup, OF 35, OF 36
worksheet(s), OF 3
   analyze numbers in, OF 17
   auditing, EA 51–61
   checking spelling, EB 71–72
   commands, review of, EB 74
   components of, EB 3–4
   copying, EB 57–58
   deleting, EB 56, EB 59
   grouping/linking multiple, EI 137–156
   inserting, EB 56–57
   linking, using 3-D references, EI 140–143
   moving, EB 57–58
   navigating, EB 6–7
   previewing and printing, EB 80–92
   printing multiple, EI 143–144
   protecting, EA 2–4
   renaming, EB 56
   sending, as HTML mail, EX 17–18
   zooming, EI 2
worksheets, formatting
   alignment of cell content, EB 35–36
   borders, adding, EB 40–42
   commands, review of, EB 45
   fonts and font styles, changing, EB 33–35
   merging cells to create titles, EB 29

   modifying size of columns and rows, EB 32–33
   number formats, EB 37–40
   rotating text and changing indents, EB 36–37
   shading, adding, EB 40, EB 42–43
   working with a series to add labels, EB 30–32
workspaces, EI 144–147
World Wide Web (WWW), OF 53, OF 62
WWW. *See* World Wide Web

X

x-axis, EB 100, EB 103

Y

Yahoo, OF 60
y-axis, EB 103

Z

z-axis, EB 103
zooming, EI 2